THE BEGINNING OF
THE U. S. ARMY
1783-1812

THE BEGINNING OF
THE U. S. ARMY

1783-1812

By James Ripley Jacobs

GREENWOOD PRESS, PUBLISHERS
WESTPORT, CONNECTICUT

Library of Congress Cataloging in Publication Data

Jacobs, James Ripley, 1886-
    The beginning of the U. S. Army, 1783-1812.

    Reprint of the ed. published by Princeton University
Press, Princeton, N.J.
    Bibliography: p.
    Includes index.
    1. United States. Army--History. 2. United States
--History, Military--To 1900. 3. United States--
History--1783-1815. I. Title.
[UA25.J33 1977]   355.3'0973   77-8427
ISBN 0-8371-9691-4

Originally published in 1947 by Princeton University Press,
Princeton

Reprinted with the permission of Princeton University Press

Reprinted in 1977 by Greenwood Press, Inc.

Library of Congress Catalog Card Number 77-8427

ISBN 0-8371-9691-4

Printed in the United States of America

355.3
517b

TO MY GIRLS:

Peggy
Jean
&
Nancy

PREFACE

During the period from 1783 to 1812, the Army of the United States had to be ready to thwart aggression from Europe and at the same time to protect a constantly increasing number of immigrants from Indian raiders in the Old Northwest. Such a difficult and important mission required a large and highly competent force; but the existing one was small, ill-paid, ill-clothed, ill-fed, and often ill-trained and ill-led. It numbered only eighty officers and men when Henry Knox was "Secretary at War" in 1784; not until 1809 did it reach its maximum strength for this period, a total of 6,954. The record of the army shows both successes and failures, but frequently the failures were from causes beyond its control.

This neglect of the army arose partly because the new federal government, still uncertain and experimental, was centering its attention on problems that it considered of greater importance. Above all, it required strengthening of its own very limited powers; otherwise, it could never expect to enjoy respect at home or abroad. Measures had to be taken to meet current expenses and to liquidate debts that were long overdue. Both a desire for economy and a deeper seated fear of military tyranny led Congressmen to keep the army small. Many politicians argued that the militia were the real bulwark of the nation. Customarily, volunteers, militia, and levies supplemented the regulars when heavy fighting was in prospect. These mixed troops usually came from the frontier and reflected its viewpoint. They were bound together by a bitter hatred of the Indians —a feeling constantly shown in the speeches, letters, and diaries that form the fabric of this book.

In solving its varied problems, the early army developed certain marked characteristics. In fighting the Indians, it became highly proficient in the tactics and supply of small groups, in marching and camping in the wilderness, in scouting and patrolling, in the use of rifle and bayonet, in the building of roads and blockhouses, and in the making of temporary defenses and shelter. Out of such experiences, officers and men established a great tradition for individuality. This tradition has set certain limitations on the army, but it has also bred a capacity for improvisation, resilience, and immeasurable courage, making the army at one and the same time the despair of martinets and the pride of generals who understand its basic character.

Although the following pages deal with the army, they, of necessity, also describe an important and somewhat neglected section of our social history. The United States Army flourished or declined according to the whims of Congress and the people. Settlers along the Ohio and the Mississippi helped mould its peculiar character; and it often decidedly influenced them. This book is therefore social as well as military history. This volume ends with the opening of the War of 1812, but subsequent volumes will carry the story forward to 1846.

UNLESS many had unselfishly helped me, I could not have completed *The Beginning of the United States Army, 1783 to 1812*. My wife, Beryl Martin Jacobs, has often relieved me of duties that were my natural share, allowing me more opportunities for writing. She has also frequently suggested better turns in thought and expression. Even in her last days of illness, my sister, Elizabeth C. Jacobs, was unsparing in her efforts to make my narrative more forceful and clear. To Major Charles W. Elliott, U.S.A. (Retired), I am deeply indebted. I have frequently drawn on his rich store of knowledge of the army during its early years; in fact, he supplied most of the data for two of my chapters. Brigadier General Asa L. Singleton and Colonel Peter F. Wolfe, U.S.A. have both repeatedly given me the benefit of their judgment covering the tactical problems confronting Harmar, St. Clair, and Wayne. Messrs. L. Thomas Rainey and Robert B. Whitsett, Jr., have been uncommonly kind in supplying information of the early Ohio country. Mr. H. Charles McBarron, Jr., saved me many hours of research by placing at my disposal the results of his detailed study of Army uniforms. Colonel A. C. M. Azoy, U.S.A. also helped me in a similar way. From Colonel A. Gibson, U.S.A. and Miss Katherine E. Greenwood, Army War College Library, Lt. Colonels E. E. Farman and W. J. Morton, U.S.A., U.S. Military Academy Library, and Miss Edna L. Jacobsen and Mr. Joseph Gavit, New York State Library, have always come very thoughtful replies to my numerous questions. Messrs. Thomas E. Roberts, University of Connecticut and Harry C. Durston, Onondaga Historical Society, have read parts of my manuscript and suggested improvements in organization and wording.

When I needed bits of information to complete my narrative, the following have supplied it: Miss Elizabeth C. Biggert, The Ohio State Archaeological and Historical Society; Mrs. Jouett Taylor Cannon, The Kentucky State Historical Society; Dr. Frederick M. Dearborn; Mr. Randolph C. Downes; Mr. Allyn B. Forbes, The Massachusetts Historical Society; Miss Mae Gilman, The Maine Historical Society; Mr. Thomas R. Hay; Mr. Milo S. King, The Fort Ticonderoga Museum; Miss Ludie J. Kinkead, The Filson Club; Mr. G. Lanctot, Public Archives of Canada; Messrs. Harlow Lindley and K. W. McKinley, The Ohio State Archaeological and Historical Society; Miss Mary E. Martin, Alabama Polytechnic Institute Library; Mr. Charles B. Montgomery, The Pennsylvania Historical Society; Mrs. John Trotwood Moore, The State of Tennessee Library; Mr. Paul A. T. Noon, The Ohio State Library; Miss Annie A. Nunns, The State Historical Society of Wisconsin; Mr. Howard H. Peckham, Indiana Historical Bureau; Mr. S. H. P. Pell, The Fort Ticonderoga Museum; Mr. M. M. Quaife, The Detroit Public Library; Mr. Stephen T. Riley, The Massachusetts Historical Society; Mr. L. Hubbard Shattuck, Chicago Historical Society; Mr. Lee Shephard, The Society of Colonial Wars in the State of Ohio; Mr. H. C. Shetrone, The Ohio Archaeological and Historical Society; Mrs. Elleine H. Stones, The Detroit Public Library, Mr. H. B. Swearingen; Colonel William J. Verbeck, U.S.A.; Miss Nancy Jane Welch, The Manlius School Library; Mr. Harry E. Wildes.

JAMES RIPLEY JACOBS
Major U.S.A., Ret'd.

Manlius, New York

CONTENTS

Preface   vii

1. Determining Influences   3

2. The First American Regiment   13

3. Harmar Tries an Offensive and Fails   40

4. St. Clair Makes New Plans   66

5. The Great Defeat   85

6. Wayne Creates a Fighting Army   124

7. Wayne and the Battle of Fallen Timbers   153

8. Wilkinson, New General-in-Chief,
   Inspects and Disposes   189

9. Short-Lived Changes and Proposals   221

10. Jefferson and Dearborn Refashion the Army   244

11. A Military Academy is Founded   280

12. The Army and the Louisiana Purchase   309

13. Drifting into War   342

14. A Country Unready for War   369

Bibliography   387

Index   399

THE BEGINNING OF
THE U.S. ARMY
1783-1812

1. *Determining Influences*

DURING the seventeenth century, many Anglo-Saxons left their old homes in Europe to establish new ones in North America. They were searching for greater freedom and more security. Generally poor and lacking ancestors of distinction, they were, for the most part, farmers, mechanics, and tradesmen who confidently expected to better their lot if permitted to work unhampered in ways that they chose. They were not disappointed. The new country possessed magnificent resources; it offered generous rewards to the honest, industrious, and intelligent. Making use of such opportunities, even some indentured servants eventually rose to leadership in their own communities; often their families were large and in turn gained still greater renown. Since heraldic quarterings of nobility had little to do with the success of the early settlers, they had slight respect for those who held positions of importance through birth or inheritance. They deemed their own manner of living best, especially if they were frontiersmen who had a high regard for individuals but none for class distinctions. In any institution either of church or state, they wanted those in control to be of their own selection and kind.

In any of their temporary armed forces no great gulf existed between officers and men, both often coming from the same social strata and frequently occupying similar positions in their respective communities. Those with commissions commonly obtained office because of leadership in politics or battle, being usually elected by members of their organization or appointed by the colonial governor. Partly for these reasons, the rank and file were treated with more consideration than if they had been serving in the armies of Europe.

Many of the militia and volunteers in America were familiar with forms of combat not emphasized abroad. During the Revolution and long before, they appropriated the best tactics current among the Indians with whom they frequently fought, becoming skillful in scouting and patrolling and well versed in the lore of woods and prairie. In advancing to the attack, the Indian was noiseless and unseen until the final rush was made with blood-curdling noise and fury. For hours at a time he could lie motionless, blending with the landscape. None of the animals that he hunted surpassed him in the use of cover or more skillfully confused pursuers along the route of his flight. On the other hand, he could trail a fugitive with uncanny skill. An upturned stone, a broken twig, a parted bush was enough to tell him which way to follow. This keenness of observation and physical control made him invaluable for the acquisition of certain kinds of information that were old to his experience. Living constantly in the open, he found little or no more difficulty in covering stretches of country by night than by day. Attacks during darkness were his particular forte; they often met with success because they came as a complete surprise and were carried through by small well-integrated bands that were ably led. As time went on, the settlers appropriated such ideas, using them with mounting success.

Nor was this all. The Indians knew the wilderness and how to weather its hardships with the means at hand. Their clothing, shelter, food, and equipment were crude but in some respects adequate. When on campaign, the soldier found deerskin shirts, jackets and breeches economical and comfortable to wear. When his shoes wore out and others could not be obtained, he made himself moccasins out of any leather available. In place of the regulation awkward three-cornered hat, he fashioned a cap of cloth or fur. If lucky he might have a greatcoat of bear skin to protect himself from wintry weather. When camp was pitched at night, it was laid out in a rectangular shape least vulnerable to attacks of the savages. If tents were lacking, windbreaks, lean-tos, and fox-holes served instead. If rations ran out, a few men went out and hunted and trapped as the Indians had shown them. Although bayonets and swords were well designed for killing, a tomahawk was often carried as well. It was really no more than a rough kind of hatchet, useful in the woods and often worth having in battle.

Fighting with Indians was mostly an individual matter. Both officers and men depended largely on their personal weapons. In the uses of some of them they often became very skillful. Whether equipped with musket, rifle, or pistol, they took pride in being excellent marksmen. They had frequent opportunity to practice in their frontier experience. Firing by volley appealed to them no more than to huntsmen when shooting game or to Indians when letting fly laboriously-made arrows at unwary settlers. They were also aware that powder and ball were expensive and never to be wasted. A method better than the common European practice was evolved. It later became known as firing "at will." Allowing a far greater freedom of action than was permitted in European armies, it harmonized more nearly with American traditions. To be successful, it presumed superior intelligence in the ranks and a highly efficient training in small arms. Both have continued to be characteristic of our army.

At the same time we were borrowing heavily from the British army. Americans had fought bravely as allies of British regulars at Louisburg, Duquesne, Ticonderoga, and elsewhere before the opening of the Revolution. From this hard school of actual combat, George Washington, Philip Schuyler, Arthur St. Clair, and others learned to solve a few of the difficult problems connected with training, tactics, and supply.

When they returned home they sought opportunity to supplement this knowledge by studying British books on military art. These were easy to obtain and widely read. Washington had some of the best in his own library. Henry Knox sold a number of them in his book store at Boston. The *Norfolk Militia Discipline*, or a modification of it, was popular in the northern colonies. It had been published in England after the passage of the Militia Bill of 1757. Another was the British *Manual of 1764*, commonly known as the "Sixty-fourth." In the South, Colonel Bland's treatise had been in vogue for years. Books like these were used in training local organizations, such as the Henrico County Militia of Virginia and the City Troops of Philadelphia.[1] And, of course, there was the "Ancient and Honorable Artillery Company of Boston" that had been organized as early as 1638; here also flourished "The Train," a rival artillery organization where Henry Knox first learned the use of heavy weapons.

Like others, Knox also had opportunity to acquire something from merely observing British organizations that came to America in constantly increasing numbers during the decade before the Revolution. They were scattered in some of the larger sea-coast towns. Boston had several hundred troops, a constant source of information and irritation. In Philadelphia the 18th Irish Infantry, as well as a company of royal artillery, took station. They were quartered in Northern Liberties and became quite friendly with some of the inhabitants.[2] Before the revolution had fully begun, New York City was familiar with the facing and marching of redcoats.

With the opening of hostilities in 1775, a number of British officers joined the Americans, gaining positions of high rank and influence. Of these Horatio Gates and Charles Lee became major generals. For a while Gates was the adjutant general of Washington's army, organizing it much as any British officer might have done. Companies, battalions, regiments, and brigades became the usual units of command. Articles of War, similar to those in the British army, were drawn up, submitted to the Continental Congress, and duly adopted and published.[3] The army itself was kept subordinate to the civil authority; it was governed by Congress, which in turn elected a civilian

[1] C. K. Bolton, *The Private Soldier under Washington*, p. 109.

[2] J. Wilkinson, *Memoirs*, etc., I, p. 13.

[3] For Articles of War Adopted in 1776, see J. F. Callan, *The Military Laws of the United States* (rev. ed.), pp. 63-85.

as "Secretary at War" to exercise certain delegated powers. He established the routine of pay and supply following the methods current in England. Salaries of officers controlling these two departments depended upon the amount of money disbursed. The system itself was bad, and was further aggravated by a scarcity of hard money and military supplies. As a result, soldiers often went without pay, rations, equipment, or clothing.

The regulation uniform closely followed that of the British. It had much the same cut, but its dominant colors were blue and buff, colors that the Whigs had adopted instead of the red and white of the Tories.[4] It had many objectionable features. The high stiff collar was always a nuisance, the cross belts constricted the chest, the coat tails easily caught on bush and bramble, the breeches were too tight for comfort, and the leggings interfered with circulation. The three-cornered hat was even worse. Usually it was poorly fitted to the head and hard to keep on. It was a convenient catch-all for wind, rain, and snow; it had no visor to protect the eyes from dazzling sunshine or driving storm. Its shape was soon lost, and it seldom looked presentable for inspection. In spite of these defects, we continued to use such a uniform until after 1812, possibly because we were basically conservative and hesitated to change.

Our chief infantry weapon was also of British make and design. It was commonly known as "Brown Bess," being a flint-lock smooth-bore, weighing about eleven pounds and measuring 4 ft. 9 in. without a bayonet. The customary 1½ oz. lead ball made a cruel wound, but only if the aim was good might the soldier expect it to hit a man-sized target about half the time at seventy-five yards. Beyond this distance results became progressively worse. Extreme range was four hundred yards. An expert could load and fire five shots a minute; in action, fewer, especially if the bayonet was fixed. Though often using "Brown Bess,"

[4] A. B. Gardner, "The Uniforms of the American Army," in *Magazine of American History*, Aug. 1877, p. 465.

Americans much preferred a rifle or Charleville musket.[5] As a rule, they did not want the bayonet attached to the muzzle, for this made loading harder, and in times of excitement the hand might be badly lacerated. They did not appreciate the bayonet as a weapon until Bunker Hill, Bemis Heights, and other bloody fights had proved its worth in combat.

Heavy weapons, too, were generally like those that the British manufactured. They were about the only kind in the Colonies when the Revolution began. Field guns were usually four, eight, or twelve pounders, made of bronze and having an extreme range of about one mile. Howitzers were classified according to diameter of the bore and weight of shot. Common projectiles were grape and canister. Guns, mounted on every conceivable kind of carriage, were hauled about by man or beast, horses or oxen being used when they could be obtained from along the line of march. Most drivers were civilians. When a company went into action it might be assigned to several guns widely different in caliber and type; all of them were loaded with bags of loose powder and fired with a slow match device.[6] With such matériel, Americans carried on during the Revolution and many years afterward.

We owe much to Baron von Steuben for teaching us how to use and care for our equipment. He will always remain prominent for what he accomplished in the training and organization of our early army. Before coming to America he belonged to the general staff of Frederick the Great, which was composed of probably "the most highly trained corps of infantry officers in the world."[7] On May 5, 1778, he was appointed inspector general of the army. He began his great work at Valley Forge, where Washington's disheartened troops were then encamped. On the 29th of March, 1779, *Steuben's Regulations for the Order and Discipline of the Troops of the United States* ap-

[5] O. L. Spaulding, *The United States Army in War and Peace*, pp. 17-18 and E. E. Curtis, *The Organization of the British Army*.

[6] O. L. Spaulding, *op. cit.*, p. 19.

[7] J. M. Palmer, *General von Steuben*, p. 29.

peared. For about thirty-three years, it continued to be our official manual. Commonly known as "The Blue Book," it contained about 100 small pages setting forth clearly and simply the fundamentals of guard duty, organization, property accountability, field operations, and drill. Movements of the soldier were minutely described. At attention.

"He is to stand straight and firm upon his legs, with the head turned to the right as far as to bring the left eye over the waistcoat buttons; the heels two inches apart; the toes turned out; the belly drawn in a little, but without constraint; the breast a little projected; the shoulders square to the front, and kept back; and the hands hanging down the sides, with the palms close to the sides."[8]

In priming and loading, the soldier learned that there were some fifteen motions. Plates illustrated just how they were to be executed. Through constant practice he became proficient.[9]

Von Steuben not only stressed what good troops must know, he did more; he created among officers a keen sense of responsibility and a very human understanding of their relations with subordinates. He called on those in commissioned grades to do more than merely mount the guard and head their organizations in battle. They were to win the ardent support of their men "by treating them with every possible kindness and humanity, inquiring into their complaints, and when well founded, seeing them redressed." They were to be sure that the sick were supplied with proper medicine and food, also "such comforts and conveniences" as lay in their power. Under such sympathetic treatment men became eagerly receptive to the training that Steuben personally demonstrated and supervised. He formed a model company and drilled it himself. By such practical methods captains learned how to instruct their own organizations with precision and uniformity. They began to value the bayonet highly as a weapon for close-in-fighting; they marched in cadence in parade and went forward into action without straggling; they kept their

[8] Steuben, *Regulations*, etc. (ed. 1803), p. 7.
[9] *Ibid.*, p. 18 *et seq.*

bodies clean and their equipment in proper condition and place. Monthly inspections revealed who were present or absent and whether or not they had all of their equipment. If a cartridge box, belt, musket, blanket, or anything else, once issued, was found to be lacking, the delinquent had the price of it charged against him in the book that his company commander kept. At one time or another a musket cost $16, a bayonet $1, and a flint 5 cents. From those of highest rank to those of lowest grade responsibility was fixed for different things, resulting in a high morale and a new evidence of power upon the field of battle.[10]

Perhaps no foreigner had ever done more to make Americans set a high value on military art and to show how it could serve our particular system to best advantage. Von Steuben accomplished this difficult feat at a time when efforts for liberty were ebbing very low. To the ultimate triumph we must assign him no small measure of credit and devotion. Americans were aware that valor was essential to victory, but he taught that valor alone is never sufficient. Training, painstaking and complete, will be forever requisite, and this above all is what Steuben admirably contributed in the formative years of the Republic.

In spite of France's alliance with us after 1777, she did not exert any great influence upon our military establishment. Though we drank French wines, we still retained our original preference for an issue of rum or whisky as part of the army ration. Sometimes we found temporary pleasure in the minuets and courtly manners of the French officers at our more formal military routs and balls. We were also thrilled with the music and uniforms of the French regiments on parade. But we seldom had the will or means to imitate. Even though many Frenchmen fought bravely and unselfishly with us during the Revolution, we did not speak their language or readily accept their point of view. Perhaps we understood Lafayette best of all. To him we must be deeply and forever grateful for what he himself gave or obtained from others that we might have

[10] *Ibid., passim.*

more money, troops, and equipment in our struggle for independence. These contributions gave us new strength and courage in our darkest hour.

When Lafayette came to America, in June 1777, the French had been long distinguished for their knowledge of artillery and engineering. We, on the other hand, had almost none who were skilled in the erecting of forts, the use and emplacement of heavy guns, or the manufacture and inspection of ordnance. To supply this lack, our agents in Paris engaged four French officers in 1777; one of these was Tronson du Coudray who was promised the position of Chief of Artillery. When Greene, Knox, and Sullivan heard of this agreement they prepared to resign. As a result du Coudray did not get what he expected; instead, he was made "inspector general of ordnance and military manufactures." In this capacity, he served for only a few months, being drowned in the Schuylkill when on his way to join one of our combat units as a volunteer captain.[11]

Louis Lebègue Duportail was another French officer similarly engaged. His influence was far more pronounced. Commissioned as a major general, he became our first chief of engineers, giving them that admirable motto, *Essayons*, which they have found no better to live by, even after more than 150 years. Upon joining Washington, he organized the defenses of Valley Forge in such formidable fashion that Howe was reluctant to attack them. When West Point required fortifications, he was consulted and his advice accepted. Later, through his technical skill, he eased and accelerated the investment and capture of Yorktown. By 1782 he had fourteen engineers working as his assistants, all of them of French descent. The Revolution over, Duportail, upon request, made recommendations covering the organization of our peacetime army.[12] One of them involved the consolidation of artillerists and engineers in a single

---

[11] L. C. Hatch, *The Administration of the American Revolutionary Army*, pp. 55-59.

[12] E. S. Kite, *Brigadier-General Louis Lebègue Duportail*, pp. iii, 7, 46-47, 96-101, 226.

organization. He thought the plan would prove highly economical and would prevent recurrent contentions between these branches. It was practical, he also pointed out, because the two were much alike and required a preliminary knowledge common to both. He also strongly urged the establishment of a military academy that would supply competent subalterns.[13] The work of Duportail would have been of more lasting value to our army if his subordinates had been Americans instead of Frenchmen who were only temporarily with us.

Molded by such influences, our Revolutionary army fought for eight long years. During this time it had been considered habitually as only a provisional force. It never gave the impression of being highly professional; generally it reflected the ideas of the people, seldom opposing mass opinion. In war it had been supported only from sheer necessity; in peace some would abolish it altogether, a few wanted no more than a single regiment. Jefferson went so far as to declare that we could not maintain a standing army because we had no paupers to compose it. Many farmers and men in a profession or trade held a similar opinion, believing it to be an expensive and unnecessary haven for the idle and dissolute. Only after exhausting all other available means to protect our settlers from Indians, did the members of Congress grudgingly consent to authorize a very small body of regular troops in 1784.

[13] *Ibid.*, pp. 264-270.

2. *The First American Regiment*

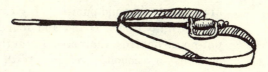

Once the Revolution had ended, Americans, with more than an ordinary share of exuberant independence, resented the imposition of any authority remotely resembling the British regime that they had abolished after eight years of continuous struggle. They found themselves wholly unable to sacrifice erroneous ideas of liberty for restrictions that were necessary for the common weal. According to the Articles of Confederation, Congress was the organ of government. But its members came and went as suited their pleasure and the wishes of the state that they represented. Some of them found Philadelphia congenial; others preferred their own homes surrounded by prosperous farms. Only those who acutely felt the call of public duty submitted to the hardships of traveling to the ambulating seat of government. Even on great occasions no more than a mere handful huddled forlornly together to legislate for some four million people scattered over 828,-844 square miles of territory. When George Washington gave up his command on December 23, 1783, just twenty members were present to acknowledge his inestimable service in helping to create the Republic.

Most Americans lived narrowly, thinking only in terms of their own state's interest; they could see no justice beyond their neighboring hills. When Pennsylvanians coveted the rich and beautiful Wyoming Valley of the Susquehanna, they hypocritically observed that the floods obliterating the New England settlers there clearly indicated divine disapproval. As partners of a chastening God, they hunted down the forlorn remnant with musket and sword, thereby passing into the inheritance of a harried and forsaken land. Without hindrance the farmers of Vermont fought with those of New York along the placid waters of the Hudson. They cared not for boundaries and gave no quarter in a no-man's land of their own making. When Massachusetts would punish its fugitives from justice, they escaped into Rhode Island and found asylum among the pot-house dotards who were constantly proposing noxious methods of economic reform. With courts working at cross purposes and money in disorder, the processes of justice were indifferently and expensively served.[1]

This generally demoralized condition throughout the Republic prevailed because Congress had no adequate powers, no practical method of increasing them, and no executive agents to enforce the few that it actually possessed.

No armed body existed to support the rule of federal law. Since the return of Washington to civil life, Major General Henry Knox had been rapidly discharging men from the army. On January 3, 1784, he reported to Congress that only 700 rank and file remained. Even this diminutive force was not to be retained. The Newburgh address of 1783 and an open mutiny of recruits a few months later had frightened the lawmakers. Like many of their constituents, they believed that a standing army in peace times was "inconsistent with the principles of republican governments, dangerous to the liberties of a free people," and might be used as an active agent in "establishing despotism." Giving these lurking fears as reasons for action, they ordered all troops to be discharged except twenty-five men at Fort Pitt and fifty-five at West Point. These, with a proper proportion of officers, were to guard post-Revolutionary equipment and stores.[2] Four score peace-loving caretakers, widely scattered on jobs of greasing and cleaning, could scarcely be expected to overthrow the government even if they were niggardly paid, clothed, and fed.

During most of 1784, the troops at Fort Pitt were under a lieutenant who took life as it came. He considered

[1] J. B. McMaster, *A History of the People of the United States*, I, pp. 211-215.
[2] *Journals of the Continental Congress, 1774-1789*, XXVII, p. 524.

that his duty consisted only in guarding, not helping to preserve, the great quantity of powder stored there. When commissioners for making the treaty of Fort McIntosh wanted some of it to help along negotiations, they found most of it worthless. The lieutenant's men were more successful; they discovered as much as they needed when they wished to go hunting. They had the easy carelessness of the neighboring Irish who lived in dirty log cabins and were prone to find joy in liquor and fighting. Two days after Christmas the garrison decided not to let the night waste away without celebration. As the hours grew late, potation followed potation. The artillery was ordered out and commanded to fire in the midst of the fort. A head-splitting noise awakened those who had peacefully taken to their beds in post and town. Those so rudely jarred from slumber hastened to make short work of the disturbers. A riot followed and did not end until the leaders were locked securely in quarters. Someone said "he never saw in his life such a rumpiss; that they were all running hurry-scurry, and when the bagnits [bayonets] were fixtured, they glomed so in the moon, as to pister me to death." As a result, the surgeon dressed a few indifferent wounds. Two officers were temporarily relieved of command, and all those in the neighborhood found a new theme of gossip to lighten their rounds of monotonous duty.[3]

Just how the other fifty-five men of the federal army spent the Christmas holidays is not duly recorded. They were at West Point, New York, and were under command of Captain John Doughty, the highest ranking officer continued in service after the Revolution. They were all that were left of Alexander Hamilton's battery. Though near the centers of population, the barracks at West Point had few of the ordinary comforts of the day. Men were not adequately clothed, and they suffered extremely when midwinter winds swept down the ice-covered Hudson. When the weather was good and the sun came out, they tried to

[3] "Journal of Arthur Lee," in J. W. Harpster, *Pen Pictures of Early Western Pennsylvania*, p. 160; *Order Book of Josiah Harmar No. 1*, Dec. 30, 1784, Jan. 9, 1785, William L. Clements Library, University of Michigan.

preserve the large stores of powder by drying it out and putting it in new kegs. Coopers were scarce and hard to hire at government wages. Hundreds of cartridge boxes had been turned in, and they required mending and oiling. There were many small arms, too, but parts had been lost or damaged; most of them were useless until artificers had made repairs.[4] Later, when the army was increased, requisitions were made on West Point and filled from this rubbish heap of discarded supplies. Broken guns, leaking cartridge boxes, and blunted bayonets went into the hands of untrained recruits to meet a crafty and resourceful enemy.

Meanwhile, Indians were hostile all along the north-western frontier. They resented the intrusion of immigrants trying to possess the land ceded to the United States by the treaty of 1783. Until savages were thoroughly beaten and the British ceased urging them on, they might be expected to continue raids into Pennsylvania and the districts of Tennessee and Kentucky. Once the English had evacuated Mackinac, Detroit, Oswego, and Niagara, the Indians would no longer have secret encouragement and a constant supply of ammunition and guns. Believing that these forts would soon be surrendered, Congress asked four of the states on June 3, 1784, for 700 men to act as garrisons and furnish general protection to the country north of the Ohio. They were to be taken from the militia and were to serve for twelve months unless sooner discharged. Connecticut was to furnish 165; New York 165; New Jersey 110, and Pennsylvania 260. The Secretary in the War Office, Major General Henry Knox, was to organize them into one regiment of infantry and two companies of artillery and govern their disposition and duties, subject to Congress while it was in session, otherwise to the Committee of the States.[5]

4 A. B. Gardner, *Register of the Army of the United States*, Jan. 1, 1784, to Jan. 1, 1785, p. 5; *Letter Book*, No. 2, U.S. Military Academy, West Point, N.Y., *passim*.

5 *Journals of the Continental Congress, 1774-1789*, XXVII, pp. 530-531. Troops so raised were to have the same pay as previously "allowed the troops of the United States."

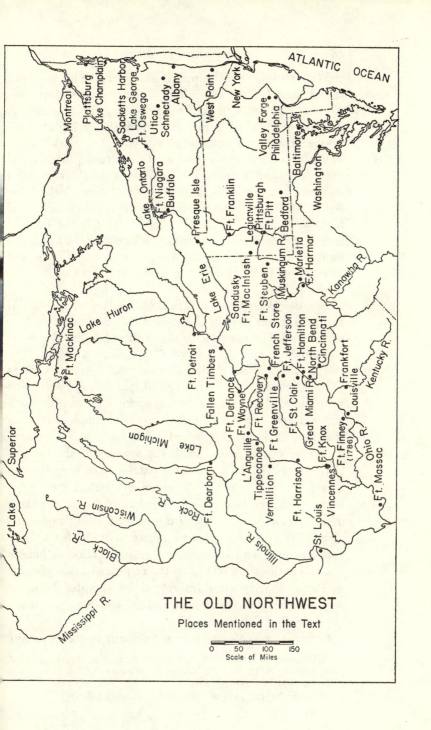

THE OLD NORTHWEST

Places Mentioned in the Text

0   50   100   150
Scale of Miles

Pennsylvania soon supplied its quota. The constant threat from Indians along its frontier had quickened compliance. New Jersey raised a single company. Connecticut delayed, not beginning to recruit until the spring of 1785. Massachusetts did nothing at all; she knew what trouble would be started once any of her troops took possession of the Oswego and Niagara country, which she still contended was hers in spite of the angry claims of New York. After Great Britain refused to make the expected surrender of forts in this area, neither of the states felt the need of immediate recruiting. Besides, New York wanted to use her own militia; she was having trouble with the Indians and was trying to make her own treaties with them in spite of the wishes of Congress.[6]

Because Pennsylvania furnished the largest number of troops, she was permitted to select the commanding officer of them all. He was to have the rank of lieutenant colonel commandant and the pay of fifty dollars a month. The thirty-one year old Josiah Harmar was appointed. Most of his life had been spent in Philadelphia among well-to-do people. For the times, his formal education had been much above average; boyhood note-books bear ample testimony that he was thoroughly instructed in Latin and Geometry by meticulous Quakers. With the opening of the Revolution he espoused the cause of the patriots, and when the war closed he had reached the grade of lieutenant colonel. Upon discharge he enjoyed a good reputation, something of an income, and the friendship of influential people. His disposition and circumstances seemed to fit him for a diplomatic errand, and Congress accordingly selected him to bear its ratification of the treaty of peace to our minister in Paris. Shortly after his return, he accepted both the responsibilities of matrimony and the command of troops for defending the frontier.[7]

Commissioned officers were not difficult to secure; many

6 Williamson to Duane, June 8, 1784; Reed to Washington, Aug. 13, 1784; both in E. C. Burnett, *Letters of Members of the Continental Congress*, VII, pp. 541-543, 584.

7 *Harmar Papers, passim.* William L. Clements Library.

of them with experience in the Revolution were without employment and eager for service in the army. The rank and file signed up more slowly. Pennsylvania wanted to enlist three seventy-man companies of infantry and a detachment of artillery fifty strong. Recruits had to be free of "fits, rupture, and other diseases." Those accepted were to have a two dollar bounty and a brand new uniform. A private was to draw $6.66 a month, a sergeant $10, and a sergeant major $15. Unlike the British army, no stoppages existed for the benefit of doctor or chaplain. "Every man had liberty to practice physic and pray for himself."[8] By September 30, 1785, nearly all Pennsylvania's troops had been recruited, equipped, organized, and were on their way from Philadelphia to Pittsburgh. Three unfortunates who were too sick for travel were left "friendless and moneyless" in Carpenters' Hall, where it was hoped that someone in the City of Brotherly Love would have enough compassion to care for them.[9]

Even for the vigorous in mind and body the march across the mountains was disheartening. By day they trudged along in chill autumn rain and at nightfall stretched their tents on sodden ground. Settlers along the route told them harrowing tales of Indian outrages. Some of the faint-hearted took fright and slunk away from the column; if caught and brought back they were summarily punished with a hundred lashes. At times troops halted a day or more to repair their wagons and obtain more rations. On these occasions, they tried to relieve their monotony in ways peculiarly their own. Twelve of them, when reaching Bedford, Pennsylvania, obtained permission to remain in town, putting up at the sign of the Blazing Star. Before long they had drunk enough whisky to send them staggering along the streets in search of adventure. After tearing up fences and turning the stock out to feed on neighboring gardens, they con-

[8] "Account of John Robert Shaw," in J. W. Harpster, *op. cit.*, pp. 166-168; J. B. McMaster, *op. cit.*, I, p. 191.

[9] McDowell to Dickinson, Sept. 30, 1784, in C. W. Butterfield *Journal of Captain Jonathan Heart*, p. 41.

tinued committing nuisances until their leader toppled into a twenty-foot well. He was bailed out by an Irish major, suffered punishment, and later became an excellent soldier and one of the most skillful well-diggers along the Ohio.[10]

Before the troops had reached Pittsburgh, Harmar had organized them into what he called the "First American Regiment."[11] Perhaps less than two hundred and fifty arrived there. During 1784 they were constantly kept on fatigue, repairing and enlarging the fort and doing odd jobs for the commissioners who were acting as agents of Pennsylvania and Congress to treat with the Indians. Most of the recruits disliked any kind of work or control. Their tasks were trying when the weather turned cold and their clothes became worn and threadbare. Before the year had ended, sixty had deserted. No chaplain had been appointed, but perhaps the wayward in soul would not have been deterred by his presence.[12]

The work around Pittsburgh was hard, ill-paid, and without chances for glory. From this base detachments were constantly dispatched in various directions for the maintenance of law and order. Fort McIntosh, thirty miles down the Ohio, was soon garrisoned, troops marching overland while their tents and baggage were being transported in barges. Although it was originally a stout stockaded work of hewn logs provided with four bastions and defended with six pieces of artillery, the fort had been abandoned toward the end of the Revolution.[13] With no one to hinder, Kentucky-bound immigrants had stripped it of everything that had any value. Harmar declared that "they had destroyed the gates, drawn all the nails from the roofs, taken off all the boards, and plundered it of every article."[14] To recondition the storehouses, palisades, and barracks required many men with ax and saw.

[10] "Account of John Robert Shaw," in J. W. Harpster, *op. cit.*, p. 162.

[11] C. W. Butterfield, *op. cit.*, p. 37.

[12] Harmar to Dickinson, Dec. 5, 1784, in C. W. Butterfield, *Journal of Captain Jonathan Heart*, p. 41.

[13] C. W. Butterfield, *op. cit.*, pp. 46–47.   [14] *Ibid.*, p. 58.

Supplies for the new post came from Fort Pitt. The downstream leg of the journey was made in a day; the return trip required two or three times as long. At least once it took four days for nine men to bring a boat back to Fort Pitt. On this occasion a barrel of whisky seems to have been the reason for their lack of haste and skill. The Quartermaster did not complain; he sent them again down the river in the more trying days of winter when the menace of ice was added to that of shoals, planters, and sawyers. Before returning they had to jump into the freezing waters and keep the boat turned upstream to prevent an upset. Two of them managed to get to the bank; and after walking four miles in heavy snow, they borrowed a canoe and salvaged the cargo.[15]

Even so, they were not as unlucky as the soldier, John Robert Shaw, who on another trip fell overboard while doing the steering. After being hauled out of the water, he was made to pull the fore oar as punishment for his carelessness. He was quickly frostbitten, and soon became ill. A few days later his boat struck a fish basket, and everything had to be jettisoned before it could be set free and floating once more. Bedridden and unable to move, Shaw was left alone on board by the rest of the fugitive crew. With better spirit and finer courage, a Lieutenant Butler came to the rescue, carrying him off to a cabin, where friends laid him in a fainting condition beside an open fire. Here they kept him tucked between two feather beds while they prepared a large tub of fresh spring water for bathing his feet and legs. A poultice of turnips was afterwards applied to the parts that had been frozen below the knees. For three weeks he lay suffering. By then the river had become navigable and he was taken to Fort McIntosh, where he was put in a barrack-room with Corporal Reed and Sergeant Major Duffy and his wife. It was next door to the apartment occupied by Lieutenant Colonel and Mrs. Harmar. During his sickness, he was carefully tended, two orderlies waiting on him and Doctors

[15] "Account of John Robert Shaw," in J. W. Harpster, op. cit., pp. 163-164.

McDowell and Allison prescribing helpful medicines. Every day Mrs. Harmar sent him the best food and wine that she had. Like all those who sustain the finest traditions of the service, she knew that no rank is worth the having unless it delights to give what is due to every faithful soldier. By August Shaw had recovered, but he and two others were declared unfit for service and recommended for a Pennsylvania pension. They were sent to Fort Pitt and told to remain there and draw rations as long as they wished. Finally Shaw hobbled away to Philadelphia, where he is reputed to have regained his accustomed health.[16]

Arthur Lee and Richard Butler fared much better than Shaw when they made a midwinter journey to Fort McIntosh about the beginning of 1785. They went there as federal commissioners to negotiate with the Wyandots, Delawares, Chippewas, and Ottawas, who had gathered to voice their complaints and listen to the government's proposals. This "ugly set of devils," as Denny called the Indians, were won over by food, drink, and the gifts of a few odds and ends. On January 25, 1785, the treaty of Fort McIntosh was signed. By its terms the four tribes present ceded most of the land lying in the area of the subsequent state of Ohio. They agreed to return all captives and surrender any of their own people guilty of robbery or murder of American citizens. They were to consider themselves under the protection of the United States and were to have the help of both federal and state authorities in getting rid of intruders upon their own lands.[17]

In fact, Harmar was already taking steps to burn the cabins and destroy the chattels of those who had unlawfully settled on the Pennsylvania land that lay between Forts McIntosh and Pitt. At about the same time he also received direction from the Commissioner of Indian Affairs to expel any squatters on areas under federal control. Ensign John Armstrong and twenty men, sent on this

[16] *Ibid.*, pp. 166-168.
[17] Harmar to Dickinson, Feb. 8, 1785, in C. W. Butterfield, *op. cit.*, p. 58.

disagreeable detail, found some of them in nearly every river bottom from Wheeling to Moravian Town. At the falls of the Hockhocking, he estimated there were three hundred families, on the Muskingum an equal number, on the Miami and Scioto about fifteen hundred. Against so many lawless and obstreperous whites, a few score soldiers could do nothing decisive.[18] Harmar wisely decided to give these squatters a little more time in which to abandon their shacks and haphazard clearings. It was better to wait until Congress should determine what should be done concerning the petitions that some of them had already made.

Harmar was becoming alarmed. His tasks were increasing while his own small force was disintegrating daily from death, desertion, and discharge. With few amusements, little clothing, indifferent rations, and scant pay, soldiers had slight reason to remain voluntarily in the service. They gloomily recalled the miles of tortuous roads that separated them from their squalid haunts of pleasure beyond the mountains. Forbidding forests, truculent Indians, continued hardships, and irritating control increased their nostalgia and created a pervasive hatred for the raw work necessary in winning the wilderness. Only the stalwart in spirit could find recompense in the comradeship that strong men enjoy; they alone could successfully meet the ever-recurrent challenges to fortitude. Those who failed waited impatiently for the day of their discharge when unrestrained they might start out once more on some untried path of adventure.

Of the two hundred or more troops in the neighborhood of Fort Pitt, 112 would finish their enlistment in August 1785 and all but ten of the rest in September.[19] By the law of April 12, 1785, the 700 previously authorized were to be continued in service for three years.[20] In consequence, Harmar immediately began to enlist Pennsylvania's quota of 260. He also sent to Governor Dickinson a list of the officers whom he believed should be retained in the service.

18 C. W. Butterfield, *op. cit.*, pp. 63-66. 19 *Ibid.*, p. 81.
20 J. F. Callan, *The Military Laws of the United States* (rev. ed.), p. 78.

At the same time, he vigorously condemned the recent reduction in pay of both officers and men.[21]

So parsimonious a step had been taken in spite of the fact that the need for more troops was constantly growing. The procastinating British were showing no inclination to surrender the forts that they held along the United States border; and the Indians, more restive than ever, were complaining bitterly against the surrender of the land west of the Ohio in accordance with the treaty of Fort Stanwix that some of their chiefs had signed in 1784. Squatters and unlicensed traders were invading the federal lands in the same general area. Harmar was ordered to move his troops down the river to a point between the Muskingum and the Great Miami and begin driving them out. For expenses Congress appropriated $600.[22]

On October 3, 1785, Captain Walter Finney and seventy men set out on such a mission. Two Indian commissioners, Richard Butler and James Monroe, accompanied them; a third, George Rogers Clark, planned to join the detachment somewhere down the Ohio. Twelve keel boats furnished most of the transportation for the men and their immediate equipment and supplies. They were usually longer but not so wide as the customary flatboat and were capable of carrying from twelve to forty tons; a four-inch square beam extended from bow to stern along the bottom, giving protection from snags and rocks. The horses, cows, and other stock were loaded on two flatboats. At this season the water was low and progress consequently slow, not more than twelve to fifteen miles being covered each day.

On October 22 they all reached the mouth of the Great Miami. Here they began building a fort on the eastern bank about 150 yards from the Ohio. Clark would have had it located on the western bank, but his wishes did not prevail. Within less than three weeks they had completed a stockaded enclosure about 100 feet square. Inside they felt safer and more comfortable; now they could readily kindle a

---

[21] Harmar to Dickinson, May 24, 1785, C. W. Butterfield, *op. cit.,* pp. 69-70.

[22] C. W. Butterfield, *op. cit.,* pp. 72-73.

fire and do their cooking beside the hearths of their clay-covered chimneys. In each corner of the stockade stood a building measuring twenty-four by eighteen feet, serving both as barracks and bastion. Elsewhere a magazine and place for contractor's goods were added. A short distance from the fort a council house was ultimately built. To honor Captain Finney the post bore his name.[23]

About the middle of 1787 the garrison left and established another fort of the same name near the falls of the Ohio. In this general vicinity the Kentuckians had become greatly alarmed over the dangers from Indians, who had become increasingly insolent since the pusillanimous expedition of George Rogers Clark against them during the autumn of 1786. The site selected for the new fort lay on a sloping bank about a half-mile from the beginning of the rapids. Between it and the river, some ninety yards distant, gardens were planted and grew luxuriantly. Quarters were comfortable and the necessities of life very cheap. Members of the garrison often found pleasure in entertaining travelers and agreeable persons of the community. But when officers visited Louisville or places nearby they carried a pistol or dirk under their coat, for there were many bullies who gloated on their prowess. One of them boasted that he had gouged out five eyes, that he had bitten off two or three noses and spat them back in the faces of the beaten. Once the very same ruffian attacked an officer and, though knocked down three or four times, did succeed in leaving on his nose a permanent scar.[24]

The first Fort Finney was not the only post established in 1785 and subsequently evacuated. Early in 1784 Congress had discussed the sale of land and the government of prospective settlers north of the Ohio. Nothing immediately resulted, but the ideas in the subsequent Northwest Ordinance began to germinate. However, a land ordinance

---

[23] For first Fort Finney, "Military Journal of Major Ebenezer Denny," *passim*, and T. Rainey, "Fort Finney," in *Cincinnati Times Star*, Dec. 13, 1937.

[24] Harmar to Knox, July 13, 1786, *Harmar Papers*, William L. Clements Library; "Diary of Erkuries Beatty," *Magazine of American History*, I, pp. 432-433.

did become effective in 1785, establishing an admirable system for surveying the national domain. In September of the same year, Harmar was particularly enjoined to protect federal surveyors laying off seven ranges just west of the Pennsylvania boundary line. For the purpose he detailed Major John Hamtramck and three companies of infantry; they were soon building a blockhouse twenty-three miles above Wheeling on the "Indian Shore," bearing the name Fort Steuben. In this general vicinity he remained for about two years.[25]

About the middle of 1787, Hamtramck was ordered to evacuate Fort Steuben and establish a post at Vincennes, where there were about three hundred families indolently living in dirty log huts along the Wabash River. They were mostly of French descent; and, according to Symmes, a most peculiar lot. He declared that the men were the greatest slaves in the world to the women, even doing the milking and cooking, in fact, all the chores inside and out of the house, except nursing the babies and washing the clothes. Perhaps such men could not be relied on to defend our most westerly outpost. Certainly Hamtramck would try to prevent any encroachment of the Indians, British, or Spaniards. For this purpose he erected a fort capable of housing three companies or more. It was christened Fort Knox in compliment to the Secretary of War.[26]

Meanwhile Harmar and the rest of his command had taken station further down the Ohio. Before the end of 1785, Fort Harmar was rising on the west side of the mouth of the Muskingum. It was made of logs and was large enough to accommodate a regiment. It was pentagonal in shape, each corner being provided with an identical bastion measuring forty feet on a side. The five bastions were two stories high. Each upper story had four and six-pound cannon to sweep away any Indians trying to scale the walls; the lower one was divided into two rooms

---

25 "Diary of Erkuries Beatty," *loc. cit.*, I, pp. 313, 382.

26 Harmar to Knox, Aug. 7, 1787, *Harmar Papers*, William L. Clements Library; and B. W. Bond, *The Correspondence of John Cleves Symmes*, pp. 288-290.

twenty feet square and was used as quarters for officers and their families. Connecting the bastions were curtains, about 120 feet long and 12 feet high, forming the outside wall of the barracks and storehouses. Roofs sloped inward so that defense might be easier and rainwater could be more readily caught. Near the center of the enclosure were the arsenal and flagstaff. On one curtain a towerlike cupola rose high above adjacent buildings. Here a sentinel was posted to scan the surrounding country for approaching enemies. If need be, troops could go out to counterattack through the sally port, which was on the land side, looking out upon a stretch of ground used for drill and parades. The main gate, called the water gate, opened on the side nearest the Muskingum. For about fifty yards from this exit the adjacent ground was some eight feet higher than the more distant and level section which lay closer to the river. This space was later used as the site for the large buildings used by blacksmiths, wheelwright, carpenters, and other artisans. Behind the fort, close to the walls, a number of gardens were laid out and carefully tended. Here officers' wives had a few beds of flowers, possibly petunias, cockscombs, four-o'clocks, zinnias, etc. They had brought the seeds with them from the East; bright blossoms made the hardships of the wilderness less difficult to bear. Vegetables, however, predominated— beans, peas, squashes, radishes, turnips, and melons. Beyond, fruit trees were planted. Captain Doughty took a great interest in an orchard, developing the "Doughty Peach," long known and enjoyed around Marietta, Ohio.[27]

By the summer of 1786 Fort Harmar was thoroughly established. Those in the reach of its protection had less fear from Indian attack. Eastern emigrants were now eager to cross the mountains and build new homes along the Ohio. In the same year General Rufus Putnam and

27 S. P. Hildreth, *Contributions to the Early History of the Northwest*, etc., pp. 215-218. A picture of Fort Harmar is given in Woodrow Wilson, *A History of the American People*, V, p. 203. At least some of the flowers and vegetables mentioned were grown around Fort Harmar, perhaps all of them. Casual references are made to them in various contemporary accounts.

several Continental officers met in Boston at the Bunch of Grapes Tavern. With their judgment sharpened by good food and drink, they decided to exchange their near-worthless paper money for good lands in the West. For this purpose they formed the Ohio Company; and through their agent, Dr. Manasseh Cutler, a well-known divine, they obtained a contract from Congress for about 1,500,-000 acres lying just west of the Pennsylvania boundary. The price was a million dollars. The land was of high quality, far better in kind than the eight-cent dollars that went for its purchase.[28]

Simultaneously Cutler obtained a grant of about 3,500,-000 acres west of the Ohio Company's land in the name of Winthrop Sargent. It went to form the holdings of the Scioto Company, composed of a number of New Yorkers who hoped to defraud the government and did succeed in swindling some of the public. One of their representatives abroad was an ex-preacher and indifferent poet by the name of Joel Barlow. Some 500 Frenchmen succumbed to his peerless mendacity concerning a Utopia for five shillings an acre. They were men of the city—carvers, gilders, dyers, and makers of coaches, wigs, and lustrous garments. After crossing the sea in storm, some of them continued on across the mountains only to find themselves in the midst of an Indian-infested wilderness on a plot of land that they did not own and knew not how to cultivate. Congress finally came to their rescue, granting them 25,200 acres between 1795 and 1798. To the swindlers who had brought them to such pitiful misery, nothing much was ever done.[29]

Besides the cheated and deluded, many well-fitted for pioneering started for the Northwest Territory. From the government or other sources they had acquired legitimate titles to the best land at extremely low prices. They determined to make the wilderness a better place than the homes that they left behind in some of the disordered states of the Union. They had reason to hope that they might live safely and democratically in the new country. On January

28 E. A. Channing, *A History of the United States*, IV, p. 542.
29 J. B. McMaster, *op. cit.*, II, pp. 146-151.

31, 1786, the Shawnees had signed a treaty surrendering all their lands north of the Ohio except a small section for hunting. On July 13 of the following year Congress had passed the Northwest Ordinance, by which settlers could expect a civil administration of law in accordance with their own conceptions. The poor with enterprise required no further inducement for coming. From October 1786 till the following May, the adjutant at Fort Harmar counted as many as 177 flatboats floating by the post. From Pittsburgh alone fifty barges, arks, broadhorns, etc. set out during the spring of 1787. In 1788, ten thousand immigrants were reputed to have passed by Marietta alone, and these were probably no more than half of the total.[30]

Not a few of them traveled under the auspices of the Ohio Company, which established its headquarters near the mouth of the Muskingum at a place called Marietta, in honor of the queen of France. Rufus Putnam, one of the directors, arrived there with some fifty settlers on April 7, 1788. They were from New England, and they came in a barge that they had built during the winter and christened the *Mayflower*. It was forty-five feet long, bullet-proof, and heavily timbered. Delighted with its coming, the officers and men of Fort Harmar quickly assembled and eagerly helped the crew bring it snugly to shore. Only a little group of Delaware Indians observing nearby evinced no enthusiasm. They looked silently and curiously on without offering aid. The whites themselves resented the Indians' presence; for they were an ill-smelling lot, and they dressed and acted like "the children of Satan." With others soon following this vanguard under Putnam, log huts began to rise where once stood huge trees of oak and sycamore. Large squares were cleared to lay the basis of a becoming city. One of these at Marietta was called Camp Martius. Here an extensive palisade enclosed a number of blockhouses. In one of them Governor Arthur St. Clair found temporary quarters when he came west in 1788 with his three daughters, Louisa, Jane, and Margaret, and his

[30] J. B. McMaster, *op. cit.*, I, p. 517.

son Arthur, twenty-one years old. These children, with a Negro housekeeper and cook, composed his menage. Mrs. St. Clair was in the East, and did not join the family until later.[31]

When the Governor was comfortably settled, the directors of the Ohio Company gave a dinner honoring him and the officers and ladies of Fort Harmar. The guests from across the Muskingum came over in a twelve-oared barge especially decorated for the occasion. It was the Fourth of July, 1788, and the booming of guns announced the character of the day. Gathering under a huge bower, they sat at a sixty-foot table loaded with a great variety of fish from the river and game from the forest. Beans, peas, and radishes were also abundantly served. Scarcely had the meal begun, when the clouds darkened and the rain descended in torrents. The food was quickly rescued, and after awhile the table was set once more. Then a second deluge came, again interrupting the eating, though not the drinking. A brimming bowl of punch was easily accessible; if any preferred grog or wine, that, too, might be had without asking. Toast followed toast. The twelfth was designed as a compliment to the ladies, being dedicated to "The Amiable Partners of Our Lives." In maudlin generosity, the thirteenth and official last was drunk to "All Mankind." About midnight the guests began to leave. It had been a "handsome dinner."[32]

Harmar enjoyed such a pleasing interruption of the frequently trying and ill-requited work constantly required of him and his men in protecting the law-abiding immigrants who were entering the Northwest in greatly increasing numbers. Many were coming at the urging of John Cleves Symmes, who had signed a contract in 1788 for 1,000,000 acres lying between the Little Miami and the Great Miami rivers. He in turn sold a small section of his tract to three speculators. The trio included an ex-schoolteacher named John Filson, who called their settlement opposite the mouth of the Licking, Losantiville, an atro-

---

[31] R. H. Gabriel, *The Lure of the Frontier*, II, pp. 78-79.
[32] R. S. Edes, *Journal and Letters of Colonel John May*, p. 79.

cious combination of Latin, Greek and French words. A few weeks later the Indians scalped Filson, but apparently not for this reason. When St. Clair visited the place in 1790 he changed the name to Cincinnati, in honor of the Revolutionary Society of which he was a member.[33]

Symmes did not visit his own holdings until 1789. On February 2 he landed at North Bend with a company of infantry commanded by Lieutenant William Kersey. The cold was intense. Rude shelters were quickly made by setting two forked saplings upright and connecting them with a ridge-pole. Boards were ripped from the boats and placed against it, forming a sort of steep-roofed hogan ventilated at both ends. One end was roughly closed and in front of the other a fire was kept burning. Six weeks passed before Symmes had a log cabin and a few rude comforts.[34]

The soldiers underwent even greater hardships. Coming almost empty-handed into the wilderness, they had to depend upon the bounty of Symmes. Food was dear and hard to obtain. Troops needed a good deal of bread and meat, especially because their service was hard and they were often scattered in small groups. When inhabitants of Columbia became fearful of an Indian raid, a sergeant and eighteen men were dispatched to protect them. They did keep the savages away, but the floods came and the waters rose to the loft of their block-house. Luckily they managed to escape in a boat that had been salvaged from the raging waters of the Ohio. On another occasion some immigrants stopped at North Bend on their way to the Falls of the Ohio. For their protection a sergeant and twelve men were detailed to go along with them. Symmes gave the detachment a little food, and the immigrants agreed to provide it with more. They did not have long to redeem their promise, for ice soon wrecked their boats and all ideas of a settlement were abandoned. With no assurance against starvation in his present location, Kersey decided to move to Fort Finney. Thus North Bend

[33] R. King, *Ohio*, pp. 213-214.
[34] Symmes to Dayton, May 18, 19, 20, 1789, in B. W. Bond, *The Correspondence of John Cleves Symmes*, pp. 55-63.

was temporarily left without troops. At other times it had five federal defenders.[35]

Symmes was incensed; he deemed the life of his settlers precarious and the action of Kersey outrageous. He was particularly irritated because a story was going the rounds that his real estate venture was petering out; so he sat down and wrote to Jonathan Dayton, business associate and rising politician in New Jersey, asking him to see Henry Knox, Secretary of War, and have Kersey punished.[36] Once Harmar learned what had happened, he ordered the lieutenant to join Captain John Mercer's company and go back with it to the settlements of Symmes along the Great Miami.

Meanwhile, Ensign Francis Luce, with seventeen rank and file, had carried on the best he could—not much protection for the "North Bend Slaughter House," as Kentuckians in derision called it. Except for guns and ammunition, the soldiers had almost nothing at all. Their stores did not include axes, hoes, saws, frows, and augers. Symmes supplied what he could; and, after working a week, they built a blockhouse of sorts. When it proved only large enough to shelter the troops in case of attack, the settlers were filled with chagrin. Symmes was also disgusted because the tools loaned to them were either very much damaged or never returned at all. Passing boatmen fell into the habit of offering whisky for axes, and once in a while a weatherbeaten soldier exchanged his instrument of toil for a jug of oblivion.[37]

Troops along the Ohio were not alone in their hardships. They fared very badly at Venango, Pennsylvania, a place that was about 150 miles above Pittsburgh on the Allegheny River. There Captain Jonathan Heart had been sent with his company and a detachment of artillery to build Fort Franklin as a protection against the Indians along the northern frontier of Pennsylvania. He was to commence hostilities only in case of "unprovoked aggression." On April 28, 1787, he left Pittsburgh with the tools

---

[35] B. W. Bond, op. cit., pp. 54-58, 61.   [36] Ibid., pp. 81-82.
[37] Ibid., pp. 55-58, 81-82.

that he needed—felling axes, picks, shovels, augers, frows, knives, and gimlets. He also carried along a grindstone, bellows, and 200 pounds of steel and iron. Arriving at French Creek on May 11, 1787, he decided to build the blockhouse on its south bank, a half-mile from its juncture with the Allegheny. This point enabled him to protect his boats more easily and to get plenty of water without digging a well. The building of the fort began immediately. Those who could do the work of artificers were given an extra ration; those who were less skillful obtained a double allowance of whisky a day. Food was always at a premium. If the soldier was lucky enough to get more than he needed, he could readily trade it off to some of his married companions or to starving Indian women and children who were constantly visiting the garrison to beg or steal.[38]

Captain Heart was openly friendly with the savages. He helped to obtain and distribute fifty bushels of corn that Major General Richard Butler had sent them. Kayashuto, a Seneca chief, was very thankful and made him promises of peace. The understanding Heart answered, "I am glad to see you hold the Chain of Peace. The Thirteen Fires put in your hands. Be strong and hold it fast. I will hold one link with both hands. You must not let it go. If you do, it will fall out of my hand. It is a great chain. I cannot hold it alone. You must help me."[39]

The Indians of the neighborhood did so. But by the end of 1787 they were very few. Smallpox came in the summer and carried away all except three men, five women, and a few children. The troops fortunately escaped the disease, but not the hardships in establishing a fort. To cover their nakedness, they cut off their coat tails to use for patches. On the coming of heavy autumn rains, they dug and ditched to keep their barracks from being overflowed. When ice covered the river and rations failed to arrive, they had to eat the flour that had been previously condemned. By the spring of 1788 few cared to reenlist. The

[38] *Letter Book of Captain Heart* (Apr. 17, 1787, to Jan. 26, 1788), *passim*, National Archives.
[39] *Ibid.*, pp. 27-28.

willing ones were mostly common drunkards whom Heart did not want. The majority of his sturdy farmer lads were eager to cross the mountains and return home. In this situation he thought best to leave Fort Franklin under another officer and go to Connecticut for recruits to fill his dwindling ranks. He did not return to the West until the spring of 1789, and then he took post on the lower Ohio.[40]

In the northwest, federal troops were now stationed all the way from the upper reaches of the Allegheny to near Louisville, Kentucky. In the East there were only two small detachments, one at West Point, New York, and another at Springfield, Massachusetts. In spite of the fact that the army greatly needed reinforcements and better maintenance, Congress had done very little. It was rent by selfish interest. The New England states had no frontiers to protect, and they did not care to spend their hard-earned money to make the Northwest Territory safe. They did not want any additional encouragement to their thrifty farmers and enterprising tradesmen to journey across the mountains and found new homes where the lands were unbelievably cheap, miraculously fertile, and blest with a more kindly climate than that of the northern Atlantic seaboard. The Southern and Middle States had different reasons, but the result was the same. Most of them, suffering from raids along their borders, were avid for federal money to keep the Indians in order; but they usually insisted that it be expended through the channel of the militia. In any event, Congressmen too often hid their narrow and selfish reasons through the commonplace tricks of demagoguery, inveighing against the expense of maintaining a force of regulars and expatiating upon the danger of a standing army to the liberties of the people.

Congress was reluctant and half-hearted in taking any action beneficial to the army. On October 20, 1786, it had authorized 1,340 more men to reinforce the 700 that presumably existed. In the preceding July only 518 were actually in ranks. Six states were to supply a certain number of recruits. Virginia's quota was sixty, Massa-

[40] C. W. Butterfield, *op. cit., passim.*

chusetts' eleven times as many. The pay and allowances
were to be the same as before. The expense entailed involved
borrowing, which was in turn to be repaid by contributions
from the states. The term of service was fixed at three
years; men were encouraged to enlist by the promise of
attractive clothing, comfortable barracks, good provisions,
and the advance of a half-month's pay. Once recruited
they were to be organized into a "legionary Corps" consisting of two troops of cavalry, one battalion of artillery,
one battalion of light troops, and three regiments of infantry.[41] With this additional force, the federal government could have successfully solved some of its most pressing problems of defense. As it was, only two companies of
artillery ever were raised; they were designed to guard
the arsenal at Springfield, Massachusetts. Lack of funds
and interstate bickering prevented the entire program from
being carried out.

Congress had better success in drawing up new rules
for the trial of Army offenders. The wide scattering of
army personnel made the maintenance of discipline particularly difficult. In the future a minimum of five officers
might compose a general court-martial; capital punishment in times of peace had to be approved by Congress;
corporal punishment was limited to 100 lashes; the rights
of the accused were to be duly protected; deserters and
cashiered officers were to be publicized in the papers.[42]
These and other provisions were designed to improve the
administration of justice in the army. As a rule, punishments were better suited to the offense and less easy to
evade than in the ordinary civil courts.

During the same year of 1786, no corresponding improvement was accomplished in the feeding of the army.
The contract for rations was let to Turnbull, Marmie, and
Co., covering the usual components of bread, meat, rum,
and a small portion of salt, vinegar, soap, and candles for
every hundred men. At Fort Pitt a ration cost $10\frac{1}{3}$ nine-

---

[41] T. H. S. Hamersly, *Complete Regular Army Register of the United States*, p. 231 (second part).

[42] J. F. Callan, *op. cit.*, pp. 78-83.

tieths of a dollar, at Fort McIntosh and Fort Harmar 11½ ninetieths. The contractor was paid in depreciated Pennsylvania currency, and he retaliated by furnishing "depreciated" rations, or none at all. During November, troops at Fort Harmar often went hungry, for they got only half their allowance of bread and meat. In the following January, they might have starved if Harmar had not advanced his own personal funds to purchase provisions. For a time conditions were so bad that he thought of abandoning the fort.[43] They began to improve in 1787, however, when the Board of the Treasury let the contract to James O'Hara, who lived in Pittsburgh. This was probably the best place for supervising the distribution of army supplies. Under him rations cost a little less than before, deliveries being made at Forts Harmar, McIntosh, and Pitt, as well as two new places, the Rapids of the Ohio (Louisville, Kentucky) and Venango, Pennsylvania.[44] Elliott and Williams, the sucessors of O'Hara, did "the business with spirit." Their contract ran until the end of 1789. By its terms, the ration cost a minimum of 7/90 of a dollar at Forts Pitt, McIntosh, and Harmar and a maximum of 16/90 of a dollar at Fort Knox (Vincennes, Indiana). Payment was made in warrants on Maryland. When officers at Vincennes needed more food for themselves and dependents, Harmar granted them an additional ration. The contractors overcame a shortage of flour at several posts by securing a little from local sources.[45] At some places venison was plentiful; turkeys and buffalo were also abundant. Once in a while a catfish weighing 100 pounds could be caught in the Ohio.[46] At the older posts

[43] R. P. Thian, *Legislative History of the General Staff of the United States*, pp. 327-328; Harmar to Doughty, Dec. 21, 1786, to Finney, Jan. 7, 1787, to Marmie, Jan. 10, 1787, *Harmar Papers*, William L. Clements Library.

[44] R. P. Thian, *op. cit.*, p. 328.

[45] *Ibid.*, p. 328; Harmar to Wyllys, July 16, 1788, to Hamtramck, Aug. 7, 1788, to Elliott and Williams, Jan. 21, 1789, *Harmar Papers*, William L. Clements Library.

[46] Harmar to Mifflin, Nov. 9, 1789, *Harmar Papers*, William L. Clements Library.

food was better and more plentiful than it had been for several years.

Not only did soldiers often go hungry; they lacked adequate clothing and proper equipment. Their near-bankrupt government almost entirely failed them. Far too often they were provided with inferior guns, bayonets, and cartridge boxes that had been turned in after the Revolution and had accumulated at West Point, Philadelphia, and other places. Since the quartermaster's department had been abolished on July 25, 1785, the contractor had taken over its duties; in other words, he was supposed to supply such articles as were "indispensably necessary" when ordered to do so in writing by Harmar or post commanders. Whatever was finally received frequently did not conform either to requisition or specification in respect to quality and quantity. During April 1786 Harmar himself reported that the shirts were skimpy, of sleazy cloth, and would wear out in a week. Shoes were too small; they were designed for twelve or fourteen-year-old boys, and the leather was bad. For a variety of reasons the hats were objectionable. Coats provided in Philadelphia were so worthless that they would not have lasted through the march to Pittsburgh unless fatigue coats had been worn for part of the time. On October 2, 1788, old soldiers were short a year's supply of clothing. They did not receive it because it had been used to fit out the recruits of 1788. The Board of the Treasury hoped, however, that they might get what was due them the next year if a contract could be negotiated.[47]

In the matter of pay, conditions were even worse. At first troops were paid in Continental currency at the monthly rate of $90 for a colonel, $45 for a captain, and $7 for a private, or equal respectively in "hard money" to $3.30, $1.55 and 26 cents. In 1786 Knox made strenuous efforts to have the troops paid in specie, directing the paymaster, Erkuries Beatty, to get an order from the Board of the Treasury for the purpose. He succeeded in getting one

[47] R. P. Thian, *op. cit.*, pp. 190-191; Harmar to Knox, July 1, 1785, *Harmar Papers*, William L. Clements Library.

amounting to $12,000 drawn on Thomas Smith of the Loan Office of Pennsylvania. But Smith had no money, and so he transferred the order to David Rittenhouse, Treasurer of Pennsylvania. But Rittenhouse had no specie, so he gave Beatty orders on several country treasurers, but only for $8,000. Hopeful of collecting even this smaller amount, Beatty set out, visiting Easton, Reading, Lebanon, Lancaster, York, etc. but obtaining little but paper money. Hearing of the result, Knox told him to take anything offered and discount enough of it to give the troops one month's pay in specie. After a second trip, Beatty collected $8,000 from "one person or another," $3,000 of which he converted into specie and $1,000 he employed to liquidate officers' and men's obligations to the contractor. The remaining $4,000 Rittenhouse promised to have ready for him on April 1, or about six months later. To Beatty, the matter was "a troublesome piece of business as ever I undertook."[48]

Because of such a scarcity of funds, troops seldom drew pay more than once or twice a year. On October 2, 1788, they had not been paid since January 1, 1787. Officers, however, had drawn their subsistence and forage money to April 1, 1788. In spite of this shabby treatment of the rank and file, a committee of Congress reported that they "appear well satisfied in this respect."[49] Perhaps troops may have become indifferent because they had little or nothing due them owing to various deductions for this or that. But it seems more likely that the committee was ignorant of the truth or unwilling to tell it.

Over this ill-fed, ill-clothed, and ill-paid force, sometimes of not more than 595 men, Henry Knox presided as "Secretary at War," Congress having elected him on March 8, 1785, and promised him $2,450 a year. Three clerks assisted him with an annual salary of $450 apiece. There was also a lone messenger who had to make $150 suffice for his living. Contingent expenses for the Secre-

48 "Diary of Erkuries Beatty," *Magazine of American History*, I, pp. 380-381.

49 R. P. Thian, *op. cit.*, p. 457.

tary's office—fuel, candles, stationery, etc.—amounted to
$176 a year.[50] So modest an overhead was in keeping with
the size of what was commonly called the army—the First
American Regiment and battalion of artillery. It was
really no more than a frontier constabulary for making
the Indians behave and a police force for protecting
arsenals and supply bases in the more populous sections
of the country.

[50] T. H. S. Hamersly, *op. cit.*, pp. 231-232 (second part).

3. *Harmar Tries an Offensive and Fails*

FROM 1783 to 1788 Congress increasingly declined in public confidence and esteem. Although its members, for the most part, were distinguished and able, they could accomplish little. Their range of legislation was entirely too restricted and no real executive power existed. In the general conduct of affairs that were essentially federal, they ignominiously failed. The states bitterly wrangled over boundaries, tariffs, and foreign treaties, and no authority was capable of bringing them to book and making them accept an equitable decision. Those who had led the nation successfully through the Revolution now wondered if they had only ushered it into political chaos. Washington and his colleagues foresaw that all their sacrifices would be in vain unless they succeeded in establishing a central government worthy of support and admiration at home and capable of convincing countries abroad of its strength and capacity to meet the responsibilities assumed by its treaties. Political leaders at Mount Vernon in 1785 and at Annapolis in 1786 became fully conscious of the fact that the Articles of Confederation must be revised. Not a few members of the moribund Congress simultaneously reacted in the very same way. This opinion finally reached such strength that delegates from the states were called to meet at Philadelphia to propose steps to be taken. Once assembled, they became known as the Constitutional Convention.

Seldom have so many able men counseled together for their country's good. George Washington, James Madison, Benjamin Franklin, John Dickinson, and Alexander Hamilton were there. Others were present whose minds were equally keen and whose patriotism was equally ardent. From May 14 until September 17, 1787, they worked with clear and far-seeing vision to draw up our present Constitution; but not until June 21, 1788, was it adopted by the necessary majority of nine states.

On April 30, 1789, Washington was inaugurated in the city of New York as the first President. Though this event was the forerunner of better times, many of the thoughtful began to wonder how he and his assistants would perform the difficult tasks soon to be theirs. The doubters were reassured when he and his colleagues sought peace in preference to almost anything else. Only if peace prevailed would the recently adopted Constitution have a chance of successful operation. Needed laws might be enacted; federal courts and executive agents would have a normal opportunity to learn their functions. On the contrary, the growing admiration for the new order would quickly dwindle away if recovery were retarded by the demoralization of war. Hence discerning statesmen earnestly worked to avoid any great struggle, whether with Indians along the frontier or with foreign peoples across the sea.

Certainly tranquility was more easily possible under the new Constitution. The federal government could now hope to keep its engagements with foreign countries, eliminate weakness that had invited exploitation, and suppress domestic violence, such as Shays' Rebellion. It now possessed direct authority to call forth "the militia, to execute the laws of the Union, suppress insurrection and repel invasion." Besides, it could "raise and support armies" and draw up rules for their government. The President was designated as Commander in Chief, and on him fell the burden of appointing officers. Upon Congress rested the responsibility of determining the size and character of our federal force. Funds might become quickly available, for now taxes could not only be laid but also collected.

When Congress met, it did not fail to use its allotted powers. On August 7, 1789, the War Department, with a Secretary, was created as one of the executive branches of the government. The Secretary was to perform any duties that the President might assign him in reference to army, navy, Indian affairs, or lands under grant for military services. He was to have a chief clerk who might act during his temporary absence or permanent removal. All employees of the department were to take an oath "well and faithfully to execute the trust committed" to them.[1] By 1792 they had grown to only ten with an average annual salary of $460.[2]

Henry Knox became Secretary at a salary of only $3,000 a year, a sum that did not go far to support his pretentious living at the temporary capital, where some spoke of him as the "Philadelphia nabob." He was then forty-two years old, over six feet tall, and weighed about 280 pounds. His appointment had come because he possessed not only the confidence but also the affection of Washington, whom he had efficiently served as chief of artillery during the Revolution. Owing to the inventive skill of Knox heavy guns had been hauled over the snow from Ticonderoga and used to batter the British out of Boston in 1776. Several months later he marched with Washington in the disheartening retreat from New York. Toward the end of the year his voice roared laggards to victory at Trenton and Princeton. During the operations around Philadelphia, he handled his artillery so well that he even elicited praise from the British. In the bitter winter at Valley Forge, he stoically and encouragingly endured with the tattered nucleus of the Continental Army. At Yorktown he saw his batteries help bring Cornwallis to surrender. When the war ended, he organized the Society of the Cincinnati; he and Washington were elected respectively its first secretary and president. On March 8, 1785, he became Secretary of War under the Articles of Confederation, a post to which he was again appointed on September 12, 1789, after its character had been changed by the Constitution. He continued in office until December 31, 1794.[3]

In 1789, the War Department's most immediate problem

[1] J. F. Callan, *Military Laws of the United States* (rev. ed.), pp. 85-86.

[2] *American State Papers, Miscellaneous Affairs*, I, p. 58.

[3] *Dictionary of American Biography*, X, pp. 475-477; *Bulletin of Fort Ticonderoga Museum*, July, 1936, pp. 30-31.

concerned the frontier. Peace with the Indians must be made and enforced with the means provided by Congress. The majority of Congressmen came from along the Atlantic seaboard. They were conservative in outlook; their interest essentially centered on the country that lay east of the Appalachians. Secure in their comforts, they could not visualize the suffering that their kinsmen endured at the hands of savages along the valleys that drained into the Ohio and the Gulf of Mexico. They were not moved to spend money on raising a regular army to be sent far into the wilderness to subdue a relentless foe that had been driven long since from the environs of their own principal towns and cities. Some were not sure that the army would be successful on such a mission; others believed that it could not be trusted and might eventually become an instrument of tyrannical oppression. The majority of the lawmakers had not enjoyed a very broad experience; they were deeply perplexed by the range and variety of their new tasks. Least of all did they care for any large expenditures of funds when Hamilton was straining every effort to make the new-born government solvent and pay in full its long overdue obligations.[4]

Out of sheer necessity, an act was passed on September 29, 1789, the very last day of the first session of the First Congress, legalizing the 840 men authorized by the law of October 3, 1787. Only about 672 of these were actually in the service. Regular troops were granted the same pay and allowances as before and made subject to the Rules and Articles of War, and the President was authorized to call out the militia to protect the settlers against Indians. Obviously the law was designed to serve only as a makeshift until the needs of the country could be thoroughly investigated.[5]

Such an investigation occurred during the second and third sessions of the First Congress. Leaders in politics

[4] E. A. Channing, IV, pp. 37-40; J. S. Bassett, *A Short History of the United States*, pp. 259-261; H. J. Ford, *Washington and his Colleagues*, pp. 26-79.

[5] J. F. Callan, *op. cit.*, p. 87; and *American State Papers, Military Affairs*, I, pp. 5-6.

and government bitterly debated measures designed for the defense of the United States against its enemies at home and abroad. In them, Henry Knox, as Secretary of War, took a very interested part. According to his ideas, "A small corps of well-disciplined and well-informed artillerists and engineers, and a legion [of 2,033 officers and men] for the protection of the frontiers and the magazines and arsenals" were all the regular troops that the United States required for its immediate needs.[6]

In addition, Knox wanted this small force supplemented by "an energetic national militia . . . the capital security of a free republic." His country could then cope with any emergency. In support of this thesis he proposed that all citizens between eighteen and sixty years of age be held liable for military service. By his plan, men eighteen, nineteen, or twenty years old were divided into three groups according to age and formed into an "Advanced Corps." Those in the two younger groups were to be trained annually for thirty days; those in the oldest group, for ten days only. After thus completing these three training periods, they were to be transferred to the "Main Corps," assembling every year for four days' instruction until they reached the age of forty-six. Then they passed to the "Reserve Corps" and reported only twice annually for routine inspection of arms.[7]

The plan was substantially the same as the one proposed by Washington in 1786 except for the reduction in time of training of the "Advanced Corps" from 126 to 70 days. In spite of the change, Congress did not support this meritorious proposal. The people could not think in terms of long-range security when they had to pay for it immediately by giving up part of their time and submitting themselves to a discipline that they very much hated. General Benjamin Lincoln declared the bill was damned because of "expense, pay of officers, no pay of men, the burden on masters, calling on the youth indiscriminately,

6 Knox to the President, Jan. 18, 1790, in *American State Papers, Military Affairs*, I, p. 7.
7 *Ibid.*, pp. 6-13.

disfranchisement for a time in certain cases, officers excluded from active service, subjection to a draft for a service of three years, etc."[8] Someone at Elizabethtown, Pennsylvania, execrated it because it was "pregnant with mischief both to the agricultural and mining interests as well as having a tendency to debauch the morals of the rising generation."[9] A correspondent in the *Gazette of the United States* avowed that the existing militia of Connecticut was all sufficient, consisting of "thirty thousand effective men, well officered and appointed, and completely armed . . . who are determined to support the Constitution and government, without the aid of a standing army, or an expensive national militia."[10] Massachusetts had even more of the same type, hypothetical soldiers assigned to imaginary brigades and divisions. They were admirable as a political machine, but for uses in battle they were utterly futile. They were dominated by an epauletted hierarchy that bulged with fat and ignorance. Not until more than a century had passed would our system of defense become reasonably efficient through unequivocal legislation.

With most of his militia program failing to win Congressional approval, Knox applied himself to obtaining a larger force of regulars. From various places along the frontier settlers were demanding that they be made safe from the raids of marauding savages. On April 15, 1790, Pierce Butler, Senator from South Carolina, declared Georgia would get help elsewhere if troops were not sent for its protection. Ralph Izard, his colleague, held similar views. When some railed at standing armies, he declared himself ready for one of 10,000; it was not because of standing armies, he added, that Rome had fallen, nor did he expect the United States to suffer for any such reason. His logic was correct but his motives were questionable. At this time the South Carolina Yazoo Company had a dubious title to 3,000,000 acres lying near the Yazoo River in lands of

---

[8] Lincoln to Knox, Feb. 12, 1790, *Knox Papers*, Massachusetts Historical Society.

[9] *Pennsylvania Packet and Advertiser*, Apr. 14, 1790, quoted in J. M. Palmer, *America in Arms*, p. 45.

[10] Quoted in J. M. Palmer, *op. cit.*, p. 44.

the Choctaws. Prominent South Carolinians, like Isaac Huger, Alexander Moultrie, and William Clay Snipes were financially interested in this piratical venture that promised miraculous profits. When troops were needed to further their unlawful designs, they turned to their senators and used them as convenient agents. The remarks of Butler and Izard were not wholly convincing, and a suggestion was made and accepted to question the senators from Georgia. In answer, Colonel James Gunn said his state of Georgia was entirely at peace with the Indians and had a fine prospect of continuing so; in fact, no more troops were wanted, and if a bill should be introduced to augment them he would vote against it.[11]

This discussion gave Richard Henry Lee a good excuse for delivering his set speech on the danger of having regulars. William Maclay, from Pennsylvania, joined forces with him. He considered untrue the reports that Knox had received from the Southwest concerning Spaniards inciting the Indians—just propaganda designed to wheedle concessions for a large army. The requests of the secretary were not worth considering. "Give Knox his army," he declared, "and he will soon have a war on hand; indeed, I am clearly of the opinion that he is aiming at this even now, and that, few as the troops that he now has under his direction, he will have a war in less than six months with the Southern Indians."[12] Only the sourly disposed Maclay would have accused the pacific Knox of being so arrantly bellicose. The senator's mind was keen but his spirit cantankerous. He was troubled with homesickness, dyspepsia, and rheumatism. Many of his favorite plans had gone awry; he had few friends, and loans to some of them had deepened his financial concern.

Although federal relations with the Indians in the Southwest were not entirely satisfactory at this time, Maclay was right in believing that Spain was not inciting them to war. Hostilities would seriously jeopardize her tenuous hold on the trade with the Creeks, Choctaws, and

11 C. A. Beard, *Journal of William Maclay*, p. 233.
12 *Ibid.*, p. 234.

Chickasaws. The half-breed Alexander McGillvray, well known for his great influence among them, also favored peace. Though having broken off negotiations with federal agents, he willingly accepted an invitation to visit the seat of government.[13] With over a score of chiefs and interpreters in wagons and on horseback, his colorful entourage set out, finally arriving at Murray's Wharf in New York during the summer of 1790. Here a military escort awaited them, as well as a huge and gaping crowd. Washington gave them a speech of welcome and so did the Secretary of War. After being crammed with food and drink and shown the sights of the town, they reciprocated by giving their hosts a masterful war dance and signing a treaty on August 7, 1790. By its terms a workable peace was arranged with the Creeks, the most powerful tribe in the Southwest.[14]

Conditions were entirely different in the Northwest, where the presence of troops was constantly required. There the Shawnees, Kickapoos, Miamis and other dominating tribes paid no attention to previous treaties. They boasted that no settlers might come north of the Ohio and live. Numerous and varied outrages followed their threat. Below the mouth of the Muskingum unwary immigrants often became captives because they had turned their flatboats toward the shore in answer to the piteous outcries of women and children whom the savages had forced to act as decoys. After visiting Fort Knox as friends, a band of young braves went out and killed members of an army patrol that had been ordered to expel squatters from lands of neighboring red men. When St. Clair invited Indians to a peace parley in the summer of 1788, the Chippewas came to the rendezvous early, falling upon the guard in the hope of stealing all the government's provisions. They failed in their object, but managed to wound several soldiers. During the same year four different

[13] A. P. Whitaker, *The Spanish-American Frontier, 1783-1795*, pp. 135-137; *Dictionary of American Biography*, XII, pp. 50-51.
[14] *Treaties between the United States of America and the Several Indian Tribes from 1778 to 1837*, pp. 29-33.

attacks were made upon convoys traveling between Fort Steuben and Fort Knox in spite of the fact that fifty or sixty soldiers usually furnished protection. From 1783 to 1790, Judge Harry Innes estimated that merely in Kentucky and along the routes leading thither, 1,500 people had been killed, 20,000 horses stolen, and immense quantities of property destroyed.[15]

The Indians had excuses of their own for such marauding. They declared that the surrender of lands north of the Ohio had never received their consent and that they were constantly pestered by filibustering frontiersmen. To prevent lawless acts of raiders and squatters, the government had established Fort Steuben near Louisville and Fort Knox at Vincennes. The Indians were confident that both of these posts were serving a directly contrary purpose, that of being used as bases from which encroaching immigrants received protection and aid. Events lent color to such a mistaken belief, especially when Major Hamtramck dared to do nothing except protest at the action of Patrick Brown and sixty Kentucky ruffians, who, after visiting Fort Knox, attacked some neighboring friendly Piankashaws and badly wounded nine of them.[16]

In the hope of stopping such undeclared war, St. Clair invited the Indians to send representatives to a conference at Fort Harmar during 1789. In January 1789, chiefs from the Senecas, Wyandots, Delawares, and a few others came. Only Cornplanter among them was distinguished. He pleaded eloquently for what he believed was his tribesmen's due, but he obtained little more than what they already enjoyed. Boundaries, as fixed by the treaties of Forts McIntosh and Stanwix, were to remain as before. The Indians might hunt in ceded lands if they behaved peacefully. Thieves, either red or white, were to be summarily punished. Ample warning was to precede any act of hostility. No traders were to be allowed in the Indians' country except those who possessed a federal license.

[15] J. B. McMaster, *A History of the People of the United States,* I, p. 597; T. Roosevelt, *The Winning of the West,* III, pp. 72, 77, 80-84.
[16] R. C. Downes, *Frontier Ohio, 1788-1803,* p. 18.

Their lands were to be bartered away only to the United States. Though assenting to these provisions, the Indians asked that no settlements be made close to their boundaries and that prices be regulated in a mutual system of trading. They also wanted a blacksmith to come and live with them in order to repair their tools and weapons of iron. As a token of friendship, St. Clair bestowed upon those present goods that were valued at $3,000.[17] The recipients were not permanently helped by this act of apparent generosity; they merely craved additional gifts and became more dependent upon the white man to supply them.

The Fort Harmar treaty, signed on January 9, 1789, and affecting the Northwestern Indians, produced only slight results. The savages continued openly hostile around Fort Knox. Farther north they sallied forth from the Maumee villages to plunder and destroy. Travelers passing the confluence of the Ohio and Scioto were frequently killed or captured. From the vicinity of Louisville, Major John Hardin of Kentucky led some two or three hundred militia against the Weas during August, 1789. His troops suffered no casualties, destroyed no towns, but did kill a dozen Indians.[18] Three similar raids were soon in the making.

As long as these exasperating but indecisive raids continued, Harmar might expect all his efforts for peace to be futile. Even so, he could not take any really preventive measures. The federal government knew that the leaders of Kentucky were already petulant because their district was not adequately protected and had not been admitted as a state in spite of all their deep-laid plans during the preceding four years. It was also aware that the Spanish agents at New Orleans were granting pensions and dispensations to prominent settlers along the Cumberland and Tennessee, hoping that this area might be induced to withdraw from the Union and become a protectorate under the Spanish crown.[19] To help win the support of

[17] *American State Papers, Indian Affairs*, I, pp. 5-7; R. C. Downes, *op. cit.*, pp. 10-13.
[18] R. C. Downes, *op. cit.*, pp. 18-19.
[19] J. R. Jacobs, *Tarnished Warrior*, pp. 70-109.

these restless borderers the government authorized Harry
Innes, federal judge in Kentucky, to call out any militia
that were needed to form any expedition that it had approved.[20]

Meanwhile St. Clair, still hoping for peace, sent Captain
Pierre Gamelin as envoy to the Wabash and Illinois Indians to ascertain what their intentions were. They gave
no encouraging answer, declaring that the Fort Harmar
treaty did not bind them and that they never would make
one except through the Indian Confederacy. They wanted
the Americans to equal the British inducements in trade
and to guarantee that the Kentuckians would not further
molest them. St. Clair received their reply at Kaskaskia.
Knowing that he could not grant their demands, he soon
left there, bent on preparing for a war that he declared
was inevitable. He reached Fort Washington in July 1790.
Here he began arranging for the means that would make
victory certain.[21]

Congress, realizing that the Northwest's demand for a
militant policy could be ignored no longer, had begun to
help in a faltering sort of way. Frontiersmen had to be
protected on lands that they had legitimately purchased
from the federal government. The law of April 30, 1790,
was the answer. By its terms the 700 existing troops were
increased to 1,216. They were to be organized into a regiment of infantry and a battalion of artillery with the
customary quota of officers. Men were enlisted and officers
commissioned for only three years. Privates' pay amounted
to $2 monthly after deductions had been made for clothing
and hospital stores; sergeants had theirs established at
$3.50 after a deduction of $1.50 for the same purposes. If
injured in line of duty, those from the ranks might obtain
a maximum monthly pension of $5, the amount varying
with the degree of disability. Under similar circumstances
commissioned officers might draw as much as one-
half their usual pay for life. In the new organization, the

20 Knox to Innes, Apr. 13, 1790, in *Filson Club Publications*, No. 31,
Littell's Political Transactions, pp. 114-115.

21 R. C. Downes, *op. cit.*, pp. 22-23; R. King, *Ohio*, pp. 241-243.

lieutenant colonel commandant had the highest rank and was paid $60 monthly; an ensign had the lowest and drew only $18. Some officers might earn $10 more a month if they were selected to perform the duties of adjutant, paymaster, or quartermaster. Both enlisted and commissioned personnel were entitled to the customary ration consisting of bread, meat, and whisky, plus a small amount of vinegar, soap, and candles. No clothing or equipment was to be furnished officers. Every enlisted man was to have a yearly issue of a hat, coat, vest, blanket, one pair of buckles, a stock and clasp, four shirts, two pairs of overalls and socks, and four of shoes. Neither overcoats nor underwear were to be supplied. Such were the arrangements made for existing troops and those that were to be recruited so that the total number of regulars would not exceed 1,216.[22]

With peace receding and the army strengthened, the government decided on an offensive policy. To reinforce the regulars, Kentucky's county lieutenants were directed to call out supporting militia. Even if this combined force could not adequately protect the entire frontier, it was deemed large enough to carry war into the Indian country, making the savages feel the weight of the white man's power by destroying their gardens, obliterating their strongholds, killing their warriors, and capturing their women and children. With such a mission in mind, two cooperating expeditions were planned; one was to march northward from Fort Washington against the Miami centers of resistance, another was to set out from Fort Knox and attack Vermillion, L'Anguille, and possibly the Wea towns.[23]

Major John F. Hamtramck planned to start with the second of these expeditions on September 25, but it was not until five days later that his troops, 330 strong, left Fort Knox. Some ninety sick and sore, lame and dejected, of his would-be campaigners were left behind as a garrison. On

[22] J. F. Callan, *op. cit.* (rev. ed.), pp. 87-90.
[23] Harmar to Hamtramck, July 15, 1790, *Durrett Mss.*, University of Wisconsin.

reaching Vermillion eleven days later, he found it completely deserted. He also discovered that only fourteen days' supply of flour and even less of beef remained for his men. If they pushed on to the Wea or Kickapoo towns, they would have to eat less. Hamtramck himself lacked courage to urge his command to accept such a temporary hardship. He left the matter to his militia officers. When they were unable to win their subordinates over, he reversed the march and made for Fort Knox.[24]

Hamtramck thus failed in the role that he was expected to play. His outlook was essentially conservative and mercantile. Though not the holder of the contract for supplies, he may have been interested in it.[25] In spite of his Revolutionary training he showed few qualities of a great soldier. He would not take the risks of Indian fighting; he would not willingly assume responsibility; and the ability to persuade was not one of his gifts.

While Hamtramck was thus proving unequal to his task, Harmar was making his own preparations to move northward against the Indian towns that were thickly clustered along the waters of the Maumee. On August 24 Knox had written him emphasizing the importance of success. The expedition, he advised, was to be "conducted in the most perfect manner"; no omissions were to be tolerated; "every plan and order" was to be duly executed; movements were to be "rapid and decisive"; "every possible precaution in the power of human foresight" was to be taken against surprise; the "mature experience and judgment of Governor St. Clair" were to be frequently consulted.[26] St. Clair, like Harmar, was then working hard to accelerate the assembling of militia to reinforce the handful of regulars. For this purpose he visited both Pennsyl-

[24] Harmar to Hamtramck, Sept. 3, 1790; Hamtramck to Harmar, Nov. 2, 1790; both *Durrett Mss.*, University of Wisconsin; Harmar to Hamtramck, July 15, 1790, *Harmar Papers*, William L. Clements Library, University of Michigan.

[25] Hamtramck to Harmar, Mar., 1790, and Elliott to Harmar, Aug. 1, 1790, *Durrett Mss.*, University of Wisconsin.

[26] Knox to Harmar, Aug. 24, 1790, *Durrett Mss.*, University of Wisconsin.

vania and Kentucky. He had traveled even as far as New York City, where he saw the President, stressed the need of offensive action, and urged the speedy dispatch of arms and supplies across the mountains and down the Ohio. By September 23 he was back at Fort Washington, ready to see Harmar and his troops start out.[27]

There Harmar had assembled a motley collection of short-time soldiers. The majority had no camp kettles, axes, or serviceable arms. Major William Ferguson, of the regular artillery, made what repairs he could; and guns were issued to those who had none. Even with weapons in their hands, some of the riff-raff did not know how to put in flints for striking fire or remove and replace gunlocks for oiling.[28] To their stupidity and awkwardness, a few added indifference; they had enlisted mostly because they wanted the government's free transportation to the West. They knew that they would be in the service for only a few months at most, and they might even be lucky enough to escape before their time had expired.

For such apathy and ignorance Harmar had no effective cure. A delay for training along the Ohio was not possible. Frost would soon come up and make the grass unfit for grazing. Then the whole system of pack horse transportation would fail from a lack of forage. Under the circumstances, the hard school of experience remained the only way for these improvised soldiers to learn the rudiments of their trade. Through actual marching, woodcraft and the ways of the Indian might be slowly acquired. No matter how costly in lives or how great the handicaps imposed on the chances of success, the expedition must start quickly. Harmar therefore ordered the militia to move forward, and by September 26 they were encamped about twenty-five miles north of Fort Washington. Four days later he himself set out with his 320 regulars. When they all got together at Turkey Creek, a tributary of the Little Miami River, on October 3, the combined forces numbered 1,453 men.[29]

[27] Rufus King, *op. cit.*, pp. 241-244.
[28] *American State Papers, Military Affairs*, I, p. 21.
[29] *Ibid.*, pp. 21, 24.

From there on, the method of advance followed a routine pattern. The marching column was led by spies and guides, followed by what was known as an advance company. Then came the pioneers commanded by John Thorp, superintendent of artificers, and protected on each flank by small bodies of cavalry. Behind them plodded a militia battalion from Kentucky; in its rear were a few pieces of artillery and a little cavalry. Still farther behind came some 578 pack horses with ammunition, baggage, flour, salt, and 175 cattle that were to be slaughtered whenever fresh beef was required. These provisions and articles of equipment were strongly protected in rear and flanks by Kentucky and Pennsylvania militia. At the end of the column, as an additional precaution, a small detachment moved sluggishly along. Such was the usual disposition of troops upon the march, flexible only in intervals and distances and in the designation of troops that occupied the different positions.[30]

In camp the plan of defense was equally stereotyped. Front, flank, and rear guards were posted so that they generally enclosed a square or rectangle in which the stores and animals were placed. Along its sides, between organizations, fires were built for use in cooking and to prevent the horses and cattle from straying away.[31] Raw troops were always slow in taking positions assigned them or in making the necessary patrols. Because of the difficulty of pitching camp and setting guards, efforts were always made to reach the place of encampment before the coming of darkness.

Battle dispositions were similarly set in hard and fast lines. Separate organizations were designated to meet the attack when it occurred in front, rear, or flanks. For this purpose they were given definite positions.[32] The regulars were placed wherever the worst fighting was anticipated. If Harmar apparently did not give enough weight to the use of reserves, the modifying influence of terrain, or the unpredictable methods of the savages, his action may have arisen from studied design rather than from neglect.

[30] *Ibid.*, p. 31.   [31] *Ibid.*, p. 32.   [32] *Ibid.*, p. 33.

Fort Washington, 1790 (from a drawing by Captain Jonathan Heart, U.S.A., 1790).

If he had acted differently his plans would have been more flexible, and those to whom they were committed would have enjoyed a greater degree of latitude. Unfortunately most of his officers were ignorant and could not meet the demands of an increased trust. Their individualism had been accentuated by the frontier; and when they were permitted a measure of initiative, they often failed because they were generally untrained and customarily thought in terms of personal prowess rather than tactical objectives.

With such troops Harmar reached French Store, some 100 miles north of Fort Washington, on October 13, 1790. Here a Shawnee captive told him that the Indians were ready to abandon their Maumee villages, about two days' marching away. Harmar decided to hasten on and strike them while they were in the midst of this movement, hoping to defeat them in detail and capture most of their supplies. He might also be able to destroy an old fort of theirs with the few pieces of artillery that he had brought along. He determined to send forward a detachment under the command of Colonel John Hardin of the Kentucky militia in order to reconnoiter and ascertain the enemy's intentions while the army advanced. Many wished to be part of it, officers casting lots to see who would go. Finally 600 men were selected. Militia predominated; only fifty were regulars, commanded by Captain David Zeigler. The raiders did not set out until about ten o'clock on the morning of the 14th, and then they made such a slow progress in the drizzling rain that at nightfall they were only four miles in advance of the main body. Next day, with a burst of effort, they covered twenty-eight miles. When they arrived at the Indian villages at three in the afternoon, they were already deserted. The savages had burned their principal settlement at Omeetown. Here Hardin's men pitched camp. In spite of repeated orders that they should not wander beyond it, parties of thirty or forty began to scatter in all directions and did not return until they were satiated with hunting for plunder. Luckily they fell into no ambuscade, for the Indians had completely abandoned their hovels and had taken refuge in the forest. With none to hinder, the

main body moved up, joining Hardin on the 17th. Next
day the work of destruction began. Five villages containing
a total of 184 cabins were burned to the ground, and a
great quantity of corn in the ear was destroyed—20,000
bushels, the victors boasted.[33]

Before the ashes of this Indian stronghold had cooled,
Colonel James Trotter of the Kentucky militia was directed
to take 300 men and reconnoiter the neighborhood. He was
expected to be gone for about three days; instead he returned on the evening of the eighteenth, the very day that
he set out, after killing two Indians and marching a few
miles. Incensed at this shameless and cowardly conduct,
Harmar ordered the same detachment to go out again on
the next morning, October 19, and redeem its blasted
reputation. Hardin was given a command of 180 militia
and 30 regulars in place of the pusillanimous Trotter.
While on the march a third of his men sneaked out of
ranks and slunk back to camp. Continuing on, the rest
came to a morass where the savages had encamped the day
before. Here the troops halted for about half an hour and
then pushed on, excepting one company that lingered behind. After marching two or three miles, Hardin discovered
what had happened and sent back some calvary to bring
the sluggards forward. Shortly afterwards scattered shots
came from the front, but no precautions were taken. Confident that the Indians would not fight, Hardin moved
carelessly on at the head of his men. Suddenly from all
sides the Indians began firing heavily into the unwary
column. Demoralization followed. Those in front would
not stand; those in rear would not move forward. Many
broke ranks and fled, never firing a shot, even throwing
their loaded muskets away. Some were so stricken with
terror that they did not halt their flight until they reached
Kentucky. Only a very few remained steadfast and wrote
their names for valor, nine militia and all the thirty regulars. These resolute men were cut to pieces, excepting six
or seven.[34]

Ensign Hartshorn was one of those who survived. His

[33] *Ibid.*, pp. 20-30.   [34] *Ibid.*, pp. 20-30.

good fortune, according to James Bachus, depended more on "the lucky circumstances of falling over a log in his retreat and by this means screening himself from the eye of his pursuers" than from any other circumstance. Lieutenant Armstrong, who commanded the party, made his escape by "plunging himself into a pond or swamp up to his neck, within two hundred yards of the field of action where he remained the whole night, a spectator to the horrid scenes that the Indians performed over the dead and wounded bodies of the poor soldiers who had fallen the preceding day—where their shrieks mixed with the horrid yells of the savages made his situation shocking."[35]

Routed by probably not more than 130 savages, Hardin collected a few of the wounded and ordered his demoralized detachment to begin a retreat that very night. He had accomplished no more than Trotter, and his losses were greater. The Indians, on the contrary, were greatly encouraged, in spite of the fact that their villages had been burned down. Harmar knew that now they would come out of their lurking places and harass his troops, who had covered eight miles on their way home.[36]

In consequence of his own estimate of the situation and Hardin's pleading, Harmar decided to send back 300 militia under Colonel John Hardin and 60 regulars under Major John P. Wyllys, 1st Regiment, in order to mop up any surviving savages. They set out about 9:00 p.m., October 21, marching in three columns with the militia on both flanks and the regulars in the center. The raiders reached one of the Maumee towns a little after sunrise. Discovering the Indians there, Wyllys sent Major Horatio Hall and his battalion to take position in their rear, while he held the regulars and remaining troops in hand to make a frontal attack. The ruse failed. The plan was disclosed when someone prematurely fired at a lone Indian. The redmen took flight, and small groups of the militia pursued them in every direction. Major Wyllys was

---

[35] Bachus to ?, Nov. 24, 1790, *Woodbridge Papers*, Detroit Public Library.

[36] *American State Papers, Military Affairs*, I, p. 29.

quickly deserted except for his sixty regulars; his contact with the other troops was entirely lost. Discovering his dilemma, the savages came out of hiding and surrounded his detachment. The major and fifty regulars who had remained by his side were killed, a useless sacrifice to the miserable conduct of some ill-led and undependable militia who saw no virtue in obedience when faced with the prospect of trivial success. Killed, wounded, and missing amounted to 180.[37]

News of this second disaster did not come to Harmar's ears until 11:00 a.m. of the 22nd. Major James Ray was then dispatched with a battalion to give aid to the fugitives. After going only a few miles he fell in with some of them helping along their wounded companions. Losing hope of doing any good by marching farther, he returned to camp, where stragglers continued to dribble in throughout the day. The surgeon gave treatment to the disabled and had litters made for those who were unable to walk.[38]

Believing other offensive action impossible with his thrice defeated militia, Harmar decided to get out of Indian country before his army disintegrated and his transportation collapsed. One third of his packhorses had died or been lost at night through fault of the guards. Frost had come, and good grazing was no longer available. On October 23 he started back with his demoralized troops. For most of the way the militia were out of control, paying little or no attention to orders. At the mouth of the Licking, Harmar was on the point of arresting some of the officers and sending them home in disgrace; but Hardin induced him to refrain, declaring they were influential characters, capable of stirring up trouble along the Ohio. Men in the ranks behaved no better, in brazen disobedience they left the column and fired their guns when and where they chose. Finally one such offender was tied down to a six-pounder and given a half-dozen lashes. Though the punishment did not equal his deserts, his father, an ignorant blathering Baptist preacher, and a few incompetent and disgruntled militia officers loudly criticized Harmar,

---

[37] *Ibid.*, pp. 27, 28, 35, *et passim.*   [38] *Ibid.*, p. 25.

declaring that he was totally unfit to lead troops in a war against Indians.[39]

Finally on November 3, 1790, Harmar reached Fort Washington. Here he immediately began to discharge the militia. He did not bitterly arraign their conduct, as he might well have done. Instead, he gave an elaborate dinner to all of his field officers and a number of his friends. Animosities were forgotten and guests drank deeply to his health.[40]

None, however, could hide the fact that the expedition had failed. Over fourteen hundred men had set out to ravage the country of the Indians and make them so fearful of the white man's power that they would cease their raids along the frontier. Instead, Harmar's troops had advertised their own incapacity and infuriated the savages into greater acts of destruction. They had inflicted only trifling losses at a very heavy cost to themselves. About one seventh were casualties; of the 320 regulars, 75 were killed and 3 wounded; of the militia, 108 were killed and 28 wounded. A great deal of equipment had been lost or destroyed; large quantities of rations had been wasted; many horses had been killed or stolen.[41] Yet no serviceable roads had been cut through the wilderness and no forts had been erected at strategic points. Though much growing corn had been destroyed, the Indians were able to subsist entirely upon meat, which they could generally obtain from game that roamed through forest and prairie.

On the other hand, the fund of knowledge about the Maumee country had been increased; and a few soldiers had learned to fight the Shawnees, Miamis, and other hostile tribes to better advantage. Some of the hard problems in transportation and supply had been partially solved for a larger number of men than had ever invaded the same section of Indian country. In addition, Harmar had kept his force reasonably well fed and had succeeded in

---

[39] *Ibid.*, pp. 25, 35, *et passim.*   [40] *Ibid.*, p. 35.

[41] *Ibid., passim*; Harmar to Knox, Nov. 4, 23, 1790, *Harmar Papers*, William L. Clements Library; B. W. Bond, *The Correspondence of John Cleves Symmes*, pp. 132-133.

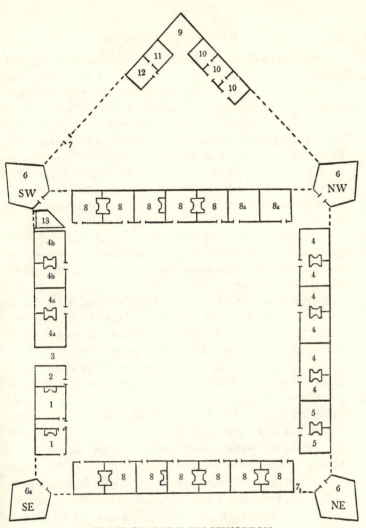

PLAN OF FORT WASHINGTON
(based on official drawings of 1790 and 1792)

1. Headquarters. Once occupied by Winthrop Sargent.
2. Clothing storehouse.
3. Main gate.
4. Officers' quarters.
4a. Quarters once occupied by General Josiah Harmar.
4b. Quarters once occupied by General Arthur St. Clair.
5. Commissary storehouse.
6. Pentagonal blockhouses. Cannon in upper story.
6a. Lower story used for Ohio territorial legislature and for General Harmar's court of inquiry.
7. Sally ports.
8. Soldiers' quarters.
9. Probably used for guard house.
10. Shops for carpenters, turners, and wheelwrights.
11. Shop for armorers.
12. Blacksmith shop.
13. Magazine.

bringing it back to its base as a tactical unit. His mixed troops of cavalry, infantry, and artillery had set out from Fort Washington on September 30 for the Miami villages situated near the subsequent site of Fort Wayne. They returned on November 3. In these thirty-four days they had fought the savages three times and covered approximately 340 miles; and this, too, when they had been hurriedly assembled and formed into organizations that had never before operated together. The country traversed was practically unmapped, devoid of roads, often heavily wooded or cut with swamps and streams. Merely to make such a march was something of an exploit. Those on it had learned a great deal. Unfortunately many of them were unwilling to help with their knowledge by going on another expedition when opportunity offered.

Harmar himself was thoroughly disgusted with results but still hoped that the Indians might be frightened into peace. He knew that both the President and Henry Knox were dissatisfied with what he had done. They shared the public opinion that he had failed on his mission. Knox declared the net result of the expedition had been to stimulate the Indians to greater hostility instead of fostering peace. At the same time, Harmar was asked to explain why he had made detachments on October 14, 19, and 21 without supporting them. He was also informed that another "more efficient expedition" must be undertaken, not under him but under St. Clair, in whom more confidence was placed. For the good of his own reputation he was advised to ask for a court of inquiry to investigate the whole of his conduct.[42] For a time he thought of resigning. This was what some of his enemies would have liked him to do. According to Wilkinson, such a step would be "unphilosophical, petulant and boyish" and should be

[42] Knox to Harmar, Jan. 31, 1791, *Durrett Mss.*, University of Wisconsin. Others also believed Harmar had failed. See: Gilman to Cass, Feb. 3, 1792. *Cass Papers*, Detroit Public Library; Journal of William Maclay, p. 340; B. W. Bond, Jr., *The Correspondence of John Cleves Symmes*, pp. 132-133. For Harmar's own account of his expedition, see Harmar to Knox, Nov. 4, 23, 1790, *Harmar Papers*, William L. Clements Library.

avoided like "plague, pestilence and famine." He further remarked that a court would convince the world of Harmar's real character and "refute the calumnies which the envenomed tongue of slander and detractions have let fly at you without mercy."[43]

Yielding to the advice of his friends and his own better judgment, Harmar requested President Washington for a board of inquiry to consider his conduct of the expeditions. The request was immediately granted. For the purpose, however, enough suitable officers were not available until they began to report at Fort Washington for St. Clair's campaign. Not until September 15, 1791, did the board begin to hold sessions in the Southeast Blockhouse at Fort Washington. Major General Richard Butler acted as president; Lieutenant Colonels George Gibson and William Darke were members. Though none of them had gone on the expedition with Harmar, they were well known along the frontier and understood its problems. For nine days they deliberated and examined a number of witnesses ranging in rank from ensign to major. The principal officers of the militia were informed of the investigation, but none of them came to testify. They were widely scattered, and had business of their own that called for attention. In addition they may have felt that the evidence that they would present might be as harmful to them as to the interests of Harmar. As a consequence, all the witnesses were regulars. On September 24 the findings were sent to St. Clair. They declared the personal conduct of Harmar was "irreproachable," that his organization of the army was calculated to foster "harmony" and "mutual confidence," that the order of march was "perfectly adapted to the country" through which it moved, that his plans for encampment and battle were judicious and simple, and that the detachments made on October 14 and 19 were well justified. The one on October 21, they declared, was based on "good principles"; failure to support it was due to the fact that

[43] Wilkinson to Harmar, June 20, 1791, *Durrett Mss.*, University of Wisconsin.

orders were "not properly executed." Thus was Harmar completely exonerated; his conduct, they believed, merited "high approbation."[44] However consoling such conclusions might be to him personally, they offered no suggestion as to how a similar expedition might avoid a repetition of error.

Most fair-minded people believed that some of the outstanding defects of the militia must be remedied before they could ever be relied on to win an important success. Someone caustically declared that the expedition had gone down in defeat because of the militia's "ignorance, imbecility, insubordination and want of equipment."[45] Certainly they had shown no willingness to cooperate or carry out orders at critical times. Many of them were skilled in woodcraft and lore of the Indians, but their knowledge had been acquired as individuals, and as individuals they did their best work. They had sometimes performed the duties of messengers, scouts, or patrols with distinction. When faced with possible annihilation in battle, they struggled as bravely and as fiercely as the regulars. But their methods were entirely their own, and were not to be changed except by considerable training. In small groups of friends under leaders of their own choice, they could perform a limited task with reasonable competence. They had learned a small degree of cooperation in log rolling, cabin building, and very minor raids against the Indians. By skillful use of such talents, a clever commander might win at least partial success. On the contrary, he was destined to fall into disaster if he made hasty efforts to reform their deficiencies or trusted them to perform a task that was hateful to their spirit or new to their experience. Harmar was not entirely ignorant of how they might best be employed; but, on account of the small number of his regulars, he had to use them on tasks for which they were unfitted because they had not been adequately trained. It is surprising, not that he lost a large percentage of his men, but that he saved the majority from annihilation on

[44] *American State Papers, Military Affairs*, I, pp. 20-30.
[45] Judge Burnet, *Notes*, p. 105.

such a long and dangerous march. As might have been expected, the new government's quickly improvised and ignorant force had failed on a difficult mission. Within the next year the same error would be repeated with more appalling results.

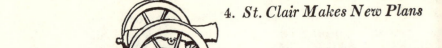

Dᴜʀɪɴɢ 1791 the United States maintained comparative peace with the tribes in the Southwest. When Creeks or other Indians came to visit General James Robertson, "father of Tennessee" and commanding general of the militia in the "Territory South of the Ohio River," he treated them kindly and gave them what he could. When one of them applied for a gun, Robertson promised to "git him one" because he was the first "Cheafe coming in friendly to this country after the piece concluded with Gen'l Nox." For several others he planned to ask help in giving each of them a blanket, for he could not "Bare the Hole exspence, being so distressed." When Chicasaws tarried with him, he killed them a "beaf," taking every step to "gain their good will."[1] Although never able to master the vagaries of his own people's spelling, Robertson understood the ways of the red men, who looked upon him with great respect because he was generous and honest and brave.

William Blount successfully dealt with the Cherokees. He was the newly appointed governor of the transmontane lands ceded to the United States by North Carolina as well as Superintendent of Indian Affairs of the Southern Department. Using sympathy and tact with both Indians and settlers, he labored for peace, succeeding in obtaining a treaty with the Cherokees on the banks of the Holston near the mouth of the French Broad on July 17, 1791. Under this agreement the United States acquired more land, promised certain annuities, and made arrangements for friendly intercourse.[2] By the summer of 1791, the

---

[1] Robertson to Smith, Nov. 14, 1791 in C. E. Carter, *Territorial Papers South of the Ohio, 1790 to 1796*, pp. 102-103.
[2] *Treaties between the United States of America, etc.*, pp. 34-38.

settlers in Georgia and North Carolina could hope for freedom from Indian raids.

Similar peaceful conditions prevailed along the Northeastern frontier of our country. During the winter of 1790-1791 Cornplanter, with a party of his Seneca warriors, paid a visit to Philadelphia, where Congress was then sitting. They wanted the Treaty of Fort Stanwix modified and more scrupulously observed, complaining that border ruffians had wantonly murdered some of their people and that the area allotted to them was not extensive enough for their needs. President Washington regretfully replied that the treaty could not be immediately altered but suggested that they might continue to occupy the small strip of land that they sought as long as they conducted themselves peacefully. Secretary Knox declared that the murderers would be punished and that the relatives and friends of the victims would receive compensation. He also agreed to give them some farming tools and to provide two good men to act as instructors for improving their methods of agriculture, and he promised to try to find some suitable person who would live among them and teach them the ways of the white men.[3] Reassured by these promises, Cornplanter and his companions departed contentedly for their homes. As long as he lived, the sturdy old Seneca chief faithfully maintained his friendship for the United States. He died in 1836 at the reputed age of one hundred and four.[4]

Unfortunately there were no other Indian chieftains north of the Ohio who followed Cornplanter's example. In all that vast region the savages were bitterly determined to expel the white settlers. During the latter part of 1790 they told Putnam that "there should not remain a Smoak on the Ohio by the time the Leaves put out." On January 2, 1791, Wyandots and Chippewas attacked Big Bottom on the Muskingum and killed thirteen of the inhabitants. About the first of February, the entire family of Thomas Dick was taken captive in Allegheny County, Pennsylvania,

---

[3] *American State Papers, Indian Affairs*, I, pp. 143, 206.
[4] C. H. Sipe, *Fort Ligonier and its Times*, pp. 657-661.

and carried away to Detroit. Next month the savages came to the home of Abraham Russ, twenty-three miles from Pittsburgh. After being received as friends and given food, they killed his aged mother, four men, and six children, pitching the bodies of the victims into the flames of his burning cabin. Terrified by such atrocities, the inhabitants of Pittsburgh sought arms and were issued 100 muskets. Those who lived in lonely places frantically fled to stations where they might have others' help and the protection of palisades.[5]

Ever since the defeat of Harmar, the Indians had turned increasingly to murder and plunder. St. Clair, as Governor of the Northwest, made a formal report of the defeat on October 29, 1790. Congress was not then in session and did not meet until December 6. On December 14 the Senate was given the details; and in spite of every effort to twist the report until a victory could be claimed, administration partisans could not hide the fact that the campaign had been a dismal failure. Knox demanded that a larger force of regulars be provided. The year before, in January 1790, he thought that the United States needed no more regulars than a well trained corps of artillerists and engineers and a legion of about 3,000 infantry. The former would look after our harbor defenses, the latter would protect our frontier and guard our magazines and arsenals. A year later, he had pruned his estimates until they called only for a battalion of 240 artillerists and two regiments of infantry of 700 men each, a total of 1,640 troops, or about twice the number actually in the service at that time.[6] Certainly the request was superlatively modest when an offensive against the Indians was planned. The safety of the frontier was in jeopardy, and the prestige of the United States was at stake.

After a good deal of wrangling, a law was enacted on March 3, 1791, the last day of the third session of the

[5] R. C. Downes, *Frontier Ohio, 1788 to 1803*, pp. 17-23, and C. H. Sipe, *op. cit.*, pp. 616 *et seq.*

[6] Knox to Washington, Jan. 18, 1790, *American State Papers, Military Affairs*, I, pp. 6-13, and Knox to Washington, Jan. 4, 1791, *American State Papers, Indian Affairs*, I, pp. 59-61.

First Congress. To the authorized strength of the regular army, it granted an increase of a single regiment of 912 men. A bounty of $6 was provided for those already enlisted or who might enlist in the future; otherwise the pay remained the same as before. The President was granted discretionary power to raise 2,000 levies and a body of militia for six months. If the ranks of the new regiment could not be filled in time for the expected campaign, the number of militia and levies was to be increased. To stimulate the efforts of recruiting officers, they were to receive a bonus of $2 for each man enlisted and mustered. A major general was to command the force, his remuneration to be fifteen rations for "daily subsistence," either in money or in kind, together with $125 as pay and $20 for forage each month. To provide for the expense of the proposed forces, $312,686.20 was appropriated, and if this modest sum could not be raised by taxes, a loan was to be negotiated.[7]

Because the law was intended primarily to furnish security and protection for the frontier, St. Clair, as governor of the Northwest Territory, had been frequently consulted. He had been in the East for several months; and because he had spent much of his time since his appointment in 1789 in negotiating with the Indians, he was presumably the chief authority on the question of relations with the tribes and their disputes over boundaries. Some naturally argued that he might well be entrusted with both military and civil functions. His experience as a general in the Revolution gave strength to their contention. On March 4, 1791, he was appointed a major general, thus making him the holder of two federal offices and the beneficiary of two salaries.[8] Combining military and civil

---

[7] J. F. Callan, *The Military Laws of the United States* (revised edition), pp. 90-91.

[8] St. Clair had a regular salary of $2,000 a year as Governor of the Northwest Territory (See American State Papers, *Miscellaneous Affairs*, I, p. 59, and Treasury Files from Jan. 1791 thru May 1792). In addition he drew $2,437.48 for pay, forage, and rations as Major General for the same length of time. (See "Statement of St. Clair's Pay Account" in *Burton Collection*, Detroit Public Library.)

functions in the same individual was an arrangement designed to be both economical and efficient. In the long run it proved to be neither one nor the other. There were plenty of political croakers and jealous personal enemies who predicted that he would never be successful because he had no knowledge of Indian fighting. General Harmar himself went so far as to forecast failure. Washington and Knox may have had their moments of doubt, but they were sure St. Clair had ability and they knew him to be loyal and brave.

Arthur St. Clair had traveled more widely and his education had been far more liberal than the majority of his associates in the Northwest. A Scotsman born, he passed his boyhood in the environment of Edinburgh, later studying medicine for a time in London. Inheriting from his mother a comfortable fortune, he purchased an ensigncy in the 60th Foot in 1757, came with Boscawan to America in 1758, served under Amherst at Louisburg and later under Wolfe at Quebec. Resigning his commission in 1762, he settled in Western Pennsylvania where he acquired a large estate with funds derived from the dowry of his wife, a half-sister of Governor James Bowdoin of Massachusetts. He took sides with the rebellious colonists during the Revolution and attained the rank of major general in 1777. He fought, though not always successfully, at Ticonderoga, Trenton, Princeton, Brandywine and Yorktown, winning the good opinion of Washington. With the advent of peace, he became a member of Congress and in 1787 was elected its president. Giving up this office to become Governor of the Northwest Territory at $2,000 a year, he went from Philadelphia to Marietta, Ohio, where he assumed his new duties in the summer of 1788.[9]

In his own person St. Clair united the executive, legislative, and judicial functions of the government in his vast domain. Winthrop Sargent, a former field officer of the Continental Army, who held the post of Secretary of the Ohio Company, was appointed to the same position in the territorial government. Samuel Holden Parsons, James

[9] *Dictionary of American Biography*, XVI, pp. 293-295.

Mitchell Varnum, and John Cleves Symmes, all soldiers or jurists of high repute, acted as judges. With these able colleagues St. Clair set himself to govern the "Territory Northwest of the Ohio River," and to keep it safe from the Indians. In 1789 he concluded the treaty of Fort Harmar. It did not restrain the savages' hankering for scalps or their zeal for plunder. Settlers were shot from ambush, their horses stolen, their cabins burned, and their families carried off into captivity. St. Clair was soon convinced that the hostile tribes would never mend their ways until a punitive expedition had brought them to heel. Harmar was selected to lead it, and St. Clair went east to see that adequate supplies were sent. Returning to the West in 1790, he saw Harmar set out confidently in September only to return a month later in defeat. St. Clair was now more than ever certain that a powerful offensive operation was imperative. He again traveled to the East, where he interviewed the President and members of the Cabinet and Congress. Partly as a result of his representations, the law of March 3, 1791, was passed and St. Clair was appointed a major general.

With his commission St. Clair received detailed instructions concerning what was expected from the army that he soon would command. It was to be about 3,000 strong exclusive of any troops that were to be used as garrisons along the Ohio. The depleted ranks of the old 1st Regiment were to be immediately filled with recruits living in New York and Maryland and the states in between. New England was to furnish the men for the 2nd Regiment except for those required to form two companies organized in South Carolina and Delaware. In all, about 2,000 levies were to be drawn from various states. Troops were to be assembled at Fort Pitt, then sent on to Fort Washington. From there Knox hoped to start a forward movement by July 10.[10]

Above everything else St. Clair was enjoined not to offend the British and to secure a "just and liberal peace"

10 Knox to St. Clair, Mar. 21, 1791, *American State Papers, Indian Affairs*, I, pp. 171-174.

with the Indians. If peace could not be gained by negotia-
tion, he was authorized to send General Charles Scott and
750 men against them. This raid might even be followed
by another if conditions warranted. Both, however, were to
be subsidiary to his own expedition, which was to establish
"a strong and permanent military post in the heart of
the Miami villages." It was to have a garrison of from
1,000 to 1,200 men, a force large enough for sending out
strong detachments to chastise the Wabash and other
unruly tribesmen.[11]

Pondering over these instructions, St. Clair left Philadelphia on March 23, 1791, and set out for the Northwest
by way of Pittsburgh. Within two days he was stricken
with a severe attack of gout. He had not fully recovered
when he reached Kentucky several weeks later. Conferences
were held there with leading citizens and plans for the
proposed campaign discussed.

Among those with whom St. Clair consulted was James
Wilkinson, a friend of Ticonderoga days who had recently
written to his Spanish pensioners that he expected to lead
an expedition against the Indians, declaring that he would
never be thwarted by the "inclemency of the season, from
Frost, from Ice and Snow, from deep and rapid Rivers."[12]
By springtime he was ready to modify this vainglorious
boast. Political leaders in Kentucky succeeded in convincing him that he would do better by serving an apprenticeship before attempting to lead. He should first go on
a raid, now in the making, commanded by General Charles
Scott.

St. Clair was eager to have Scott's minor operation
promptly started and swiftly carried out. He wanted the
Indians punished at once and no opportunity given them
to prepare against the major offensive that he planned to
conduct himself. In the meantime, however, the federal
government initiated one more attempt to conciliate the
tribes and achieve a lasting settlement of border questions.

11 *Ibid.*
12 Wilkinson to Miro, Dec. 17, 1790, A.G.I. Seville, *Papeles de Cuba*,
leg., 2374.

Colonel Thomas Procter and Captain Michael Gabriel Houdin were sent as emissaries of peace to the belligerent Indians north of the Ohio. They were instructed to go first to Cornplanter's towns and, if possible, induce him and other friendly chiefs to accompany them. The delegation was then to visit the Wabash and Miami tribes and to urge them to make another treaty at Fort Washington. Six hundred dollars were allowed for general expenses. Colonel Procter was promised $500 personally if he succeeded in his mission. In the not unlikely event that he should lose his life during the course of his negotiations, his orphan children were to be recommended for seven and a half years' pay of a lieutenant colonel. When he arrived at Buffalo Creek with his fellow envoys, Procter asked permission of Colonel A. Gordon, the British commander at Niagara, to charter one of his vessels to carry them to Sandusky. The Senecas were fearful and unwilling to make the journey either by land or in their own canoes. On May 18, 1791, Gordon refused this request; the mission collapsed, and Procter returned to Philadelphia.[13]

St. Clair's preparations for militant expedition naturally hung fire until the result of this mission was learned. When the news of Procter's failure became known in the West, General Scott, now a $4-a-day brigadier, began to collect troops near the mouth of the Kentucky River. There companies and battalions were organized and officers duly elected. The force was 800 strong, volunteers signing up for a month to harry the villages of the Kickapoos with fire and sword. They went out as planned and burned a few wretched hovels and destroyed a few acres of growing corn. On May 23, 1791, they returned, exhibiting as proof of their prowess an odd assortment of Indian princesses, half-starved children, and a number of ill-smelling, flea-bitten squaws. The damage done to the savages was not extensive, but it was enough to rouse them to anger and spur them on to revenge. The volunteers suffered five casualties, and the cost to the federal government was $20,000.[14]

13 *American State Papers, Indian Affairs*, I, pp. 145-164.
14 *Ibid.*, I, pp. 131-133.

The distribution of so much hard money was always welcomed by the frontiersmen, and Kentuckians liked to do a little fighting and have an opportunity for vengeance. Despite the obvious inefficacy of such raids, St. Clair continued to favor them. He wanted the savages harried again. Many of the whites were willing to go, and Colonel James Wilkinson was eager to lead them. Having now served his apprenticeship under Scott, he believed himself admirably fitted for the task. The Kentucky Board of War selected him to command a body of 532 mounted volunteers who were expected to take the Indian town of L'Anguille, situated about 100 miles north of Fort Washington. On or about August 1, 1791, they set out. L'Anguille was taken and burned; 430 acres of corn were destroyed. After riding 451 miles through a rough and hostile country, they returned. Their casualties were two killed and one man severely wounded. Again some mangy squaws were brought back as captives, much to the dismay of those who had to abide their presence at Fort Washington. The twenty-day raid, barren of results, expensive and useless, was hailed as a prodigious success. Both St. Clair and Knox thanked Wilkinson for his "good conduct . . . of the expedition." No one seemed to realize what a hornet's nest had been stirred. L'Anguille was the capital and metropolis of Little Turtle's own sub-tribe, the Eel River Miamis. Within a few months this truculent chieftain would exact a long-remembered vengeance for its destruction.[15]

While Scott was making war after his own fashion on the Indians north of the Ohio, St. Clair was journeying from Kentucky to Fort Washington. After an hour or two on the road from Lexington, he and his companions passed the tavern called the Sign of the Plow and Oxen, the last place where they could find shelter for the seventy-five miles remaining. Constantly drenched by rain, they made their beds on the water-soaked ground. St. Clair was soon suffering from a bilious attack, which was quickly succeeded by a recurrence of gout, a frequent affliction of his. For relief he was accustomed to take a teaspoonful of

15 *Ibid.*, I, pp. 133-135.

brimstone flour in the morning before breakfast. Possibly from such dosing or better living conditions, he seemed to improve in health after reaching Fort Washington on May 15, 1791.[16]

The fort was located in the rude, frontier village of Cincinnati, at that time numbering only a few score civilian inhabitants. Most of them were Scotch-Irish settlers, generous and hospitable, but much given to liquor and fighting. A whisky still of 100 gallons capacity could be traded there for more than 200 acres of good land. Most of the people were Protestants of high emotional tension. Until churches were built, they held their religious services in the open air beneath the trees. The New Lights were accustomed to keep pace with the fervor of their backwoods preachers by frequent "grunts and groans," "raving and roaring like so many bulls." Constantly they yelled their Amens, shouting "Fire and Damnation" at the top of their lungs, or falling down in fits and seeing visions of a "new heaven and a new earth."[17]

They wanted to escape their rounds of hardship. Passionately they yearned for a better world, a world in which they might have plenty to eat and suitable and becoming clothing. Usually they were lucky if they had enough bread to go with their meat and fish. Until they had planted, cultivated, and brought a few vegetables to maturity, a "mess of greens" represented about the only exception to their simple and monotonous fare. Too often their gardens yielded only a pitiful return despite the hard work required to protect them from the ravages of drouth, blight, insects, and marauding wild animals. The constant toil soon wore their clothing threadbare. It could not be replaced until flax was raised, wool spun, or deerskins cured and dressed. Occasionally a settler might barter something for materials that could be turned into garments. In exchange for a broken slate, a certain John Peat

[16] A. St. Clair, *Narrative*, etc., p. 57; and E. S. McClay, *The Journal of William McClay*, p. 369.

[17] Judge Wilkinson, "Early Recollection of the West," *Pioneer*, II, p. 163; and B. W. Bond, *Correspondence of John Cleves Symmes*, p. 300.

acquired two fawn skins. His wife made them into a "petti-coat for Mary, and Mary wore the petticoat until she outgrew it; then Rhoda took it till she outgrew it; then Susan had it till she outgrew it; then it fell to Abigail, and she wore it out."[18]

There was no escape from such bitter poverty for poor little Abigail until her father made the ground produce its due. His crop harvested, he might have some surplus to barter for the things that all of them needed. But neither he nor the settlers north of the Ohio dared to venture far from their cabins to till the fields with sluggish oxen and home-made plows and hoes until they and their families could feel safe from the savages. When the settlers learned that soldiers were traveling to Fort Washington and a campaign was on foot to punish the tribes to the north, they were delighted. But their enthusiasm began to cool when they heard that Governor St. Clair was to be the commanding general; many were convinced that he had slight understanding of their problems and was wholly unfit to conduct a war against the Indians.[19] His appoint-ment of Winthrop Sargent as Secretary of the Territory did nothing to lessen their unflattering opinions. The con-firmed Federalism and dour New England training of the conscientious Sargent made him unpopular with the West-erners, who thought him "sour and frigid." As leaders they desired men of their own type, like Scott and Wilkin-son. It was only their desperate need for protection and hard money and their keen love of adventure that induced them to serve under the new major general in the capacity of volunteers or militia.

Available regular troops were few. When St. Clair assumed active command at Fort Washington in about the middle of May 1791, he counted only eighty-five privates present and fit for duty. From Forts Harmar, Steuben, and Knox he withdrew reinforcements until the 1st Regi-ment numbered 427 rank and file.[20] Additional increments

[18] J. W. Harpster, *Pen Pictures of Early Western Pennsylvania,* p. 233.

[19] R. M. McElroy, *Kentucky in the Nation's History,* p. 156.

[20] St. Clair, *op. cit.,* p. 10.

came slowly. Maryland was laggard in recruiting its battalion; Massachusetts failed to measure up to expectations; Pennsylvania did no better. Soon word came that the levies and regulars would not reach Fort Washington until the last of July; in fact, many were uselessly held at Pittsburgh until the last days of August. Next came a warning that there would be something like 500 less than the 3,000 troops originally planned. St. Clair was told to make up the deficiency by drafts on the nearby frontier, perhaps from Pennsylvania, Virginia, and the District of Kentucky.[21]

There were many reasons why enlistments were few. A shortage of labor existed in even the most populous sections of the country, and all who had the will to work found ready employment. In spite of the $6 bounty, good men eyed enlistment papers askance. Many of them believed that the army represented the very system they had fought to destroy during the days of the Revolution. If they wanted to go westward, marching as enlisted men offered the least congenial way. A private's pay of $3 a month was not much of a lure, especially when one third of it was inevitably deducted for clothing and medical care and usually some more for lost or damaged equipment. If these drawbacks failed to keep a prospective recruit from joining the colors, fear of the Indians might, for everyone knew that they were skillful in individual fighting and delighted in the barbaric torture of captives.

At best, the life of a recruit was hard. The government made it worse by failing to keep implied or direct promises. Pay was always behind. On March 21, 1791, Knox informed St. Clair that he was sending enough money to liquidate "arrearages" for the previous year. During the last week of June, Captain Erkuries Beatty set out for the Northwest with $17,840.50, which was to form a sort of "Military chest," St. Clair being authorized to spend $5,000 of it to pay the regulars up to March 31 and to use the balance in giving the other troops a month of their earnings. He availed himself little of such power. He

---

21 Knox to St. Clair, May 5, 12, 19, 26, June 23, 26, 30, and Aug. 25, 1791, *American State Papers, Indian Affairs*, I, pp. 175-182.

apparently thought that he could not control $3 men with $1 whisky in reach. The year ended, and some were even discharged without receiving a cent of the money due them.[22]

Similar inadequate steps were taken to provide troops with much needed clothing. Although some of it was inferior in quality and wore out quickly on campaign, Knox tried to issue less than the minimum. He directed that recruits for the 1st Regiment were to draw theirs, about 550 suits, from a presumable surplus on the frontier. All of them were to have blankets. From a fourth of them "completely clothed, the officers will make arrangements for rendering all of the men comfortable." This direction did not include the 2nd Regiment, for he unctuously added "it will be clothed." In blankets, however, there was soon to be a considerable shortage. As he explained, they "shall be issued here [in Philadelphia] of the number of which you shall be informed, a deduction must be made from the clothing for the troops on the frontiers, and a transfer thereof made to the Indian Department for the purpose of the proposed treaty."[23] Thus were part of the blankets originally deemed essential for replacement or original issue set aside for gifts to the Indians. As a result, some of St. Clair's men lacked an essential article of equipment, either because they did not get it originally or had subsequently lost it. But usually they paid for it wholly or partially anyway.

With pay uncertain and clothing inadequate, St. Clair's men could not even feel sure that they would have enough to eat, especially when they were far from bases of supply. Under the circumstances, enlistment appealed to only a few. Usually they were aimless drifters at best—ignorant, shiftless, and with little sense of responsibility. Not infrequently they were Irish immigrants who had always suffered the extremes of poverty. They might be miserable hangers-on who did chores about a slovenly grog-shop or

[22] Knox to St. Clair, Mar. 21, 1791, *ibid.*, I, pp. 171-174.
[23] Knox to St. Clair, June 23, 1791, *ibid.*, I, p. 178, and *American State Papers, Military Affairs*, I, p. 43.

tavern; often they were sailors who had missed their ships by lying too long with their doxies. Some were lads or older men who lay in vermin-infested jails for lack of money to pay debts or fines; some were farmer boys or apprentices already broken on the wheel of toil. Recruiting parties knew the haunts of these unfortunates; they sounded fife and drum on the village common where the poor and homeless gathered; they marched through the main streets and darkened alleys of the towns and cities, beating more loudly and blowing more shrilly as they passed noisome inns and passed in the shadows of the whorehouses. Thus were the dregs of population led to forsake their lurking places and respond to the call of the colors.

Drawn from such sources, recruits were even more lonely and friendless when transferred to the frontier. Yet more than one of them learned to endure wilderness hardships with fortitude and to fight resolutely in battle. Their deeds of heroism were accepted by the nation and their comrades in arms as merely a part of inescapable duty. Although they won for the republic the range of an empire, the annals of the Northwest are barren of their deeds. Only here and there do forgotten mounds of earth and simple headstones mark the resting places of their moldering bones. In their own day they were looked upon as mere hirelings of the government, grudgingly considered necessary at times but generally distrusted by the majority of the people.

Not infrequently ignorant and indifferent men have been transferred into skillful and heroic soldiers through the alchemy of able leadership, training, and adequate supplies—three things forever stressed in the regular service. Unfortunately the army of St. Clair lacked these essentials. He himself evoked neither temporary enthusiasm nor sustained confidence. Sargent, his adjutant general, was a man of brittle mind and unbending manner. Loyal, energetic and in many ways able, his habitual austerity and chilly aloofness, as well as his ill-concealed contempt for the frontiersmen, repelled and alienated the

very ones with whom he was compelled to work. He was
wholly unfitted to break down the animosity that habitually
existed between regulars and militia when serving together.
Neither was he able to win the whole-hearted support of
the higher ranking officers. Major General Richard Butler
disliked Sargent and to some extent this explains, but does
not excuse, the perfunctory service rendered by the second-
in-command. Samuel Hodgdon, the quartermaster, was
more friendly with the adjutant general, but was himself
a hopeless incompetent. Though a veteran of the Revolution, Hodgdon did not realize the necessity of forwarding
adequate supplies quickly even while he remained in Philadelphia. When he arrived at Fort Washington his extem-
poraneous bustling merely aggravated the prevailing confusion. The Secretary of War himself must accept some
portion of the blame for failure to supply the army speed-
ily and properly. Henry Knox was growing fat and seldom
inspired haste. In addition, the Secretary of the Treasury,
Alexander Hamilton, was governed by a pernicious economy in the purchase of army supplies. The price allowed
for rations was so low that it permitted only a very small
margin of profit for the contractors, who, as might have
been expected, usually resorted to chicanery. William
Duer, the contractor for 1791, was no exception to the
general rule.

St. Clair's success depended much upon Hodgdon, who,
though incompetent, was neither dishonest nor venal.
Part of the equipment that he supplied was as useless as
some of the broken-down derelicts who lied to the recruiting officer about their age. Many of the small arms were in
need of repairs, particularly the guns furnished the militia.
Parts had been lost or were wholly lacking; in some cases
guns had been fashioned without even adding the touchhole. The artillery carriages used by Harmar on his expedition were rickety and worn out. Cartridge boxes that
had been gathering mold in the damp storehouse at West
Point were oiled and blackened and sent on to Fort Washington where they had to be again refurbished before they
were fit to be issued. The haversacks were poorly made and

of inferior material; most of them had to be waterproofed
with heavy coats of paint, usually of Spanish brown. The
soldiers of the 1st Regiment had previously covered theirs
with bearskin at a cost of thirty-five or forty cents each.
Thus the few articles carried in them were better protected
from the weather, and the regiment had a characteristic
piece of equipment of which it was distinctly proud. Axes,
saws, frows, and other tools were entirely too few for the
immense task of cutting a road through the wilderness
and building log forts at important points. Camp kettles
were lacking, and so few bells were issued that horses
could not be turned out to graze without the danger that
they would wander off and be lost. The scarcity of tents and
the poor quality of those issued made the troops realize
that they would not be protected from rain or snow after
the campaign had really begun. Any casualty from sickness
or wounds could hope for only the most indifferent medical
care; the surgeon had almost nothing on hand to relieve
pain or promote recovery.[24]

To remedy these deficiencies both raw materials and
skillful laborers were needed. Artisans were drafted arbi-
trarily wherever found. Organizations were often crippled
in this way, much to the anger of some commanding officers.
Under the supervision of the chief of artificers and Major
William Ferguson, the mechanics and their helpers were
kept hard at work in the newly established workshop at
Fort Washington. A blacksmith turned out kettles, canis-
ters for shot, and bells for horses and oxen. Gunsmiths
replaced or repaired innumerable springs, triggers, ram-
rods, and bayonets for both levies and militia. When a
supply of paper arrived, cartridges were made not only
for marching troops, but also for the garrisons that were
to be established along the line of communications. New
stocks were turned out for guns, spokes for wheels, and
handles for shovels. Worn-out traces were replaced with
rope, sets of harness patched, and pack-saddles altered to
fit the small western horses. Splints, litters, and other

[24] Knox to St. Clair, Mar. 21, 1791, *American State Papers, Indian
Affairs*, I, pp. 171-174.

hospital supplies were improvised from whatever suitable materials were handy. Men grew weary turning grindstones for sharpening the cutting tools so badly needed for hewing a way through the forests to the towns of the Indians.[25]

Samuel Hodgdon, the Quartermaster, who was responsible for the supervision of all this work, lingered in Philadelphia and did not reach Fort Washington until September 10, only seven days before the campaign actually began. Owing to his negligence, St. Clair received not much more than a trickle of supplies. His delay in going west would have been less reprehensible if troops had received what they needed; but essentials were lacking in quality, quantity, and kind.

No long march could be made successfully with the transportation available. Horses were too few and their handling was incompetent. When a hundred of them arrived at Fort Washington, they were put ashore on the Virginia side of the Ohio where pasturage was excellent and raids by the Indians unlikely. Within twenty-four hours, seventy of them were temporarily missing. The forage-master, who was short of both bells and hobbles, knew nothing of wood-craft, and some said he should himself have worn a bell. At feeding time the grain was scattered on the ground instead of being placed in troughs, thus wasting a large part of it. While trying to get a mouthful, horses injured each other by kicking and biting; some swallowed dirt and rubbish with their feed and died as a consequence. For a time they were tied to fences at Fort Washington and given little or no feed. When the mounted detachment needed an officer, one with infantry training only was selected. Though his unfitness was soon proved, he was nevertheless retained; the only remedy taken was to make someone else of higher rank and more suitable qualifications his immediate commander.[26]

While Samuel Hodgdon was adding failure to delay,

25 St. Clair, *op. cit., passim,* and *American State Papers, Military Affairs,* I, pp. 36-44.
26 St. Clair, *op. cit.,* pp. 41-44.

William Duer, the contractor for supplying the army with rations, was adding deception to failure. The Secretary of the Treasury, Alexander Hamilton, let the contract and occasionally advanced considerable funds to purchase flour, meat, and whisky, requiring in turn that a final and detailed settlement of accounts be made to his office. Dominated by rules of economy, the Treasury all too often failed to meet the pressing needs of troops actually in the field. When rations were lacking in quality or quantity the commanding officer might exert his authority and direct his quartermaster to supply the deficiency and charge the cost to the contractor. On short notice in a country barren of stores, this procedure was of little help, no matter how capable the quartermaster concerned might be. Farmers were not tempted by high prices when their own cupboards were almost empty. As a result, soldiers often went hungry and strategic movements were not infrequently determined in the tent of the contractor instead of in the marquee of the general.

The problem of William Duer and his agent, Israel Ludlow, was to accumulate enough stores for the frontier garrisons and at the same time feed an army of 2,500 men. It called for organizing ability of the first order. Duer further complicated the problem by eagerness for personal profit and a canny unwillingness to take financial risks. On June 9 Knox had written to General Richard Butler that rations for six months would be required for the posts to be established along the line of communications, adding cheerfully that they would certainly be furnished.[27] Two months later Ludlow was complaining that he still lacked authority to buy animals to transport provisions, although by this time most of the troops had already arrived at Fort Washington. On his own responsibility, St. Clair directed the purchase of six or seven hundred horses, reporting his action to Knox.[28] Soon some of them were stolen or killed by Indians; others had little feed and were quickly

27 Knox to Butler, June 9, 1791, W. H. Smith, *op. cit.*, pp. 216-217.
28 *American State Papers, Military Affairs*, I, p. 38.

worn down by hard work and constant abuse by ignorant drivers who had no interest in tending them properly.

Notwithstanding the fact that the army was far from ready for active service, the troops began to move from Ludlow's Station, five miles from Cincinnati, on September 17. General Butler, the Quartermaster, the contractor's agent for transportation, and the final detachment of troops had not yet arrived.[29] Key men and essential supplies were still lacking. The rank and file were indifferent and listless. They were being led by a general now fifty-seven years old, afflicted with gout and harassed by a host of worries and apprehensions. His strength had passed its meridian and the iron of his spirit was eaten away. One of his prime necessities was a good staff; his seldom rose above the level of mediocrity. His army was no more than a rabble, conscious only of its inferiority and unmindful of the future. It was entering a wilderness that few white men knew; it had no maps to follow, no competent scouts to guide. In contrast the Indians possessed a minute knowledge of the woods, streams, and trails that lay in the theater of operations. In the type of fighting soon to be employed, they were experts of the first order. Confident in the sagacity of their chiefs and animated by a thirst for revenge, they bided their time, waiting for the moment when they could fall on the disorderly column and cut it to pieces. Then would the country that the Great Spirit had given to them be redeemed from the invading hosts that were sweeping northward from the "Beautiful River."

[29] St. Clair, *op. cit.*, p. 140.

5. *The Great Defeat*

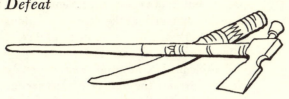

O<small>N</small> August 7, 1791, St. Clair, leading an untrained and bickering army, inadequately equipped and short of rations and transportation, moved from Fort Washington to Ludlow's Station, six miles distant.[1] Five weeks had already elapsed since the date originally set for the opening of the campaign. Although some declared this change of station was made only to enable the contractor to collect approximately fifteen cents for the ration instead of the seven cents allowed at Cincinnati,[2] more cogent reasons for the movement existed. The march, short as it was, would probably reveal weaknesses that could be remedied. The horses and oxen had exhausted the pasturage about Cincinnati and it was necessary to find new grazing areas. The health of the troops might also be improved. Certainly they could receive more efficient training in camp routine and they would be farther removed from the vicious grog shops along the river. Passing boatmen needing hands would have fewer opportunities to induce the discontented to leave the colors and travel southward with them. Already advertisements were appearing in the *Kentucky Gazette* offering rewards of ten dollars for the apprehension of deserters.[3] If the troops now numbering 2,300 men, exclusive of militia, could be better organized and more closely controlled, the blight of desertion might be checked.

In his new location Sargent, the adjutant general, worked indefatigably to improve the unfortunate conditions in the army, but with such impersonal coldness that nobody gave him support. Every hour of delay at Ludlow's Station diminished the probability of a successful cam-

[1] St. Clair, *Narrative*, p. 13.
[2] *American State Papers, Military Affairs*, I, p. 37.
[3] *Kentucky Gazette*, Lexington, Ky., July 2, 9, 1791.

paign; but it was not until September 17 that the ram-
shackle command broke camp and plunged forward into
the wilderness. Forty-one days of favorable weather and
valuable time had been lost.

President Washington was seriously concerned. He
clearly foresaw the danger of further inaction, but hoped
that St. Clair might overcome the handicaps imposed by
previous delays in recruiting, organizing, equipping, and
training the troops raised under the law of March 3, 1791.
On July 21, even before the regiments had reached Fort
Washington, the President was strongly advising "decisive
measures." On August 4 he urged that operations begin
at "the earliest moment." A week later he expressed the
hope that the utmost would be done to accelerate the
campaign. As his anxiety grew, Washington charged St.
Clair, by "every principle that is sacred," to stimulate
his exertions "in the highest degree and to move as rapidly
as the lateness of the season and the nature of the case
will possibly admit."[4]

It was, indeed, high time for the President and his
Secretary of War, Henry Knox, to be disturbed. Their
original plans called for the beginning of the campaign on
the first of July. Later they postponed the date to the 10th.
Two months later not all the troops earmarked for the
operations had arrived at the general rendezvous at Fort
Washington. The War Department held some of them at
Pittsburgh for local defense; others were unable to descend
the river because Hodgdon, the incompetent quartermaster, failed to furnish necessary boats. Knox never succeeded in prodding him into vigorous action. The Secretary
himself moved majestically, but seldom swiftly. Although
genial and loyal, he had lost those relentless and dynamic
qualities that he had displayed during the Revolution when
hauling cannon from Ticonderoga or crossing the Delaware above Trenton. Key officers also delayed beyond
reason. The quartermaster and the contractor's agent for
transportation did not reach Fort Washington until
September 10. On the same late date Major General Rich-

4 St. Clair, *op. cit.*, p. 5.

ard Butler arrived. Washington, despite misgivings as to his competency, had appointed him second-in-command of the army. Butler remained at the fort several weeks to investigate Harmar's campaign, not joining the main body until the 27th.[5]

Meanwhile the army had been moving slowly northward, taking three days to cover the eighteen miles between Ludlow's Station and the banks of the Great Miami. For the entire distance a road had to be cut through heavy timber—beech, maple, walnut, hickory, and oak. Good axes, as well as expert axmen, were lacking. Because of improper tempering, blades often "bent like dumplings."[6] To keep them serviceable, men were constantly busy at forge and grindstone. After enormous labor a way was finally opened through the forest for carts, wagons, pack horses, and artillery. Fortunately for the cumbersome column, the Indians did not attack. By the 19th of September, troops had completed the march through intervening swamp and woods and pitched a camp on the prairie near a crossing of the Great Miami.[7] Here St. Clair began the construction of Fort Hamilton, which was to be his first fort and place of deposit on his prospective line of communications.

The fort was a work of considerable size close by the river. To build it required much labor and consumed valuable time. The adjacent area was carefully cleared for two or three hundred yards. In a trench, three feet deep and following the ground plan, were set upright two thousand log pickets, dragged from the distant forest. They were twenty feet in length, of uniform size, well butted, and carefully trimmed so that they would fit closely together. A ribband was run around near the top of the pickets to hold them securely in position; at the bottom the earth was rammed hard about their bases. On the inside of the wall, between every two pickets, another was snugly fitted, making the whole impenetrable to Indian missiles. The whole provided a stout stockade in the form of a

5 *Ibid.*, pp. 97, 140.
6 Testimony of Major Zeigler, in Smith, *St. Clair Papers*, II, pp. 206-210.
7 Denny, *Diary*, in Smith, *op. cit.*, II, p. 252.

square, measuring 150 yards on each side. At the four corners bastions were built to cover the approaches; two of them were provided with platforms from which cannon could sweep the ground in front. Quarters for the officers and men and storehouses for equipment and supplies were built inside the enclosure.[8]

Two weeks were required to build Fort Hamilton. Much or all of this time might have been saved had detachments been forwarded from Ludlow's Station to do the work while the rest of the troops were being organized and equipped. Such a base was obviously necessary, but why the entire army should have been delayed a fortnight to construct it is not equally clear.

On October 4 the army once more started northward. The leaves of the forest had begun to yellow, goldenrod along the trail was turning brown, and an autumn chill occasionally set the ill-clad soldiers to shivering. Reveille was sounded early enough for all to be awakened and under arms before dawn, the favorite time for Indian attack. Usually camp was not broken until about nine o'clock. Surveyors and riflemen set out first, traveling far ahead on a compass bearing and marking out the road. St. Clair had been unable to engage either Indians or frontiersmen competent to act as guides. Next came the woodcutters and their protecting detachment, a little ahead of the advance party. In rear of the latter group, the main body, divided into two columns with pieces of artillery scattered here and there, trudged along. Packers and drovers followed, driving heavily laden horses and rawboned cattle; often the forest re-echoed as they urged a stumbling beast forward with blows and profanity. With them also marched a detail of troops to fend off a sudden attack. A hundred yards or more from the route of the main body the cavalry reconnoitered the flanks. Farther out, detachments of riflemen filtered through the woods. Ahead of these, selected scouts moved swiftly but cautiously. A customary rear guard protected the tail of the long column.[9]

8 St. Clair, *op. cit.*, pp. 152-154; Smith, *op. cit.*, pp. 292-293.
9 St. Clair, *op. cit.*, pp. 270-271.

In such fashion the army advanced through woods, swamps, and open stretches of plain from the 4th to the 14th of October. Seldom did it cover more than six miles a day. As hardships increased and the signs of Indians became more frequent, the fighting spirit of the combatants showed a marked decline. On the night before the army's departure from Fort Hamilton, twenty-one deserted. It became necessary to select patrols and messengers with care; such details too often failed to return to their organizations.[10] From time to time, detachments of recruits arrived, but their quality and appearance was not such as to encourage their officers. When, on the 10th of October, Lieutenant Colonel William Oldham appeared with a body of newly enlisted reinforcements, the adjutant general declared that they were the "off-scourings of large towns and cities, enervated by idleness, debaucheries and every species of vice. . . . They were, moreover, badly clothed, badly paid, and badly fed." Never, asserted Sargent, could such trash be trained to fight.[11] All that kept these and many others with the colors was their terror of the Indians, their dread of a hundred lashes as punishment for desertion, and the great hardships they would have to undergo in trying to escape the forbidding and all-encircling wilderness.

For somewhat different reasons the column was accompanied by a considerable number of camp followers. General St. Clair had with him a little Indian boy whom he called Billy; Captain Heart had brought along his son, a youngster in his teens. There were the many civilian employees of the contractor and quartermaster. Both sexes and all ages were represented in the motley throng of hangers-on; some women carried babies, others were pregnant. Four women were usually allowed to each company as washerwomen. These, with the wives and mistresses of officers and men, may have numbered two hundred or more.[12]

10 St. Clair to Knox, Oct. 6, 1791, Smith, *op. cit.*, II, pp. 245-246.
11 Sargent, *op. cit.*, p. 242.
12 Sargent indicates in his *Diary, Ohio Archaeol. and Hist. Soc. Pub.*, XXXIII, p. 269, that there were only about thirty-three women with the army. He probably had in mind only those officially authorized to accompany it and draw rations. Many others were doubtless present—

The enlisted women were something more than their scarlet sisters who lived in frontier bordellos and took the common wages of shame. It is true that they were not beautiful and virtue was not one of their strong points. Drunkenness and carnal sin were their frequent diversions but they were not always prone to make of either a habit or a profession. They recognized the fact that life was hard and they made what they could of it, gratefully accepting the government's rations and pay and whatever else the soldiers might spare them. In return they washed for the living, nursed the sick, and bound up the wounded. Only the most robust of their sex could endure the long hard marches, the cold and dreary camps, the scanty food, often unfit to be eaten. If these women had been weak, they would not have chosen the ill-paid scarecrows of the new republic as husbands or lovers. Had they not been strong, they could never have survived the hardships that they suffered. Like the frontier, they were rough in language and action; their conversation was often shot through with profanity, their conduct earthy and unregenerate. They suffered stoically and when necessary they would, and did, fight bravely. They hated the Indians as fiercely as any. When one of their men went down, they seized a musket and leveled it at the oncoming savages, rejoicing when bullets tore into the advancing redmen. They did not blench when they heard the blood-curdling yells of Miamis, Shawnees, or Delawares, well knowing that, if captured, roasting or crucifixion might be their fate. Although these women along the Ohio did not meet the niceties of conventional standards, they played an important role in winning the Northwest.

All these camp followers imposed an added burden on the contractor. As the line of communications constantly lengthened, the problem of supply became more complicated. Provisions ran low. St. Clair's anxieties doubled when he realized that unless flour was brought up by

wives of officers, non-commissioned officers, and privates. The militia were prone to take with them whomever they pleased. For Atwater's figures, see *A History of the State of Ohio*, p. 142.

the 10th, there would not be an ounce left in the wagons. Israel Ludlow, the agent for the contractor, was mainly interested in the accumulation of profits for his principal; the feeding of the army was a secondary consideration. While the rank and file hungered, he was prolific in excuses. On October 8 St. Clair wrote indignantly to him:

"It seems to me, sir, to be idle to talk about disappointments in drivers, and horses thereby unemployed, in a business where the honor and the interests of the United States are so deeply concerned as in the present. No disappointments should have happened which was in the power of money to prevent, and money could certainly have prevented any here. A competent number of horses were provided to your hand; how they have been employed I know not; certainly one half of them have never been upon the road, or we should not have been in our present situation; and take notice that the want of drivers will be no excuse to a starving army and a disappointed people."[13]

The venal contractor was not the only one who failed to give the harassed general the help that was requisite to success. There were officers of high rank who fell far short of expectations. Colonel Sargent, the conscientious and energetic adjutant general, fearing the total disintegration of the army, tried as remedy an incessant round of floggings for the men and courts-martial for the officers. This method of disciplining troops did not succeed. The human material with which he dealt was poor in body and mind; the time was entirely too short for transforming it into an efficient fighting force. Although he was an experienced veteran acquainted with the system, Sargent did not understand the art of creating a great army. He aroused fear and deep-seated hatred, but little else. Major General Richard Butler, St. Clair's second-in-command, finally joined the expedition during the last week in September. He was soon differing with his chief on the manner in which the column should march. His desire for an independent command made him loath to cooperate. When his ideas

[13] St. Clair to Ludlow, Oct. 8, 1791, in Smith, *op. cit.*, II, pp. 246-247.

were not accepted, he became restive and dissatisfied. Lieutenant Colonel William Darke, of the 1st Regiment of Levies, was consumed by a burning desire to slaughter Indians with his own hands; but he did not know how to lead a group of men to accomplish it on a large scale. St. Clair believed him two-faced and had little confidence in him. Lieutenant Colonel William Oldham, 2nd Regiment of Levies, was made of better stuff. He had been a captain in the Revolutionary Army, resigning his commission in 1779 and settling at the Falls of the Ohio. He was familiar with the methods of Indian warfare, but the raw Kentucky levies that made up his command were of the poorest quality. He knew that he could not use them on missions demanding obedience and courage. Lieutenant Colonel George Gibson, a competent and enterprising Pennsylvanian with an excellent Revolutionary War record, was opposed to an advance beyond Fort Jefferson because the enlistment terms of many of his men would soon expire. He was not happy over his rank as a junior to Darke.[14] Another field officer was, in Sargent's opinion, a "damned bad soldier for peace or war" . . . a perfect disgrace to the profession of arms.[15] Without a speedy or practical method of ridding himself of incompetent officers, St. Clair proved himself incapable of inspiring and integrating the efforts of those who were really able, although he did lean heavily upon loyal and energetic officers like Major William Ferguson, Major John Hamtramck and a few others.

Unfortunately the powers of able subordinates were limited and the troops with which they worked were not always dependable. The regulars, militia, and levies proved to be elements that could not be fused. The militia cavalry were paid two-thirds of a dollar a day. When they refused to do their share of the necessary fatigue, they were assigned more patrolling and reconnaissance, both of which they performed in a slovenly fashion. They looked contemptuously upon the ill-paid infantry as hirelings who had joined the colors only to evade jail or starvation. Although most of the regulars were little more than recruits,

---

[14] St. Clair, *op. cit.*, pp. 29-37.   [15] Sargent, *op. cit.*, p. 267.

their very name and the prestige attached to the federal service tended to quicken their pride and nourish a contempt for the improvised soldiers who filled the ranks of the levies. Most of the older regular officers were veterans of long and varied experience. Hard service under Washington in the Revolution had taught them how to handle their long-suffering subordinates; if rations or equipment were at all available, they usually saw to it that their organizations obtained their full share. A few of the field officers and company commanders among the levies were reasonably competent. Their men, however, were almost invariably a wretched lot; they had to wait until the regulars were supplied before they got their clothing and arms, or else they were issued what no other troops would have.

Heading a force so little deserving the name of an army, General St. Clair reached a point forty-five miles north of Fort Hamilton on October 13, 1791. His marches had averaged only five miles a day. Before advancing farther into hostile territory, he determined to establish a base and build another fort. The site selected for Fort Jefferson, as it was later called, lay on rising ground that sloped gently away to a prairie on the east and west. There was a good spring close at hand and game was plentiful in the woods nearby. About thirty miles distant were numerous Indian villages. On the 14th of October a detail of 200 men reported to Major Ferguson and work on the fort began. Not so large as Fort Hamilton, the ground plan measured only thirty-five yards on each side. Built of logs horizontally laid, it had a bastion at each corner with curtains forming the outside walls of the storehouses and barracks within. Construction progressed slowly, weather being bad and tools few. The quartermaster could supply only eighty axes, thirteen of which he had borrowed from the troops. Luckily the only saw that the army possessed was still serviceable, and somebody managed to find a frow. A lone grindstone edged all the tools. Spades and mattocks were plentiful enough. By the 23rd of October the fort was completed, and Captain Joseph Shaylor with ninety men, most of them invalids, moved in as a garrison.[16]

During the ten days spent on construction, the troops suffered many discomforts. From the 18th to the 23rd the weather was cold and the rains descended daily. In each cheap leaky canvas tent eight or more men were crowded together; the camp site was a bog and the soldiers went about wet to the skin. The sky was overcast and they had little opportunity to dry out their things. On the 19th strong winds blew, and for two short hours around noon there was cheering sunshine. For a day or two the weather was fine, then it turned colder and flurries of snow warned of approaching winter. Ice was half an inch thick on the creeks during the night of the 21st. The levies shivered in their wretched clothing that now hung on them in rags. A few were able to obtain coats and overalls from the paymaster when their officers guaranteed that he would be reimbursed. Some of them, when their terms of service expired, enlisted in the regular regiments rather than face the hard journey back to Fort Washington with almost nothing to wear. Secretary of War Knox had seen the clothing of the levies in Philadelphia and knew that it was fit only for scarecrows. Even so, he had exerted himself little to provide any better.[17]

Not only did troops have slight protection from wind and weather, they also went hungry for much of the time. Everybody grumbled at the "unpardonable mismanagement in the provision department." On October 17, the last of the flour was issued—only enough for a single day. Two days later the officers entitled to double rations had to be content with one, and certificates of indebtedness for the balance due them. When these certificates were presented later at the War Department, Knox refused to approve them because they brought no profit to the contractor, his partner in real estate ventures.[18] On the 20th troops received one half their allowance of flour, next day

16 *Ibid.*, p. 245.
17 *Ibid.*, pp. 244-247; St. Clair, *op. cit.*, pp. 199-201, 219.
18 St. Clair, *op. cit.*, p. 115.

it was only a fourth. Whisky ran out, and many a soldier yearned for his allowance of it on bleak winter mornings. There was usually enough meat; but the cattle, herded along with the column and slaughtered from day to day, were rawboned and on the point of starvation. Grazing was scant and no forage available. St. Clair's wrathful letter of October 8 had resulted in no continued improvement in the amount of provisions. Ludlow declared later that not a ration could be furnished beyond Fort Jefferson because he could not obtain pack horses. The general directed Hodgdon to spare no expense in securing them.[19] They could not be purchased promptly, no matter how zealously the well-meaning but incompetent quartermaster tried.

Living as they were, from hand to mouth in a comfortless present, the soldiers looked forward with even less satisfaction to a forbidding future. Order and system in the army rapidly deteriorated. The militia were soon beyond all control, performing only such tasks as suited their whim, untrustworthy even at these. Twenty of them deserted in a body on October 21. The next day an officer with sixty men went out and brought them back.[20] The levies insisted that their term of service was for six months only, and that it had begun when they were sworn in, not when they reached Fort Washington or some other rendezvous. A few seem to have argued the point successfully and to have obtained their discharge. Those who remained with the colors might well have been granted the same privilege; they became only more disorderly and riotous. The morale of the troops, even in the 1st Regiment, ebbed constantly lower. During the first few days at Fort Jefferson four men from this organization slipped away. Others followed, despite the fact that Indians were close by and white settlements were many miles distant. Courts-martial were frequent. On Sunday, October 22, the grisly punishment of three privates was formally carried out.

[19] Sargent, *op. cit.*, pp. 245-247; Denny, *op. cit.*, pp. 253-255; St. Clair to Hodgdon, Oct. 21, 1791, in Smith, *op. cit.*, pp. 11, 253-255.
[20] Denny, *op. cit.*, pp. 254-255.

The day was fair, and a northwest wind blew the dying leaves from the near-naked trees. At half-past two in the afternoon a subaltern, two non-commissioned officers and twenty privates brought a murderer and a pair of deserters to the grand parade where all the troops were assembled.[21] The sentence was read, a chaplain exhorted, and the condemned struggled for a moment beneath a gallows that the quartermaster had made. The punishment, while not undeserved, had little effect in deterring others from similar crimes. Most of those who witnessed the execution had already lost the will to fight and the spirit to endure. They could not be changed by the means employed; they faced their responsibilities with no more hardihood or resolution than before; they listlessly performed their daily tasks with a growing sense of impending disaster.

Officers and men alike realized that the twenty-four days of delay involved in the building of the two forts had brought them almost face to face with a winter campaign, and they knew that as yet no measures had been taken for making war in the Indian country during such a season. With all their temerity, Scott, Wilkinson, and Harmar never would have attempted the double-headed, equivocal program of fighting and fort building after the 20th of September. St. Clair, whose thinking and scheming was too often wishful in character, still hoped to eke out some sort of victory, in spite of the fact that his tatterdemalion army was neither clothed nor equipped for another month in the wilderness and supplies were dwindling with each mile that it advanced from its base. Had he halted his troops at Fort Jefferson and sent out a mobile detachment to harry the Indians, a small success might have rewarded his efforts. But to go on, as he determined to do, knowing that his ill-supplied men had lost faith in their cause and their leader, was a clear revelation of poor thinking and inexcusable obstinacy. St. Clair himself was sick and old. He was utterly lacking in those soldierly qualities that enable great generals to make swift and

21 Crawford, *Orderly Book*, Oct. 23, 1791 (no page numbering); Sargent, *op. cit.*, pp. 247-248.

unerring decisions, irrespective of public opinion. Sitting among the ashes of hope, without the comforts of wisdom, he failed to see that his original mission could not be accomplished. If disaster were to be averted that mission must be drastically revised.

St. Clair prepared to continue the march northward. At nine o'clock on the morning of October 24, the troops broke camp and started for the Indian towns about thirty miles distant. St. Clair accompanied the column, although he might well have been left at Fort Jefferson with the rest of the invalids. He was suffering great physical pain as well as mental distress. Wrapped in flannels, he was carried in a litter by some of his men. The route followed an old Indian trail, winding through the seemingly endless forests of oak, ash, and hickory. By late afternoon the army had progressed only six miles. A halt was called and canvas stretched again, this time on the banks of a "handsome creek running east." The camp site was on ground where later rose the town of Greenville, Ohio.[22]

Here the army remained five days, waiting impatiently for the arrival of additional rations. Rain began to fall the first night, continuing until dawn. Cloudy weather followed. Then, to add to the universal misery, hail and snow descended by turns. Those whose time was expiring clamored for their discharge; each day little groups hastened southward over the path so recently traversed. As sickness and discharges diminished the number on the rolls, signs of Indians multiplied. On the 27th a body of fifty militia stumbled into a group of about five of them. They failed to capture a single warrior, but they brought in a few dollars' worth of plunder. On the next day, two of the men, having wandered off three miles from the camp, were attacked. One of them was killed and scalped, the other was wounded but managed to escape. Precautions were taken to prevent the camp from being surprised. The troops were ordered to be under arms before daylight and to continue so until dismissed. At night they were permitted

22 Denny, *op. cit.*, p. 255; Sargent, *op. cit.*, p. 248; *American State Papers, Indian Affairs*, I, pp. 136-137.

to remove only their coats, vests, and shoes; cartridges and firelocks were to be always ready for instant use; sentinels on post were to be relieved precisely as prescribed in orders and regulations.[23]

Each day alarms and discomforts increased. On the 28th a three-day issue of flour was made in the hope that more horses might be released for transporting provisions from the base. On the 30th the advance was resumed. Twenty Chickasaws had joined the army several days before. This tribe had a treaty of peace and friendship with the United States and its warriors were bitterly hostile to all Indians living north of the Ohio River; they hated the Kickapoos especially. These friendly allies might have served St. Clair well for local reconnaissance, but he foolishly sent them on a distant scouting expedition that served no immediate purpose. The army groped its way along as blindly as before, finally pitching a camp in the midst of a dense forest after marching only seven miles. Complaints multiplied, especially since a lack of transportation had forced the troops to leave behind much tentage and baggage. There was little shelter from the incessant rain and cold. Scarcely had they bedded down when a violent wind tore through the woods, accompanied by terrifying lightning and deafening peals of thunder. Limbs and even trees crashed down. Bewildered sentries, believing that they had discovered Indians, fired their muskets wildly. Unable to sleep at night and constantly wretched during the day, troops failed to do their duty. The militia grew mutinous. Sixty or seventy of them tramped off in a body, swearing that they would stop the pack horses en route from Fort Washington and take what they wanted. St. Clair sent his most dependable regiment, the 1st, after them, not to bring them back but to prevent the looting of the oncoming stores.[24]

The convoy arrived safely on October 31, with 212 horses loaded with flour. Still no immediate movement was made. Fatigue details were chopping out a road to the

[23] Denny, *op. cit.*, pp. 255-256; Sargent, *op. cit.*, pp. 248-250.
[24] Sargent, *op. cit.*, pp. 250-251.

front, and a place of deposit had to be made for the heavy articles so that the loads of the overworked pack horses could be lightened. Sadly behind in his official correspondence, the general took a day off to compose a report to the War Department. Not until November 2 was he ready to resume the advance.[25] All that day a light snow fell. The country was flat and marshy, criss-crossed with creeks. Troops wallowed in the mire, wet to the skin. After an eight-mile march they halted late in the afternoon, camping in two lines, the artillery parked between. They were now close to the heart of the redmen's country. The danger of attack was acute, and guards were posted with more than usual care.

The night passed without incident, and on the morning of November 3 they set out again. As usual, the quartermaster rode ahead to select a camp site. His choice not meeting with the General's approval, the army was halted while Captain Edward Butler went off in search of another. When he failed to find suitable ground, another officer was sent on the same errand. St. Clair waited impatiently, finally riding forward with Butler to discover the cause of delay. They came up with the officer and learned that there was good camping ground a mile and a half further on. The selection was approved, and the troops wearily resumed the march. It was about sunset when they halted and eight o'clock before they were bedded down—hungry, exhausted, and chilled to the bone. The fire of their offensive spirit had flickered out.[26]

The army was now ninety-seven miles from Fort Washington. The new camp, facing west, lay close to the east bank of the upper Wabash, in what became Mercer County, Ohio, about 50 miles from the Fort Wayne of a later day. The ground was not well drained; towards both flanks and to the rear it was low and wet. All of it was timbered. When brush and snow had been cleared away, tents and improvised shelters were arranged in two roughly paralleled

[25] *Ibid.*, p. 251.
[26] St. Clair, *op. cit.*, pp. 214-273; T. Irwin, "St. Clair's Defeat" in *Ohio Archaeol. and Hist. Soc. Pub.*, X, pp. 378-380.

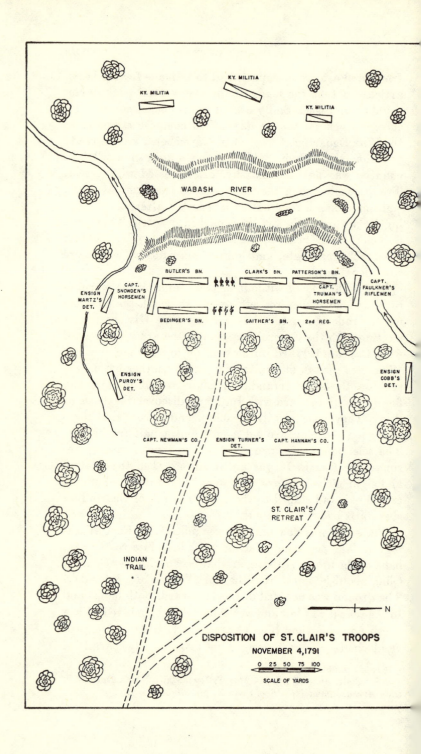

KY. MILITIA

KY. MILITIA

KY. MILITIA

WABASH RIVER

BUTLER'S BN. CLARK'S BN. PATTERSON'S BN.

CAPT. SNOWDEN'S HORSEMEN

ENSIGN MARTZ'S DET.

CAPT. TRUMAN'S HORSEMEN

CAPT. FAULKNER'S RIFLEMEN

BEDINGER'S BN. GAITHER'S BN. 2nd REG.

ENSIGN PURDY'S DET.

ENSIGN COBB'S DET.

CAPT. NEWMAN'S CO. ENSIGN TURNER'S DET. CAPT. HANNAH'S CO.

ST. CLAIR'S RETREAT

INDIAN TRAIL

N

DISPOSITION OF ST. CLAIR'S TROOPS

NOVEMBER 4, 1791

0   25   50   75   100

SCALE OF YARDS

lines about 350 yards long and 70 yards apart. Within this rectangular area horses were tethered, stores piled, and fires built for cooking rations and warming the shivering men. In front of the camp the Wabash was from fifteen to twenty yards wide and was covered with a thin coat of ice; it was shallow enough to be crossed by men on foot. On each side of the river for about 50 yards stretched bottom land. Farther to the west the ground was higher; and there, in the covering of open woods, the outpost commander placed an advanced detachment of about 300 militia.[27]

In some respects, the camp site had points in its favor. Fuel, water, and partial shelter were all available. Its defects consisted in tactical disadvantages. Obviously, it would be difficult to defend against the kind of attack that might reasonably be expected. From nearly all directions the Indians could advance under good cover, fighting in the manner that suited them best. The approaches were known to them—in fact, when the army appeared in the neighborhood some of the savages had fled from the very place where tents were pitched a few hours later. Not more than two or three miles away several hundred braves were comfortably encamped.[28] Dimly realizing that his situation was anything but secure, St. Clair toyed with the idea of throwing up hasty entrenchments or breastworks. But his men were weary, the hour was late, and the danger was not openly apparent. Nothing was done. Thus what might have saved an army from destruction proved no more than a general's passing thought.

Unaware, or unconvinced, that the woods nearby were swarming with savages, St. Clair did no more than establish a routine defense. If his scouts had performed their duties properly, he could hardly have escaped the conclusion that the enemy was closer at hand and more numerous than before and that he must immediately take special

[27] Irwin, *op. cit.*, pp. 378-380; "Military Journal of Major Ebenezer Denny," in *Memoirs of the Historical Society of Pennsylvania*, VII, p. 368.

[28] Sargent, *op. cit.*, p. 271.

precautions for the safety of his command. Unluckily, on November 3, reconnaissance beyond the outguards had been left largely to chance. Worse than that, important information once gained was never used.

One case of such neglect was especially reprehensible. When a certain Captain Slough of the levies was getting his own shelter ready for the night, Colonel Gibson turned up carrying a fat raccoon. He suggested that the captain come with him and learn a good way of getting it ready for eating. The two went off together. They were joined by Captain Edward Butler who boasted how easily a patrol might capture a few of the Indian horsethieves believed to be lurking nearby. Slough warmed to the idea, promising to lead such a patrol if some good men could be persuaded to go with him. Butler promised to collect enough of the right sort from Gibson's regiment and bring them to General Richard Butler's tent. Twenty-three volunteers were assembled, most of them sergeants from various companies. Slough took charge of the detachment, receiving his orders from General Butler. He was given the countersign and advised to be careful. One of St. Clair's aides, Captain Ebenezer Denny, was also present, taking a glass of wine with the others to wish good luck to the venture. Slough went off to talk to Colonel Oldham who warned him that his patrol would probably be cut off because the army would undoubtedly be attacked in the morning. In spite of such a prediction, Slough proceeded to the "picquet guard" where he arranged for a password with the officer in charge so that his men would not be fired upon when they returned. After going about a mile westward from the camp he halted his patrol and divided it into two groups, placing one on each side of an Indian trail that they had been following. Scarcely had they hidden when six or seven savages came along. At a range of about fifteen yards, the groups on the left opened fire, killing one of the braves. The rest of them managed to escape. Again Slough's men lay down among the snow-covered leaves and quietly waited. Soon a much larger party came from the same direction. After stopping and coughing and trying to discover the members of the patrol, the Indians pushed on toward the camp. A few minutes later more warriors passed by. Uneasy at all this activity, Slough and his guide, George Adams, decided that they should return to the camp lest they be surrounded and taken. Moving as rapidly and as quietly as possible, they started back in single file. Every fifteen or twenty yards, they heard noises on each side of them but could not determine the cause. About midnight they reached camp in safety. Slough immediately went to Colonel Oldham, who was just then in the act of going to tell St. Clair that he expected an attack before sunrise. After they had talked together, he decided not to go, entrusting the errand to Slough instead. Slough then went and made a report to Colonel Gibson, who asked him to go and tell all he had learned to General Butler, the second in command. He found the general standing before a fire in front of his tent. When they had withdrawn far enough to prevent the sentry from hearing their conversation, Slough told all about his reconnaissance, suggesting that the army commander should be informed of its results. Butler, however, demurred, suggesting instead that Slough go and lie down and get a little rest. The captain followed this piece of advice, although he afterwards insisted that he felt sure an attack on the camp was imminent.[29]

Thus three of the highest ranking officers of the army, Gibson, Oldham, and Butler, had been informed that the Indians were numerous in the nearby woods and were drawing closer to the camp. Slough's information was certainly corroborated by the unusually frequent firing of muskets by the outguards. Had Oldham obeyed his orders and sent out early morning patrols, doubts would have no longer ruled his vacillating mind. Even had his patrols been attacked and wiped out, the consequent alarm would have forced the troops to stand to their arms and might have prevented the appalling disaster that happened a few hours later. His proffered excuse, that his men could not be trusted and would not obey, merely confirms the con-

29 Testimony of Slough, St. Clair, *op. cit.*, pp. 213-218.

clusion that as an officer and a soldier he was lacking in the fundamental qualities essential to the exercise of command. It is true that St. Clair was ill, and that the Adjutant General, Sargent, was captious and irascible; but at least Gibson and Butler should have had enough regard for duty to make sure that their own commanding general was informed of all that they knew. Such neglect clearly discloses that they lacked loyalty to their chief and inexcusably disregarded a primary obligation to their subordinates. The fact that both Colonel Oldham and General Butler later went down in slaughter does not free them from the damning indictment that they miserably failed at a critical juncture to perform a simple act that might have saved the lives of many of their own men.

Swiftly the reckoning for this neglect fell upon the luckless rank and file. Ordinarily troops were paraded ten minutes before daylight and held under arms until sunrise. On November 4 the schedule was altered. Reveille was blown and the drums began to beat much earlier, an indication that a general uneasiness pervaded the camp. Troops had spent the night lying on their arms, with all equipment for instant use. When they fell into ranks before daylight, it was customary to hold them assembled until objects could be distinguished at three hundred yards. On that fatal morning they were dismissed several minutes earlier so that they might have a little more time before beginning the tedious labor of making a place of deposit on the camp site. A few of them had been sent out to collect the grazing horses that were to be sent back as soon as possible to Fort Jefferson for bringing up additional supplies.[30]

While the men were forming in ranks, Sargent was busy inspecting the militia outpost across the Wabash. These troops occupied a much better defensive position than did any of the others. For about 400 yards to their front the woods were more or less open, offering little cover for hostile approach. To their rear there was bottom land,

[30] Sargent, *op. cit.*, p. 258; Denny, *op. cit.*, p. 258; "McDowell's Story" in Henry Howe, *Historical Collection of Ohio*, II, pp. 490-491.

dropping abruptly away to a level stretch thirty feet below. If Indians attacked from this direction they would come under fire not only of the militia, but of the regulars and levies in the main camp as well. The flanks of the position were also easy to defend. When he had completed his inspection, Sargent regretted that this area had not been selected for the camp of the main body. While so engaged, he received the disconcerting information that Colonel Oldham had failed to send out morning patrols in compliance with orders issued to him. Sargent returned to his headquarters on the left of the camp, apparently in complete ignorance of the fact that the surrounding woods were already swarming with savages.[31]

It was a half hour before sunrise. The troops had been dismissed and had gone back to their tents or were huddling around the fires preparing breakfast. Suddenly Sargent heard yells of Indians rushing through the forest to attack them. To him the sound seemed neither terrible nor blood-curdling; he thought it was like that of an infinite number of horsebells ringing at the same time. An ominous quiet followed; then a burst of musket fire and the whistling drone of bullets broke the silence. The militia received the first impact of attack. Although their position was naturally strong, they fired only a few scattered shots and fled headlong, crossing the open bottom land and the Wabash, breaking through the first line of the main body and spreading confusion and terror in the second. Their flight was halted only when they perceived that another body of the savages had encircled the camp and were attacking it from the rear. Some of the militia were tomahawked and scalped during this race for life; those who escaped owed deliverance to their fleetness of foot rather than to their valor.[32] Sargent recorded that with few exceptions they behaved like a lot of shameless cowards. He seemed to forget that this was not their permanent character; they were merely illustrating what any troops without training and discipline will always do in strenuous moments of battle.

[31] Sargent, *op. cit.*, p. 258.   [32] *Ibid.*, p. 259; Denny, *op. cit.*, p. 258.

Led by a chief in a long red coat, the painted warriors pursued the fleeing militia, rushing upon the first line commanded by General Butler. The fire of the regulars temporarily halted their onset. The few who continued to come on had their ardor chilled by the cold steel of bayonet. Swerving to the right and left, the attackers cut off and slaughtered the outguards, completely surrounding the camp. Hiding behind fallen logs and trees and utilizing any cover offered by the broken terrain, they fired with deadly accuracy on the milling and disorganized troops. A great pall of powder smoke hung close to the ground and aided concealment. Most of it came from the three and six pounders that were kept constantly firing; they made a great noise but did little execution with the round shot and canister that had been so laboriously hauled for almost a hundred miles. Most of the gunners were killed and not a single artillery officer survived unwounded. Small-arms fire proved little more effective. The recruits had not yet been trained to use their muskets; many of them, ignorant lads from the streets of Eastern cities, had never fired a gun before. Terror-stricken, their fingers numb with cold and their hands trembling, they loaded clumsily and flinched from the heavy recoil, their bullets going wide of the mark and often merely cutting the twigs from the upper branches of the distant trees.[33]

The Indians, approximately 1,000 strong, exhibited considerable skill in butchering St. Clair's army.[34] They aimed with care, and their bullets and arrows found many a mark in flesh and bone. Relentlessly pushing their advantage, they swept forward under cunning and revengeful leaders. Simon Girty ("The Great Renegade"), Little Turtle, the fiery chief of the Miamis, and others equally able, once having organized the attack, now dashingly led it. Soon the troops posted on the left of the camp were in disorder. St. Clair decided to join them. Because the

[33] Irwin, *op. cit.*, p. 380; St. Clair, *op. cit.*, pp. 28, 220-221.
[34] McKee to Johnson, Dec. 5, 1791, Public Archives of Canada; Wilkinson to Brown, Dec. 12, 1791, *New Eng. Hist. and Gen. Register*, XXI, pp. 339-340.

general's gout was so bad that he could scarcely walk, a
horse was brought up. Four men tried to help him into the
saddle but before they succeeded the horse was shot in the
head and his orderly was wounded in the arm. A soldier
then caught another horse; both were immediately killed.
The general's rheumatism abated. In his own words: "I
could wait no longer; my pains were forgotten, and for a
considerable time I could walk with a degree of ease and
alertness that surprised everybody."[35] No longer handi-
capped by personal infirmities, he gathered about him a
little group of determined men and at their head drove
back the savages who had gained a foothold on the left.
Lieutenant Colonel Darke, the officer who had a consuming
desire to slice off Indians' heads, was ordered to charge with
a part of the second line. He drove the redskins from cover
and westward across the Wabash, but he was unable to
maintain this temporary advantage because of a lack of
riflemen and cavalry. His men could neither kill the fugitives nor hold the ground that they themselves had won.
The charge ended; the troops fell back; the Delawares,
Shawnees, and their allies again closed in.

Three separate charges were made in rapid succession by
troops from the 2d Regiment and other organizations.
Many of the men followed their officers without flinching,
using their bayonets and gunbutts to drive the savages
from cover. But valor alone was not enough. After each
rush forward they had to fall back once more; each time
the ring of hostile flame around the camp grew smaller.
Between the lines the dead lay thick upon the ground. In
the 2nd Regiment only two officers escaped alive, and one of
these was wounded.[36] Although these makeshift regulars
had been only a few months in uniform, some of them made
a shining record of brave deeds. Their acts have added
luster to the tradition of the United States Army.

As counterattacks failed one after another, the Indians
pressed closer and picked off their victims more readily
as the range decreased. By some miracle St. Clair himself
escaped unwounded; eight bullets cut his clothing and one

his whitening hair. Had he worn his customary uniform he might have been singled out as a special target and shot down. Dressed in a plain coarse coat and a commonplace three-cornered hat, he was not recognized as the commanding general. Colonel Oldham, failing to check the panic-stricken militia, took a post near the artillery and fought bravely until about half an hour before the retreat began, when he was mortally wounded. In a small area near the guns, thirty men lay scalped. The Indians did their work well; all the hair was skinned away, leaving only bloody pools. A Captain Smith was such a victim, "sitting on his backside, his head smoking like a chimney," and inquiring if the battle was not almost over. Major General Butler fell while moving up and down the lines encouraging and directing his men. Shot first through the arm and then through the body, he was carried to a tent where two surgeons tried to dress his wounds. While thus engaged, one of them was struck in the hip by a ball and mortally wounded. Even so he managed to kill an Indian who rushed into the tent and attempted to scalp the general. The savages greatly admired Butler for his dauntless courage. After gaining complete possession of the camp, they secured his body, cut out his heart, and devoured it in the hope of acquiring some of his valorous qualities. Major Ferguson, an officer who had from the beginning of the campaign acted with ability and dependable energy, retained the character that he had always shown.[37] He died while serving his guns. About him were piled the bodies of his men; they followed him to the end—the highest tribute that any officer may ever hope to have in battle. Captain Price, of the 1st Regiment of Levies, was equally brave; he was killed while urging forward one of the charges.[38] Dr. Victor Grasson, a surgeon's mate in the same organization, died while coolly attending the wounded; he was

[37] Smith, *op. cit.*, I, pp. 220-221; St. Clair, *op. cit.*, pp. 220-221; McDonough to McDonough, Nov. 10, 1791, William L. Clements Library, University of Michigan.

[38] Sargent, *op. cit.*, pp. 267-268; Stelle, *Wayne and the Pennsylvania Line*, p. 320; "Unveiling of Fort Recovery," *Ohio Archaeol. and Hist. Quarterly*, July 1913, pp. 420-424.

the first medical officer to fall in action since the days of the Revolution.[39]

General demoralization followed these great losses. Most of the officers were casualties, and men began to leave the ranks, loot the tents, and hunt places of safety. Many, stricken senseless with terror, milled aimlessly about in small groups, easy targets for the well-trained redskins. Surviving officers endeavored by threats and entreaties to induce those still able to return to their places in the broken lines of defense. St. Clair drew his pistol, swearing to shoot down anyone who refused to fight. Others kicked or cursed the cringing cowards who unresistingly waited to be toma-hawked and scalped. Many of the women evinced the heroic spirit that does not quail at the imminence of death, keep-ing up the fight after their men had fallen. They shamed the weaker into redeeming acts of valor. They "drove out the skulking militia and fugitives of other Corps from under wagons and hiding places by firebrands and the usual weapons of their sex."[40] On that bleak November day these women rose high above the reputation that they some-times bore. In the course of a few hours nearly all of them had been "inhumanly butchered, with every indecent and aggravated circumstance of cruelty." Only three are said to have escaped.

As the panic became general, retreat or annihilation remained the only alternatives. About nine o'clock St. Clair decided to abandon the camp. All equipment and stores, as well as all the severely wounded, were to be left behind. There was no time for preparation, every moment of delay lessened the chance of escape. On the right flank men were quickly assembled. Led by St. Clair and Darke, they desperately charged the Indians who encircled the camp's rear and blocked the way to the road that had been cut through the woods on the preceding day. Dis-concerted by the vigor of the attack, the warriors fell back in both directions, permitting two hundred or more of the soldiers to pass through like "a drove of bullocks."

[39] H. E. Brown, *Medical Department of the U. S. Army*, p. 73.
[40] Sargent, *op. cit.*, p. 269.

Then the hordes of yelling savages closed in again and very few others got by them to safety. Had the Indians kept up pursuit, none of the fugitives might have escaped. As it was, after a pursuit of only two or three miles, they returned to camp to sate themselves with blood and loot. In their frenzy of victory they inflicted on the luckless captives every species of cruelty that savage ingenuity could devise. They danced and laughed and howled at the screams of prisoners roasting at the stake; they pulled out men's intestines bit by bit; they flayed others alive and slowly hacked or wrenched their limbs away. They dashed out the brains of children against the trunks of trees and then flung their battered bodies into the brush. Some of the women were stretched naked upon the ground and run through with wooden stakes; others were cut in two after their breasts had been hacked away.[41]

The fortunate few who escaped this horrible butchery made a headlong flight to Fort Jefferson, twenty-nine miles distant. The older men and the wounded had slight chance of getting there without the aid of their comrades or some kind of transportation. The commanding general himself finally secured a worn-out pack horse that could seldom be spurred out of a walk. Unable to halt the fleet of foot in the vanguard of retreat in order to allow the others to catch up, St. Clair selected two dependable officers and a dozen or more stout-hearted men and posted them along the line of flight. By their efforts the craven militia were temporarily checked.[42] The majority of troops were frantic with terror, without an ounce of fight left in them. Nearly all of them threw away whatever encumbered them in the race for life—guns, cartridges, bayonets, belts, knapsacks, blankets, and coats.

The line of flight was marked by acts of heroism as well as cowardice. An Irish soldier passed a wounded comrade

[41] St. Clair to Sec. of War, Nov. 9, 1791; Smith, *op. cit.*, II, pp. 261-267; Sargent, *op. cit.*, p. 269; Howe, *Historical Collection*, II, p. 493; McDonough to McDonough, Nov. 10, 1791, William L. Clements Library.

[42] St. Clair, *op. cit.*, pp. 50-51, 225.

hobbling along the trail, halted and refreshed him with liquor and bread and set him on a horse. Another, seeing one of his friends lying helpless on the ground with a broken thigh and begging for aid, hoisted him to his back and carried him for several hundred yards. Mounted men passed by unheeding; none would stop and relieve the good Samaritan of his burden. With the Indians drawing nearer and his own strength ebbing fast, he could not rid himself of the unhappy man until he took out his knife and cut off his clutching fingers. Then the wretch rolled off in a heap, and the savages soon came along and tomahawked him out of his misery.[43] A mother, unable to carry her infant son any longer, threw him into a snowbank. The Indians picked him up, carried him away, and eventually raised him to manhood.[44] A $15-a-month packer named Van Cleve came across a badly wounded young man who had been brought up in his own family and whom he loved like a brother. He put him on a horse, but riding was impossible for one shot through the hips. Before long he fell off and his scalp was soon added to the bloody trophies at a Shawnee's belt. A small boy, whom the same Van Cleve placed behind two men riding another horse, shared a like fate. The packer himself, suffering from cramps, was barely able to walk. Removing his shoes, he found that the touch of his bare feet upon the frozen ground revived him so that he was able to continue to Stillwater. Here, about twelve miles from the battlefield, he fell in with Lieutenant Shaumburgh, Corporal Mott, and a tall, strong woman known as "Red-headed Nance." Mott and Nance were both weeping bitterly; the corporal had lost his wife and the woman her child. The lieutenant's strength was nearly spent; he hung on the corporal's arm, turning over his fusee and equipment to the indomitable Van Cleve. With Nance in the lead, this oddly mixed quartet reached Fort Jefferson about sunset. For hours afterwards, the shattered remnants of the routed

---

[43] Irwin, *op. cit.*, p. 492.

[44] "McDowell's Story," Howe, *Historical Collection of Ohio*, II, pp. 490-491.

army straggled in and sank exhausted upon the nearby prairie.[45]

Even the fort proved to be no haven of refuge. The place was overcrowded due to the presence of most of the 1st Regiment, which had been previously detached to protect an oncoming pack train from loot-hungry deserters. After Major Hamtramck, commander of this detachment, had accomplished his mission, he and his men were encamped five miles south of Fort Jefferson, expecting to rejoin St. Clair in a few days. Early on the morning of November 4 they broke camp and started out. They soon heard distant firing of cannon. This was enough to make them hasten more rapidly to the fort. Here they rested a little while. Then leaving the shoeless behind, the others marched on for six more miles. By then it was eleven o'clock, and all were hungry for their breakfast. After halting long enough to eat, they again set out along the trail. They had covered no more than a mile and a half when a waggoner and an artilleryman who had been with St. Clair brought them word of the disastrous defeat, some twenty-three miles distant. Not until after dark could Hamtramck ever expect to reach the field of battle of which he knew nothing at all. He would have been foolish to risk the hazards of a night attack by his greatly inferior force, which was ignorant of the terrain and would be utterly weary from thirty-five miles of wilderness marching. He therefore started back to Fort Jefferson, expecting to defend it in case the need arose. The day after his arrival, he dispatched some of his men to go out and escort a supply train that was approaching; it had to be saved, for the garrison had no meat and only 300 pounds of flour.[46]

With rations so low, St. Clair, who had reached Fort Jefferson at dusk on the 4th, resolved against using the place as a rallying point for his fugitive forces. Fearing that it would soon be invested, he reluctantly arranged

---

[45] "Memoirs of Benjamin Van Cleve," in *Pub. of Hist. and Phil. Soc. of Ohio,* XVII, pp. 151-152.

[46] Denny, *op. cit.,* pp. 260-261; Sargent, *op. cit.,* p. 262.

to leave behind all those who were unable to travel. With the other wretched remnants of his army, he prepared to leave for Fort Washington as quickly as possible. He knew that the fighting spirit of his men was gone, their equipment was lost, and they had nothing to eat. He was only too well aware that the militia and levies could not be restrained, once they learned there was no bread or meat in the neighborhood. To ward off starvation and mutiny, his officers were eager to keep their men moving. They hoped soon to meet a pack train in order to obtain a little food for themselves and hasten the remaining supplies forward for the sick and wounded at Fort Jefferson.

Spurred on by fear, the panic-stricken troops started southward that very night, back through beech swamps and over ice-covered ponds. For hours they splashed and wallowed through the darkness. Many were without shoes, and their feet cruelly bruised and cut by roots and stones. When they reached high ground, many fell out to rest until they were able to go on. One of them afterwards declared that he slept at the foot of a tree, "passing the night very coolly." One group halted to build a fire and make a kettle of soup from some beef and flour stolen at Fort Jefferson. Their strength renewed, they pushed on, finally halting several miles beyond a bend in the road. Fearing ambush, they waited until St. Clair and others came up. The two groups continued together until daybreak. They had covered about seven miles, or between thirty-six and forty since the preceding morning.[47]

About 9:00 a.m. on November 5, they all set out again. After going three or four miles they met a supply train— fifty horses loaded with flour, and a small drove of cattle. The escort consisted of fifty men of the 1st Regiment, the only organization in the army that had not been in battle and was still fit for duty. Two pounds of flour for each man were taken from the packs, and the train was sent on to Fort Jefferson. After finding water suitable for cooking, St. Clair halted his men until one o'clock in the afternoon.

[47] *Ibid.,* p. 138; Van Cleve, *op. cit.,* pp. 152-153.

This was the first food for some of them since the evening of the 3rd. When night overtook them, they kindled their campfires fifteen miles from Fort Hamilton, or about sixty miles from their rout on the Wabash.[48]

Setting out before dawn on November 6, they arrived at Fort Hamilton during the afternoon. Others, with less spirit and strength, did not straggle in until much later. Believing themselves far in the rear and the Indians near, they had abandoned the road and wandered through the forests until they were in the neighborhood of the Great Miami. Many of them, wounded and without weapons, had eaten little or nothing for seven or eight days. As they reached Fort Hamilton by twos and threes, they were taken in and given their full share of the little that the post afforded in food and shelter.[49]

At about noon on the 7th all those able to travel set out on the road to Fort Washington. They covered about half the distance that day and came to the banks of the Ohio during the next afternoon. The long flight was there ended; it had tested the strength and spirit of men. Some had shown disgraceful weakness of mind and character; others had proved their valor in hours of extremity. From one indomitable officer, the Adjutant John Crawford, then fifty years old, many drew new courage, quickening their faltering steps. Sargent, in his report, makes clear the reasons for such inspiration: "It deserves to be remembered that very early in the action he [Crawford] received a brace of balls in his body, but that notwithstanding he continued with cheerfulness and spirit to discharge his duty during the service, and marched with the army ninety-seven miles to Fort Washington, on foot, in bad roads, without a murmur or complaint, and scarcely ever betraying the symptoms of fatigue or that he was wounded."[50] St. Clair's campaign was a bitter ordeal, but there was some compensation in suffering it with men like Crawford.

Once the army had reached Fort Washington, the full extent of the disaster became obvious. Thirty-five com-

---

[48] Denny, *op. cit.*, p. 261. [49] *Ibid.*; Sargent, *op. cit.*, p. 263.
[50] Sargent, *op. cit.*, p. 268.

missioned officers had been slain on the field of battle. Six hundred and twenty-two non-commissioned officers, privates, and civilian employees had been killed. Of the wounded, 29 were commissioned officers and 242 of the rank and file. According to these figures the total casualties numbered 918, exclusive of about 30 women who accompanied the column under proper authority. Only about one in three had escaped unharmed.[51] "The only regular regiment present lost every officer killed or wounded."[52]

The loss of stores and equipment was practically complete. All the artillery was abandoned, as well as the baggage wagons, tents, and traveling forges. About four hundred riding and pack horses were left behind, and this number did not include many belonging to the contractor's department. Few carried with them over the hundred miles of their flight anything but the clothes that they wore and the food that they hoped would keep them from starving. The money chest containing $1,938, as well as a great number of axes, spades, mattocks, and the tools of the blacksmiths, carpenters, armorers, and tinsmiths, fell into savage hands. Much of the spoil was what the Indians needed and knew how to use. They gorged themselves on the abandoned bread and meat. They found less satisfaction in some of the hospital stores. By trial and error they finally learned to distinguish the purgatives from whatever else was found in the medicine chest.[53]

While the Indians were thus revelling in plunder and the torture of prisoners, the battered fragments of what was once an army forlornly gathered at Fort Washington. Clothing and blankets were lacking; wounds, long un-

[51] These figures are from Sargent's Diary, p. 260. Caleb Atwater's total is 901 as given in *A History of Ohio*, p. 140. Roosevelt states total casualties were 910 in *Winning of the West*, III, part I, pp. 168-169. The number 915 is given in Smith, *op. cit.*, I, p. 176. All of these figures are apparently based on the losses of persons officially authorized to accompany the army. There seem to have been many others. Hence the above estimates represent a minimum rather than a maximum.

[52] Roosevelt, *op. cit.*, III, part I, p. 161.

[53] Sargent, *op. cit.*, p. 265; "Statement of St. Clair's account," in *Burton Coll.*, Detroit Public Library.

tended, had become infected. Shelter was insufficient and winter beginning. Except in the 1st and 2nd Regiments, discipline and military control no longer existed. One problem was quickly solved for the unhappy general—the militia went home. Some of the levies, aware that they had only a short time to serve, paid no attention to their officers, spending most of their time in annoying the neighboring public. Their excesses, committed in the town, aroused a fervent hope that they, too, would soon be gone. A few of the officers made halfhearted attempts to reestablish their authority and correct these abuses; others were either indifferent or so grievously wounded that they could do nothing at all. General St. Clair did not bestir himself to get his men paid and discharged. The acting paymaster general, Joseph Howell, Jr., then residing in Philadelphia and enjoying a salary of $1,200 a year, had no deputies around Fort Washington. The general himself declared that he had more important business than the examination of pay rolls. In his abated strength he failed to recognize a primary duty of any officer, that of being honest and fair with subordinates. Most of the levies got very little of what they had been promised for their six months' service. Few or none of them obtained $12 in cash. With their discharges, they received a final statement that an unknown amount of money and clothing had been furnished them. Usually they exchanged these ambiguous certificates of indebtedness for varying quantities of frontier whisky.[54] Sordid bouts of drunkenness often followed, the soldier's final compensation for all his months of hardship and suffering.

The complete story of St. Clair's rout was slow in reaching the East. An aide, Major Ebenezer Denny, was the official courier sent by the general to the temporary capital at Philadelphia. He left Fort Washington early in November, but because of the ice in the Ohio River and the difficulties of overland travel, he did not reach Wheeling until twenty days later. For ten days more he

[54] St. Clair, *op. cit.*, pp. 47, 124; *American State Papers, Military Affairs*, I, p. 38.

rode across snow-covered mountains and passed through valleys filled with rushing water. He did not reach Philadelphia to knock at the imposing residence of the corpulent Knox until December 19. Having read the dispatches, Knox decided that he must inform the President without a moment's delay. Washington was dining with guests, but he excused himself long enough to learn the story of the dreadful disaster. Rejoining his friends at the table he gave no indication of the disturbing news that he had just received. Not until the last guest had taken his departure did he give vent to the wrath that was searing his soul. Striding back and forth in his library he damned St. Clair for the misfortunes that he had brought upon the Republic. He recalled that in that very room he had warned St. Clair against surprise, only to have him repeat, with less reason, the blunders of the pigheaded Braddock. Yes, exclaimed the incensed commander-in-chief, he had suffered his army "to be cut to pieces, hacked, butchered, tomahawked, by a surprise, the very thing I guarded him against! O God! O God! He is worse than a murderer! How can he answer to his country?" Washington's anger was great, but his sense of fairness was even greater. After his first outburst he was silent for a few moments, and then, in a calmer voice, he spoke once more. "General St. Clair shall have justice—I will hear him without prejudice; he shall have full justice!"[55]

The President unswervingly held to this decision. Congress had met on October 24 and was still in session. An investigation could easily be arranged after witnesses and documents had been assembled. St. Clair himself did not leave Fort Washington until December 9; he was still unwell, and he needed time to collect data for his defense. When he reached Philadelphia in January he subsequently called on the President and expressed his willingness to resign his commission as major general after an investigation had been concluded. Although Washington received him kindly, he insisted upon a resignation beforehand. St. Clair complied in a letter written on April 7, 1792.

[55] Roosevelt, *op. cit.*, pp. 170-173.

The investigation of his campaign was already under way. A committee from the House of Representatives had been appointed for this purpose on March 27. It was composed of seven members, Thomas Fitzsimmons, a wealthy merchant of Philadelphia, being the chairman. For about a month and a half he and his colleagues examined a mass of papers and a multitude of witnesses. Those who gave testimony received a dollar a day for their services. On May 8, 1792, the final day of the first session of the Second Congress, the report of the committee was presented to the House, remaining there without any action being taken until the following November.[56]

The committee reported that the causes of the disaster arose from delay in passing the act which provided for the bulk of St. Clair's forces, in "the gross and various mismanagements in the Quartermaster's and contractor's departments," and in the lack of "discipline and experience in the troops." The general himself was completely exonerated. It was the committee's opinion that "the failure of the late expedition can in no respect be imputed to his conduct, either at any time before or during the action."[57]

These might be the real causes for such a national disaster, but they were not sufficiently specific to satisfy the public. Many believed that Congress, by its procastination and evasion of responsibility, deserved a large share of blame. As early as December 8, 1790, the President had invited its attention to the need of active operations against the Indians. Harmar's handful of regulars and militia had already demonstrated that a small force could not bring peace to the frontier. Twice during the month of January 1791 the House and Senate had been informed that the depredations of the savages were continuing. Not until March 3 was the law passed providing for additional troops. By then, as the committee confessed, the time was "hardly sufficient to complete and discipline an army for such an expedition during the summer months of the same

---

[56] *Journal of the House*, 1st Session, 1st Congress, I, pp. 552, 605, 733.

[57] *American State Papers, Military Affairs*, I, pp. 38-39.

year." Undoubtedly Congress had failed. At least a few of its members were honest enough to confess publicly that such was the case. As experienced soldiers, Knox and St. Clair must have realized how slim were the chances of success with so little time for preparation. Once they had accepted the responsibility for performing their mission, however, the utmost haste was mandatory. When every moment was precious, they both dawdled inexcusably.

This was especially true in the case of supplies. From July 25, 1785, until March 4, 1791, organization commanders obtained supplies from various depots after requisitions had been approved by Harmar or St. Clair. Faced with the prospect of a campaign against the Indians, the President thought it best to make use of the authority granted him and revive the office of quartermaster general. The appointment of Hodgdon followed. He was genuinely unfitted for this office. Knox had known him intimately during the Revolution and was certainly acquainted with his capacity. The genial secretary may have been blinded by friendship, wishfully thinking that his former subordinate could perform a task that would have tried a genius. Hodgdon did not lack willingness, but his ability was slight. When his service as quartermaster ended he was happy to accept a post as a government storekeeper at $500 a year. In this less exacting role he displayed both courage and faithfulness when the yellow fever raged in Philadelphia in 1793.[58]

The case of William Duer, the contractor, is very different. He was both dishonest and mercenary. In 1786 he had been Secretary to the Treasury Board; three years later he was Assistant Secretary of the Treasury, resigning in 1790 to embark on a career as a contractor and speculator. St. Clair's investigators disclosed his relations with the government. The original contract for supplying troops beyond Fort Pitt had been given to Theodosius Fowler, who had guaranteed its execution under a $100,000 bond. In January 1790 the contract was transferred to Duer,

---

[58] J. B. McMaster, *A History of the People of the United States,* p. 11, *passim.*

and in March he was also awarded another covering troops at Fort Pitt or on the way there. For fulfilling these two, Duer gave no security except an unsecured $4,000 bond. Both contracts were let by the secretary of the treasury, Alexander Hamilton, who also favored Duer with advances amounting to $85,000 between March 23 and July 20, 1791. With these funds in hand, and having promised to transport rations beyond Fort Washington, Duer neglected to authorize his agent, Israel Ludlow, to purchase the necessary horses. St. Clair ordered them bought and the cost charged against the contractor. The bills amounted to $17,000, the amount being paid later by the treasury in spite of Duer's protests.

While engaged in this phase of army supply, Duer was speculating in scrip. On April 27, 1791, he was so hard pressed for funds in spite of advances by Hamilton that he asked Knox for a loan of $100 until the following Saturday. By October his finances were much better, apparently due to Knox's "aid and friendly advice." In fact, the secretary was asked to do some speculating for him. Putnam was to furnish $10,000 for the purpose. Results did not tally with Duer's hopes; his prestige began to wane. A suit was brought against him for financial irregularities committed in 1786, and his credit was ruined. He was arrested for debt and was actually in jail while the campaign of 1791 was under investigation. Except for an interval of freedom obtained through the intercession of Secretary Hamilton, Duer spent the rest of his life in prison, where he died in 1799. It is little to be wondered at that the army was often on the verge of starvation when its supplying contractor was a felon at large, not under military control, had no financial responsibility, and was concerned more with personal profits than with feeding the soldiers.[59]

Naturally Henry Knox and Samuel Hodgdon resented that part of the committee's findings which reflected on

[59] *American State Papers, Military Affairs*, I, pp. 37, 38, 41, 42; *D.A.B.*, V, pp. 486-487; Duer to Knox, Apr. 27, and Duer to Knox (?), Oct. 30, 1791, in *Knox Papers* (Boston Public Library).

them. When Congress reassembled on November 5, 1792, they asked permission to supply "information and explanations" concerning St. Clair's defeat. Shortly afterwards they submitted a sheaf of sworn statements that were obviously the product of interested parties.[60] A "revisionary report" was made to the House on February 15, 1793. It differed very little from the original one, and the findings remained the same. Knox and Hodgdon were still blamed as heavily as before.[61]

In striking contrast, St. Clair was completely exonerated —a distinct mark of the committee's confidence in his integrity and ability. Few denied that he sometimes showed qualities of greatness, but they also had to admit that he possessed weaknesses that were fatal to the successful exercise of high command. His power of analysis was not equal to the dimensions of his task. He had no adequate appreciation of the fundamentals of Indian fighting. From Scott, Wilkinson, and Harmar he might have learned what personnel, supplies, and transportation were necessary; they had all campaigned in his own theater of operations. But even after consulting with them and others he did not focus his efforts on these three important requirements. His mind was not incisive; at times he was mentally indolent; frequently he was procrastinating; always he was hopeful that he might accomplish his mission through some fortuitous accident or circumstance. As a consequence, his army degenerated into a disorderly, half-fed multitude that could not move quickly because it never had enough carts or packhorses. If he ever clearly visualized the reasons for these defects, he utterly failed to apply the proper remedial measures. He was old, and his energy was drained by physical infirmities. When he was sick he reasoned unsteadily and his driving power abated. He could not bring himself to make decisions quickly or convincingly.

[60] Hodgdon's letter to the committee is not impressive. It is without date, consists of thirty-five pages, and refers to numerous unconvincing affidavits that were apparently supplied as ordered. They may be found in a bundle of the St. Clair papers in the National Archives.

[61] *American State Papers, Military Affairs*, I, p. 44.

When surrounded with difficulties, he hesitated to be ruthless in solving them; for he was wholly unable to commit himself entirely to an irrevocable course of action. As a result, he quenched in his followers the zeal and enthusiasm with which a lesser man might have won great objectives. The militia, especially, became perfunctory in the performance of duty; and when no heavy punishment fell upon them, they disregarded orders more frequently. St. Clair could not generate confidence or inspire ardor for victory. Men followed him only with faltering steps, and in battle they did not trust him to save them.

Nevertheless, St. Clair was brave and loyal to an eminent degree. He constantly tried to meet the wishes of his superiors, even if doing so ran counter to his better judgment and resulted in the injury of his own reputation. When he failed, he accepted his share of blame with philosophical calm. Criticism did not arouse in him a mean anger that vented itself in the aspersion of his superiors or the castigation of his subordinates. There was something essentially patrician in his dignity, much that was praiseworthy in his sense of justice, and a good deal that was splendid in his acceptance of responsibility. Though a failure as a general, many still considered him a man of unquestionable worth. He was therefore permitted to continue as Governor of the Northwest Territory. Another man more skillful in the art of war and enjoying a larger measure of federal support would finally come and strike terror among the savages with fire and sword.[62]

[62] The official report of the defeat is found in the letter of St. Clair to the Secretary of War, November 9, 1791 (*American State Papers, Indian Affairs*, I, pp. 136-138). Sargent gives his version in "Sargent's Diary" (*Ohio Archaeological and Historical Society Publications*, XXXIII, pp. 238-282). Sargent's *Order Book* is in the Massachusetts Historical Society Library. It has not been published. It contains no orders from the third to the ninth of November, 1791. "The Diary of Major Ebenezer Denny" (Smith, *St. Clair Papers*, II, pp. 251-262), who was an aide of St. Clair, covers the time from September 1 to November 7. Other contemporary accounts are given by the following individuals: Benjamin Van Cleve (*American Pioneer*, II, pp. 150-153); Captain Daniel Bradley (*Journal of Captain Daniel Bradley*, Jobes & Son, Greenville, Ohio); Thomas Irwin (*Ohio Archaeological and Historical Society Publications*, X, pp. 378-380); McDonough to

McDonough, Nov. 10, 1791 (William L. Clements Library); McDowell (*Historical Collection of Ohio*, II, pp. 490-491); an unknown person (*American Pioneer*, II, pp. 135-138). The results of the Congressional investigation of St. Clair's defeat are in *American State Papers, Military Affairs*, I, pp. 36-44. St. Clair tried to defend his conduct of the campaign in *A Narrative of the manner in which the Campaign—was conducted, etc.* (Published in Philadelphia, 1812). Knox and Hodgdon endeavored to exculpate themselves of responsibility for the defeat by a number of *ex parte* affidavits, which are in the National Archives, Washington, D.C. Contemporary newspaper accounts of St. Clair's defeat may be found in the *New York Journal & Patriotic Register* for December 14, 1791; in the *Columbian Centinel* (Boston) for December 17 and 19; in the *Maryland Gazette* (Baltimore, Md.) for December 9, and in the *Maryland Gazette* (Annapolis, Md.) for December 22. The *Palladium* (Frankfort, Ky.) for August 21, 1806, hints that James Wilkinson helped the Indians by indirectly informing them where they might best attack St. Clair. Secondary accounts are given in Theodore Roosevelt, *The Winning of the West*, III, part 1, pp. 137-147, and J. B. McMaster, *A History of the People of the United States*, II, pp. 44-47.

6. *Wayne Creates a Fighting Army*

On October 24, 1791, the first session of the Second Congress met in Philadelphia, continuing there for 197 days. Once its members had learned of St. Clair's disastrous defeat, discussion immediately centered on means of defense. Some argued that no war should have occurred in the first place, for the whites were the aggressors and the lands that they coveted were not worth having. But as long as the British retained forts within our borders, we were bound to have trouble with Indians. If troops were needed, we should raise regulars for garrisons, militia for campaign. Levies were equal, militia superior to regulars. This was the general opinion; the campaigns of Scott and Wilkinson were thought to have proved it. Proposing a force of 5,168 men when the British had only 1,000 in the limits of our country seemed ridiculous. The annual expense entailed would amount to $1,250,000 although our treasury was empty; when people were already objecting to taxes, they would hate to be burdened with more.[1]

Others took the directly opposite view. If there ever was a just war, this was one. It was not for conquest; it was to defend our own people. From 1783 to 1790, fifteen hundred settlers in Kentucky or travelers going there had been massacred or carried away into captivity. Those along the frontiers of Pennsylvania and Virginia had likewise suffered. Even during 1790 while a treaty was pending and a truce had been solemnly ratified, Indians had either killed or captured 120 Kentuckians. The savages had rejected overtures for peace and taunted the whites to come and

---

[1] *The Debates and Proceedings in the Congress of the United States,* Second Congress, pp. 338-355, 418-423, 430-435. T. H. Benton, *Abridgement of the Debates of Congress from 1789 to 1856,* pp. 341-348, 410-414.

take the lands that the British were holding. Men and money must be raised. War could not be avoided while Indians plundered and murdered. There were then about 1,200 warriors from twenty-three tribes, and more stood ready to join these because of their confidence in victory. Measures must insure success. Militia would not do. Their efficiency varied widely with each state; often they were physically unfit for hard service; they had no sense of subordination; they would break and flee in the presence of disaster. As someone remarked, regular troops with equal experience would be found "infinitely superior to any militia upon earth"; if the former were not employed, nothing effectual could be done.[2]

As a result of this welter of argument, a law was passed on March 5, 1792, providing for the better "protection of the frontiers of the United States." The defense of our borders was to be entrusted no longer to a few improvised troops, unpaid and scantily equipped. The regular battalion of artillery and two regiments of infantry were to be brought up to strength. These would be reinforced by three regiments of infantry enlisted for three years, unless peace with the Indians made their earlier discharge possible. In addition there were authorized four troops of light dragoons, who might be required to serve dismounted if occasion demanded. With a better face of honesty, deductions for clothing and hospital supplies were no longer made from the $3-a-month pay of the private soldier; non-commissioned officers were likewise exempted and drew one dollar more in their various grades. For past and future enlistments an $8 bounty was offered. The lowest ranking commissioned officer, an ensign or coronet, had to make $25-a-month and two rations suffice for his living, a major general could do a little better on $166 plus fifteen rations and $20 for forage. Paymasters and adjutants were to be detailed from the line and were to have $10 extra as monthly compensation. Quartermasters were similarly selected but were paid $2 less.[3]

[2] *Ibid.*

[3] J. F. Callan, *The Military Laws of the United States* (revised edition), pp. 92-93.

It was not easy to find a person who could successfully lead this enlarged and reorganized force now known as the Legion of the United States. For such an important command Washington reviewed all of his former high-ranking subordinates who were still living and might be fitted for the task. He thought deeply on the qualities of nine former generals, wondering which one of them would be most desirable. Benjamin Lincoln, to whom O'Hara had surrendered his sword at Yorktown twenty years before, was thoughtfully considered. He was "sober, honest, brave, and sensible" but was nearing sixty, was well satisfied with his lucrative job as Collector of the Port of Boston, and was indifferent to further military adventures. William Moultrie, of course, was brave, tractable, and had dealt successfully with the Cherokees, but Washington seems to have known little more about him. In the cases of Lachlan McIntosh, George Weedon, Edward Hand, Charles Scott, or Jedediah Huntington, all had one or more heavy counts against them: old age, lack of enterprise, mediocre ability, too great a love of pleasure, etc. Von Steuben might suit, but after all he was a foreigner. Charles Cotesworth Pinckney had points in his favor. He was brave, honorable, sensible, and studious, but he was junior to the others and was little known outside of South Carolina.[4] Washington himself preferred Light Horse Harry Lee; others bitterly opposed this selection because Lee had never risen higher than lieutenant colonel during the Revolution. Besides, Virginia already had more than her share of important posts in the federal government.[5] As for Anthony Wayne— he had qualities of leadership but his defects were great. He was "more active and enterprising than Judicious & cautious. No economist it is feared:—open to flattery— vain—easily imposed upon and liable to be drawn into scrapes. Too indulgent (the effect perhaps of some of the causes just mentioned) to his officers and men.—Whether

4 "Washington's Opinion of General Officers," *Magazine of American History*, III, part I, 1879, pp. 81-88.
5 H. E. Wildes, *Anthony Wayne*, etc., pp. 348-349.

sober—or little addicted to the bottle," Washington knew not.[6]

Pondering upon a selection, the President recognized that the federal government had little money or prestige, and could not risk another disastrous defeat in the North-west. It was still on trial, and upon his shoulders rested the heavy responsibility of making the Constitution the beneficent instrument that its makers had planned. He could not fail the great trust the people had confided to him. Their welfare could not be jeopardized by the weak-nesses of Wayne. Unwittingly the President was exaggerat-ing them. His error was very natural, because in the light of the times they seemed portentous: they appeared to be the very characteristics that a commanding general should not have. In his anxiety for national safety, he had become hypercritical.

Washington, however, was not unaware that Wayne possessed the fundamentals of greatness; eight trying years of the Revolution had engraved this fact upon his impartial mind. Many knew how Wayne had suffered starv-ing misery and looked upon putrefying death in Canada and at Ticonderoga and had come through with his patri-otism unshaken and his will unbroken. Wherever brave and brilliant adventure found a hearing his capture of Stony Point had been repeatedly told. Farther up the Hudson, he had saved West Point from the treachery of Arnold. For his work in the South, he had won the deep admiration and intimate friendship of Nathanael Greene.[7] From such a record, Washington was convinced that Wayne possessed one quality preeminently—a dominating desire to meet and annihilate the enemy. None of the others had it in such an outstanding degree. Washington knew that all successful commanders must have this offensive spirit; he assumed that it would be rightly employed for defeating the Indians and making them beg for peace. At the same time, he fore-saw that if Wayne spent too freely, Hamilton and Knox

6 "Washington's Opinion of General Officers," *Magazine of Amer-ican History*, III, part I, 1879, pp. 82-83.

7 *Dictionary of American Biography*, XIX, pp. 563-565.

could tighten the purse strings; if Wayne wanted to begin the campaign too early, he might be restrained until the time was propitious and his troops were supplied and trained. As Washington thought, "under a full view of all circumstances, he appeared to be the most eligible," even though he was a repudiated Congressman and a business failure.[8] When his appointment was submitted to the Senate, confirmation, as Madison observed, followed "rather against the bristles," on March 5, 1792.[9] Some had misgivings, but the highest hopes of the President were to be fully realized.

Wayne had greater chances of success than his predecessor St. Clair. His troops were twice as numerous; they were better paid and supplied, and federal funds for campaign were not nearly so scant. Besides, the time for training his men was longer, due primarily to the fact that the government wished to exhaust all efforts for peace before permission was given to begin active operations.

For a few months after appointments, Wayne remained in Philadelphia arranging for supplies and conferring with those who knew something of the Northwest—traders, trappers, missionaries, land speculators, and government officials. Then he pushed on with his escort to Pittsburgh, passing through rolling mountainous stretches of country where men danced beneath Liberty Poles deriding the excise tax that Hamilton and his colleagues had recently imposed. Sometime in June he reached Pittsburgh, where "Whisky Boys," brothels, and "demoncrats" flourished in all their unwashed prime.[10] As the largest settlement along the headwaters of the Ohio, it was a desirable place for the organization and training of the army until it moved westward against the Indians. In this general neighborhood he fretfully remained for over a year.

Wayne made his headquarters at Fort Fayette, which was then garrisoned by a detachment of the 2nd Infantry

8 Thomas Boyd, *Mad Anthony Wayne*, p. 249.
9 Madison to Henry Lee, Apr. 15, 1792, in R. Worthington, *Letters and Other Writings of James Madison*, IV, p. 553.
10 H. E. Wildes, *op. cit.*, pp. 355-358.

under Captain Thomas Hughes. Built shortly after St. Clair's defeat, the fort stood near the center of the town of Pittsburgh, being situated between the Allegheny river and the thoroughfares later known as Liberty Avenue, Ninth Street, and Garrison Way. Its walls, formed by a wooden palisade some sixteen feet high, followed the general outline of a square. Each of the four corners faced a cardinal point; in three of them a blockhouse had been built, in the other a magazine. Within the enclosure, quarters for officers were nearest Liberty Avenue; barracks for the men were on the opposite side closest the river. The principal gate opened on the road to town. The heaviest armament consisted of six pounders, and only two of these were in position and ready for firing.[11]

Since the fort was designed to accommodate only a company, Wayne placed his men in tents nearby. The camp proved entirely too close to Pittsburgh, where the inhabitants found profit in pandering to the lowest wants of the soldier. Liquor and women became the most important articles in the rounds of a nefarious trade. Everybody knew that squaws were cheap, and that other women were only passably high. Stories were told that an ensign was acting as pimp for those who had need of either. Even Wayne was erroneously reputed to have a mistress who lived in a neighboring orchard. Lured by the tawdry blandishments of sin, the newly arrived recruit frequently lost his $8 bounty, the pay that he drew, and the money that he got from selling his equipment or clothing. Heavy punishments failed to deter him from such dissipation. Refusal of passes except to the excellent in character did not prevent many of the dissolute and idle from sneaking by the chain of sentinels and going about their evil business as freely as before. Topers escaping into town fell into mud holes where wandering hogs were wont to lie.[12] Attributing most of the army's troubles to the "baneful poison of whisky," Wayne took vigorous steps to curtail its use upon the

[11] E. M. Davis, "Fort Fayette," in *Western Pennsylvania Historical Magazine*, Apr. 1927, pp. 65–67.
[12] H. E. Wildes, *op. cit.*, p. 358.

reservation. He could not do the same in Pittsburgh. When he tried to use military law there, the civil authorities defied him; they yielded only when armed detachments enforced his orders. Strong measures were not desirable on every occasion, especially since his authority for the purpose was entirely equivocal. Nor did he care to start a quarrel with the "Whisky Boys," the lawless young blades who blatantly defied the collection of the excise tax. They had even sworn they would tar, feather, and castrate Captain William Faulkner if he took sides against them.[13]

Because of these conditions Wayne decided to move his troops. After reconnoitering, he found a suitable place twenty-two miles down the Ohio from Pittsburgh. The ground was high above the river, well drained, and covered with timber suitable for huts. On November 30 most of the troops were on barges ready for the change in station. When the flotilla got under way, artillerymen fired a salute of fifteen guns "as an acknowledgement of the politeness and hospitality which the officers of the legion had experienced from the inhabitants of Pittsburgh."[14] Some in the army, like Captain Faulkner, may have seen slight reason for such a friendly gesture; nearly all could agree that the whims of Wayne were not easy to fathom.

At their journey's end the troops pitched camp. They were soon hard at work building huts like those which once had sheltered Washington's army at Valley Forge. Some forty at least were needed for the infantry alone, for others a proportionate number. Each one was made of logs, had a fireplace of its own, and was large enough for perhaps a dozen or more men. Not until the December snow began to fly were most of them finished. Those for officers and for headquarters were built last; several weeks of the new year had passed before they were ready to be occupied.[15]

This new post in the wilderness was called Legionville, presumably in allusion to the new name of the regular army, which had been designated as the Legion of the

13 *Ibid.*, p. 379.   14 *Ibid.*, p. 368.
15 Wayne, *Order Book*, entries for Dec. 4, 30, 1792.

United States. As early as 1784 von Steuben had written to Washington outlining a plan for organizing the militia and a small regular force into legions of some 3,000 men each.[16] When Knox became Secretary of War in 1789 the name legion seemed to have pleased him. Though reminiscent of the days of Julius Caesar, it did allow a partial escape from English terms. Ever since he had been a bookseller in Boston, the classics had been dear to Knox's heart. He was wise enough, however, to introduce only a few Latin words, well knowing how disagreeably a grizzled old veteran would react if he had to pass as a tribune or call his organization a cohort.

According to the tables of organizations, the legion had a strength of 5,120 officers and men, exclusive of the commanding general and his staff. It was in turn divided into four sub-legions, each 1,280 strong and composed of sensible proportions of infantry, cavalry, and artillery.[17] Thus the sub-legion appeared admirably suited for the real business of fighting. If the sub-legion could be held together instead of being badly scattered in small detachments, each arm might learn better its special functions when operating with the other two. Team work in battle might be more easily attained with the new sub-legions; ignorance and jealousy might diminish; the field officers might learn to understand the measure of their tasks; and Congress would find it more difficult to pare and prune the army away. The country had a small well balanced force of great possibilities.

Under Wayne, the legion became an offensive weapon of power. When recruits arrived at Pittsburgh and Legionville, they started learning the cardinal virtues of a soldier. As in the case of St. Clair's men, they were mostly waifs of misfortune who had been little used to the cleanliness and neatness that Wayne demanded. He rightly insisted that officers set an example; not one of them failed to

---

[16] Baron von Steuben, *A letter on the Subject of an Established Militia and Military Arrangements Addressed to the Inhabitants of the United States, 1784* (Library of Congress).

[17] *American State Papers, Military Affairs*, I, pp. 40-41.

appear on parade with his espontoon and his habiliments as prescribed. Ensign Gazaway was reprimanded publicly for "wearing clothing not uniform at the head of his guard." Since Knox had succeeded in supplying a reasonable amount of clothing, Wayne was determined that his men should keep it presentable. Needles, thread, and patches were issued to all organizations. If anyone did not turn out properly at reveille, he was deprived of his half gill of whisky—a loss that was keenly felt in the cold gray hours of a wintry dawn. Men detailed for guard duty were minutely inspected; they had to be "fresh shaved and powdered" and to have their "arms in most perfect order." Every week the contractor issued a ration of the "bread kind" for dusting the hair. With only a few razors and strong lye soap, shaving was more difficult. Some of the careless and lazy soiled their uniforms with blood and grease by carrying rations in their hats or pockets. For every offense of this kind, the general worked reformation by assessing a penalty of twenty lashes.[18] A company that was conspicuous for its slovenliness was detailed for "Standard Fatigue in Camp" until it improved.

Believing that the health of his men depended much upon proper conditions around them, Wayne kept Legionville thoroughly policed. The quartermaster was responsible for seeing that enough latrines were dug. Fatigue details kept them in order. Kitchens were placed at the front of the camp and were regularly inspected. The day was unlucky for anyone dropping rubbish on the parade ground. Company washerwomen were compelled to do the work assigned them, and when they littered their washing place with filth, they were ordered to go elsewhere. Disobedience was punished by a triplicate ducking in the waters of the Ohio; few cared to break December ice for such a ceremony.[19]

While trying to make Legionville clean, Wayne endeavored to secure proper medical attention for his men. When they fell sick they were sent to the hospital in spite of their

[18] Wayne, *op. cit.*, Nov. 3, 1792, Jan. 17, 19, Feb. 11, 1793.
[19] *Ibid.*, Dec. 22, 1792.

Major General Anthony Wayne (from a portrait by Edward Savage in the New York Historical Society).

frequent efforts to remain in their huts and be cared for by companions.[20] For years they had believed that one seldom or never returned from a trip to the hospital. There was reason for this belief. Diagnosis and therapy were little beyond the practices of the savages. As late as 1812 the surgeon general of the army believed that the Indian tepee was the best form for a hospital and that typhoid fever patients should be subjected to rigorous vomiting.[21] Many of his civilian colleagues were even more ignorant; they often mixed the practice of their profession with mesmerism and witchery. The small amount of helpful knowledge that they possessed had been acquired through the devious route of apprentice. It consisted largely of trying to cure most human ills by a dreary round of cathartics, bleeding, and blistering plasters. The treatment for wounds was more strenuous, and without the use of anesthetics.

Soldiers were therefore reluctant to trust themselves to professional care. They much resembled Wayne, who, when troubled with flux and vomiting, ignored the doctor's orders and spurned his pills.[22] Assuring his men that he was working for their health and comfort above everything else, he placed Surgeon John Francis Carmichael in charge of the hospital, telling him to make requisitions for the things that he needed. Organizations were inspected and men needing treatment were given it. Those not immune from smallpox were ordered to be inoculated. With the idea of improving the diet of patients, their daily half-gill of whisky was bartered away for roots and vegetables. Men were detailed from companies to provide a few enlisted helpers for the hospital. These were generally from the riff-raff whom a captain was very willing to spare. To cure this defect, Carmichael was bidden to inquire for two "industrious humane and honest matrons to assist in nursing and cooking for the sick." They were to be paid

20 *Ibid.*, Aug. 19, 1792.
21 P. M. Ashburn, "American Hospitals of the Revolution and War of 1812," in *Bulletin of Johns Hopkins Hospital*, No. 46, 1930, p. 48.
22 Wildes, *op. cit.*, pp. 369-370 *et passim*.

$8 per month, and if found incompetent, were to be quickly discharged. Of the eighteen doctors allowed for the legion and garrison duty, each sub-legion was presumed to have one surgeon and two mates—a generous allowance for contemporary units of similar size. With all these assistants and the general's support, Carmichael did a good deal for his patients.[23]

Simultaneously Wayne cultivated esprit de corps in various ways. The quartermaster was directed to supply "16 Camp Coulers," white, red, yellow, or green, according to the sub-legion for which it was designed. Thus each troop of dragoons, company of artillery, and battalion of infantry had a distinguishing flag around which they might rally. In addition, the uniform was made more distinctive and serviceable. Cocked and rounded hats in British style were discarded as being unfit for wear along the frontier. Caps were fashioned, instead, and were ornamented with the tails of cattle that had been slaughtered for rations. Each sub-legion had a characteristic headdress, according to its colors. The 1st sub-legion had one with white bindings; in the 2nd, 3rd, and 4th they were respectively red, yellow, and green. On ceremonial occasions, men wore their hair white in odd-numbered organizations; in even-numbered, black. During the winter they cut up bearskins to cover their heads. Sometimes moccasins and leather jackets were worn. Even if a member of the Legion was far from his own row of huts, his uniform and equipment would disclose the organization to which he belonged.[24]

From men so well cared for, Wayne demanded efficient performance in drill and tactical exercises. Every company officer was issued a copy of *Regulations for the Order and Discipline of the Troops of the United States*. This book of approximately one hundred small pages was written by von Steuben during the winter of 1778-1779. It contained the rules for close-order drill and exercises in the field according to a modified French system. When

23 Wayne, *op. cit.*, July 17, Aug. 19, Oct. 2, 1792.
24 *Ibid.*, Sept. 11, 23, Oct. 6, 13, Dec. 24, 30, etc.

errors were made at parade officers were ordered to study the chapters of which they had shown ignorance. Some of them, like Captain William Eaton, certainly needed to consult the "Blue Book," as it was called. At one formation he had the rear of his company in front and its right on the left. The adjutant was too hotheaded to damn him for ignorance; he damned instead for disobedience. Sword and espontoon were about to clash when Wayne rode up and settled the dispute. In time such errors became less frequent; column, line, and order of battle were formed with ease and precision. Cavalry and artillery also learned their functions. Lieutenant Robert M. Campbell was often seen on a January morning teaching recruits how to ride; the ground was frozen and those who fell off remembered well. Sometimes the three arms of the service made a practice march together, solving advance-guard and outpost problems and learning the routine of marching. When combat exercises were staged, blank ammunition was frequently used.[25]

Unlike the British, who depended on volley firing, Wayne took pains to see that his men learned how to shoot as individuals. On field problems, blank ammunition made from inferior powder was used; at other times flints were removed and firing was simulated with wooden snappers. Plugging up the regular touchhole and drilling a new and larger one obliquely into the barrel enabled pieces to be primed much more easily when troops were in movement.[26] On fair days, they were turned out to fire at "marks" for an hour. To the best shots of the infantry and riflemen was awarded a gill of whisky, to runners-up half as much, provided always that the riflemen would forfeit theirs if the infantry excelled. About half the time the riflemen won nothing to drink. The poorest shots paid for their ineptness by salvaging lead from the targets or the ground nearby. From the standing position the most expert could hit within an inch or two of the center of the target some

---

[25] *Ibid.*, July 21, Aug. 26, Sept. 20, 1792, Jan. 22, 1793; Wildes, *op. cit.*, pp. 372-380.

[26] Wayne to Knox, July 7, 13, in *Wayne Papers*, XX, pp. 61, 74.

fifty-five yards away.[27] In this target practice, cartridges apparently contained only a single ball; for actual service conditions, they usually had three or more buckshot besides. As a rule, pieces were French muskets, model of 1777, or closely resembling them; their point blank range was about 100 yards.

Recruits often evinced an open dislike for this strenuous training. They were irked at a routine that they could not evade. Shortcomings were frequent. For minor infractions punishment was inevitable but seldom severe. Delinquents had to spend a few extra hours at woodcutting, taking care of the sinks, or general police of the camp. Equipment or clothing lost was charged against the loser. For every charge of powder and ball that could not be accounted for, a stoppage of one eighth of a dollar was entered upon the rolls. If men of good character overstayed their pass, they might expect to be deprived of their whisky at least. On March 17, all the sons of Hibernia were customarily given a holiday in honor of St. Patrick, a "holy and good man," as the general order read. Most of them spent it in joyful sprees. By the end of the day, the guard was uncomfortably busy; for arrant misbehavior a few lashes were commonly ordered. Even then the punishment was often remitted, especially if the defense had been committed against a fellow Irishman.[28]

Noncommissioned officers were treated with more consideration. Reprimands usually served as a corrective. Reduction was considered a punishment heavy enough except for the most serious offenses. There was the case of Sergeant Hopkins. Like several others, he kept a concubine; unlike them, he was less clever in exercising control. When she would not behave, he riotously beat her and was very profane. They both yelled very loudly, and the sick in hospital as well as others in garrison were greatly disturbed. On ordering the sergeant to cease chastening his strumpet, Dr. Carmichael got only abuse, threats, and indecent gestures to repay him for his pains. The guard was

---

[27] Wayne, *op. cit.*, July 21, Aug. 24, 1792, and Wildes, *op. cit.*, p. 374.
[28] *Ibid.*, Nov. 11, 1792, Jan. 21, Mar. 16, 1793.

called and it quickly took both of the culprits away. Before long the sergeant had to face a general court-martial, which saw no reason to justify his wicked and insubordinate conduct. He was accordingly sentenced to be reduced to the grade of private.[29]

Except in the case of the most serious military offences, the army was more lenient than the civil courts in meting out punishment. The times were revoltingly brutal. Idiots were herded with criminals and often flogged to death or until their spirit was broken. In at least one Connecticut prison, men were shackled, thrown into underground holes of filth and vermin, had their food thrown to them like dogs, and were kept at work until they fainted in their fetters—all because they had fallen into debt or were petty thieves or harmless vagrants. The penalty for killing a slave in South Carolina was only a fine. In Kentucky persons might be executed for stealing a horse. Massachusetts, in all its pride of sovereignty, exercised no clemency when a witless woman gained a few shillings in highway robbery. She was duly hanged. In frontier communities, spectators exulted and chortled when a bully pinned down his opponent and smashed his testicles, chewed off an ear, or gouged out an eye. Branding, flogging, ear cropping, nose slitting, and castration were often visited on those for whom the thrifty deemed a term in jail too expensive.[30]

Although influenced by the conventional punishments of the day, officers realized that men are of little value to the service if either their health or spirit is broken. Fighting Indians required brawn and initiative. Both were often forfeited by the British through unmerciful flogging— 500 to 1,000 lashes. Seeing the futility of such an example, Americans did not fall so deeply into error. Officers often came from the same social strata as their men and knew that employing such a system of degrading brutality would end in mutiny. Hence only the offences that threatened

29 *Ibid.,* Nov. 11, 1792, Jan. 21, Mar. 16, 1793.
30 N. A. Phelps, *A History of Simsbury,* Chapters IX and X; Edward Channing, *A History of the United States,* III, pp. 571-572; J. B. McMaster, *A History of the United States,* II, pp. 5-10.

demoralization or ruin to any military organization were punished with a heavy hand.

Chronic thieves were given short shrift. On one occasion a soldier entered Wayne's marquee, stealing clothing and a purse containing gold and silver coins. He was sentenced to walk the gantlet naked and at a slow step, to have his head and eyebrows closely shaved, to be branded on the forehead and the palms of both hands with the letter T, and to be drummed out of camp with a halter round his neck. When another had counterfeited orders on the commissary and storekeeper, thereby defrauding noncommissioned officers and privates of parts of the ration, he was made to walk the gantlet twice, wearing a label around his neck on which was written "The Fatal Effects of Forgery." He was then drummed out of the legion.[31] In this way the army took steps to be rid of some of its undesirables. Battered and forlorn, they were left to find their way back to the dunghills from which they had been recently recruited. There or in prison they soon rotted away, for the rest of the world was even less interested in redeeming them to honesty and decency.

Desertion was even more rigorously punished. If it became common the legion would dwindle away. On the other hand, recruits were irked with the system of control and were stricken with fear when told how hideously Shawnees, Delawares, Wyandots, and Miamis tortured their captives. Once when a detachment was en route from Carlisle to Pittsburgh fifty-seven recruits left in a body. At Legionville they sneaked away from time to time. Anyone bringing a deserter back was paid $10 plus reasonable expenses. A general court-martial tried the culprit, usually sentencing him to be given from fifty to one hundred lashes. Sometimes drumming out of camp was added. Punishment occurred on the parade ground in the presence of troops, usually between eight and eleven o'clock in the morning. The prisoner was tied to a post, and lashes were laid on at half-minute intervals. Only the very hardy could stand a hundred without serious injury, so the tendency was to give only

[31] Wayne, *op. cit.*, Feb. 17, 1793.

twenty-five at a time. Seeing a bloody, writhing, half-naked man being beaten beside a post may have deterred a few from their evil ways. A much larger number honorably served their country under company commanders who were understanding and able.

When offenders were considered incorrigible and their acts disrupted military control, capital punishment was sometimes ordered. Perhaps there were a dozen such cases while Wayne was at Pittsburgh and Legionville, although only a few of them were actually carried into effect. On August 4, 1792, Henry Hamilton was scheduled to be hanged for mutiny; he had attempted to kill Ensign William Devin. Wayne pardoned him on the day of execution, restoring him to duty. In doing so, the General expressed hope that this would be the last as well as the first time when he had to pass on a death sentence. The future proved otherwise. About a month later one of the dragoons deserted, stealing a horse and accoutrements. His record was otherwise bad. On September 30, he was duly hanged in accordance with the sentence of a court. During October two others were shot for somewhat similar offenses. Next month a sergeant forfeited his life because he had been convicted of the same thing with aggravating circumstances. When executions occurred, troops were paraded, the adjutant being present to read the orders and see that they were carried out. The main or camp guard acted as a firing squad. When a gallows was used, the quartermaster was responsible for its erection and the fact that it worked. He also had to see that the corpse was taken away and buried.[32]

Though officers were never executed, they did not escape punishment. Ignorance, weakness, disobedience, neglect, and dissipation brought down the full weight of Wayne's anger. Those guilty of errors at drill were made to study. A slovenly company was given fatigue until it reformed; the captain concerned had to do the supervising. When a lieutenant talked out of the side of his mouth at parade, he was driven out of the service. The same thing happened

[32] *Ibid.*, July 24, Aug. 4, Sept. 29, Oct. 2, 1792, *et passim.*

to a young ensign who was caught weeping at the execution of a deserter. Applications for leave were seldom granted; if men had to spend their days in a comfortless camp, so must the officers. When resignations were offered, Wayne disapproved them, vociferously damning their authors.[33]

In some respects, however, Wayne's hands were tied. He could only approve or disapprove of court-martial sentences. There was the case of Captain Ballard Smith who sneered at Major George Michael Bedinger because he used to be a street singer. Once when Smith was drunk, he had in his tent an unruly wench whom he declared to be his nurse. In reality she had been married to a private in the legion but was the hand-me-down wife of Sergeant Sprague. Joining the captain over his bottle, she gloated over her rise in rank and slashed with a sword at those who questioned. When a noncommissioned officer came, at Bedinger's bidding, to take her in hand, she jumped on her patron's bed and grabbed a pair of pistols. Heaping upon him all the billingsgate that she had learned in her sordid past, she declared herself the "little queen" who could lick any sergeant. As for him, she would shoot him in the crotch if he came any nearer. Smith, standing laughingly by, ordered the noncommissioned officer to get a written order if he would disturb the captain and "his lady." Soon he and Major Bedinger returned and between them Smith was arrested and the "little queen" Polly was quelled. Though she escaped any subsequent punishment, Smith was suspended six months from the service. Wayne considered the sentence entirely too light, but he could do nothing to increase it.[34]

While Wayne was trying to train and discipline the majority of the legion in the neighborhood of Pittsburgh, his second in command, Brigadier General James Wilkinson, was near Fort Washington with several hundred men who once composed a part of St. Clair's luckless army. As a

[33] *Ibid.*, May 9, 1793; Wildes, *op. cit.*, p. 378.
[34] *Wayne Papers*, XXII, 40; XLIX, 35, 38; Wayne to Knox, Nov. 14, 1792, *ibid.*, XLIX, p. 47.

brilliant young officer of the Revolution, Wilkinson had enjoyed spectacular success interrupted by failure. On the coming of peace he had gone to Kentucky and carried on large-scale tobacco trading with the Spaniards at New Orleans. They succumbed to his wiles, rewarding him with a $2,000 yearly pension and various other dispensations. For about twenty years he continued the beneficiary of their bounty. Though suspecting him of double dealing, the borderers were won over by his easy manners, unusual affability, and generous hospitality. Wanting hard money and rough sport, they eagerly volunteered to go with him on an Indian foray in 1791. The praise resulting from its commonplace success was sweet music to their unwashed ears. Partly because of his leadership in Western politics and military affairs, he was commissioned a lieutenant colonel of regulars on October 22, 1791; on March 5 of the following year, he was raised to the rank of brigadier general. In the army, as in civil life, he changed his sails with every political gust that blew, with the result that he was never able to continue long on a direct course to a fixed objective. As an aide during the Revolution, he had become thoroughly acquainted with army routine and the value of attention to details. This knowledge made him helpful as an assistant, but frequently led him, even when a general officer, to invade the province of low-ranking subordinates, waste his energies on small things, and criticize bitterly any methods that failed to fit the pattern of his own preconceived ideas. He never became expert in emphasizing the significant and discarding the unimportant. In the fog of war he seldom discerned clearly what was best in strategy or tactics.[35]

According to instructions from Knox, Wilkinson's mission in the Northwest consisted of three parts: to assure the Indians of the federal government's desire for peace and to find out all that he could about them; to establish one or more posts along the line of communications between Forts Hamilton and Jefferson; and to lay in all the stores that he could at the posts north of Fort Washington in

[35] J. R. Jacobs, *Tarnished Warrior, passim.*

addition to any that might be needed to last the garrisons for three or four months.[36] In carrying out this three-sided program, Wilkinson largely operated as an independent commander in spite of the fact that he was a subordinate of Wayne. Giving him such latitude was based on good reasoning; on this type of problem he worked better when free from supervision; the transmission of orders was slow and often interrupted; most problems could be solved locally to better advantage. In return, Wilkinson often corresponded directly with Knox, not infrequently disparaging Wayne.

So pronounced was Wilkinson's egotism that he had little patience with the ideas of others. He had a very low opinion of his associates. He arraigned his officers as a group of incompetents who had a "painful deficiency of service and talents." He declared that some of them in the 1st Regiment were "pedlars, others drunkards, and nearly all of them fools." A few had gone only a "little past the hornbook," others could scarcely sign their names.[37] Major David Zeigler was as "obstinate as a German Boor . . . a most insensible blockhead, as seditious as any old Sargent and destitute of any Ray of duty beyond the police of a company and the minutiae of the parade."[38] Lieutenant Colonel Samuel Hodgdon, the quartermaster, was "irritable, unaccommodating," without any "comprehension, capacity or resource for the office he fills," but "exact in his accounts, scrupulously tenacious of public property," and possessed of "great integrity." These redeeming points were enough in Wilkinson's opinion to prevent him from being put in the guardhouse to placate the "pigheaded" Zeigler. Had he been confined, he might have escaped the beating that Captain Mahlon Ford vigorously administered on the threshold of the general's quarters. After

[36] Knox to Wilkinson, Feb. 11, 1792, *Wilkinson Papers* (Chicago Historical Society).

[37] Wilkinson to Wadsworth, Sept. 18, 1792, *Wilkinson Papers* (Library of Congress).

[38] Wilkinson to C. Biddle, Mar. 13, 1792, *Wilkinson Papers* (Detroit Public Library).

being arrested, the captain still swore vengeance; and Hodgdon in terror applied to Wilkinson for protection.[39]

If officers had been as bad as Wilkinson painted them, little might have been expected from the army. As it was, he seldom or never judged without bias. To those whom he disliked, he never gave their due. He had a habit of making sweeping statements without regard to obvious exceptions. Certainly Cushing, Harrison, and many others merited high praise. They could think clearly and fight bravely. True enough, the frontier and army service had modified their character. They were intensely individual, disputatious concerning regulations, and dogmatic in their beliefs; but they were sturdy in their friendships, deep in their patriotism, and patient and uncomplaining in privation and suffering. Under a skillful leader, they might be fashioned into an admirable fighting force. Wilkinson was not the man to do it. He was essentially an accomplished politician, never a great general.

As a rule, he was on easy terms with the neighboring settlers. He knew their value and cultivated their friendship. They could frequently aid in promoting his interests, adjusting differences between soldiers and civilians, supplying horses and rations, and acting as boatmen, artificers, scouts, pack drivers, and Indian agents. He determined to win their good will. Judges, federal commissioners, and other prominent people in the Northwest often called on him for protecting escorts. Usually they were cheerfully furnished. St. Clair, Sargent, and others stayed at his house and broke his bread. He and Mrs. Wilkinson set a high standard of frontier hospitality after she had joined him at Fort Washington early in 1792. On May 1 they entertained elaborately in a huge wigwam erected especially for the occasion on the banks of the Ohio in front of the garrison. At three o'clock, "the principal officers, most respectable citizens," and "a small but genteel female group" sat down to a "most sumptuous dinner." With plenty of noise and loquacity, the afternoon quickly

[39] *Ibid.*

passed, many cannon booming and sixteen toasts being offered and drunk. Thus were friendships strengthened and hardships temporarily forgotten.[40]

Wilkinson had been on agreeable terms with most of the militia for a long while. The tasks that he usually gave them were seldom too onerous, and a chance for a frolic generally existed whenever he led them. About the first of the year 1792, he circulated the news that he was planning to go on an expedition to the site of St. Clair's defeat and from there he might launch an attack against the Indians. Even if he never carried out the last part of his plan, he had other very substantial reasons for going. By riding over the whole length of his line of communications, he might obtain first-hand knowledge of how troops and supplies could best be sent in safety over it. During January, 1792, he easily assembled about 200 regulars and 150 volunteers near Cincinnati. Many were dressed like woodsmen—moccasins, hunting shirts, knives, and tomahawks. After an "eloquent" address on the purpose of the expedition, Wilkinson started his men on their hundred-mile journey. The weather was severe. The heaviest snow in years had fallen; the ice was so thick in the streams that it would sustain mounted men; sometimes a trooper, awakening in the morning, found his cue frozen to the ground. After a week's marching, they reached Fort Jefferson; here all ideas of a raid against the Indians were wisely abandoned. The regulars, composed entirely of infantry, returned to Fort Washington; the mounted volunteers pushed on to the battlefield, where they arrived about noon on the first day of February. As they rode about through twenty inches of snow, the hooves of their horses exposed the blackened and mutilated bodies of what once were men. In such a dismal spot, they cleared a space and pitched a camp. Next day, they gathered together all the human fragments that they could pry loose from frozen ground and placed them in a common grave. For the last time, Wilkinson, Sargent, and others looked upon the distorted faces of former friends whom the savages had tortured. After this

[40] *Kentucky Gazette*, May 26, 1792.

tribute to their comrades, the volunteers salvaged what
equipment they could and destroyed what they were unable to carry with them. Then they turned their faces
homeward.[41]

On the way back, Wilkinson stopped at Fort St. Clair,
situated about twenty miles north of Fort Hamilton. Its
construction had started as early as December 15, 1791,
under the directions of Major John S. Gano, of the Territorial militia. To prevent any interruption by Indians, he
constantly maintained a very strong guard, the members
of which suffered extremely because they had neither fire
nor shelter. By the end of January, a stockade measuring
130 feet on a side was completed; and around it twenty
acres were fully cleared. Later a blockhouse a little larger
than the one at Fort Jefferson was added. For such efficient service, Wilkinson sent Gano a highly commendatory
letter. He also assumed much credit for himself, informing
Harry Innes, federal judge in Kentucky, that he had established a work equal to Forts Hamilton or Jefferson in
strength and extent. And he also declared that he had done
all of this in less time and with fewer men.[42] Washington
himself was well pleased with the result; his previous
doubts were now changed to deep satisfaction. A new link
had been forged in the chain of defences that stretched
some seventy miles northward.

Back at Fort Washington, Wilkinson was soon faced
with an entirely different problem. The people at Cincinnati disliked soldiers except for the protection that they
furnished and the money that they spent. Men on pass
were not careful of civilian rights and property, especially after drinking the low-grade whisky sold in the dives
along the river. Recently there had been near riots on
several occasions. Once a sergeant of the 1st Regiment
committed "a most lawless outrage" upon a petty magis-

---

41 F. E. Wilson, *Journal of Capt. Daniel Bradley*, pp. 35-36;
F. Cleves, *Old Tippecanoe, etc.*, p. 11; W. C. Miller, "History of Fort
Hamilton," *Ohio Archaeol. and Hist. Society Pub.*, XIII, p. 102.
42 Wilkinson to Innes, Apr. 3, 1792, *Innes Papers*, XXIII, p. 60;
F. Cleves, *op. cit.*, p. 12.

trate of the town. He was sentenced by a local judge to pay a fine of $3, to suffer fifteen stripes, and to obtain someone to guarantee his conduct for six months. Through influences at work in St. Clair's office, the whipping was remitted.[43] Hoping to improve the situation, Wilkinson ordered that any soldier found drunk outside of the fort would be given fifty lashes immediately. It was not long until Ensign William Henry Harrison found an inebriated artificer and gave him the prescribed fifty lashes. His companion received ten lashes for objectionable interference. Claiming damages because of alleged exemption from military control, the pair hired two "rascally lawyers" to handle their case, resulting in the issue of a warrant for Harrison's arrest. Thereupon Wilkinson exempted the artificers from any such punishment in the future, but he forbade service of the warrant on the reservation. Judge William Goforth ordered Harrison's arrest wherever found. When the deputy sheriff attempted it, the ensign knocked him sprawling. On second thought, however, he gave himself up, took a scolding, and for twenty-four hours was locked up in McHenry's Tavern, where he spent a rollicking time with boon companions.[44] Deeming the artificers an "extremely seditious" lot and Harrison one of the "most promising" officers in the army, Wilkinson decided to do no more in the matter except to get him out of the neighborhood. He therefore detailed the young ensign to accompany Mrs. Wilkinson and her three boys to Pittsburgh. From there Wayne directed him to continue on with them to Philadelphia.[45]

Meanwhile, Wilkinson continued to center his attention on strengthening and supplying the posts that lay north of his Fort Washington headquarters. The nearest of these was Fort Hamilton, about twenty-five miles distant. It was situated on the banks of the Great Miami in the midst of a country where the land was rich and the woods were filled with game. Ducks were plentiful in the quiet stretches of

[43] Sargent to Wilkinson, Feb. 17, 1792, in C. E. Carter, *Territorial Papers of the United States*, III, pp. 365-366.
[44] F. Cleves, *Old Tippecanoe, etc.*, p. 12.   [45] *Ibid.*, p. 13.

the river, and sometimes a multitude of carrier pigeons huddled closely together after nightfall on the branches of the trees. Wild turkeys could be readily trapped if a brush pen was made and a little grain scattered inside. Seins were improvised and netted an abundance of fish. Bear and deer were often seen beyond the stockade; they proved a chronic nuisance to those who had growing gardens. Vegetables were assiduously cultivated because they were not included in the army rations and because food on the frontier was usually scarce. General and Mrs. Wilkinson often supplied seeds for the different garrisons. By the summer of 1792, Captain John Armstrong, commanding at Hamilton, was raising beans, peas, corn, and even strawberries in spite of cut worms, yellow bugs, caterpillars, and grasshoppers. With his cupboards filled and the rooms of the fort made more comfortable through additional conveniences, the Captain wrote and asked "the General to make him a visit, hinting that if only a cow was supplied they might enjoy berries and cream together." Mrs. Wilkinson was also invited; if she would only come, he promised that the flowers would be "taught to smile at her approach and droop as she retires." Unfortunately she could not attend, so the flowers were not required to perform.[46]

In addition to laying by enough food for visitors and his own men, Armstrong had to accumulate a large amount of other supplies. A great deal of grain and hay were needed for the oxen and horses that worked around the post and transported rations and equipment from distant places. Grazing alone was not enough for them or for the mounts used for messengers, scouts, or cavalry. Feed, for the most part, had to be supplied locally; it was too bulky to be brought from distant places. For raising it, land for grain and hay was hard to clear around Hamilton. Timber was thick and heavy, and marauding Indians

[46] Armstrong to Wilkinson, Mar. 17, 1792, in *The Cincinnati Miscellany*, I, p. 210, and other letters in *ibid.*, I and II; Wilkinson to Sargent, Sept. 27, 1792 in *Sargent Papers* (Massachusetts Historical Society).

sometimes scalped the wood choppers. After completing this part of the work, the ground was broken with a heavy hoe instead of a plow. This required great effort and resulted in a small area of cultivation. If the ensuing crop escaped drought or being fired by the savages, all available soldiers were turned out to help with the harvesting. For a day's work of this kind, they sometimes received an extra half gill of whisky or had a dime added to their pay. Toward sunset, sentinels might hear the sound of small iron bells, for the oxen were approaching with huge wagon loads of hay. Close by marched a guard and workers with pitchforks and scythes. Not far from the stockade they tossed off the load and ricked it high in rounded stacks. In this fashion Armstrong accumulated a hundred or more tons of hay.[47]

Other post commanders were faced with similar problems but were not so well situated for solving them. The nearer the Indian country, the greater were the number of men needed for guard duty and the fewer that could be spared for farming. At the same time difficulties increased with every mile added to transportation by wagon or pack horse. Fort Jefferson lay about seventy miles north of Cincinnati, and was harder to reach than other forts in the Northwest. It was smaller than the rest and had been hastily constructed. Cluttered with sick and wounded after St. Clair's defeat, it made slight progress toward self-sufficiency in food and forage during 1792. A little hay was cut from the meadows, but men and beasts were dependent mostly upon government stores that were brought up the long trail from Fort Washington. There was seldom more than enough on hand for immediate needs.

At Fort Knox, located on the site of the later city of Vincennes, Indiana, the neighboring inhabitants were mostly turbulent, shiftless Frenchmen ruled by fickle, indolent wives. The land nearby was very fertile and could be cultivated without interference from the Indians. Here farming was done on such a scale that the training of troops was sometimes badly neglected. Rations, clothing,

[47] J. R. Jacobs, *op. cit.,* pp. 123-124.

and equipment could be shipped conveniently down the Ohio and brought up the Wabash when the water was high. Thus the garrison, unlike troops stationed elsewhere, did not usually suffer from a dearth of supplies. Being too far removed from the best route to the Miami villages, Fort Knox did not concern Wilkinson as an advanced base. Its principal function was to serve as a barrier to Spanish or Indian aggression from the West or Northwest.

Since Fort St. Clair was still incomplete, the energy of its garrison was largely spent during 1792 in increasing its defenses, improving its barracks, and enlarging its storehouses. With this work done, the spring of 1793 saw a chain of forts guarding the line of communications stretching northward in an almost straight line from Cincinnati to the neighborhood of the Great Lakes. Blockhouses had been sturdily built, but they contained few stores. These would have to be considerably increased if offensive measures were to be taken.

Just then the federal government was trying to avoid hostilities, and at the same time it was endeavoring to persuade the Indians to acknowledge its ownership and control of the territory north of the Ohio. Washington and his colleagues recognized that time and tranquillity were the prime needs of their country. The Constitution and its mechanism were still on trial. It could not operate without money; and this was almost impossible to get in peace, much less in war. Taxes were deeply resented, and the one on whisky was so hateful that rebellion was stirring in western Pennsylvania. European nations were unwilling to make loans until the United States had proved its stability. The British continued to consider our independence as spurious, having no minister at our capital and treating our envoy at the Court of St. James with "pointed rudeness and neglect." With arrogance halting just a little short of war, they used the Indians as pawns in a reach for dominion, endeavoring to prevent American immigration north of the Ohio. The Spaniards were equally contemptuous in the Southwest, spreading disloyalty and treason among the settlers there, even trying to seduce

the District of Kentucky into an alliance with Spain.
France, our ally of the Revolution, was likewise against us.
She wanted the alliance of 1778 continued in full force, no
matter how harmful it might be to our interests. With
conditions so precarious, Washington was fully determined
to maintain peace with the nations abroad and the Indians
at home.

While our diplomatic agents were working toward the
same end, the army was ordered to abstain from any hostilities and give the savages every token of friendship.
Wayne accordingly invited Cornplanter, New Arrow, Big
Tree, and the "old sachem Guasutha" to visit him at
Legionville, where they were hospitably entertained. In
spite of his efforts to the contrary, they insisted that the
Ohio must "continue to run and remain the boundary
between the White and the Red people on its opposite
shores." In a similar attempt Wilkinson met with no better
success. He saw that visiting chiefs were stuffed with food
and drink and ate at the same table with him. They liked
to bolt the victuals and belch the liquor with which they
were freely supplied; they were flattered to eat from the
same bowl with their hosts. Even if one of them died from
too violent an appetite or some other accident, his last
rites were those accorded a hero. After the warrior Olle
had started for eternity, Wayne had three rounds of blank
ammunition fired at his grave.[48] When old Nawiatchtenos
died while visiting at Fort Washington, he was laid away
with military honors in the cemetery of the post. Some
whose hatred did not yield to this charitable policy of
government twice disinterred him and set him upright in
the street. Fearing punishment, the ghouls left his bones
alone after they had been buried for the third time. Others
may have suffered equal disrespect in death,[49] but few have
had a greater number or variety of frontier obsequies.

While the army was thus entertaining the Indians and
restraining the frontiersman from vengeance, the federal

48 Wayne, *op. cit.*, July 9; Thomas Boyd, *op. cit.*, p. 256.
49 "Narrative of John Heckewelder's Journey," etc., in *Pennsylvania
Magazine of History and Biography* (1888), pp. 34-54.

government was working for a permanent peace. Colonel
John Hardin, hard-riding cavalryman from Kentucky,
and Captain Alexander Trueman, of Revolutionary fame,
were dispatched to invite the red men to a parley. In June
1792 the two started out on their ill-starred mission. After
they had been received with every mark of friendship, the
savages, without the least provocation, suddenly murdered them both. In brazen impudence, the chiefs declared
that some of their "foolish young men" had done it; they
offered no regrets and took no steps to punish the guilty.[50]
Dispatched on a similar errand, Brigadier General Rufus
Putnam managed to keep his life and gain a limited success.
After he had conferred with the Wabash and Illinois Indians, they agreed to cease hostilities and come under
federal protection.[51] Through the agency of Major Hamtramck the Wea and Eel River tribes consented to be
peaceful.

Knox was even less successful with other Indians in the
Northwest. In the hope of furthering peace, fifty chiefs of
the Six Nations were invited to Philadelphia. Among them
was Joseph Brant, the distinguished Mohawk. Generous
rewards in money and land were promised him if he would
bend all his efforts to induce the western savages to come
to a conference. He refused; but others, like Captain Hedrick, a Stockbridge Indian, were more pliant. With little
hope or enthusiasm on either side, the representatives of
twenty-four tribes assembled at Grand Glaize on October
1, 1792. Here Hedrick argued in behalf of the federal for-
mula for peace, only to be howled down. The Seneca Chiefs,
Red Jacket and Farmer's Brother, fared no better. Painted
Pole, prominent among the Shawnees, declared that these
peace-loving speechmakers had been bribed and could never
be trusted. In the end a majority spurned a truce unless
the settlers should withdraw from lands north of the Ohio
and destroy the forts that were there. If this were promised
them, they might meet again when the trees began to swell
and bud. With the interest of both so diametrically op-

50 *American State Papers, Indian Affairs*, I, pp. 243-244.
51 *Ibid.*, I, pp. 234, 241, 319, 338.

posed, the conference broke up.[52] Before long, bands of marauding Indians redoubled their raids upon the settlers. Spies soon brought word that the English and Shawnees were eager for a full fledged war and would soon begin it. Possessed of this information, Knox gave permission in April 1793 for the legion to move down the Ohio.[53] The lands north of the "Beautiful River" were going to be held.[54]

[52] *Ibid.*, I, p. 235.   [53] *Ibid.*, I, pp. 233, 322, 346.

[54] Primary source material for this chapter is derived chiefly from Wayne, *Order Books* for 1792 and 1793 (U.S. Military Academy Library and Library of Congress), *Wayne Papers* (Pennsylvania Historical Society), *Wilkinson Papers* (Library of Congress, Detroit Public Library, and Chicago Historical Society), *Innes Papers* (Library of Congress), and Wilkinson-Armstrong correspondence published in *The Cincinnati Miscellany*, I and II.

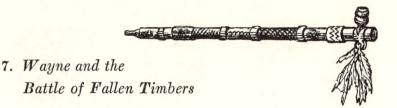

7. *Wayne and the Battle of Fallen Timbers*

By the last part of April Wayne's barges began drifting down the Ohio on their way south. The best time for traveling was at hand. The river was free of ice, the waters were high, the bitterness of winter had passed, and enough soldiers were on board to perform all of the routine duties without individual hardship. Every day en route a new landscape appeared, constantly revealing the marvelous richness of the throbbing earth. If settlers could only come and cultivate it in peace, years of abundance would surely follow. Some were hopeful that this happy condition might result after negotiations with the Indians had been finished; Wayne was confident that it could be achieved only by a victorious campaign. Most of those in the Northwest shared his opinion. Settlers at Wheeling, Marietta, and Cincinnati rejoiced when they heard bugle and drum announcing the approach of the army; to them it was the herald of a better day for which they had long waited. As the barges drew near Cincinnati, 1,100 spectators on the neighboring hills watched them approach. Troops were lined up along the shore; they rousingly welcomed their comrades in arms with cheer after cheer. The six-pounders crashed out a fifteen-gun salute. Not to be outdone, the musicians on the boats vigorously played their instruments in reply. After the general and his officers had disembarked, they were given an elaborate banquet by the leading characters of the town.[1]

Unfortunately no one could tell Wayne of a suitable camping place nearby. Finally he selected a site along the river bank about a mile west of Fort Washington. He did not like it, but he could find no better place. Hence it was

[1] H. E. Wildes, *Anthony Wayne,* pp. 382-385.

named Hobson's Choice. The site was level except for an Indian mound high enough to give an excellent view of the surrounding country; the rest was low, heavily timbered, and often flooded. Even after being cleared and drained, the camp was neither attractive nor comfortable. From Hobson's Choice as his headquarters, Wayne began issuing orders on May 9, 1793, not leaving there until autumn.[2]

Meanwhile Wayne was active in perfecting the training and organization of the legion. Often its personnel annoyed him greatly. Severe punishments did not appreciably diminish the number of desertions. Disputes between officers were frequent. Wrangles over rank were settled by drawing lots, others were aired before courts-martial. Lieutenant William Diven was either a plaintiff or defendant three times in eight months. At the same time two factions were destroying teamwork in the legion. For the most part, older officers allied themselves with Wilkinson, calling Wayne "Old Tony," "Old Horse," or "Mars" whenever they dared. Subalterns followed the lead of their elders, taking one side or the other. Both principals lacked any spirit of compromise. Wilkinson was disloyal, unbridled in speech, and deceitful in manner; Wayne was vindictive, irritable, and sometimes dogmatic and overbearing. Wilkinson and Wayne could never serve harmoniously in the same organization.[3]

To make matters worse, troops made slow progress in training. Wayne was disturbed because his infantry officers were not adept at maneuvers designed to teach them how to meet an attack on their organization's front, rear, or flanks. They did not understand the signals quickly and were unable to "form with velocity." For the cavalry, Wayne laid down the unalterable rule that they were "to charge in very open Order, to move easy" until in front of the light infantry, then advance quickly, "every Man Charging Twenty Indians" after they had been put to

[2] T. Boyd, *Mad Anthony Wayne*, pp. 288-289, and Anthony Wayne, *Order Book*, May 9, 1793.

[3] Wayne, *Order Books, Michigan Historical Collections*, XXXIV, pp. 341-733, June 6, 21, July 13, Aug. 5, Sept. 6, 1793; and Wildes, *op. cit.*, p. 389.

flight. "In other Words they must Adopt that kind of Manoeuvers suitable to the Country and Service for which they were intended," forgetting the principles laid down by "Blinn, Dalrymple and others for Charging Squadrons of Dragoons or Battalions of Infantry on the plains of Jumatry."[4] Even though the advice imposed odds of twenty to one, the principle was good and Wayne was not temperate in driving it home. All summer long, he kept his cavalrymen riding hard on their sorrels, grays, chestnuts, and bays through rough wooded country in the neighborhood of Bellerophontia, the high-sounding name of their camp, which was situated just across the Ohio near the mouth of the Licking.[5]

As he had done at Legionville, Wayne insisted that his men keep their equipment in order and be experts in using it. He stressed the use of musket and bayonet, declaring that these two were the "most formidable weapons." Rifles, he insisted, were useful only in the hands of real riflemen, and these he set about training. All equipment had to be kept ready for inspection. Broken or lost parts were charged against the one to whom they had been issued. When the weather permitted, cartridges were dried out on blankets, powder in the horns was shaken and exposed to the sun.[6] The general was determined that there should be no misfiring as had occurred during his own maneuvers or on that fearful day when St. Clair's men were butchered on the banks of the Wabash.

The army was being transformed into a formidable force that would hurdle disaster. Wayne was succeeding but without growing in personal popularity. Though eager to be fair, he was stern, short-tempered, often sick. He frequently changed his orders and his demands bore heavily upon his men. They had little in camp to relieve the monotonous round of building, policing, and training. Only those whose records were clean had the privilege of leaving Hobson's Choice and visiting the Sodom and

4 Wayne, *op. cit.,* Sept. 5, 1793.
5 F. E. Wilson, *The Peace of Mad Anthony,* p. 86-87.
6 Wayne, *op. cit.,* May 25, June 19, Aug. 22, 1793.

Gomorrah of Cincinnati. Once there they had no money for liquor or women. Even as late as March 1793, some troops at Fort Washington and Fort Hamilton had not received a cent since the preceding August.[7] The government was short of funds and the paymaster in the Northwest was rheumatic and indifferent. Hoping for better things, many deserted.

The French notions of liberty, equality, and fraternity, then sweeping the country, may have fed their discontent. Many civilians living around frontier posts propagated such ideas as the chief articles of their faith. Obviously, the army, modeled along British lines, gave little comfort to those who championed such levelling theories; it could not, from its very nature, thrive on democracy. Unfortunately Wayne was not flexible and ingenious enough to work out a system of discipline and control that would meet military requirements and harmonize more nearly with the spirit of those who greatly influenced, but were not a part of, the army. He was growing old, strong-willed, and was constantly tortured with gout. Though he failed to achieve popularity, he had a keen appreciation of the needs of his mission, skillfully accomplishing it in spite of all difficulties and personal hardships.

Most of the officers and men looked upon Wayne as a martinet. He spared neither himself nor subordinates. Though meticulous in having his own orders obeyed, he often ignored regulations or customs of the service for the benefit of those whom he liked. Out of regard for his Revolutionary comrade, Richard Butler, he gave his one-eyed, immature son an appointment as ensign, only to have it subsequently revoked by Knox. When he needed horses for his personal use, he took them from the dragoons and used them as he pleased. In spite of the protests from a number of older officers against Captain Edward Butler for arrogance and incompetence, Wayne retained him as deputy adjutant general.[8]

---

[7] Wayne, *op. cit.*, Sept. 20, 1793.   [8] H. E. Wildes, *op. cit.*

The general was loyal to his friends and helped them whenever possible. He could scarcely refuse a request when worded like this:

> "My poor Boy being but a short time with me put it out of my power to write by him. But I flatter myself it is not too late for me to recommend to your goodness an excellent Son and affectionate Brother. All the misfortunes that he has at present is that he is poor and of course has few friends—he is just setting out in life and in a way that is not altogether agreeable to himself. I have only to beg that you will honour him with your friendship and advise in anything that you think proper.
>
> "That I cannot doubt from your known goodness of Heart and love of all mankind, more particularly for one who is the son of a man who held you dearest in his friendship.
>
> "Ann hopes you will look upon Jefe as her tender and much loved Brother.
>
> "May all the happiness this world can give attend you is the wish of
> MARGARET McDOWELL."[9]

In spite of the good wishes of Margaret McDowell, Wayne began to think he was working to no purpose. He was greatly discouraged because he feared that the legion would never be used to crush the Indians completely, and he believed that only in this way would a lasting peace be achieved. Instead, he had to wait until all other methods had proved ineffective. Negotiations seemed endless to him. During May 1793, three federal commissioners, Benjamin Lincoln, Beverly Randolph, and Timothy Pickering, had started for the frontier for the purpose of holding a final conference with the Indians. Reaching Niagara, they remained there for six weeks enjoying the hospitality of John Graves Simcoe, lieutenant governor of Upper Can-

[9] McDowell to Wayne, July 5, 1793, *Wayne Papers*, XXVII, p. 85, Pennsylvania Historical Society Library.

ada. While they waited for a British vessel to carry them to the far end of Lake Erie, they held several meetings, trying to win the approval of neighboring chiefs to the federal government's conditions for peace. Unfortunately they blundered egregiously: they boasted that the United States would combine with the Six Nations to nullify any efforts which any other Indians would make, looking either to a great confederacy of their own or an alliance with Great Britain. After these impolitic remarks the commissioners went on to Detroit, finding shelter in the house of Matthew Elliott, who had been long on the payrolls of the British Crown. At this place, other chiefs heard the commissioners, but they refused all proffers of peace unless the Americans would agree to the Ohio River as the boundary line between themselves and the red men. Since the United States would not consider such a proposal and the Miamis, Shawnees, Delawares, and Wyandots were burning for war, the conference broke up with nothing accomplished.[10]

On September 11, Wayne received news that the commissioners had failed and hostilities might soon be expected. With no alternative left but war, Knox gave the general permission to wage it. At the same time he directed Wayne to hazard nothing and always be aware that his force was adequate for victory, and he warned him defeat would be highly pernicious to the interests of the Republic. Soon officers and men knew that the "Emortal Washington" had ordered "the Old Hero, Gen'l Wayne and his well disciplined legion" to destroy the "savage foe."[11]

On October 7, 1793, the legion broke camp at Hobson's Choice and headed north. On the march, troops employed the same general formations that St. Clair's men had used, but with much more confidence and skill. They usually halted about three o'clock in the afternoon, if by then the quartermaster and several of the general's staff had been able to select a camp site. At the camping place they immediately established a "front guard" about a half

10 *American State Papers, Indian Affairs*, I, pp. 340-346, 357.
11 T. Boyd, *op. cit.*, p. 762.

mile in advance and a "rear guard" at a similar distance in the opposite direction. Both were composed of not less than a company, usually more. About 300 yards from camp "picket guards" were posted. They often consisted of a captain, subaltern, sergeant, two corporals, and from thirty-six to forty-eight privates; sometimes they were made up of only a subaltern, sergeant, corporal, and from twenty-one to thirty-six privates. Pickets were divided into first, second, and third reliefs, each of which took post at a place selected by the quartermaster, continuing on duty there for two hours. Sentinels were placed about 100 yards apart, thus completely encircling the camp. Additional protection was provided by a rough kind of breastworks, a section of which each company had to erect.[12] After taking all these precautions, troops, animals, and stores were little disturbed by Indians. Such arrangements, in principle, did not vary greatly from those of the Romans when they fought the Germans along the Rhine.

These precautionary measures disconcerted the savages. They believed the story that Wayne never slept; they knew he could not be surprised. They were also aware that his army, in contrast with St. Clair's, covered the same distances about twice as fast. It traveled along straight and well cleared roads connecting sturdy forts, which had been established at twenty-five-mile intervals and could be depended upon to furnish reinforcements and supplies. Never before had they seen a campaign so carefully planned and so vigorously executed.

By October 14, 1793, Wayne was issuing orders near the southwest branch of the Maumee, six miles north of Fort Jefferson. Here he soon decided to pass the winter. Conditions of weather and supply were against continuing the advance. At the time, his line of communication was often cut. On October 17, Lieutenant John Lowry and Ensign Boyd were on their way to Greenville with twenty-one wagons loaded mostly with grain. Just about sunrise, when they were about six miles north of Fort St. Clair, the Indians suddenly swooped down upon them. Pierced with

12 *Pioneer,* II, pp. 291-292.

bullets and arrows and battered with tomahawks, the lieutenant, ensign, and a few others slumped beside the train that they bravely tried to defend. The remaining ninety riflemen showed no symptoms of valor. Stricken with terror, they sought safety in flight. Left in possession, the Indians cut sixty-four horses loose from the wagons and quickly rode off, taking with them whatever else they could easily carry along. In their haste, they failed to fire the wagons and run down the fugitives. But they could gloat over capturing the horses, routing the escort, and inflicting a number of casualties. Once the disastrous news was received, Colonel John Adair went in pursuit with 100 militia, only to return in two or three days without ever catching sight of the raiders. Although most of the wagons were salvaged, Wayne was disturbed because the loss of horses would delay the arrival of needed supplies; he was particularly incensed because a detachment of riflemen had acted so cravenly. Subsequent courts-martial disclosed that some troops were still ignorant of the customary tactics of the Indians and had no desire to meet them in battle.[13]

Wayne knew his legion would become more formidable if it remained for the winter on the border of hostile country. Therefore he determined to keep his troops where they were while he erected a fort that would repel any attack and furnish another base for a subsequent advance when conditions warranted. He immediately set fatigue details working on a stockade that enclosed a rectangular area of about fifty acres; in the corners they erected stout, rude bastions where light guns were placed. After finishing six huts apiece for each company, they started on the housing for officers. Later, buildings for headquarters, bakeries, mess halls, etc. were added. With shelter and defenses completed, Wayne called the place Fort Greenville in honor of Major General Nathanael Greene, his old friend of Revolutionary days.[14]

This newly established post was not generally popular

13 T. E. Wilson, *Journal of Capt. Daniel Bradley*, pp. 54-55.
14 T. E. Wilson, *The Peace of Mad Anthony*, p. 91.

with the members of the hard-working garrison. A number of them fell sick. Rations were not always wholesome or adequate. Robert Elliott and Eli Williams were the contractors for 1793 and 1794. They were small-scale frontier merchants who lacked both the experience and capital necessary for supplying the army adequately. They chronically failed to fulfill their promises. Wayne wanted 270,000 rations collected before the end of 1793; only enough were supplied to meet the daily requirements of his troops. The quartermaster, James O'Hara, estimated that the contractors needed 1,700 horses to function properly; they had only 300. Under the circumstances no offensive campaign could be planned.[15] During April, Wayne angrily wrote the contractors:

"I will be no longer imposed upon or trifled with, nor shall the army be starved nor shall the Interest, honor, and Dignity of the Nation suffer through your neglect and non-compliance with positive and repeated Demands, admonitions and Orders upon this interesting subject. . . . You have repeatedly been called on to increase your means of transport. . . . I must once more insist on an immediate and punctual compliance with orders."[16]

With this vigorous protest ringing in their ears, the contractors somewhat bestirred themselves. They still worked under a system that favored themselves instead of the troops. According to Wayne, "some more effectual and certain mode of supplying the army than that of private contract" was absolutely necessary. He argued that, "a voracious individual will always consult their own private interests . . . they will not part with a great sum of money . . . to purchase a large quantity of provisions in advance and more particularly the means of transport . . . but content themselves if they can only supply the troops from hand to mouth . . . whilst the principal part of the money advanced by the treasury may PROFITABLY be other-

[15] Wayne to Elliott and Williams, Oct. 16, 1793, *Wayne Papers*, XXX, Pennsylvania Historical Society.
[16] Wayne to Elliott and Williams, Apr. 20, 1794, *Wayne Papers*, XXXIV, p. 41, Pennsylvania Historical Society Library.

wise employed ... they run no risks of loss from an enemy
... always require an escort ... should an accident happen
to any ... convoy the legion would be reduced to the last
distress for want of provisions."[17]

At the same time, Wayne might have mentioned that all
contracts for rations were made, not by the War Department, the natural agency for this purpose, but by the
Treasury, which was more interested in economy than army
efficiency. He might have added that, in rare cases, officers
were in collusion with the contractors, closing their eyes
when rations were poor or insufficient. Wayne half suspected that something like this was then going on. Wilkinson may have had his hand in the profits of Elliott; the
two were friendly and corresponded secretly. For years
Wilkinson had been a pensioner of Spain and was not
averse to questionable methods of earning a dollar. It
would have been very easy for Elliott to recompense him
either in money or supplies just as James Morrison did in
a similar case fifteen years later.[18] If Wilkinson was innocent it was more because Wayne was constantly watchful,
giving him small chance to be profitably dishonest.

Wayne knew that some of his officers could not be
trusted. On October 14, 1793, near Fort Hamilton he expressed his "Most grateful Thanks to Brigadier Genl
Posey, and to the officers of the Legion in general, for the
ready cheerfullness with which they have executed every
order." At the same time he observes "with Concern and
Regret the Apparent want of Harmony, and due Subordination, in a few, in a very few Gentlemen of the Legion."[19]
Wilkinson was not mentioned; he therefore concluded that
he was classified among the disgruntled few. There were
reasons for this assumption. Although second in command,
he declared that he was considered no more than a cipher
at headquarters. Wayne never asked Wilkinson's advice
or always acted against it when gratuitously given. Wil-

---

17 Wayne to Knox, May 7, 1794, *ibid.*, XXXIV, p. 99.
18 Morrison to Wilkinson, July 28, 1809, *Wilkinson Papers*, III, Chicago Historical Society.
19 Wayne, *Order Book*, Oct. 14, 1793.

kinson resented the fact that his authority to order general courts had been curtailed and his plan to win the war through the use of mounted volunteers had been ignored.[20] Wayne did not always evince great patience when suggestions became too insistent and frequent, especially when they originated with long-winded subordinates who were suspected of being disloyal.

Nevertheless, they both knew that they had to make a pretense of harmony. Wilkinson, at least, recognized the obligation and wisdom of being outwardly courteous to his commanding general. On December 20, he wrote as follows from Fort Jefferson to Wayne at Greenville, six miles distant:

"Mrs. W. ventures to hope your Excellency may find it convenient & consistent to take dinner with Her on the 25th inst. with your suite, & any eight or ten gentlemen of your cantonment you may think proper to attend you; she begs leave to assure you the Dinner shall be a Christian one in commemoration of the Day, and in Honor of Her Guest, and on my part I will promise a welcome from the Heart, a warm fire, and a big bellied Bottle of the veritable Lachrymae Christi. We pray your answer."[21]

Wayne did not accept. He might have been happier if he had dined at the right of the charming Ann Wilkinson and talked with her of mutual friends and of earlier Philadelphia days. Beside the warming glow of an open fire he might have found his gout improving and the solution of some of his complicated problems made somewhat easier. He may have yearned to be among the guests, for he was very lonely and his life was hard. But his sense of duty was strong and his regard for Wilkinson slight.

Instead of going to Fort Jefferson, he and eight companies set out on Christmas eve for the site of St. Clair's defeat. Some ten months before, Wilkinson had gone there with 200 mounted men, salvaging a little matériel and burying the remains of many who had been slain in 1791.

20 J. R. Jacobs, *Tarnished Warrior*, pp. 139-140.
21 Wilkinson to Wayne, Dec. 20, *Autograph Letters*, II, Pennsylvania Historical Society Library.

This time Wayne planned to do more; he was going to reconnoiter the neighborhood and establish a fort. Upon arrival, he cleared the place of human bones, pitched his tents, and began to build Fort Recovery. In a few weeks it was completed.[22] Another advanced base confronted the savages, who looked on with dismay. They had no weapons to destroy these newly made centers of defense; and, if this was not done, the advance of the Long Knives could never be stayed.

The Indians were also perturbed because of Wayne's continuous vigilance. He spared no efforts to improve the fighting quality of his legion; he knew he could not afford to be lax at such a critical juncture. Indians were all around him. Some of them had come to Greenville during the winter, showing an inordinate appetite for government rations and a limited willingness to discuss conditions of peace. Upon their refusal to return all their white captives, negotiations ceased. Statements and acts of British officials had much to do with their obstinacy. Lord Dorchester, Governor General of Canada, addressed delegates of the Seven Nations on February 10, 1794, telling them that the British would probably be at war with the Americans before the end of the year. If so, the Indians might expect to regain the lands that they had lost by the treaty of 1783.[23] Inflamed by these words, the red men became even more confident when, with the coming of spring, they saw soldiers of the Crown erecting a sturdy fort on American soil along the waters of the Maumee. In addition, Colonel Alexander McKee set himself up close by as a trader; his buildings were substantial and his stores considerable. From him belligerent tribes obtained plenty of powder and ball.[24] Possessing both allies and weapons, they believed themselves and their property secure. They were confident that they could halt Wayne's advance, harvesting, as usual, abundant crops from the fruitful valley of the Maumee.

[22] H. E. Wildes, *op. cit.*, pp. 408-409.
[23] R. C. Downes, *Frontier Ohio, 1788-1803*, p. 38.
[24] T. Boyd, *op. cit.*, pp. 270-273.

If the frontiersmen in the Northwest were angry at the British for inciting the Indians, so were the merchants along the Atlantic seaboard for reasons that they considered both good and sufficient. They were incensed at the high-handed acts of British privateers and the royal navy. In June 1793, England had declared breadstuffs contraband; in November she had forbidden all trade with the French West Indies, where many a Yankee captain was reaping enticing profits. All through the early months of 1794, newspapers were filled with lists of American vessels condemned at Jamaica, Antigua, Dominica, Montserrat, St. Kitts, Nassau, and Bermuda. Along the Atlantic and in the Caribbean, few escaped British or Spanish privateers, frequently manned by Negroes and mulattoes who made rules of their own for the capture of cargoes. If Americans tried to trade with the British instead, they became spoil for the French and were treated no better.[25]

Far too often, American ships were taken unjustly and condemned illegally by admiralty courts. When cargoes were not confiscated, they often rotted away before inspection was completed and masters were permitted to clear from the harbor; meanwhile hulls had been battered and masts had gone down from the force of wind and waves. Crews were often treated even worse. Poor and sometimes jailed, they fell sick and died before they saw their ship lift anchor and sails fill with a homeward breeze. As a result, few ships from Charleston, Philadelphia, New York, and Boston sailed out into the open sea. Captains and mates grew dour and swore heavily while bottoms accumulated barnacles and seams gaped wider. Those who once sanded decks and set up rigging became aimless vagrants covered with lice and tatters. No longer did brigs and snows make hasty trips with barrels of flour and quintals of fish. Trade was at a standstill even though granaries were bursting with wheat and corn and on the Grand Banks cod and herring were as plentiful as ever. The fishermen

[25] J. B. McMaster, *A History of the People of the United States*, II, pp. 166-168; R. G. Albion and J. B. Pope, *Sea Lanes in War Time*, pp. 73-74.

laid aside their nets, the farmers their scythes, joining the crowds of the disgusted and idle. Our surplus could not be sold; few imports arrived—our foreign trade was withering away.[26]

With the United States helpless, British men-of-war arrogantly entered and left our harbors without hindrance in spite of all the wrongs done our vessels upon the high seas. If the British were not enough to stir us to action, the Algerian pirates were. In the fall of 1793, they had captured eleven of our vessels and thrown the crews into prison.[27] Congress reacted to the rising anger of the people, enacting laws to create a navy and erect fortifications. Arrangements were made for building six frigates. Forts and redoubts were planned for Portland, Portsmouth, Boston, Newport, New London, Philadelphia, New York, Baltimore, Alexandria, Charleston, Savannah, and ten other ports. Orders were issued for the purchase of 350 cannon, the largest of them capable of firing a 32-pound ball. Foundries started work on 250 tons of cannon shot. Four arsenals were authorized with the personnel needed to repair and manufacture small arms. Through state cession or federal purchase, sites were acquired for fortifications. Henry Knox, then secretary of war, temporarily engaged eight engineers of French origin to build them, enough competent Americans not being then available.[28] Thus foreigners with whose country we were then on the eve of war were supervising the construction of our important defenses.

People in the East dramatically responded to the plans for making our harbors safe. For New York City, Governor's Island was chosen as a strong point for defense. Here from spring until summer, men of every station in life toiled without pay. On April 21, 1794, the Democratic Society began work with shovel and spade. Other organizations soon followed. Each had a rendezvous from which it went to do its patriotic stint—the tallow-chandlers, from

²⁶ J. B. McMaster, *op. cit.*, II, pp. 169-170.
²⁷ R. G. Albion and J. B. Pope, *op. cit.*, p. 132.
²⁸ *American State Papers, Military Affairs*, I, pp. 68-108.

the Exchange; the grocers, from the Old Coffee House; the coopers, from Whitehall dock; Republican bakers, from the flag pole; and students, from Columbia College. Thus people in this section endeavored to make their city safe from attack by sea.[29]

The same spirit animated the South, where bitter memories of redcoats prevailed. Engineers were loudly cheered at Baltimore when they came to mark off a fort. Militia companies enthusiastically reported for breaking ground and putting cannon in condition. At Charleston, the people furnished slave labor, donated 7,000 feet of timber, and subscribed between 700 and 800 pounds. The South Carolinian governor was not worried by expense; but he was greatly perturbed lest the "vehement fury of the waves undermine the foundations of the harbor's defenses."[30] Here and elsewhere work was not always well done, guns not scientifically placed, and forts not strategically located.

The act of May 9, 1794, made modest provision for manning these forts. Some 764 noncommissioned officers and privates were added to the corps of artillerists and engineers, thus increasing it to a total strength of 992 exclusive of 56 commissioned officers. Though designed for sea coast garrisons, they could be ordered elsewhere. To encourage enlistment in all branches of the service, pay was never to be in arrears more than two months at a time, and the President was authorized to increase the beef, flour, whisky, and salt components of the ration at certain places and times. The widow or children of an officer dying from wounds in battle were granted a maximum of a lieutenant colonel's half pay for five years. In spite of these added inducements to serve in the army, the organization of artillerists and engineers was not quickly completed. The same number of officers and men were again authorized by the Act of March 3, 1795.[31]

While the federal government was diplomatically strug-

[29] J. B. McMaster, *op. cit.*, II, pp. 172-173.
[30] *American State Papers, Military Affairs*, I, pp. 103-104.
[31] T. H. S. Hamersly, *Complete Regular Army Register*, etc., p. 275 (2nd part); J. F. Callan, *The Military Laws of the United States* (revised edition), p. 105.

gling to halt British depredations on the high seas and Indian raids along the frontier, insurrectionists were on the march in the very heart of our country. During the summer of 1794 the Whisky Rebellion was in full swing west of the Alleghenies. Snug in the hills near Pittsburgh, the revolters refused to pay the excise tax of 9 to 25 cents a gallon on distilled liquor. Riots followed. Thomas Mifflin, governor of Pennsylvania, dallied with the lawless in hope of political gain. President Washington acted immediately, improvising an army of militia from adjacent states and putting it in motion against them. Resistance collapsed, and the ringleaders were eventually taken.[32]

To provide against similar contingencies, two laws were enacted in January and February 1795 concerning militia that might be called into federal service for repelling invasion or suppressing insurrection. As a result, the President was fully authorized to employ such improvised troops when occasion demanded; their pay, allowances, rations, and bounties became definitely fixed. At about the same time, the regular army was put on a better footing and continued at existing strength, largely because it had already demonstrated its value against the Indians and might prove to be an even more effective agency than the militia in the maintenance of domestic law and order.[33]

During 1794 Wayne had full proof of the fine quality of his regular troops. Knowing that war was inevitable with the savages, he was ready when it started. The first blow was struck when Little Turtle, Simon Girty, Blue Jacket, and other chieftains induced 2,000 Wyandots, Delawares, Shawnees, Miamis, and Weas to follow them on an extensive raid. Encouraged by their Canadian friends, they selected Fort Recovery as their first objective. Here they expected to repeat the great victory that they had won on the same ground less than three years before.

By June 29, 1794, they had come within striking distance of the fort and were making ready to attack it. That very day 300 horseloads of flour had arrived for the use of the garrison. The accompanying escort was commanded by Major William MacMahon and consisted of ninety riflemen and fifty dragoons. Early next morning these troops broke camp outside the stockade and started on the way back to Greenville. Scarcely had they swung into column along the south trace when the Indians began firing upon them from lurking places in the high grass. With the raiders were men painted like savages but who acted and were dressed as if they were Englishmen. Mac-Mahon's advance party was quickly cut to pieces, and those in the rear sought safety under the walls of the fort. Around the fort the ground had been cleared for several hundred yards except for scattered stumps that laborious effort had failed to remove. Using these as cover, the savages crawled close to the fort, trying to silence the men who stood by the loopholes and met the assault with accurate fire. Confident of their prowess and skill in the use of their weapons, Captain Alexander Gibson and his defenders were fully determined that the fort should not be taken; they also well knew what torture awaited them in case they were captured. They aimed carefully, and their bullets found a mark in painted faces and greasy mops of shining hair. On that bright summer day many warriors were killed outright; others were so badly wounded that they never returned to the fruitful valleys of the Maumee. Chiefs saw that their losses were useless; they realized that resistance would continue unbroken while sturdy walls and bastions stood. They would have battered them down with the cannon that St. Clair had abandoned, but with all of their searching they found none to use. They did not know that the shot falling among them came from these very pieces, which Wayne had salvaged and mounted once more.[34]

Toward nightfall the Indians perceived that their first efforts had failed. They withdrew from around the fort and assembled about a mile distant. Here by the Wabash they cooked their food and planned another attack. It was

[34] H. E. Wildes, *op. cit.*, pp. 414-415; F. E. Wilson, *Journal of Captain Daniel Bradley*, pp. 62-66; Jacob Burnet, "Notes," in Henry Howe, *Historical Collections*, etc., II, pp. 495-496.

misting and the moon was obscured. With the weather favoring and many of the garrison disabled, they hoped to scale the walls and rout the defenders. They moved out quietly and approached even more stealthily when they saw the dim outlines of the fort. Their precautions served no purpose. Sentinels were watchful; loopholes blazed with light; savages who had come close to the stockade were cut with slugs and buckshot and fell writhing upon the ground. Some crawled away beyond the range of fire. With this assault repelled, Blue Jacket spent the remaining hours of darkness in collecting his wounded. When the sun rose the attack was resumed, but with results as futile as before. By then MacMahon's men had got inside the fort, giving renewed courage to the defenders. Toward the end of the day the Indians saw that their chances of victory had passed; encumbered with many wounded, they started back to the Lakes in humiliating retreat.[35]

Although Fort Recovery had not been taken, casualties were heavy. Twenty-two officers and men had been killed; thirty others had been wounded. Early in the attack Major MacMahon had been shot in the forehead. He and others had died as becomes brave men. With a few changes of detail, the death of Captain Asa Hartshorn was typical; it was described in this letter to his father:

"After he was left by his troops he defended himself with his spontoon against the enemy until they despaired being able to Tomahawk him while alive. One of them lodged an Arrow in his vitals, which in a moment ended his life. His dead body was treated by the savages after their usual manner. They however were filled with admiration of the brave officer who had fallen, and put two leathern hearts into an incision they made in his breast, as testimony that he had courage enough for two men."[36]

Next day the bodies of Captain Hartshorn and others were buried with the honors of war inside of the stockade.

[35] *Ibid.*
[36] Bachus to Hartshorn, Dec. 26, 1794, *Kingsbury Paper*, I, Library of Congress.

Years later they were removed to the cemetery of the neighboring village.[37]

Though exacting a costly toll, the savages could not stay the advance of the white men; they could not cope with those who were skilled in the art of war and provided with all the means for success. Some 1,500 to 2,000 warriors had vainly attacked one-tenth of their number of regulars. As on other occasions, they lacked the common essentials of victory—stamina and supplies. Without them, their most gifted leaders saw that they were destined to fail; to them a negotiated peace was therefore better than the uncompromising terms of a conqueror. But others who wanted revenge and coveted the spoils of war would not listen to talk of peace; and their wishes prevailed.

Wayne was not slow in accepting their challenge. On July 26 Major General Charles Scott reached Greenville with 1,500 mounted volunteers. Two mornings later, with guns booming and trumpets blaring, 3,500 troops set out for the country where St. Clair had been ignominiously defeated three years before. For twelve days they marched north, seldom or never covering more than a dozen miles in twenty-four hours. With this "Velocity," they tramped through "Thickets almost impervious, thro Marassies, Defiles & beads of Nettles more than waist high & miles in length." Mosquitoes were bad, water was scant, and heat intense. After camp was reached, guards were posted, defenses erected, meals cooked, drums beaten, trumpets "blowed," and soldiers bedded down upon the ground. Once in a while their sleep was broken by a violent wind or rain; sometimes prowling Indians were detected, causing them to lie upon their arms for hours at a time.[38]

Moving forward in this fashion, the army reached the confluence of the Maumee and the Auglaize on August 8, 1794. The Indian village there had been abandoned, and nearby plenty of vegetables were growing luxuriantly. The volunteers found a good deal of corn. It might have been

[37] H. Howe, *Historical Collection*, II, p. 496.
[38] "Journal of Lieutenant Boyer," in J. J. Jacob, *Life of Michael Cresap*, pp. 420-421.

saved for the cavalry but instead they sold it to the government for $3 a bushel—a private's pay for a month. Wayne remained in this location for a week, sending overtures for peace, reconnoitering the neighborhood, capturing a few warriors and squaws, and building a stronghold that he called Fort Defiance. In his opinion he now had a fort that could shatter every effort of "the English, Indians, and all the devils in hell to take."[39]

With this added protection in the rear, Wayne crossed the Maumee on August 15, expecting to continue his march down the north bank until he reached Fort Miami, a stronghold that the British had erected on American soil near Lake Erie. Upon his approach, the Indians sent messengers under a flag of truce professing eagerness for peace and requesting that he halt the legion for ten days and discontinue his erection of forts. Wayne was not deceived; he did not yield to their subterfuges for gaining more time to gather their warriors. He did not even deign to reply. Next morning, August 18, he pressed resolutely on, reaching a point about ten miles from Fort Miami. During the day some of his scouts fell into an ambuscade; and one of them, William May, was captured and carried away. He told the Indians that they were to be attacked on the 19th.[40]

With signs of hostility increasing, Wayne expected to encounter hardy resistance. Accordingly he decided to halt and throw up a rude work where all his equipment and stores not essential for immediate combat could be temporarily stored. After a day's hard labor, "the citadel," as they called it, was completed except for one side. Leaving here a detachment of 100 regulars and an equal number of volunteers, Wayne planned to push on.[41]

[39] "Journal of Lieutenant Boyer," in J. J. Jacob, *Life of Michael Cresap*, p. 424; and *Dictionary of American History*, II, pp. 127-128.
[40] "William Clark's Journal of General Wayne's Campaign," in *Misssssippi Valley Historical Review*, I, pp. 426-428; and Wilkinson to Brown, Aug. 28, 1794, in *Mississippi Valley Historical Review*, XVI, pp. 81-90; McKee to Chew, Aug. 27, 1794, in E. A. Cruikshank, *The Correspondence of . . . Simcoe*, etc., III, pp. 7-8.
[41] Wayne, *op. cit.*, Aug. 19, 1794, (U.S. Military Academy Library); "William Clark's Journal," etc., p. 428.

On the morning of August 20 the army started. The day was hot and clear. Troops carried only two rations and were "divested of every species of Baggage except their Blankets." The line of march, following the northwest bank of the Maumee, cut across swamps, "luxuriant meadows," and high ground that was thickly wooded and traversed by short and deep ravines. Wilkinson had command of the right wing; Hamtramck, of the left. The legion's right flank was covered by the river; its left by General Robert Todd's brigade of mounted volunteers; its rear by a similar force under General Joshua Barbee. Far to the front rode more volunteers—a select battalion commanded by Major William Price.[42]

Near ten o'clock, after an advance of about five miles, Wilkinson and De Butts, an aide of General Wayne, rode forward to high ground from where they could see the British fort and McKee's store. From this point, they saw some of Price's men racing across the prairie in terrified retreat, not more than a quarter of a mile distant. Before De Butts could ride off and report this piece of bad news, some of the fugitives came rushing upon him. According to one story, Wilkinson temporarily halted them, only to have them make another break for the rear as soon as he galloped away to see what was happening on his own right wing. On reaching the left end of it, he found that Captain Thomas Lewis and the light infantry had fallen back and were badly mixed with other units. Captain R. M. Campbell was in command of the legion cavalry—the very same Campbell who had many friends and deemed himself rich and happy if he had "health of Body, Peace of Mind, a Pretty girl, a clean shirt, and a guinea." He was intent on withdrawing his troops in good order when Wilkinson rode up and told him to keep moving to the rear and there "form squadron." Troops being in confusion, Wilkinson refused a request of Captain Jacob Kingsbury with his infantry to charge the Indians, who were not more than a few hundred yards to the front.[43]

[42] T. Boyd, *op. cit.*, pp. 290-291.
[43] "James Wilkinson's Account of Battle of Fallen Timbers." Photostat in *Burton Collection*, Detroit Public Library; original in *John*

Possibly there were 1,300 of them in the neighborhood awaiting the army's approach. But some 400 savages and 60 Canadian militia formed the real core of resistance. They were occupying a position facing Wayne's line of march and lying in a path that a tornado had cut through the forest years before. In this tangled mass of broken and uprooted trees, the chiefs and their warriors were well protected and hidden, confidently awaiting attack. At night they were accustomed to return to the main body, four of more miles to the rear, to get their only meal in twenty-four hours. After three days of this constant watching and partial fasting, scouts brought word that an attack was unlikely on the 20th. Hence, on the very day of the battle of Fallen Timbers, a number of the savages had abandoned their advanced posts and were several miles away, either gorging themselves with food or drawing provisions at the British fort where they were habitually supplied.[44]

On learning that the fight had begun, Wayne moved forward. Believing that the Indians were in full force in his immediate front, he directed his second line to move up and reinforce the first. A charge was then ordered. With arms trailed and bayonets fixed, troops made for the savages hidden behind logs and trees. When close in, they delivered a well aimed fire, immediately rushing forward. Without chance to reload, the bravest of the warriors quailed before such a relentless attack. Driven from their protection, they broke into headlong flight. In the course of an hour they were chased two miles through woods and prairie. Scott might have made the rout complete with his mounted volunteers, but he failed to encircle the right of the savages. They were entirely too fast for him. He could not overtake them as they fled at top speed over the rough, timbered ground. The legion cavalry under Campbell, however, managed to turn their left flank. The going along

Pratt Collection, Connecticut State Library. Campbell to Van Rensselaer, July 29, 1794, in C. V. R. Bonney, *A Legacy of Historical Gleanings*, I, p. 96.

[44] A. L. Burt, *The United States, Great Britain, and British North America*, pp. 7-11, 139; I. Weld, "Travels," in E. A. Cruikshank, *op. cit.*, III, p. 11.

the river was easier. His troopers chased the red men at full gallop, cutting them down with broad swords, not halting the pursuit until the threatening walls of Fort Miami were reached and passed.[45] During the battle the jovial Captain Campbell was mortally wounded.

In forty-five minutes the battle was over. About 1,000 of the legion had been attacking less than 500 Indians. Wayne reported his losses as 33 killed and 100 wounded. According to McKee, the same classes of losses for the Indians were only 19 and 2 respectively, but these casualties included some of the most valiant chiefs of the Wyandots and Ottawas, as well as one from the Shawnees who was quartered alive. In retaliation, the savages cut an American officer into pound pieces. It was a ruthless, barbaric fight, unrelieved by any chivalrous acts of war.[46]

The Indians might replace their losses, but they could not halt the Americans sweeping northward in ever increasing numbers. They now perceived the folly of those who had roused them to war; they might better have followed Little Turtle and his program of peace. Wayne had proved himself a general against whom they could not stand. They knew that they should not rely any longer upon the French traders. They bitterly realized that the British would try to incite them to action, but would not support them as allies in battle. When they had fled to Fort Miami for refuge, they had found the gates of the blockhouse slammed in their faces.

Major William Campbell, commanding the post, was wise enough not to espouse their precarious cause, no matter how exasperating Wayne's army might be. Even then he could see Wayne's men feeding their horses on McKee's island. Before many hours the trader's houses and stores would be in smoldering ruins. In one direction the gardens

[45] "William Clark's Journal" etc., p. 429; *Journal of Capt. Daniel Bradley*, p. 69; Wayne to Secretary of War, Aug. 28, 1794, in *American State Papers, Indian Affairs*, I, pp. 491-492.
[46] Wayne to Secretary of War, Aug. 28, 1794, in *American State Papers, Indian Affairs*, I, pp. 491-492; McKee to Chew, Aug. 27, 1794, and Jarvis to Peters, Sept. 3, 1794, in *Correspondence of . . . Simcoe*, III, pp. 7-8, 29-30.

that the members of the garrison had laboriously planted were being robbed and destroyed; in another, the graves of the Indians were being desecrated, their cornfields obliterated, and their villages reduced to ashes. The invaders themselves were insolently encamped on the high ground that lay just beyond the range of his guns; he could easily hear them sounding their horns and beating their drums. Once in apparent bravado, some cavalrymen came riding so close to the walls that he had a gun pointed, a match lighted and was ready to fire when they wheeled and rode quickly away.[47] By this narrow margin Campbell escaped joining battle and committing his country to war.[48]

On the day after the engagement of Fallen Timbers, Major Campbell sent an officer to Wayne asking why the United States Army had advanced so near to His Majesty's garrison. Wayne blusteringly replied that his glorious victory on the day before should furnish an answer. The victory had been achieved in spite of any possible aid to the savages from the British fort

[47] A. L. Burt, *op. cit.*, pp. 139-140.

[48] The official report of Fallen Timbers is in Wayne's letter to the Secretary of War, Aug. 28, 1794. See H. B. Dawson, *Battles of the United States by Sea and Land*, II, pp. 24-26. Wilkinson wrote at least two accounts of the battle, both of which are highly critical of Wayne. One of these, unpublished, is in the *John Pratt Collection*, Connecticut State Library; the other is contained in a letter of Wilkinson to John Brown, Aug. 28, 1794 (*Mississippi Valley Historical Review*, XVI, pp. 81-90). Other accounts giving fewer details but showing less bias may be found in "William Clark's Journal of General Wayne's Campaign" (*Mississippi Historical Review*, I, pp. 419-444); *Journal of Capt. Daniel Bradley*, edited by Frazer E. Wilson; and Lieutenant Henry Bowyer, "A Journal of Wayne's Campaign," in J. J. Jacob, *Life of Michael Cresap*.

British contemporary remarks concerning Fallen Timbers have been published in the third and fourth volumes of E. A. Cruikshank, *The Correspondence of Lieutenant Governor John Graves Simcoe with Allied Documents relating to his Administration of the Government of Upper Canada*. There they are found in McKee to Chew, Aug. 27, 1794, III, pp. 7-8; extracts from I. Weld, *Travels*, etc., III, p. 11; "Testimony of John Bevan," III, pp. 13-14; Simcoe to Dundas, Aug. 30, 1794, III, pp. 19-20; Jarvis to Peters, Sept. 3, 1794, III, pp. 29-30; extracts from "Diary of J. G. Simcoe," III, pp. 97-100; Cartwright to Lethbridge, Oct. 10, 1794, III, pp. 118-119; Simcoe to Portland, Nov. 10, 1794, III, pp. 176-177; Burke to Littlehales, May 27, 1795, IV, pp. 21-23.

illegally built on American soil. Campbell in turn wrote that his patience was nearly exhausted, and anything more might provoke him into fighting. Thereupon Wayne sent word that he and his garrison must immediately move to the nearest post England had occupied in 1783.[49] The British did not budge, the Americans did not attack.

While engaged in this exchange of "courtesies," Wayne was issuing an order congratulating his army, bringing up more supplies, and preparing litters for those who had been wounded. After three days in the vicinity, he started back along the route over which he had come. Defeated and angry, the tribes along the Maumee became more obnoxious than ever. An officer declared that, on the night of August 25, "The savage was around my redoubt, late at night, making most Dreadful yells, Howling like wolves, & crying like owls, which kept me up all night & my men under arms, expecting hourly a charge from the Enemy, as I was 300 yards from Camp."[50]

The Indians were merely venting their impotent anger. They did not have enough supplies or teamwork for any large-scale attack. Moving quickly in small bodies to ambush or steal they sometimes did succeed in killing a few unwary travelers or destroying a diminutive detachment that was operating alone. Wayne was determined to stop this sporadic and irritating warfare. After halting for about eighteen days to strengthen the ramparts of Fort Defiance and to arrange for the comfortable care of his wounded, he advanced to Ke-Kiong-gay, commonly called the Miami Villages. Here the Miamis had established their capital; here they had defied and defeated Harmar.[51]

But soon their hegemony in the valleys of St. Marys and St. Josephs would pass. Near the juncture of these two rivers, troops began cutting timber. By October 22, a fort was completed and ready to be occupied. On that day, nearby Indians could hear a fifteen-gun salute, three

[49] A. L. Burt, *op. cit.*, pp. 139-140.
[50] "William Clark's Journal," etc., p. 433.
[51] H. E. Wildes, *op. cit.*, p. 425.

hearty cheers, and a lively beating of drums while Colonel John F. Hamtramck and six companies of infantry marched in and took possession. The newly made stronghold bore Wayne's name.[52]

With Hamtramck's detachment left behind, Wayne set the rest of his troops in motion for Greenville. There on November 2, the six-pounders boomed a welcome with twenty-four rounds. His troops had legged many a weary mile since leaving their long row of huts and starting their victorious campaign against the Indians. They had left their women and children during the dog days; now it was "cloudy and like for snow."[53] In spite of the monotony of garrison duty, they did enjoy being united with their families and comfortably housed. They were also freed from the weariness of continued marching and the recurrent toil of building forts and barricades.

For over a year Wayne was to remain in the vicinity administering the army and negotiating with the Indians. Whether he realized it or not, his conquest of the Northwest was now practically completed. He had succeeded admirably. Fallen Timbers was the natural fruit of his methodical and far-sighted plans. On December 29 he was able to read to his paraded troops the thanks of Washington and the House of Representatives for their splendid achievement.[54] It was particularly gratifying to Wayne to receive this public commendation of the President for his industry, judgment, and vigilance when only three years before his commission as major general had been recommended with serious misgivings. It quickened his pride to know that the House appreciated his "Good conduct and Bravery," even if it had refused to allow him to sit in its honorable body in 1792. And it must have been additionally pleasing to perceive that the rank and file were beginning to value him more as commanding general. Many had experienced his severity, but they also knew that he was forever unbending in demanding that penny pinching contractors,

---

[52] T. Boyd, *op. cit.*, p. 300. [53] *Ibid.*, pp. 301-302.
[54] *Ibid.*, pp. 303-304.

indolent paymasters, and profiteering sutlers should deal honestly and reasonably with them.

The savages, too, were conscious that here was a man of power whose eyes seemed never to close. They likened him to a tornado that swept all before it. His campaign had proved disastrous to them. Their fruitful valleys were not yielding their annual abundance of beans, corn, and pumpkins. The game, too, had vanished as blockhouses rose and settlers chopped the woods away to raise their cabins and plant their crops.

With the coming of winter the Miamis, Shawnees, Delawares, Potawatomies, Chippewas, and others were not far from starvation. Mounting their rawboned horses, some of them rode with a white flag to Fort Wayne, where they resignedly asked if Americans were still willing to talk peace. Before long they were traveling on to army headquarters. In late January they stood waiting outside the stockade at Greenville, hungry and cold, hoping that Wayne would take them in and give them food even if he would not grant anything else that they wanted. When they entered the council house, dejected and tattered, the general greeted them in all the glory of his uniformed magnificence. The contrast was marked, and the savages did not fail to notice it. They learned that peace might be had, but not on the terms that they wished or by those who had come to seek it. The Ohio would not be considered as the boundary between the white and the red man's country; those present were not representatives and were entirely too few to make binding engagements. Therefore, Wayne suggested that they and other Indians return all white prisoners and agree to a six month's armistice, coming back at the end of it to discuss the articles of a treaty. They dourly consented, leaving hostages as surety for good faith. They had learned that British promises were vain and to continue a war without allies was futile.

The chiefs held their warriors in check, and for a while the Northwest was relatively peaceful. The whites did not keep the agreement equally well. Kentuckians went into the Illinois country and took two Indian prisoners from the civil authorities and brutally murdered them. Somewhat later a party under the leadership of a parson by the name of Findlay plundered a Potawatomie camp on the Scioto. St. Clair, as governor of the Northwest Territory, did not succeed in bringing the offenders to trial and giving them the punishment that they deserved. He contented himself with philosophically hoping that the Indians' acts of retaliation would fall upon those who were guilty.[55]

During this time Wayne remained at Greenville. After winter had passed and crops had been planted, the Miamis, Delawares, Potawatomies, Shawnees, Weas, Piankashaws, Ottawas, Wyandots, and Chippewas began to assemble. With them came their distinguished chiefs, Little Turtle, Blue Jacket, Bockongelas, Red Feather, Moses, White Pigeon, and others. They numbered 1,130 all told. On June 16, deliberations began with a round of wearisome preliminaries. On the 20th Wayne made an address, reminding those present of the treaty of Fort Harmar and his offers of peace before the battle of Fallen Timbers. He also expressed a desire to know what lay deep in their hearts. Two days later Little Turtle replied. He would have the white men remember that the Great Spirit had charged his people never to alienate their land but to preserve it for posterity. Wayne answered on the 24th, observing that the tribes must have been recreant to their trust, for they had surrendered large areas to the English and French years before. Although they had already been twice paid for the land that he wanted, he stood ready to do so again with liberal bounties. At the same time he read them a section of the Jay treaty that representatives of England and the United States had lately agreed upon; it stated that troops of the Crown were to evacuate all of the forts on the United States' side of the Great Lakes. With this startling news, the Indians despaired of any more aid from the British. They wanted peace before, but now they realized that they had no other alternative.[56]

On August 3 a treaty was signed. By its terms hostilities ceased, prisoners were to be exchanged, and $20,000 worth

[55] *Ibid.*, pp. 305-309.   [56] *Ibid.*, pp. 312-322.

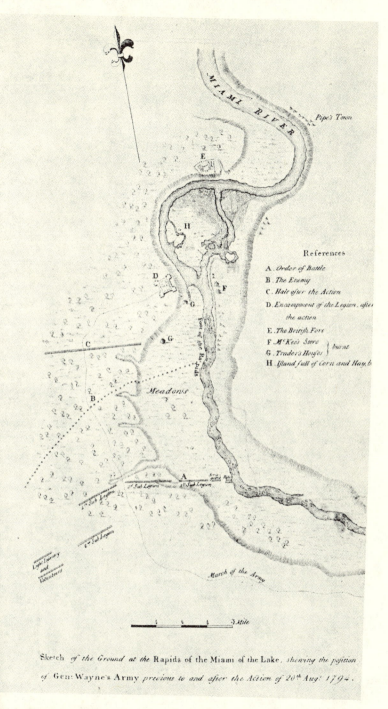

References

A . *Order of Battle*
B . *The Enemy*
C . *Halt after the Action*
D . *Encampment of the Legion, after the action*
E . *The British Fort*
F . *MᶜKee's Store* ⎫ *burnt*
G . *Trader's Houses* ⎬
H . *Island full of Corn and Hay, b*

Sketch of the Ground at the Rapids of the Miami of the Lake, shewing the position of Genᵗ Wayne's Army previous to and after the Action of 20ᵗʰ Augᵗ 1794.

THE BATTLEFIELD OF FALLEN TIMBERS (from an old print in the Burton Historical Collection of the Detroit Public Library).

of goods was to be delivered to the Indians immediately. In the future the leading tribes were to receive $1,000 yearly in merchandise; the other tribes, half as much. And most important of all, boundaries were fixed. The United States acquired most of the territory forming the subsequent state of Ohio and a small section of the eastern part of Indiana as well as considerable areas around the forts that Wayne had built and those that the British would soon evacuate. The red men also agreed to abandon any claims to 150,000 acres near the Falls of the Ohio that the government had previously granted to George Rogers Clark and his soldiers.[57] Thus the peace that Knox had worked and hoped for was not achieved until seven months after his resignation as secretary of war on December 31, 1794.

Settlers in the Northwest now enjoyed a real security for their lives and property. This happy condition had come only after the fumbling efforts of part-time soldiers, self-seeking demagogues, and religious crackpots had delayed or thwarted the thoughtful plans of able statesmen. Appreciating and properly assessing democracy's weaknesses, especially in great emergencies, Washington and his colleagues had made every effort to support Wayne in all his varied difficulties. He well repaid their confidence and aid. The treaty of Greenville naturally resulted from his successful campaign. It gave sustaining strength and prestige to the new liberal political system.

His most important work now accomplished, Wayne lingered only a few months more in the West, seeing that the treaty was observed and his troops strategically placed and properly supplied. By December 1795, he felt that his presence was no longer necessary. On the 14th, he bade his men farewell in this general order:

"The Commander in Chief cannot take leave of the Legion, compos'd of Officers and Soldiers whom he sincerely loves . . . without expressing the high Idea he entertains of the Worth and Merit of a Corps, who by their good Conduct, Fortitude and Prowess, have put a Glorious

[57] *American State Papers, Indian Affairs*, I, pp. 562-563.

Period to a distructive Indian War, and who can with truth & justice say 'Deserved well of their country' . . . With a Heart feelingly alive with Extreme Gratitude and Affection, the Commander in Chief bids a Temporary Adieu to the Legion."[58]

Two days later another order was published, proclaiming that Wilkinson had assumed command. He also announced to the army "his regard for its fame and Welfare by Avowing his Determination to inculcate, to enforce and maintain a Uniform System of Subordination and Discipline through all Ranks, without Partiality, Prejudice, Favour, or Affection, & he calls on his Officers one and all for their aid and Cooperation in the Arduous Undertaking. . . . He therefore entreats, he Exhorts and Commands the Officers of the Army to give the past to Oblivion, and to restore that Harmony, Confidence and Exchange of good Offices, which should mark a band of Brothers who have mixed Blood in the same Cause and who are liable at the Call of the States to fight, to bleed and die together."[59]

With this vainglorious blast, Wilkinson advertised Wayne's greatest fault and his own ameliorating virtues.

Meanwhile Wayne had started to the East. The time was ripe for such a journey. The legion was then engaged in routine work, which Wilkinson could easily supervise. By visiting the seat of government, Wayne hoped to accomplish several things. Perhaps he might succeed Henry Knox as Secretary of War; certainly he could accelerate the ratification of the treaty that he had drawn up at Greenville and contradict the ugly tales that were being circulated concerning his administration of the army. At the same time he might be able to frustrate the efforts of shortsighted economists who were planning to reduce its personnel. Several Senators and Representatives were already discussing how they could prune away officers and men. Wayne wanted the army maintained at existing strength to accomplish the mission assigned him. In the Northwest, he had to garrison the forts recently built and

[58] Wayne, *op. cit.*, Dec. 14, 1795.
[59] *Ibid.*, Dec. 16, 1795.

those soon to be surrendered by Great Britain; in the Southwest the Spaniards had to be watched in spite of the fact that they had ratified the Pinckney treaty. He hoped that Congress would appreciate the situation; it was then sitting in Philadelphia, where he had a great number of friends.

Returning there in the full tide of a great success made his blood flow faster, even though he had grown heavier and he limped a little more because of an old wound. His friends might not notice his infirmities, for they, too, were feeling the burden of years. He thought of them often as he rode along over slumbering hills pockmarked with snow. Soon he would be with them. The banked fires of memory would flame a little brighter if he could sit at the City Tavern and sip his sherry or madeira with his Revolutionary cronies while they exchanged tales of mutual experiences. It would also gratify him to strike a new note, to tell of a country the others had never seen, the like of which they had never dreamed. He was not very fluent, of course, but people will listen to the words of heroes.

On February 6, 1796, Wayne reached Philadelphia. The inhabitants had learned of his coming and were ready to receive him. On the outskirts, the Philadelphia Light-Horse rode up and escorted him into the city. As he moved down Market Street the shops were closed and a multitude of spectators enthusiastically watched the pageantry of his entry. From Center Square the artillery boomed a salute of fifteen rounds. He made his way to the City Tavern where old friends and city fathers welcomed him with numerous toasts and expressions of friendship. Close by a great display of fireworks brightened the evening sky. Over on High Street, between 7th and 8th, a triumphal arch had been erected. Accompanied by a huge crowd, Wayne passed beneath it while flickering gas lights disclosed the forms of its adorning figures of Peace, Justice, Liberty, Plenty, and Reason. Thus did Philadelphia extend itself on the first day of Wayne's arrival.[60]

But this was not all. More honors followed for the "Old

60 Wildes, *op. cit.*, p. 448.

Hero," turning gray and fifty-one. Even the First City Troop, chock full of Jeffersonian Democrats, gave a dinner in his honor at Richardet's Tavern. A week later, the Volunteer Greens, strongly Federalists, entertained him in a similar way at Weed's Tavern.[61] With these he must have felt more at home; certainly his political sympathies were with them. The Federalists favored the Jay treaty, an arrangement that greatly concerned Wayne and the army.

After the Jay treaty had been ratified and the strength of the army fixed as before, Wayne knew better what his duties would be. Without delay he prepared to return to the West. Soon he was traveling across the mountains. At Pittsburgh he found a government barge, the *Federal*, awaiting him. On it he traveled quickly to Fort Washington, where he conferred with officers and men. From here he rode the trail to Greenville, where Wilkinson met him and filled his ears with news of the salutary changes effected during Wayne's absence in Philadelphia. Wilkinson wanted to go there himself; for this purpose the *Federal* was placed at his disposal.[62] Wayne could not very easily prevent his second in command from traveling on a government boat that was soon scheduled to make a return trip up the river. Since he could not abide Wilkinson's presence, he was probably glad to give him a leave and provide facilities for his departure. He might not have been so apparently courteous if he had been acquainted with the depths of his subordinate's treachery.

But Wayne did not take time to investigate; on the contrary, he hurried north on a trip of inspection. During the first days of August he reached Fort Defiance. From here he embarked in a Kentucky boat, and went down the Maumee as far as the Rapids. By the 7th he was going over the battlefield of Fallen Timbers, explaining to his escort the details of what had happened there nearly two years before. For four days he remained near Fort Miami. He was happy to see the United States flag with its fifteen stars and stripes now fluttering over the ramparts, even

[61] T. Boyd, *op. cit.*, pp. 325-326.   [62] *Ibid.*, pp. 331-332.

though he had not been able to raise it there in 1794. When the keel boat *Adventure* was completed he went aboard. Soon it was sailing north over the waters of Lake Erie.[63]

On Saturday, August 13, 1796, he encamped within three leagues of Fort Detroit "at the Indian settlement of the Hurons." Next day 1,200 Indians accompanied him into the town. They welcomed him with ear-splitting yells and spasmodic rounds of musketry. They tired him with vigorous handshaking and grunting protestations of friendship. Except for the hazard of fire, he found the fort well able to withstand attack; its sturdy walls, embrasures, ditches, stockade, and abatis made it almost impregnable. He took quarters in the house of Alexander McKee, and here he held long interviews with Indian chiefs. He sympathized, in part, with Little Turtle and Blue Jacket, requesting that the government win their favor by building them a "Special mansion under the walls of the fort." The scouts, too, he thought should be more liberally rewarded. Toward officers and men he seemed more considerate and friendly.[64]

Wayne remained in or around Detroit for about three months. The place was comfortable and he was not well. From here he sent out the necessary orders to his widely scattered troops. The forts that the British had been evacuating in accordance with the Jay treaty required garrisons and supplies. Fort Mackinac, the last one to surrender, was occupied by the Americans on September 11.

In the Southwest the Indians were restless. A "complete troop" of cavalry was ordered to be prepared for service in Georgia. Seventy horses were purchased for organizations already in Tennessee. Although the Pinckney treaty had been signed, the Spaniards continued their annoying tactics. While at Greenville, Wayne had to warn them not to establish a fort at Chickasaw Bluffs or opposite the mouth of the Ohio.[65]

[63] *Ibid.*, p. 333.   [64] H. E. Wildes, *op. cit.*, pp. 455-456.
[65] Wayne to Quartermaster General, Sept. 5, 1796, and Wilkinson to Quartermaster General, Mar. 16, 1797, *John Wilkins Papers*, Detroit Public Library; H. E. Wildes, *op. cit.*, p. 453.

Fort Massac lay nearest to this troublesome area. It had been built in May 1794 on the north bank of the Ohio about thirty-seven miles from the Mississippi. Its original purpose was to prevent filibusterers inspired by French agents from raiding Spanish territory across the Mississippi. It also helped to preserve law and order near the confluence of the two mighty rivers that furnished the best routes to the fabled lands of the great Southwest. The importance of Fort Massac increased with the growth of traffic to and from New Orleans. Although the garrison consisted of only a company of infantry and a few artillerists, it was strong enough to enforce the inspection of passing boats.[66]

When Wayne heard that a good deal of money was coming to Wilkinson from Carondelet, Spanish governor of Louisiana, he ordered that the boat suspected of carrying it be carefully searched at Fort Massac. Nothing was found by a boarding party commanded by a lieutenant, in spite of the fact that $9,640 in silver was hidden in barrels of sugar and coffee. Later the barrels were opened in the store of Montgomery Brown at Frankfort, and all of the money except $640 was delivered to Wilkinson. Wayne never ascertained the amount received or why it was sent, but he felt sure that his second in command had not honestly earned it.[67]

At this time Captain Zebulon Pike had been at Fort Massac since 1795. Wayne had ordered him there to replace Captain Isaac Guion, who, in spite of a fine mind and considerable skill as an engineer, was charged with living in open concubinage with a particularly disreputable squaw. Except for short intervals, Pike remained continuously in command of the post until 1803, making friends of the nearby settlers and entertaining interesting travelers when they journeyed that way. During these years Captain and Mrs. Pike and their four children found happiness. The place was reasonably healthy, food was plentiful, and boats

66 M. T. Scott, "Old Fort Massac," pp. 50-64, in Transactions of Illinois State Historical Society, 1903.

67 J. R. Jacobs, op. cit., pp. 150-152.

brought down the river any luxuries the garrison could afford. Of the children, Zebulon Montgomery became best known. He not only secured an appointment as a cadet in the 3rd Regiment, but was also assigned for duty at Fort Massac. At the same time he considerably supplemented his income by acting as an agent of the contractor. Here on the Ohio he began to give evidence of those high qualities that would lead others to follow him loyally through the cruellest hardships of the wilderness and the most fearsome moments of battle.[68]

Other posts besides Fort Massac required Wayne's attention. Fort Mackinac had been recently evacuated by the British. It was situated on an island lying in the Strait of Mackinac, where the waters of Lakes Huron and Michigan meet. English, French, and Indian traders and trappers frequented the island because it was a convenient stopping place for their keel-boats and canoes. Some believed that British troops from Canada might pass that way in case they were bent on raiding Spanish territory along the Mississippi. A garrison at Fort Mackinac was imperative. Major Henry Burbeck, with something over a company, was ordered there. He did not long delay going, for, like other post commanders along the Lakes, he had to make sure that he was well established before winter interrupted all communications. On September 11, 1796, he and his men took possession of the fort.[69]

After making these and other dispositions, Wayne believed that he should return to the East. The sloop *Detroit* was prepared to carry him across the lake. Several reasons urged his early departure. Soon ice and snow would make the journey harder than ever. He had not enjoyed traveling during the preceding winter, and now his health and strength had declined. Perhaps physicians in Philadelphia could relieve his almost continuous pain. He really needed to go there again, for a new President would soon be in office and important army legislation was pending. Besides, dark stories had come to him that Wilkinson was trying

[68] Data on the Pikes supplied by T. R. Hay, Locust Valley, N.Y.
[69] E. O. Wood, *Historical Mackinac*, I, p. 479.

to ruin his reputation by carping criticism of almost
everything that the legion had done in the Northwest. On
November 13 the citizens and soldiers of the post and town
came down to the wharf and wished him a happy farewell.[70]

After five days' sailing across Lake Erie, the *Detroit*
cast anchor in the quiet waters off Presque Isle. Here was
a small garrison and a pentagonal fort that Lieutenant
Bissell commanded. After receiving the usual honors and
making the customary inspection, he considered plans for
an adjacent town and road that would link it with Pittsburgh. Thus a week or more slipped by while Wayne's
sickness daily grew worse. He could no longer acknowledge
salutes in his old-time vigorous way. Friends attended
him, putting him in a comfortable bed in the main blockhouse. They awkwardly did the best they could, but swath-
ing him in white flannel did not allay the pain or stop the
swelling of his leg. No physician was present, and none
arrived until too late. With torture increasing, Wayne's
hope of living passed. The days dragged on painfully, and
on the evening of December 15, 1796, he asked that they
bury him at the foot of the flag pole. Soon afterwards he
died. Then soldiers dug deeply in the frozen earth to make
a grave where they might place the hard oak coffin in which
their general lay dressed in full uniform. There he peacefully rested until prideful relatives removed his body to
a Pennsylvania churchyard so that they might lie beside
him in adjacent glory.[71]

70 H. E. Wildes, *op. cit.*, pp. 458-462.
71 *Ibid.*, pp. 462-463. For the removal of Wayne's remains to Pennsylvania, see G. B. Catlin, "Wayne Mss.," in *Burton Collection,* Detroit Public Library.

8. *Wilkinson, the New General-in-Chief, Inspects and Disposes*

DURING the first week of October 1796, Wilkinson, as we have seen, had started east in the *Federal*. Remaining at Pittsburgh only long enough to secure transportation across the mountains, he traveled quickly on to Philadelphia, where senators and representatives were now beginning to assemble in anticipation of the second session of the Fourth Congress. His eagerness to reach the City of Brotherly Love was based on the meanest of motives. On September 22 he had written to Baron de Carondelet de Noyelles, Governor of Louisiana, that he was going to Philadelphia to "keep down the military establishment, to disgrace my commander, and secure myself the command of the Army."[1] Wilkinson did not want a reduction of the army, but he knew that any apparent efforts to accomplish it would meet with high favor from his Spanish paymasters, whom he was trying very hard to impress.

Ever since 1789 he had enjoyed one of their $2,000 pensions. During 1792, a year after he had been commissioned in the army, he received $4,000; in 1794 Carondelet sent him $12,000, of which he ultimately obtained about half; in 1796, $9,000 more came up the Mississippi from New Orleans and was duly delivered to his agent at Frankfort, Kentucky. All these sums had been paid for aid that was mostly fictitious. Although Wilkinson's advice to the Spaniards was seldom based upon facts, they continued to trust him. When he told them something of value, they had neither the ability nor means to use it for the benefit of the Crown.[2]

---

[1] Wilkinson to Carondelet, Sept. 22, 1796, Seville, *Papeles de Cuba*, leg. 2375.

[2] J. R. Jacobs, *Tarnished Warrior*, p. 152.

The other alleged reasons for Wilkinson's visit to the seat of government were true. His ambition was unlimited. He had no loyalty except to his own interest. In December 1794, while writing to Harry Innes, a federal judge from Kentucky, he had characterized Wayne as a "liar, a drunkard, a Fool, the associate of the lowest order of Society, and the companion of their vices, of desperate Fortunes, my rancorous enemy, a Coward, a Hypocrite, and the contempt of every man of sense and virtue."[3] In spite of all evidence to the contrary, Wilkinson was trying to induce others to accept this malicious opinion. To help spread this idea, he formulated several general charges against Wayne and sent them on to Philadelphia. Their precise contents are unknown; they seem to have been concerned with wastefulness, partiality, lack of self-control, and tactical absurdities.[4] Once informed of their character, Wayne wrote a long letter to Knox on January 25, 1795, declaring them as unexpected as they were false —"the idle Phantom of a disturbed imagination."[5] For the time being he could do no more; he had to remain in the Northwest and complete the task assigned him. When this was accomplished, in January 1796, he set out for Philadelphia. His enthusiastic welcome in the East routed the plans of his enemies.

Upon Wayne's return to the Northwest, the next move was up to Wilkinson. Having collected evidence that might be injurious to the reputation of his commanding general, he obtained a leave and was soon on his way to Philadelphia. There he planned to sustain or withdraw the charges that he had preferred and prevent any investigation of his own very questionable conduct. His relations with the Spaniards were already causing unfavorable comment; his connection with Robert Newman had also aroused a good deal of suspicion. Newman had deserted just before

3 Wilkinson to Innes, Dec., 1794, *Innes Papers*, XXIII, Library of Congress.

4 H. E. Wildes, *Anthony Wayne*, pp. 427-429, 485-486; J. R. Jacobs, *op. cit.*, pp. 144-146.

5 Wayne to Butts, Jan. 25, 1795, *Wayne Papers*, XXXIX, Pennsylvania Historical Society.

the battle of Fallen Timbers, carrying letters to the British from apparent friends of theirs in the American camp. A tale circulated that Wilkinson had a hand in writing them, but this was never proved. He declared that he could not eat for days while such a hideous slander was being bandied about. The amount of truth in the story is still unknown. Strangely enough, Newman was never severely punished for desertion in the presence of the enemy, and apparently he had a pocket full of money after his return to the army.[6]

Wilkinson wanted official support to damn Wayne and clear himself. Timothy Pickering, secretary of war from January 2, 1795, to December 10, 1795, now headed the Department of State. Washington had tried to find a successor in C. C. Pinckney, Edward Carrington, or John Eager Howard; but they were all unwilling to serve. Both Anthony Wayne and Henry Lee wanted the position, but their financial troubles prevented any very serious consideration of either. As a last resort, Washington had turned to James McHenry, who became secretary very willingly on January 27, 1796.[7] Without unusual talents, McHenry was appointed because the President really liked him. His manners were engaging, and his views corresponded with those that the Federalists held. He also had considerable means, and hence was not solely dependent upon the impecunious salary that Congress had granted. Wilkinson had very little respect for the new secretary, referring to him as a "mock minister."[8]

Upon learning of Wayne's death, Wilkinson wanted the charges against his former commanding general no longer considered—a request that McHenry easily granted. At the same time he asked for an investigation of his own "aspersed reputation," but nothing was done.[9] This was no time to have the new general-in-chief of the army before

[6] H. E. Wildes, op. cit., pp. 431-435.

[7] B. C. Steiner, The Life and Correspondence of James McHenry, pp. 163-164.

[8] Wilkinson to Pratt, Dec. 27, 1797, Pratt Papers, Connecticut State Library; Wilkinson to Sargent, Jan. 3, 1798, Sargent Papers, Massachusetts Historical Society.

[9] J. Wilkinson, Memoirs, etc., II, appendix, no. XXXVIII.

any kind of court. Relations with foreign countries were precarious; a new administration was coming in; our whole defensive system was in process of change.

The act of May 30, 1796, abolishing the legion, had become effective on October 31, 1796. From then on, the army was to consist of four regiments, two companies of light dragoons, and the existing corps of artillerists and engineers. Two generals, a major and a brigadier, were to command this reorganized force. Provisions for rations, bounties, and retirement were almost the same as before. Court-martial sentences extending to capital punishment or "dismission of an officer" had to be confirmed by the President.[10]

Before the end of the second session of the Fourth Congress, two staff positions were again authorized, and another was created that had not existed since the days of the Revolution. The need for a judge advocate had become obvious because of the increase of army personnel and court-martial cases. Hence one was provided for in the law of March 3, 1797. He was to be detailed from the "commissioned officers of the line" and to have, in addition to his regular pay and allowances, two extra rations a day and $25 a month. Captain Campbell Smith began his duties as the first incumbent on June 2.[11]

John Wilkins Jr. was continued as quartermaster general, having replaced James O'Hara, the successor of Samuel Hodgdon, on June 1, 1796. Nevertheless, O'Hara still maintained close contact with the government. Making use of former connections, he obtained the contract for supplying the army with rations for a year, beginning to fulfill it on the very day that he ceased being quartermaster. Wilkins held office for six years, drawing the pay and allowances of a lieutenant colonel for the first half of the time; afterwards, until superseded by military agents in 1802, he enjoyed the perquisites of a major general. Much of his work consisted in arranging for the transpor-

10 J. F. Callan, *The Military Laws of the United States* (rev. ed.), pp. 114-117.

11 *Ibid.*, p. 118; and R. P. Thian, *Legislative History of the General Staff*, etc., p. 121.

tation of supplies. Not until July 16, 1798, did purchase pass from the supervision of the Treasury to the War Department, and then it was arranged through a Purveyor of Public Supplies.[12]

The office of paymaster general was likewise retained. On May 8, 1792, Caleb Swan, a $500-a-year clerk in the War Department, had succeeded Joseph Howell Jr., continuing in this capacity until 1808. Swan was directed to reside near the headquarters of the troops, to see that they were promptly paid, and to prevent any assignments of money due them. In return for this work he was given a salary of $60 a month plus a major's allowance of rations and forage. That the government might never be a loser through his own peculation, he was compelled to furnish a bond of $20,000.[13] With the pay of soldiers still inexcusably lagging, the subsequent act of June 7, 1797, specifically directed that it should never be more than two months in arrears. Even so, the rank and file got their earnings only a little more frequently than before.

In having a paymaster general, a quartermaster general, and a judge advocate, the army's arrangements were greatly improved. In addition, the act of March 3, 1797, raised the pay of subalterns, and the ration allowance of post commanders was doubled. Officers "deranged" in accordance with the preceding law of May 30, 1796, were granted six months' pay and subsistence. Thirty-four were discharged; some of them the army could ill afford to spare.[14] Wilkinson's grade was retained, but that of major general was abolished. For the time being he saw no hope for promotion. In spite of personal disappointment, he showed no resentment in public.

Ever since his arrival in Philadelphia during the autumn of 1796, Wilkinson had assiduously cultivated those who stood high in government. When John Adams was inaugurated as President, March 4, 1797, the general sat in

---

[12] Wayne, *Order Book*, May 22, 1796, in *Michigan Historical Collections*, vol. 34, p. 693; R. P. Thian, *op. cit.*, pp. 140, 193-195.

[13] *Ibid.*, pp. 457-460.

[14] J. F. Callan, *op. cit.*, p. 118; R. H. Hall, *Register of the Army of the United States for 1796.*

honorable place among the august few and saw him take the oath of office. The two became friendly. They were both sympathetic toward closer relations with England; they detested the radical, democratic ideas that the French Revolution had spawned; they yearned for a government run by "the rich, well born, and able." Often being the victim of unmerited abuse, Adams sympathized with Wilkinson when dark rumor circulated about his dubious relations with Spain. Adams comfortingly told the general that "nobody escaped accusation" and that he would have ample opportunity to defend himself if occasion required.[15]

Having won the support of the President and become commanding general of the army, Wilkinson left Philadelphia a few weeks after the inauguration, setting out for Pittsburgh with his family. On him now devolved the task of so training and disposing of the armed forces that our country could be protected from foes within and without. A few garrisons along the coast would be required. The Jay, Pinckney, and Grenville treaties had resulted in new federal responsibilities along the frontier. These had to be met.

Peculiar conditions in the new-born state of Tennessee called for immediate attention. Several months after its admission into the Union, William Blount, Senator from Tennessee, and several others hatched a scheme to seize Spanish territory for British benefit. Perhaps Wilkinson and Jefferson were ignorant of such plotting, even though they had dined with Blount during the winter of 1796.[16] At least, these two did not accelerate his ruin as his colleagues did by expelling him from the Senate. Though Blount was thus exposed and thwarted, his conspiracy still appealed to those who hated the Spaniards. His associates, too, were not entirely cured of trying other illegal enterprises.

Zachariah Cox, one of this group, was the chief promoter of the Tennessee Land Company, which had obtained extensive holdings from the crooked legislature of Georgia. He bent every effort toward establishing a

15 J. Wilkinson, *op. cit.*, II, pp. 154-156.
16 A. P. Whitaker, *The Mississippi Question, 1795-1803*, pp. 104-115.

settlement on lands reserved to the Cherokees. His past record was as questionable as his attempted speculation. The federal government had to take steps to prevent such landgrabbers and filibusterers from complicating our relations with Indians, Spaniards, British, and honest immigrants. A detachment of the army was accordingly prepared to move into Tennessee.

Sometime before his death, Wayne had requested the quartermaster general to purchase seventy mounts for the dragoons selected to be sent into this troubled area. The army horses surviving St. Clair's defeat and Fallen Timbers were old and rawboned, and their equipment was useless from "time and hard service." When Wilkinson became commanding general, he stipulated that remounts for these dragoons must be "sound in limb and wind, active and justly formed, five feet high at the least, and between four and eight years of age; uniformity in color is desirable, and bays to be preferred." They ranged in price from $90 to $130 apiece, the average being a little over $100. They were collected at Fort Washington, where Wilkinson arrived in May 1797. Here orders to embark for Tennessee were issued to seven companies of the 4th Regiment, Ford's artillery, and Van Rensselaer's dragoons. Colonel Thomas Butler was to command the detachment. Soldiers incapable of field service were to be left behind. Before departure, rolls were to be prepared and men mustered so that they could draw their pay from November 1, 1796, to March 31, 1797. A six months' supply of camp equipment, clothing, rations, medicines, and other military stores was drawn and packed away. Bulky articles had to be kept to a minimum; for after the troops had traveled a long way up the Cumberland River, they would still have to go 135 miles through an overland wilderness before they reached their station in or around Knoxville.[17] They expected to arrive in July.

[17] General Orders, Fort Washington, May 12, 18, 1797, in Wilkinson, *Order Book, 1797-1807*, National Archives; and C. V. R. Bonney, *A Legacy of Historical Gleanings*, I, pp. 140-145.

Scarcely had Butler and his men started down the Ohio before two companies of the 3rd Regiment and a few artillerists under Captain Isaac Guion set out into the wilderness. They were on their way to take over the forts that the Spaniards were expected to evacuate on the lower Mississippi in compliance with the Pinckney treaty. They left Fort Washington on May 26, and two weeks later they reached Fort Massac, where they were hospitably received by Captain Zebulon Pike, father of the redoubtable Zebulon Montgomery. While here, Guion won the good will of neighboring Cherokees by gifts of beef, flour, salt, and a few pounds of tobacco. At the same time he heard rumors that the Spaniards were strengthening Walnut Hills (Vicksburg) and planning to seize Chickasaw Bluffs (Memphis). In an effort to anticipate them, he hurried on, reaching the "infernal bluffs," as he called them, on July 24. He courted the Chickasaws with federal bounty. Forty barrels of flour went down their gullets, along with a considerable amount of meat and whisky. Some may have been condemned supplies that his own men could not eat. The weather was extremely hot, and no medicines were available for those who fell sick. Work went slowly, and the fort was not completed until October 22. It was called Fort Adams in honor of the President, and was duly christened with appropriate salutes and an issue of whisky. When the rest of the troops resumed their journey down the river, a temporary garrison of some thirty men was left behind under Lieutenant Joseph Campbell of the artillery. Guion was glad to be rid of Campbell, who had been keeping as a mistress the most "dissolute prostitute" in all the detachment. The post did not long remain in such questionable hands. Major William Kersey of the 3rd Regiment soon arrived with two companies and assumed command. Meanwhile Guion had reached Natchez on December 6 after passing by Walnut Hills which the procrastinating Spaniards were unwilling to surrender. In his new location, Guion's duty was to obtain a prompt observance of the Pinckney treaty and to administer civil law until the arrival of

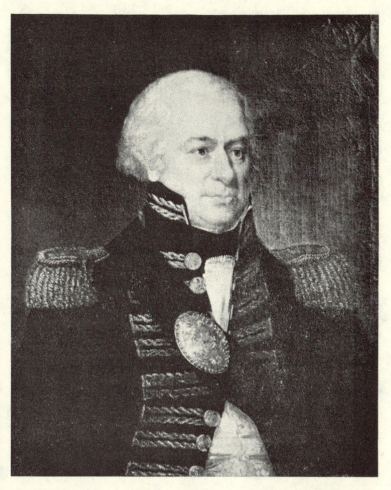

Major General James Wilkinson (from a portrait owned by the
Filson Club and reputedly painted by John Wesley Jarvis).

Winthrop Sargent, the recently appointed governor of Mississippi Territory.[18]

While Butler and Guion were traveling through the wilderness, Fort Washington was undergoing reformation. Wilkinson ordered officers to get rid of their concubines and soldiers had to do without more than their regular allowance of washerwomen. To prevent gambling, cards and dice was forbidden in quarters. Backgammon, considered entirely innocuous, was generally allowed. A soldier could not be absent from his organization on jobs of personal service unless permission was first given by the commanding officer of a district, department, or regiment. When employed by officers they were to be paid one-third of a dollar a day—pay so high that only a few were likely to be engaged. By such regulations, Wilkinson hoped to force all men back to the ranks where they belonged. Entirely too many were on detached service working as boatmen, waiters, messengers, etc. Some, under mercenary officers, were cultivating crops. Raising grain was generally profitable, immigrants and contractors being always ready to buy up any surplus. At the time, James O'Hara, previous quartermaster general, held the contract for supplying rations. To preserve them from theft and useless waste, Wilkinson ordered post commanders to provide adequate guards and storehouses. At the same time he warned against peculation of clothing or Indian goods.[19]

To learn more of conditions and to correct abuses elsewhere in the army, Wilkinson left Fort Washington to visit the scattered posts that lay to the north. In June he reached French Store. Here he found that most of his troops had turned farmers. On the 12th he issued a general order, angrily declaring such a practice must stop:

"The Spirit of cropping which is almost everywhere to be seen, is repugnant to the principles of soldiership, destructive to the Service and disgraceful to those who

---

[18] "Military Journal of Captain Isaac Guion, 1797-1799," in *Fifth Annual Report . . . of Archives . . . of Mississippi*, pp. 25-113.

[19] General Orders, Fort Washington, May 10, 12, 22, June 12, 1797, in Wilkinson, *Order Book, 1797-1807*, National Archives.

indulge in it. . . . The national bounty is expended not to improve the agricultural arts, but to instruct men in the use of arms; the hoe and the plow must be laid aside, and every moment of professional duty, devoted to form, instruct, and train them in the glorious Science of War. . . . Planting and improving of corn fields is prohibited. Gardens sufficient for the accommodation of officers and soldiers are proper and necessary, and it is obligatory on all commanding officers to pay attention to this subject, the labor is however to be done by detail; the idea of an officer farming for profit is inadmissible, as it tends to neglect of duty, a relaxation of discipline, abuse of the Public Service, and the disgrace of the profession."[20]

With this stinging rebuke to a commanding officer who had forgotten his mission, Wilkinson left for Fort Wayne, where he wrote Major James Bruff that he found conditions "truly deplorable." The army in this quarter "presents a frightful picture to the scientific soldier; ignorance and licentiousness have been fostered, while intelligence and virtue have been persecuted and exiled; the consequences were that factions have been generated to sanction enormity, and it follows that all ideas of system, economy, order, subordination, and discipline were banished, and that disorder, vice, absurdity, and abuse infected every member of the corps militarie."[21]

Wilkinson had a habit of exaggerating ills so that he might gain more credit for employing successful medication. He never doubted that he had the best antidote. It generally consisted of changing officers and men to new stations, court-martialing some, and reprimanding others. Though often deficient in judgment, his methods were forceful. He often made others believe that he could "cleanse the Augean stables of anarchy and confusion."

At Detroit reformation was less needed. When he arrived there in June he found things much more to his liking.

[20] General Orders, Loramies, June 12, 1797, in Wilkinson, *Order Book, 1797-1807*, National Archives.
[21] Wilkinson to Bruff, June 18, 1797, in *American State Papers, Miscellaneous Affairs*, I, p. 586.

Colonel John F. Hamtramck, something of a martinet, was in command of the post. In an effort to improve the soldier's food, Wilkinson ordered the contractor to furnish eighteen ounces of "good quality bread" with every ration; otherwise the customary allowance of flour was to be issued to troops or baked by the quartermaster at government expense. When the whisky component was not supplied, post commanders were authorized to make purchases and charge the cost against the contractor's account. He saw that meat unfit for use was inspected and condemned. Provisions were to be issued daily before seven in the morning. Quartermaster General John Wilkins Jr. was requested to supply each organization with enough camp kettles so that all might cook and eat at the same time. Thus better food might be more conveniently prepared and movements in the field considerably accelerated. With these improvements, soldiers listened more attentively for the mess call, *Peas upon a Trencher*, especially after long hours of drill or fatigue.[22]

The training of the five companies at Detroit went on during the summer without interruption. Unless otherwise engaged, troops drilled daily from five to seven, eleven to one and four to six o'clock under the supervision of two officers who were regularly detailed for the purpose. Instruction was based upon the regulations that Baron von Steuben had drawn up years before when Washington camped at Valley Forge. This text book was used by the army until 1812. In its pages, movements at drill and the duties of officers and men were clearly and simply set forth. The soldier without arms was taught "to stand straight and firm upon his legs." In marching the step was twenty-four inches, the cadence seventy-five to the minute. The leading element set the pace for those in rear. The platoon was the smallest division of the company, the squad not coming into existence until much later. With arms in their hands, soldiers executed a number of movements that corre-

[22] General Orders, Detroit, July 9, 1797, in Wilkinson, *Order Book, 1797-1807*, National Archives.

sponded to what was later known as the manual. In loading their muskets, fifteen distinct movements were involved.[23]

When winter really began, troops in northern posts did little close-order drill. The weather outside was too severe, indoors there was not enough room. Besides, men were kept so busy in the maintenance of supplies, shelter, and communications, and routine performance of guard duty, that they had little time for their own or other purposes. Regulations sometimes lapsed. Beginning in December, officers at Detroit had been permitted, except on guard and other special duty, to wear a "Short Regimental Coat, a Short Red Vest, Blue Overalls or Breeches." When Wilkinson arrived, apparently he did not abolish this dispensation. When the neighboring priest asked the commissioned personnel to attend a special service to celebrate Washington's birthday, they turned out in a body, as becomingly and as uniformly dressed as they could. Sometimes soldiers wore almost whatever they pleased, especially during active operations or while doing fatigue around the post. Hamtramck permitted his men to cut up their old blankets and turn them into long coats.[24] At best, they often went about in rags and tatters. Breeches or overalls seldom lasted until a new issue was made, especially because of the rough hard work required in field or garrison.

At Detroit there was always an unending number of daily and casual chores. The barracks and adjacent grounds called for constant policing. Sanitation was seldom neglected. Two sets of latrines had to be dug, one for day, the other for night use, respectively outside and inside the palisade. Punishment fell heavily upon those guilty of a nuisance elsewhere. Buildings were made of wood. Danger from fires was great. In 1805 a fire totally destroyed all houses in both town and fort. Every two weeks chimneys were carefully swept out, in winter twice as often. As an additional precaution, kegs in barracks were filled with water every evening before the gates were

[23] Steuben, *Regulations*, etc., *passim.*
[24] *Order Book, 1st U.S. Infantry*, entries from Nov. 17, 1796, to Mar. 7, 1797, in Detroit Public Library.

shut. The wickets were closed later, at ten o'clock, when
tattoo was blown. From then on no one was allowed to
pass or repass until the gates were "unfolded" at sunrise.
To see that all entrances and exits were carefully watched,
as well as to prevent any disorders about the post, thirty-
six privates, corporals, and sergeants were regularly
detailed for interior guard duty.[25]

Sometimes soldiers were known to scale the walls and
take their fling. Often they failed to return by tattoo.
Charles Kennedy, one of these culprits, was sentenced to
wear a pair of leg bolts for a week. Thieving and desertion
were common offenses, usually committed in moments of
drunkenness. Forbidden sales of liquor often originated
with sutlers or camp-followers like William Mitchell and
Lydia Conner. For repeated bootlegging, both were sentenced to be drummed out of the fort and town in front
of the paraded troops. Keeping step to the Rogue's March,
the two made their unhappy exit, joined hand in hand, with
a bottle suspended from the neck of each one. Never again
were they to enter the fort at Detroit. When the case was
reviewed, Mitchell was spared the drumming, and the delinquent Lydia had to suffer the hoots and howls of her former
clients alone.[26]

In spite of rigorous punishments, desertion was common
at Detroit. The guilty usually were given 100 lashes,
twenty-five being laid on at four separate times. In the
case of Henry Seavy the offense was particularly aggravated; he was ordered shot to death between the hours of
eleven and twelve o'clock on the morning of July 4, 1797.
On that day all officers and men not on duty assembled
on the parade, afterwards marching to the area in front
of the fort. Here with loaded arms they formed a crescent
fronting the glacis. A subaltern and twelve noncommissioned officers and privates were then dispatched for the
prisoner, who, preceded by his coffin, was marched to this

[25] Wayne, *Order Book*, entries from July 12 to Aug. 20, 1797, in
Michigan Historical Collections, vol. 34, pp. 697-730; Duncan to
Kingsbury, June 21, 1805, in *Kingsbury Papers*, Chicago Historical
Society.
[26] *Entries* of July 14, 20, 1797, in *ibid.*

place of execution. With troops standing at present arms, the adjutant was then to read the sentence. The grave had already been dug, under the supervision of the quartermaster. At "precisely fifty minutes past eleven o'clock," the prisoner was then to be shot to death at the command of the subaltern in charge of the escort. But the sentence was never carried out. Hoping that the prisoner's "escape from the jaws of death" would produce reflection upon the enormity of his crime and that pardon would stimulate "a future course of honorable action" and would impress him "with a due sense of gratitude to the author of his salvation," Wilkinson ordered that he "be conducted to the standard where kneeling and grasping the staff with his right hand, his left uplifted, he is to renew his oath of fidelity, to be administered by the judge advocate. He is then to be reconducted to the main guard, discharged from confinement and join his corps."[27] Existing records do not reveal whether the prisoner was thoroughly reformed by so narrow an escape.

Apparently other soldiers were not deterred from evil ways. Because of desertion, licentiousness, drunkenness, and disorderly conduct, Wilkinson ordered that martial law prevail within the limits of the government reservation. As a result some civilian offenders illegally living in this area were tried by court-martial and punished; others thought it best to flee the neighborhood. Sutlers bitterly complained, and the order was somewhat modified.[28] The sale of liquor, however, was soon better controlled.

With these changes effected, Wilkinson and the paymaster, Caleb Swan, left for the north end of Lake Huron on August 4. They sailed in a seventy-ton sloop to an island that the Indians called Michilimackinac because its outline resembled a very large turtle. It lay in the strait of Mackinac where the bright waters of Huron and Michigan rush rapidly by. Upon arrival, they cast anchor in a crescent-shaped harbor enclosed by high white cliffs rising abruptly

27 General Orders, Detroit, July 4, 1797, in War Department, Adjutant General's Office, Old Records, National Archives.
28 Proclamation of Wilkinson, July 12, 1797, and Askin to Wilkinson, July 24, 31, 1797, in *Askin Papers*, Detroit Public Library.

from a pebbly shore. Here they were heartily received and escorted up hill to the post, closely hemmed in by thick forests of maples, beeches, white-cedars, and firs. Major Henry Burbeck and something more than a company of artillerists and engineers composed the garrison. His troops, like all others, were happy to be paid but not to be inspected. Wilkinson was therefore the less welcome of the two visiting officers. For several weeks he remained in the neighborhood, going as far as the shores of Lake Superior in the hope of discovering the copper mines reputed to be there. He apparently succeeded, later declaring that he might have cut out a 200-pound chunk of ore if tools had been sharp enough. As it was, he obtained a few samples, made daily entries in his meteorological journals, issued a number of orders, and then started back to Detroit.[29]

Arriving there about October 1, Wilkinson found a well-known messenger bearing important dispatches from New Orleans. His name was Thomas Power. He was then acting as a secret agent of Baron de Carondelet, Spanish governor of Louisiana, whose half-penny mind became frequently befuddled with alluring dreams of a self-created empire. At the time Carondelet was offering $100,000 to anyone who would stir up trouble in Kentucky and Tennessee. He wanted to organize a new Spanish province in the area that lay east of the Mississippi between the Ohio and the Yazoo. If this revolution should be successful, more money and munitions would give it such a momentum that Wilkinson, as its military leader, might seize trans-Mississippi territory to add to their joint domain. Here, in a realm split by a mighty river, Americans and Spaniards would live harmoniously, giving allegiance to a flag of their own choosing.[30]

29 E. O. Wood, *Historic Mackinac*, I, p. 479; II, pp. 149, 389, 399, etc.; *American History Magazine*, Jan., 1888, pp. 74-75; J. Wilkinson, *Memoirs*, etc., II, Appendix, XXXVII; *Early Minutes of the American Philosophical Society*, Dec. 7, 1798 and Dec. 6, 1799.

30 I. J. Cox, "Wilkinson's First Break with the Spaniards," in *Biennial Reports, Archives and History of West Virginia, 1911-1914*, pp. 49-56.

This diverting scheme had already been told to those whose ears were open but whose tongues would not easily wag. In his progress north, Power had sent back letters in which he lyingly told of those who had succumbed to his intriguing plans. He claimed that Wilkinson, George Rogers Clark, and others equally prominent had become his converts and would arouse the common folk to revolt. Stirred by this deceptive news, Carondelet's palsied mind became enthusiastic and his purse strings loosened for his agent's benefit.

Power did not snare Wilkinson so readily. The general put him under arrest in officers' quarters. Some of the garrison had already heard of this ubiquitous stranger and believed that he must be on some mischievous errand. Therefore Wilkinson could make no friendly overtures, no matter how eager he might be to gain information. He also refused to subscribe to Power's chimerical scheme in spite of a promise of land in Illinois and a pension of $4,000 a year—$2,000 more than he was then receiving. He did, however, send word that the British would not be allowed to invade Spanish territory by the north; and if they tried to do so, he would effectively stop them. These, of course, would be reassuring words to Carondelet. Wilkinson could scarcely send him others; he had been directly ordered to prevent any violation of our territory. He was very happy to send such a message, because he hated the British for enticing his men to desert and wanted to curry favor with the Spaniards whose money he drew. He also advised the Spaniards to carry out the treaty, warning them that the western people had no real cause of complaint since the Pinckney treaty had given them the navigation of the Mississippi. He also declared that his present position would not allow him to play his former role; in fact, he had destroyed his code and his Spanish correspondence. But he was still unwilling to sever entirely his nefarious connection; he asked for the $640 that the Spaniards still presumably owed him and incidentally remarked that if he became governor at Natchez opportunities might then be presented for making new plans.[31]

Failing to get anything but fantastic schemes out of Power, the general decided to send him quickly back to Louisiana with his answer. Captain Benjamin Shaumburgh and several men were to escort him as a prisoner until he reached the borders of Spanish territory. By this singular arrangement embarrassing rumors might be dissipated and the curious prevented from searching and finding on Power any papers that might incriminate the general. Being returned by the Wabash-Massac route, Power could see with his own eyes that American troops had already been disposed to prevent a British descent on Spanish territory. He was also traveling the shortest way back. Thus Carondelet's fears would soon be allayed even if his secret hopes stood little chance of fulfillment.[32]

Soon after Power's departure, Wilkinson also left Detroit. The place was too remote from the center of affairs for him to administer the army efficiently, especially in winter when communications were long interrupted. For nearly two months, Wilkinson traveled across snow-covered country with the temperature often around zero. Accompanied by Little Turtle, chief of the Miamis, ex-Senator Mitchell's son, and a few others, he reached Pittsburgh about the middle of December. He decided not to continue on for another 297-mile journey across the mountains to Philadelphia, where "mock minister" McHenry was neglecting official correspondence and trying to make the army a victim of ignorant and untimely experiments.[33] At Pittsburgh Wilkinson could conveniently dispatch and receive orders and enjoy his family and friends. His wife and his two boys were with him, and the time went quickly and happily by. They entertained with easy and generous hospitality in quarters that had been newly papered and plastered for their comfort.

[31] J. R. Jacobs, op. cit., pp. 164-166.   [32] Ibid.
[33] Wilkinson to Owen Biddle, Dec. 24, 1797, copy of letter supplied by T. R. Hay, Locust Valley, N.Y.; Wilkinson to Pratt, Dec. 27, 1797, Pratt Papers, Connecticut State Library; Wilkinson to Sargent, Jan. 3, 1798, Sargent Papers, Massachusetts Historical Society.

Affairs were less troubled at Pittsburgh than at the seat of government where the President and his colleagues were greatly disturbed over our relations with France. Hoping to obtain our aid in a war that she had begun with Great Britain, she wanted us to continue the alliance that we had made with her in 1778. On May 15, 1797, Congress had met in special session. John Adams told the members of the House and Senate that C. C. Pinckney had been expelled from France after he had arrived there to act as United States Minister. In his anger, Adams declared that such an insult must be repelled "with a decision which will convince France and the world that we are not a degraded people, humiliated under a colonial spirit of fear and sense of inferiority."[34] He therefore recommended building a navy, increasing the army, fortifying our ports, and equipping and organizing the militia. In support of these ideas, a law was enacted June 23, 1797, appropriating $115,000 to fortify our harbors. States might supplement this amount by using the money that they owed the federal government, provided that the land on which fortifications were erected became federal property.[35]

Shortly after passing this legislation, Congress adjourned, not meeting again until November 13. Then it continued in session for 246 days, a longer period of meeting than occurred again for forty-five years. Meanwhile our relations with France kept growing worse. On April 3, 1798, Adams transmitted to both houses papers disclosing the outrageous treatment of John Marshall, Elbridge Gerry, and C. C. Pinckney. As the price of recognition for our envoys, secret agents of the French government demanded that Adams apologize for his anti-French speeches to Congress, that the United States make a generous loan to France, and that the agents themselves be advanced $250,000 as a personal bribe. The United States replied to such brazen affrontery by authorizing privateers to prey upon French vessels in the West Indies and

---

[34] Adams to Congress, May 16, 1797, in J. Richardson, *Messages and Papers of the Presidents*, I, pp. 233-239.
[35] J. F. Callan, *op. cit.*, pp. 118-119.

elsewhere. By 1800 we had lost a number of ships and eighty-four belonging to France had been captured or destroyed.

This undeclared war upon the high seas resulted in an improvement of our defenses on land. The law of April 27, 1798, increased the regular army by a regiment of engineers and artillerists, who, it was hoped, would prepare seacoast defenses against any possible attack. Six days later $250,000 was added to previous appropriations for fortifying our ports. On May 4, the expenditure of $800,- 000 was authorized for artillery and small arms. If these could not be purchased, the President might buy or lease armories and foundries where they could be manufactured.[36]

Deeming these measures insufficient, Congress also gave the President authority to raise a temporary army of 10,000 men for a period not exceeding three years, in case the interests of the United States became more endangered. Men who enlisted were to be given a $10 bounty and to be exempted from arrest for debt or contract during their term of service. A lieutenant general was to command, receiving $250 a month and liberal allowances for forage and rations; he was also entitled to a maximum of four aides and two secretaries. If need be, an inspector general, adjutant general, quartermaster general, physician general, and paymaster general might be appointed. This new force was to be subject to whatever rules the President should prescribe. Some $600,000 was appropriated for the purchase of arms and equipment.[37] As it turned out, none of the 10,000 troops were ever raised.

Instead, the regular army was sensibly strengthened. After July 16, 1798, each regiment was to have nine more commissioned officers. Thus the authorized officer personnel for a company (a captain, lieutenant, and ensign) would be depleted no longer to furnish those needed for staff duty. The regiment was also increased by eight sergeants, eight corporals, four musicians, and 184 privates. The pay of each grade was raised one dollar a month. The ration,

36 *Ibid.*, pp. 119-121.   37 *Ibid.*, pp. 122-125.

too, was made more generous; beef was increased one-quarter of a pound, bread two ounces, rum one-half a gill, and the allowances of salt, vinegar, and soap were doubled. The quality, too, many hoped, would improve; for the business of purchases and contracts for supplies and services was taken from the treasury and turned over to the War Department, where it logically belonged. Hereafter the secretary of war was entirely responsible for the proper feeding, clothing, and equipping of the army, provided that Congress allowed him adequate funds.

To supplement this force of regulars the President was given authority to recruit twelve regiments of infantry and six troops of light dragoons to serve during "the continuance of the existing differences between the United States and the French Republic."[38] Believing that the emergency was not sufficiently threatening to justify action, Adams failed to organize this short-time force or commission the two major and three brigadier generals who were designed to lead it.

During these recurrent spasms of legislation, Wilkinson was at Pittsburgh or on his way to the Southwest. He was probably not averse to doing a little lobbying at the seat of government, but he did not care to do it in the way that McHenry wanted. Besides, someone had to remain at Pittsburgh and administer the widely scattered garrisons in the Northwest. In addition, Fort Fayette was a healthy place. All the attractions of Philadelphia were no compensation for the horrors of yellow fever that had swept the city in recent years and might do so again.

Wilkinson knew that he would soon be traveling to a distant station. When the ice began to break up in the Ohio, he made arrangements for journeying to the Southwest, where his duties were calling him. There the Pinckney treaty still remained to become fully operative. It had been signed in 1795, and by its terms Americans were granted the use of the Mississippi and the "right of deposit" at New Orleans. The boundary line between the United States and Spain was also fixed at the 31st parallel. Andrew Elli-

[38] *Ibid.*, pp. 127-128.

cott was trying to survey it; his methods were distasteful to the Spaniards, who delayed evacuation of several posts that now lay within the enlarged area of the United States. These had been taken over and new ones established. In this general area our relations with the Indians had changed. Wilkinson was known to be valuable in solving such problems because of his knowledge of the Southwest and its people.

Whether his efforts would be entirely beneficial for the United States was another question. On March 5, 1798, he wrote two letters. One of these was to Winthrop Sargent, advising him to get rid of any British subjects enjoying federal office in the Northwest Territory; failure to do so might bring on embarrassing investigation.[39] Wilkinson's own ghosts of the past were speaking. In 1787 he had signed a paper that the Spaniards accepted, making him a citizen of Spain. Few knew of this or the fact that he was enjoying a Spanish pension. But many had become suspicious and he greatly feared disclosure. Hence, on the same day, he wrote another letter to Gayoso, the Spanish governor at Natchez:

"Observed everywhere, I dare not communicate with you, nor should you try to do so with me; Humphrey Marshall has attacked my honor and fidelity. You should not trust the western people, because some are traitors. Fortify your frontiers well. While I remain as at present all is safe. Have buried my cipher, but I will recover it. You have many spies in your country. Do not mention me nor write my name. I implore you in the name of God and our friendship. Fort Pitt, fifth March."[40]

Thus, for both personal and official reasons, Wilkinson wished to be stationed along the Spanish-American frontier. In the early days of June 1798, he had a government barge fitted out with hangings, sails, a "portable kitchen,"

[39] Wilkinson to Sargent, Mar. 5, 1798, *Sargent Papers*, in Massachusetts Historical Society.
[40] Wilkinson to Gayoso, Mar. 5, 1798, A. G. I. Seville, *Papeles de Cuba*, leg. 2374.

and other conveniences.[41] His wife and the two boys were planning to go down the Ohio with him. By the 14th they had all reached Cincinnati. Here the general remained for a while, deeply immersed in army administration. He had to solve the chronic problem of how best to dispose of his troops and keep them adequately supplied and properly trained. Reports and personal visits acquainted him with conditions in the neighboring garrisons; spies and secret agents brought him the news of what the Spaniards and Indians were doing.

In keeping with War Department plans, Wilkinson assiduously cultivated the friendship of the Indians. During the winter, he had elicited complacent grunts from Mrs. Little Turtle when he gave her twelve and a half yards of calico and two pairs of black silk gloves to drape her swarthy figure and protect her calloused hands. Her husband, the great Miami chief, fared even better. Through Wilkinson's kindness at Pittsburgh, he was able to put on a new shirt every day for a week, have a drink of liquor when he chose, and play a musical instrument if he pleased. He was also provided with boots, bridle, firearms, two pots, and a letter of introduction to Philadelphia personages. He journeyed to Philadelphia, saw the President, members of the Philosophical Society, and others less distinguished. After making the rounds of the city, he recrossed the mountains and again sought out his patron, who was then on his way to Fort Washington. Here the government paid Little Turtle's board at the rate of $4 a week, making it possible for him and several of his friends to gorge themselves frequently at public expense. They were particularly fond of the wine, brandy, gin, and bounce that the tavern keeper William Austin very willingly supplied, thus just about doubling the amount of his revenue. They also very gladly attended the $85 dinner that Wilkinson gave to some visiting neighborhood chiefs. In fact, Little Turtle and his fellow savages might have remained at Fort Washington longer if the wells of federal hospi-

[41] *Expenditures in the Naval and Military Establishments*, 1797-1801, pp. 42, 47, 59, etc.

tality had continued to flow. But the general had left for the Southwest, where he expected to enforce observance of the Pinckney treaty.[42]

On his way Wilkinson stopped at Fort Massac during the first days of August. It was situated thirty-eight miles from the Mississippi on the north bank of the Ohio. On ground only twenty feet above high-water mark, the fort looked down upon the river sweeping majestically by. The site, once defended by French and English, was not occupied by the federal government until 1794. Then, to prevent filibusters from invading Spanish territory at the instigation of the maladroit Genet, Wayne ordered Major Thomas Doyle to take a company of infantry and seven artillerymen to this strategic point. Leaving Fort Washington in ten boats, Doyle arrived at Massac on the evening of June 12. Work on a blockhouse and redoubt quickly followed. The resulting fort fulfilled not only the original purpose but also proved a rallying point for Kentucky militia who assembled to halt Indian depredations along the lower reaches of the Tennessee and the Cumberland. Doyle was not popular either with the settlers or the members of his own command. When the act of 1796 became effective, he was one of the surplus officers discharged. The fort was subsequently commanded by Captain Zebulon Pike who was both friendly and able. By then the garrison had been increased to about eighty men, and some thirty families were living close by.[43]

Wilkinson did not linger at Fort Massac. Soon his rough-hewn armada of twenty-seven boats was sweeping over the broad waters of the Mississippi on its way south. The rank and file beheld a new world opening before them. Brilliant days were followed by brilliant sunsets, and nights were bright with many stars. When the sun rose, the teeming life of the lower country began to stir. Sometimes reveille was intermingled with the song of the mocking

42 *Ibid., passim*; bill of William Austin, in *Gratz Collection*, Pennsylvania Historical Society.
43 Mrs. M. T. Scott, "Old Fort Massac," in *Transactions of Illinois State Historical Society, 1903*, pp. 50-64.

bird. Occasionally soldiers might see the sky suddenly darkened and hear the sound of moving wings; passenger pigeons were traveling to a land of sunshine and plentiful rain. Occasionally bears came down to the water's edge, gazing about with a sort of wistful awkwardness and afterwards thrashing back to their dens in the deep encircling forest. Deer appeared, and bounded quickly and gracefully away. After nightfall the howling of wolves, the cry of panthers, the croaking of frogs, the hooting of owls and the buzzing of innumerable insects mingled with the sound of waters breaking against the clumsy barges and keel-boats that were moored along the river bank.

As a rule no traveling was done after sunset. The flotilla drew close to shore at a convenient stopping place; and after outguards had been posted extending inland from the boats, a temporary camp was pitched, meals cooked, and arrangements made for early departure. A shot from the general's boat, always in the lead, was a signal for the others to get under way. Each boat had a definite place that it usually held in spite of wind, currents, and other obstacles. Only when squalls arose did they break formation; then each made for the shore by the shortest route. When a boat sprang a leak or ran on a sand-bar the flotilla stopped and sent hands to the rescue. Since such emergencies were rare and fatigue and guard details small, moving by water was less arduous than traveling by land, with its road cutting, bridge building, and long tedious marches through wilderness and swamps infested with "varmints" and Indians. Free from such hardships, Wilkinson and his men floated leisurely down the Mississippi, requiring only a few to keep watch, pull at the oars, and steady the helm. On the long stretches of open water a cool breeze modified the torrid heat by day and made sleep come easier at night. Before going to bed, soldiers often cleaned and refreshed themselves by swimming in the river. To thwart pestering mosquitoes and avoid the "noxious air," they tried to close themselves in when they lay down to rest.[44]

[44] Wilkinson, *Order Book, 1797-1807*, entries of Aug. 8, 9, 10, 1798, in National Archives.

Traveling in this way, Wilkinson reached Natchez on September 27, 1798. He soon went on to Loftus Heights, seven miles farther down the Mississippi. Here, on the east side of the river, just above the Spanish boundary line that had been fixed by the Pinckney treaty, he tied up his boats and began to establish a camp, named Fort Adams in honor of the President. This fort was strategically important. It was closer to Spanish territory than any other army post; it could control any large-scale traffic up or down the Mississippi; and the ground on which it was situated was high enough to offer prospects of reasonable health and successful defense. With the idea of making the place impregnable, Wilkinson soon began expending $80,000 for fortifications.[45]

At Fort Adams, Wilkinson's essential military duties proved to be only a very small part of his daily routine. He had to lend constant support to Winthrop Sargent, who had been appointed governor of the newly organized Mississippi Territory, which lay between the 31st and 35th parallels and the Mississippi and the Chattahoochee rivers. In this area the frontiersmen were often lawless and turbulent, the Indians thieving and resentful, and the Spaniards deceitful and procrastinating. To solve the resulting problems required much firmness and tact. Sargent was ill-suited to this task—his horizon was narrow, his mind brittle. Wilkinson was more effective, especially in dealing with the Spaniards.

Relations with the Spaniards had been strained for some time. For over a year Andrew Ellicott, chief of the federal surveyors, had been wrangling with Gayoso de Lemos, Spanish governor of Natchez. At first Gayoso seemed entirely willing to cooperate; later he put as many stumbling blocks as possible in the way of the literal-minded Ellicott, who, meanwhile, could do nothing but putter and fume. During the same time the nearby settlers became enraged because the urbane Gayoso had thrown a loud mouthed, trouble-making Baptist preacher into the stocks. To escape their vengeance, Gayoso took refuge

<hr>

45 B. C. Steiner, *op. cit.*, p. 450.

within the walls of the Spanish fort. While he looked on impotently from this point of refuge, a committee of inhabitants and Captain Isaac Guion kept law and order until Sargent arrived, on August 6, 1798, to assume the reins of government.[46]

Wilkinson aided Sargent in establishing the new regime. Natchez was a lawless place, particularly "under the hill," where frontier riff-raff concentrated. Here flat-boaters, slaves, Indians, and others made Sunday hideous with their debauchery. Filled with taffia or corn whisky, men, roaring drunk, cut and gouged each other over snaggle-toothed whores covered with sores and vermin. Sargent asked for troops to maintain order; he also wanted to prohibit soldiers from drinking in the town. A few of his requests were granted. He got a sentinel to keep watch in front of his quarters. Sometimes army rations were issued to him, his friends, or visiting Indians. But some of the buildings that the Spaniards had evacuated were denied him; Wilkinson believed that the army needed them more.[47]

The governor and the general, though never intimate, knew that as two agents of the government with related interests they must work together. Harmony was necessary if they were to accomplish their missions. They were about the same age, possessed similar backgrounds of Revolutionary experience, were well educated, and had been living for a number of years along the frontier. They were better at enforcing the letter than in interpreting the spirit of law. They could not understand why a frontiersman could make sport of their dignity or question their authority. They considered any opposition to their plans as disloyal to the government and a personal affront to themselves. Without a saving sense of humor when subjected to ridicule, each tried to prosecute for slander whoever caused him chagrin. By birth and training, they believed themselves destined to rule over those less fortunate and able.

[46] J. R. Jacobs, *op. cit.*, p. 176.
[47] Sargent to Wilkinson, Nov. 14, 1798, in D. Rowland, *Mississippi Territorial Archives, 1798-1803*, I, pp. 82-83; Wilkinson to Sargent, Oct. 28, 1798, in *Sargent Papers*, Massachusetts Historical Society.

Influenced by such theories and feeling the need of each other's support, they frequently conferred. Sometimes a personal matter concerned them. Once when the general was eager to have his family with him, he asked Sargent to write a few lines to Mrs. Wilkinson "commendatory of the climate and society" of the neighborhood.[48] And this was when the governor abominated Natchez and was recovering from a month's sickness; in addition, Mrs. Sargent was pregnant and ailing. Ellicott was steadfastly dosing himself with pills made of calomel, gamboge, and soap. A number of the soldiers were too ill for duty, and some had deserted. Wilkinson himself, though reasonably well, would soon suffer from "vernal floods" and summer heat. His disposition soured. He bitterly hated some of the local characters and tried to run them out of the territory.

One of these was Zachariah Cox, who had necessitated the sending of Colonel Butler with a detachment into Tennessee. After establishing an illegal settlement at Smithland, Cox had descended the Mississippi to explore the western country and make a commercial connection at New Orleans. Seven days after his arrival at Natchez, on August 18, 1798, he was arrested by Captain Isaac Guion and kept in jail for over a month with a motley collection of horse thieves. This strong-armed measure had been taken on the order of Wilkinson, who explained that Cox had settled on lands guaranteed to the Indians, organized an armed force enlisted for twelve months, and erected tribunals that had inflicted punishments "unknown to the nation." The general believed that the best way to "stifle the monster in Embryo," "to unmask the imposter . . . and to blow up the whole combination was to seize the chief actor." Cox was accordingly confined at Fort Panmure under secret charges until the night of September 26, when he escaped by climbing over the walls while the guard was, perhaps intentionally, negligent. He fled to New Orleans, but failed to arrive before Wilkinson sent word to the

---

[48] Wilkinson to Sargent, Oct. 20, 1798, *Sargent Papers*, Massachusetts Historical Society.

Spanish governor warning him that a leader of bandits was coming to stir up disorder and tumult. Gayoso merely issued a proclamation advising the inhabitants to be on their guard. Cox was not arrested in spite of Wilkinson's most urgent request. On hearing that the fugitive was returning north to "rescue his Brethren in confinement," the general offered Sargent $300 from federal funds to capture Cox. Cox was taken in the lower towns of the Choctaws. Samuel Mitchell, the federal Indian agent, interposed his authority, sending the adventurer under guard to Tennessee, the very place that he wanted to go. Though Wilkinson was partially thwarted, he had rid Natchez of a trouble-maker and had advertised himself as a stern and uncompromising enemy of transgressors. He had tried to enhance his reputation by eliminating a minor annoyance; later he would follow the same pattern of conduct on a larger scale—when Burr was dabbling in ambiguous schemes of conspiracy.[49]

By magnifying the difficulty of his task, Wilkinson hoped to gain more assistance from the War Department and to win greater recognition of his own feverish efforts. In 1798 no really valuable opportunity existed for self advertising. At the beginning of the year the Spaniards had agreed to fulfill their engagements under the Pinckney treaty. Gayoso, who had succeeded Carondelet as Governor of Louisiana, was a person of ability and charm. Though indifferent about stimulating activity toward the payment of the general's Spanish pension, he very willingly cooperated in evacuating the area recently ceded to the United States. He even allowed incoming American troops to be supplied over the more convenient routes passing through Spanish territory, accepting assurances that they came, not for aggression, but for the maintenance of law and order. Both agreed on a mutual surrender of deserters; each country's nationals guilty of offenses in the territory of the other were treated with consideration. When Matias

---

[49] I. J. Cox, "Documents Relating to Zachariah Cox," in *Quarterly Publications of Historical and Philosophical Society of Ohio*, VIII, pp. 31-114; J. R. Jacobs, *op. cit.*, pp. 174-175.

Augustin sold taffia without a permit to soldiers at three bits a pint, he was sentenced to 100 lashes and drumming out of camp with two bottles tied around his neck. Out of friendliness for Spain, the general remitted the lashes, informing Gayoso of what he had done. Soon Gayoso wrote a letter thanking him for the clemency that he had shown.[50]

Wilkinson clearly saw that both his official and personal interests would be helped by cultivating the good will of Gayoso. He knew that the government wanted the details of the Pinckney treaty amicably adjusted; he hoped that the Spaniards would continue to pay him liberally for fictitious services. He was still daring and venal enough to contrive enticing ruses for obtaining money. He wanted more than the $25,000 that the Spaniards had previously remitted to him at different times; but he was deeply perturbed lest the public become more fully acquainted with this phase of his conduct. In November 1797 Ellicott had written Timothy Pickering, who was then Secretary of State, that General Wilkinson, Senator John Brown of Kentucky, Benjamin Sebastian, and several other prominent persons along the Ohio, all enjoyed "annual stipends" from Carondelet and were suspected of trying to seduce Kentucky and Tennessee into an alliance with Spain so that a new empire might be created with Mexico as its center.[51] No official action was openly taken on this startling information. Perhaps it was thought to be wholly untrue. Public knowledge of such a scandal might have wrecked the administration of Adams. Investigation would have achieved little, especially since most of the incriminating evidence was in the hands of Spanish officials who could not be induced to testify. As a matter of fact, Adams may have considered their schemes so highly impractical that he permitted Wilkinson to continue his dubious role in order to learn what the agents of His Catholic Majesty were plotting at Natchez and New Orleans. If this be true,

[50] Wilkinson to Hamilton, Apr. 10, May 24, 1799, respectively in XXXIX and XLII of *Hamilton Papers*; Wilkinson, *Order Book, 1797-1807*, entry Nov. 19, 1798.

[51] Ellicott to Pickering, Nov. 14, 1797, *Pickering Papers*, Massachusetts Historical Society.

the federal government obtained its information for little, while the Spaniards paid Wilkinson handsomely to abet schemes that he never materially helped.

Nevertheless, having no desire that any of his shoddy transactions be reported through the agency of Ellicott, Wilkinson courted his friendship, cleverly winning his gratitude by lessening some of his troubles. Ellicott had plenty. One concerned his chief assistant, Thomas Freeman, who often went absent without leave, frequently became hilariously drunk, brandishing a sword and reciting Shakespeare without limit. He also kept up a "seditious correspondence" with Captain Isaac Guion, whom Ellicott hated. If this were not enough, there were other serious counts against him—he was "an idle, lying, troublesome, discontented, mischief-making man." Eager to be rid of Freeman and Lieutenant John McClary, a lazy fellow "under hostile influence" who commanded the escort, Ellicott appealed to Wilkinson, who in turn relieved the lieutenant and supported the discharge of Freeman for "impropriety," "disobedience," and "inflammatory conversation." Somewhat later Freeman was employed at Loftus Heights by Wilkinson who needed a surveyor and hoped to extract from him all that he knew about Ellicott and Spanish intrigues along the lower Mississippi. By then Ellicott had left the neighborhood and was indifferent as to what happened to his ex-employee. Wilkinson explained to Ellicott that he had hired Freeman from necessity, and meant "no deadening of affection" for Ellicott.[52] This excuse was apparently accepted.

In December 1798, Ellicott heard Wilkinson's name mentioned "in a manner that astonished" him. The whole thing was so bad that he did not have the temerity to "commit any part of it to paper." In writing to Wilkinson, he consolingly remarked that in its "most material point" he did not consider it true. The news was enough to startle Wilkinson and to confirm him in what he already suspected. In the preceding November he had written Gayoso that our "personal friendships have been interpreted into the most sinister designs, and falsehoods and fictions have been invented, from Natchez to Philadelphia, to rob me of my fame and fortune." Apparently Wilkinson believed that one of the best ways to stop the circulation of these embarrassing tales was to have Gayoso muzzle the affable Power, who, as a secret agent of Spain, was constantly traveling in the Southwest and was apparently responsible for the revealing letter from which Ellicott's information had been gleaned.[53]

The general continued on friendly terms with Gayoso. In fact, their intimacy seemed to grow. When Mrs. Wilkinson and the two boys came down the Mississippi in the spring of 1799, the governor offered them the use of Concordia, his country seat near Natchez; and it was eventually accepted on terms that may have had something to do with the general's pension. A certain Joseph Collins apparently acted as intermediary in the transaction when he went to New Orleans on a visit. He carried some cranberries with him—a gift from Mrs. Wilkinson to Madame Gayoso, the former Miss Watts, whose father was a Mississippi planter. The general could not refrain from informing her how rare they were in the South and how fine their "aromatic" flavor when properly prepared. So highly did he regard the Gayosos that he once thought of sending his elder son to New Orleans where he might improve his French and polish his manners under their tutelage. Once when Gayoso's daughter was traveling up the river, she stayed overnight with the Wilkinsons, and they were delighted with her. Later her family was invited to come and visit the Wilkinsons at Bayou Tara where they were planning to spend the summer.[54]

All such plans went awry because Wilkinson had to make a trip to the East. Washington and Hamilton insisted that he come and give advice about the organization and disposition of the enlarged forces of the army that had been

---

[53] Ellicott to Wilkinson, Dec. 16, 1798, *Ellicott Papers*, I, Library of Congress; Wilkinson to Gayoso, Nov. 19, 1798, A. G. I. Seville, *Papeles de Cuba*, leg. 2375.

[54] J. R. Jacobs, *op. cit.*, pp. 184-185.

authorized in the early months of 1799. Reluctantly Wilkinson prepared to leave. Mrs. Wilkinson very much wanted to go with him. She had made few friends in and around Natchez, and the responsibility of their two boys bore heavily upon her. In hope of dissuading her, he asked Gayoso to write and tell her of the trials and dangers of making a voyage from New Orleans to New York. When the time of departure came, she was pitifully distraught, fearing more than ever that misfortune would befall her beloved husband.

After making arrangements for her care at Concordia, the general set out for New Orleans, arriving there in June and becoming a house guest of the Gayosos. He greatly enjoyed his stay with them. Although the governor had little real estate, only a few slaves, and scant furniture, his conversation was "easy and affable and his politeness was of that superior cast, which showed it to be the effect of early habit, rather than the accomplishment merely intended to render him agreeable."[55]

When Wilkinson took passage in the "clumsy ship" waiting to carry him east, he did not realize that he would never again enjoy the friendship of his charming host. Fever took the governor away before the general had covered half his journey.

[55] *Journal of Andrew Ellicott*, p. 216.

9. *Short-lived Changes and Proposals*

THE treaties of 1795 settled some but not all of the existing difficulties with the British, Spanish, and Indians. In Tennessee the Cherokees murdered and stole wherever immigrants encroached on their lands or showed any weakness in defending themselves and their families. Tribes farther south were no more dependable, though less belligerent. Along the Canadian border British agents stirred up the savages, enticed our soldiers to desert, and made sport of the government that had recently taken over their evacuated forts. Even so, Spain believed that we were ready to help England seize St. Louis, New Madrid, New Orleans, and all the intervening territory. Moved by these unreasonable fears, she laid plans to strengthen her forces in the Southwest, alienate the frontiersmen from their federal allegiance, and cultivate friendly relations with the Creeks to our disadvantage. On the western border, from the Great Lakes to the Gulf, conditions were distracting and the minds of the people were filled with rumors of impending struggle.

In the East, war seemed even closer at hand. Our ships, once outside of their home ports, often encountered the British who showed no respect for American rights on the open seas. Pirates harried our Mediterranean trade. In a fit of nonsensical foreign policy we decided to build the pirates a warship hoping that they might despoil others instead of ourselves. In apparent forgetfulness, we were quickly and fervently declaring: "Millions for defense but not one cent for tribute." This ringing slogan was our answer to the French Directory's demand for apologies and bribes before our envoys might put a foot in Talleyrand's door. An undeclared war soon followed. In the two years between 1798 and 1800 we succeeded in capturing eighty French armed ships.

On January 24, 1798, Adams met the Cabinet and asked advice of his colleagues. McHenry had no helpful answers, but he did write immediately to Hamilton asking for suggestions. They came quickly, suggesting a regular force of 20,000 and a provisional army of 30,000 men. At the same time he added, "Let the President recommend a day to be observed as a day of fasting, humiliation, and prayer. On religious grounds, this is very proper; on political, it is very expedient." By February 15 the well-meaning but futile McHenry submitted a report, embodying practically all that Hamilton had recommended.[1]

Nothing immediately resulted. During the next three months there was only piecemeal legislation. An additional regiment of artillerists and engineers was authorized for five years; $250,000 was appropriated for fortification, and $800,000 was set aside to purchase heavy and small arms. Hamilton thought that we needed 1,000 cannons, ranging from eighteen pounds to thirty-two pounders, chiefly 32's. During 1794 and 1796 we had let contracts to domestic manufacturers for 358 cannons of this general type; by April 1798 only 183 of them had been delivered. The future held no promise that they would be more rapidly supplied. Hence, in spite of such measures of Congress, the people along the sea-coast could not feel that they would be adequately protected. Often forts had been poorly constructed, garrisons were too small, and armament inadequate or antiquated.[2]

More effective steps were taken to strengthen our mobile forces by the act of May 28, 1798, providing for a three-year provisional army of 10,000 men whenever President Adams believed it should be raised. Volunteers were to be accepted; as a rule they had to be armed, clothed, and equipped at their own expense unless they

[1] B. C. Steiner, *The Life and Correspondence of James McHenry*, pp. 291-295.

[2] J. F. Callan, *The Military Laws of the United States* (revised edition), pp. 199-222; B. C. Steiner, *op. cit.*, p. 361; T. H. S. Hamersly, *Army Register* (second part), p. 237.

belonged to the artillery. In this case, they, like the militia, might be loaned arms and accoutrements by the federal government. Equipment for 3,000 cavalry was to be purchased and stored at places convenient for distribution. To accelerate preparedness, the government offered to sell 30,000 stands of arms to the states. The command of this new force was to rest in the hands of a lieutenant general, who had as staff a quartermaster general, paymaster general, inspector general, and other important assistants.[3]

Immediately the eyes of the people turned toward Washington to lead these troops in battle. John Adams had said of him the year before: "His name may still be a rampart, and the knowledge that he lives, a bulwark against all open or secret enemies of his country's peace." Therefore, as President, he wrote and urged him to accept the command of the contemplated forces, knowing that his presence would lend strength and prestige to the army and that under him "all hearts and all hands" would be united. At this time Washington was sixty-six years old. He expressed reluctance to venture from retirement unless his country was actually invaded. Even so, the Senate quickly ratified his appointment as a lieutenant general on July 7, 1798. Adams declared that if he could have submitted his name for President, he would have done so "with less hesitation and more pleasure."[4] In accepting his commission Washington asked not to assume any duties or receive any pay until he actually took the field. Subordinates were to be entrusted with the preliminary organization and supply. A little more than a year went by. Washington did not again put on his buff and blue uniform and gird his sword around him; instead, he lived quietly at Mount Vernon for two more autumns, supervising the harvesting of his crops from the rounded hills and watching the steel-gray waters of the Potomac flow by. Death took him on December 14, 1799. Even the boisterous and ignorant

[3] J. F. Callan, *op. cit.*, pp. 122-125.
[4] T. H. S. Hamersly, *op. cit.* (second part), p. 235.

were silent, because they knew a great man had passed and his virtues would bless their country no more.[5]

Unlike the choice of Washington, there was nothing unanimous in the choice of his principal subordinates. When the news leaked out that his major generals would be Alexander Hamilton, C. C. Pinckney, and Henry Knox, in order of rank, Adams was angry, believing New England had been treated unfairly. Knox, in disgust, said that he never would serve—and did not. In addition, Adams wanted his son-in-law, W. S. Smith, made adjutant general with the rank of brigadier general—a scheme hateful to Timothy Pickering, secretary of state, who much preferred Jonathan Dayton. Pickering also wanted John Sevier made a general. McHenry believed Sevier had no principles, but was willing to approve his appointment because he believed it would be merely nominal and would certainly please Tennessee. When Smith's name reached the Senate, Pickering succeeded in having it rejected. Later, after being ousted from the Cabinet, Pickering declared Smith to be a "swindler," in spite of having previously stated to McHenry, secretary of war, that he would make a "good officer." Adams declared the whole thing an intrigue, that his son-in-law was not in debt any more than Knox or Henry Lee, and that his creditors were satisfied with his conduct.[6] In spite of the efforts of his family, Smith was not commissioned in the army.

The initial burden of organization and training largely fell upon the new major generals, Alexander Hamilton and C. C. Pinckney. Thanks to them and others, various acts were passed to increase the army and make it more effective. After July 16, 1798, each infantry regiment was to have 704 enlisted men and 39 officers who did duty with one of ten companies or were members of the regimental staff. The staff consisted of a surgeon, two mates, an adjutant, quartermaster, and paymaster. Another improvement allowed privates, corporals, and sergeants to receive a pay increase of a dollar a month. A larger ration allowance,

5 *Dictionary of American Biography*, XIX, pp. 509-527.
6 B. C. Steiner, *op. cit.*, pp. 311-314.

once drawn by frontier troops only, was supplied the army as a whole. Since artillerists needed instruction and guidance, four civilian teachers and an officer as an inspector were provided for them. To stimulate enlistment, recruits were lured with a $12 bounty. Many would be needed if the President decided to raise, as Congress had authorized, twelve new regiments of infantry and six troops of light dragoons "for and during the continuance of the existing differences between the United States and the French Republic."[7] Believing conditions did not justify these additional troops, Adams refrained from recruiting them.

At the same time, July 16, 1798, another law transferred the purchase of supplies for the army from the Treasury to the War Department. This was a constructive change long overdue. The Purveyor of Public Supplies did the actual purchasing at the direction of the secretary of war. The expenditures and accounts, however, were still subject to inspection and revision by the Treasury Department.[8]

About seven and a half months later, the medical department underwent reorganization. Since none could foresee the requirements of war, a framework was established by the law of March 2, 1799, permitting almost any degree of expansion if occasion demanded. A physician general had supervision of all hospitals and medical service; a purveyor acted as purchasing agent for medical supplies, which an apothecary general was either to store or send wherever needed. The exact number of surgeons and mates might vary with conditions; they could be detached from their organizations to duty with hospitals that might be established. Hospitals were to be provided with stewards, nurses, and other attendants; they were to be no haven of refuge for idlers, skulkers, or gamblers. Officers in charge must keep the hospitals clean and see that no infectious disease spread there or elsewhere.[9]

On the same day that these changes in the medical department were being translated into law, the President

---

[7] J. F. Callan, *op. cit.*, pp. 127-128. [8] *Ibid.*, p. 129.
[9] *Ibid.*, pp. 129-131.

was authorized to raise twenty-four regiments of infantry and three of cavalry, a regiment and a battalion of riflemen, and a battalion of artillerists and engineers, in case war should occur or invasion be threatened. For the purpose of filling the ranks, each state was allotted a quota, and those whom a state raised were not to be ordered beyond its borders for more than three months.[10] Thus Congress had tried to shift responsibility to the shoulders of the President and had simultaneously prevented his effective use of any increased forces by forbidding him to send them wherever conditions warranted. Whether for this reason, for economy, improved foreign relations, or something else, he did not see fit to raise any of the troops at all.

On the day following this false gesture of preparedness, the last session of the Fifth Congress ended. In accordance with the law of March 3, the strength of infantry and cavalry regiments was to be 1,026 men, 29 officers, and 10 cadets. Artillery regiments were larger than either: 1,043 men, 59 officers, and 32 cadets. The names ensign and coronet were discontinued and second lieutenant was substituted for both. In a few cases, the monthly pay of officers was increased. Majors of cavalry and artillery were to have $5 more than those in the infantry; regimental paymasters, quartermasters, and adjutants were given $16 more, $6 of which was considered their allowance for forage. The whisky ration was cut to one-half a gill, and its issue depended upon the wish of the commanding officer. To help the soldier look more presentable, the price for altering his clothing was fixed at twenty-five cents for a coat and eight for a vest, breeches, or overalls. For all of the troops so organized and previously authorized "a general of the armies of the United States" was to be appointed. In addition to his aides, he was to have a staff of a quartermaster general, inspector general, adjutant general, and a paymaster general. They in turn were to have an adequate number of assistants. When troops were discharged, they were to have pay and rations for the num-

10 *Ibid.,* pp. 131-133.

ber of days necessary for them to travel home. Twenty miles was regarded as a day's journey.[11]

While this whirlwind of army legislation was bowling over the pacifists and rendering our country dubiously safe, Alexander Hamilton wrote to Wilkinson asking him to come to the seat of government in order to help in working out some of the practical details of reorganization and to bring the latest information about the actions of the Spaniards, Indians, and settlers in the Southwest. On August 1, 1799, Wilkinson arrived in New York from New Orleans. He immediately called on Hamilton, now a major general and his senior. Wilkinson, having outranked him during the Revolution, did not enjoy his subordinate position; but, thanks to Hamilton's preeminent ability and unfailing tact, Wilkinson tried to serve him reasonably well.[12]

Possibly Wilkinson was aware that Hamilton had previously urged his promotion in a letter to McHenry. In it he declared that "half confidence is always bad." Since Wilkinson had adopted military life as a profession, "what," Hamilton asked, "can his ambition do better than be faithful to the government if it gives him fair play?" McHenry replied that "until the commercial pursuits of this gentleman, with his expectations from Spain, are annihilated, he will not deserve the confidence of government." But at the same time he added that he would not oppose his promotion if Washington desired it. Washington did nothing, declaring that other officers had been appointed without consulting him and that he did not expect the administration to shoulder off on him its own responsibility in dubious cases. There the matter rested when Wilkinson arrived to take orders from Major General Hamilton.[13]

The two often conferred at length. They discussed settlers on the frontier, Indians, and Spaniards, the best

11 *Ibid.*, pp. 133-139.
12 J. Wilkinson, *Memoirs of My Own Times*, I, pp. 437-438.
13 B. C. Steiner, *op. cit.*, pp. 396-397.

defensive and offensive plans for the Ohio and Mississippi country, and how an army there could best obtain supplies and maintain communications with the Atlantic seaboard. To make his own suggestions more definite, Wilkinson drew up a letter of some eighteen pages addressed to Hamilton. In it he gave his estimate of the situation as it concerned the western country from Canada to East Florida. To prevent any hostile irruption from Canada, he suggested a wiser and more economical use of our troops. Such forts as "Oswego, Presqu'isle, Fort Fayette, Fort Washington, Fort Wayne, and Fort Knox" should be abandoned. Garrisons at these places were no longer needed to defend the neighboring inhabitants from Indian raids; they ought to be concentrated at a few strategic points where they would be more adequately trained and have less chance of being beaten in detail. His theory was correct, but the program was scuttled then, as similar plans have been scuttled many times since by politicians with purely local minds. In the Southwest an entirely different condition prevailed. The "imbecility" and weakness of the Spaniards invited attack by the "gallant Louisianians." If this occurred, the Union might be dismembered. To prevent such a disaster and keep this area free from Indian menace, he believed three infantry regiments, three companies of artillery, two troops of cavalry, and two galleys would prove sufficient. He declared that the organizations there must be concentrated. The ranks, too, should be filled. Returns from the 1st, 2nd, and 3rd Regiments of infantry and a battalion of artillery disclosed that they were widely scattered in small detachments, seldom more than a company at any one post, and that they were short nearly three-fifths of their authorized personnel. They lacked eleven lieutenants, five surgeon's mates, thirty cadets, three sergeant majors, five quartermaster sergeants, five senior musicians, sixty sergeants, fifty-one corporals, ten drummers, sixteen fifers, and one thousand and fifty-one privates. In addition, eighteen captains and forty-four lieutenants were reported absent. For seven years the colonel of the 3rd Regiment had not seen his organization; for three, the senior major had been enjoying a leave.[14]

In addition to these glaring defects, Wilkinson might have added that the health of some of the troops in the Southwest was so poor that they could not be used effectively. The climate was debilitating and the treatment of local maladies was not well understood. Medicines and hospital supplies had been put off at Fort Massac for disposition by the officer commanding Mississippi Territory; months slipped by before they ever were forwarded to the posts where they were acutely needed. On July 22, 1799, Captain Zebulon Pike wrote that he and most of his company were sick at Fort Pickering, once Fort Adams. The only man able to make out a return was too ill to do it; no medicines were on hand for his cure. By October the shirts for those on fatigue had completely worn out; he declared that to have his men work with such a shortage of clothing was "inhuman." In addition, his acting carpenter was down with a rupture and of his six oxen three were dead, one mad, and the other two were having fits of distemper. Pike could neither build nor repair. His men were querulous and yearned to be elsewhere. Three of them had been sent down the river to be tried for desertion. Two others had recently had a fight, using "the weapons God Almighty had furnished them." As a result, one was dead, the other was in irons awaiting the orders of Wilkinson. As Pike thought of his unhappy command, he felt in no mood to write any more. He was a good officer, but the conditions with which he had to cope were almost overwhelming.[15]

Perhaps Captain Benjamin Shaumburgh, 2nd Infantry, was no better off. He was the commanding officer at Fort Stoddert, which had been established during 1799. Many of his troops were ailing, and by July he had used up all medicines with only slight prospect of soon getting any more. Being a firm believer in the therapeutic value of

[14] Wilkinson to Hamilton, Sept. 4, 1799, in J. Wilkinson, *op. cit.*, I, pp. 440-458.

[15] Pike to Cushing, July 22, Oct. 13, 1799, in *Military Book*, No. 154, The National Archives.

liquor and eggnogs, he went out and purchased for his hospital patients fifteen gallons of brandy, twice as much wine, and a small amount of chocolate. Before long the government reprimanded him for unwarranted extravagance. While the government considered itself too poor to approve such purchases, it was allowing the commissary at Mobile, fifty miles distant, to issue gratuitously every month 300 bushels of corn to the neighboring Indians. Although the law required that the pay of soldiers be promptly settled, those at Fort Stoddert had drawn none for eight or ten months. Hence they could not buy the fever and dysentery remedies that the hospital could not furnish. Surgical cases also fared badly. Since the post surgeon had reported without any instruments, the quartermaster had to furnish a broad ax when an amputation became necessary. Owing to these conditions and unusual rains, the sick list continued to grow. In great anxiety Shaumburgh exclaimed, "God knows when it will stop." During July his drummer died; the records of others who followed him were closed in August and September. In the following winter the camp doctor came to a singular end—caused by a "fall on a full bottle of rum which he carried in his pocket. He expired almost instantaneously."[16]

With so many casualties, work on the fortifications lagged, although the able-bodied labored eight hours daily upon them. When the guns were in position, they could not be fired long or easily, for Shaumburgh had no slow match and only a little powder. With things as they were, soldiers were discontented and restless. Some deserted, but most of them were apprehended and brought back. Three such offenders had to pay $100 for their capture and walk the gantlet through the troops of the post eighteen times while switches were well laid on. Shaumburgh, though German and stern in discipline, had to admit that such a "damned out of the way place" without any interest gave his men excuses for leaving. He himself was a little more fortunate. Occasionally he could go to New Orleans or

16 Shaumburgh to Cushing, July 19, Aug. 31, Oct. 20, Dec. 1, 1799, in *Military Book*, No. 154, The National Archives.

entertain travelers passing by. Once on December 26, 1800, a pair of lovers accompanied by a large party of friends turned up at sunrise and wanted him to act as a parson and marry them—for him a singular role that he never had filled. But he finally consented. He pronounced them man and wife, bade them go home, behave themselves and "multiply and replenish the Tensaw country." They are reputed to have acted accordingly.[17]

North of the Ohio and along the Atlantic seaboard, troops were healthier and better cared for than in the Southwest. In 1799 the five companies at Detroit were reasonably contented and fairly well supplied with essentials. They even received a few luxuries that came mostly by water down the Ohio and across the Great Lakes. Game and crops were usually abundant in the neighborhood. Settlers generally lived in rude plenty. Hoping to remain at Detroit for years, officers and men made permanent improvements, bought land, and purchased cows, horses, and tools. Colonel Hamtramck himself owned three stills; he and Robert Abbott planned to establish a distillery for the purpose of selling liquor to settlers, army contractors, trappers, and traders. When some of the troops had to change station in 1800, they very grudgingly sacrificed their local investments.[18]

At Fort Washington, troops fared equally well. The Ohio River was a constantly traveled thoroughfare from the East, and things that could not be raised or manufactured locally came down the river at a price only a little above that demanded in the large cities along the Atlantic coast. At Pittsburgh many an immigrant was also willing to part with his surplus at a very small profit. Garrisons at Presque Isle, Niagara, and other out-of-the-way places were not equally fortunate: they had few luxuries and often lacked necessities. Troops around Philadelphia, Baltimore, New York, and Boston were better off than

---

[17] Ibid.; A. J. Pickett, History of Alabama, II, pp. 183-184.
[18] Agreement Abbott and Hamtramck, Aug. 24, 1799, Hamphor receipts, Jan. 22, 1800, and Audian to Hamtramck, Apr. 17, 1800, in Hamtramck Papers, 1783-1803, Burton Collection, Detroit Public Library.

those anywhere else. Usually they were healthy, drew their pay more frequently, and had all the allowances and equipment that the government had promised them. They were much nearer bases of supply and closer to the seats of the mighty; their complaints could not be conveniently ignored and were more easily satisfied.

The frequent dearth of supplies at frontier posts often came about for two reasons—difficulties of transportation and unreasonable government economy. In respect to hospital stores, a general ignorance of medicine and therapy also contributed. Though McHenry, Dearborn, Eustis, and Wilkinson were all doctors, none of them did anything significant to improve the health of the army. Usually supplies could not be contracted for until appropriations were made for them. McHenry tried to obtain double appropriations so that medical supplies could be bought a year in advance, but he did not succeed.[19] No matter how plentiful things were in the East, they could not be sent to Mackinac, Detroit, and Presque Isle when ice closed the Great Lakes to shipping. When forwarded, they were usually put up in separate bundles addressed to the captain of the company. In 1799 hospital stores for different sections varied little; wine, brandy, and chocolate were included in all of them. Some Congressmen considered these inexcusable luxuries and thought that $10,000 was plenty of money to buy everything that the sick in the army needed for a year.[20] Officers could never feel sure that their requisitions would be completely filled. During 1799 McHenry declared that some of the articles requested were not included because they were deemed unessential, too costly, or could not be purchased.[21] Not even the best hospital supplies and medical treatment of the time could have saved all of the sick, but at least a much larger number of them should have escaped a four-dollar coffin and a burying hole on a neigh-

[19] McHenry to Wilkinson, Jan. 31, 1799, in *Wilkinson Papers*, Chicago Historical Society.

[20] T. H. Benton, *Abridgment of the Debates of Congress from 1789 to 1856*, II, p. 93.

[21] McHenry to Wilkinson, Jan. 31, 1799, in *Wilkinson Papers*, Chicago Historical Society.

boring hill. Those left behind would not have heard so frequently the distressing notes of the funeral march that announced that one of their comrades had left the ranks without his final papers.

Sometimes a shortage of clothing arose from other causes. Materials could not be obtained, needlewomen were scarce, and regulations were exacting. During Adams's time the right kinds of cloth could not be bought in large enough quantities at home or imported from abroad. Soldiers went without new vests, coats, or other articles. Hamilton did not help the situation. He made changes in the uniform that were highly decorative but had nothing to do with the business of fighting. The commanding general of the army was to join battle in magnificent array. He was to wear a full cocked hat with a white plume and a golden eagle, an elaborately embroidered blue coat with numerous trimmings in buff, a pair of golden epaulettes with three stars in each, white or buff breeches with buttons and buckles, a vest of the same hue with horizontal pocket flaps, black stiff-topped boots that were lined with red morocco, plated gold spurs, and a cut-and-thrust sword some twenty-eight inches long with a golden hilt. Other general officers, major and brigadier generals, had similar but not equally resplendent uniforms—plumes differed in color, stars were fewer, and half boots and pantaloons were permissible. For the lower commissioned grades, shoulder straps were introduced; field officers wore two epaulettes, those of inferior grade a single one. Worsted epaulettes marked the rank of noncommissioned officers. All ranks wore cocked hats decorated with a cockade and an eagle. For enlisted men the cockade was leather and the eagle tin. In the infantry and artillery, coats were blue with red facings; in the cavalry, green with white facings. The regimental number of each soldier was marked on his white buttons.[22]

[22] General Orders, Fort Adams, Mar. 30, 1800, Old Records, Adjutant General's Office, National Archives. See also A. B. Gardner, "The Uniforms of the American Army," in *Magazine of American History*, Aug., 1877, pp. 461-492.

One of the major causes of the lack of clothing, medicines, rations, et cetera, was the poor organization of the supply department. Hamilton pointed it out when he declared to McHenry that the management of the supply agents was "ridiculously bad. Besides the extreme delay, which attends every operation, articles go forward in the most incomplete manner. Coats without a corresponding number of vests. Cartouche boxes without belts, etc., nothing entire—nothing systematic. 'Tis the scene of the worst periods of our Revolution acted over again even with caricature—materials for tents were purchased here [in New York City] and sent to Philadelphia. This was done in regard to clothing and it is truly farcical—proving that the microscopic eye of the Purveyor can see nothing beyond Philadelphia . . . unless you immediately employ more competent agents to procure and forward supplies, the services will deeply suffer and the head of the War Department will be completely discredited."

"You must immediately get a more efficient Purveyor and I believe a more efficient superintendent—or nothing can prosper."

Though familiar with such incompetence, McHenry did nothing to eliminate it. He retained the purveyor, Tench Francis, but gave him an assistant. Colonel Stevens, the superintendent, was too strongly supported for anything to be done. As a result, the business of supply went on as before. It proceeded "heavily without order or punctuality," "disjointed and piece-meal," "ill-adapted to economy" and "the contentment of the Army."[23]

Leaving Hamilton to solve these and other difficult problems, Wilkinson started on his journey to the Southwest. He had now been in the East for four and a half months and had given the government all his information. Major Thomas H. Cushing, senior officer at Natchez, was not very adept at solving the irritating problems that were constantly arising along the Spanish-American frontier.

[23] Hamilton to McHenry, June 14, 1799, McHenry to Hamilton, June 15, 1799; Hamilton to McHenry, Aug. 19, 1799. All of the above in B. C. Steiner, *op. cit.*, pp. 390-391, 409-413.

By February 11, 1800, Wilkinson was back at New Orleans, endeavoring to carry out the War Department's program.

On the 12th, the Marquis de Casa Calvo and his officers made a ceremonial call. Wilkinson was considerably impressed, believing that, like the late Gayoso de Lemos, Casa Calvo was eager to cooperate with him. Both reiterated their desire for peaceful relations between their countries and agreed to continue the existing arrangement for the mutual surrender of deserters. Believing that the aims of the United States were friendly, the Spaniards granted permission for army supplies to pass through New Orleans without any duty. With Indian annuities, these were considerable. This dispensation was important to the United States. Sending the same things across the Pennsylvania mountains and then down the Ohio and Mississippi involved much more time and greater expense. The Spaniards saw no reason to oppose the Americans, particularly when they knew that they could do nothing but cause irritation. In addition they wanted our help in keeping the Indians at peace, especially requesting that Wilkinson apprehend William Augustus Bowles, an able renegade who was stirring up trouble among the Creeks. Wilkinson promised to prevent him from using the United States territory as a haven of refuge or base of operations, suggesting to Hamilton that he be "put out of the way on fair principles."[24] Calvo did not want Bowles to cause trouble at this time because the British were threatening to attack both Pensacola and New Orleans from Jamaica. Nor did the United States care to see any power stronger than Spain in control of the Mississippi area. Wilkinson, therefore, found it relatively easy to work out a rapprochement between the two countries.

While the general was negotiating with the Spaniards and keeping a sharp eye on the Indians, our relations with

[24] Wilkinson to Hamilton, Feb. 12, 1800, in *Hamilton Papers*, LXIX, The Library of Congress. This letter differs from the one referred to in note 25. See also Wilkinson to Hamilton, Mar. 7, 1800, *Hamilton Papers*, LXX, The Library of Congress.

the French were improving. On November 9 and 10, 1799, the Directory had been overthrown and the government of France had fallen into the abler and firmer hands of Napoleon, who wanted the friendship of the United States when Europe was swarming with his enemies. With brighter prospects of peace, Adams and his colleagues halted increase of defenses. He stopped recruiting the twelve new regiments of infantry previously authorized. They were to be numbered from 5 to 16 inclusive. In accordance with the records nearest to January 2, 1800, some 3,399 men had already been enlisted for this new force, exclusive of the 5th Regiment. They were stationed in Massachusetts, New Jersey, Virginia, and Georgia.[25] In May they were ordered to be discharged beginning on June 15, both officers and men receiving three months' pay as an aid toward adjusting themselves to civil pursuits. The recruiting of six troops of light dragoons had not begun. The only organizations to be retained in the service were two troops of cavalry, 116 strong, two regiments totaling 1,501 artillerists and engineers, and four regiments of infantry consisting of 1,812 men. Although war was still threatening, the United States was left with only 3,429 regulars. Except for a single battalion scattered along the frontier, the artillerists and engineers were stationed in small detachments along the Atlantic seaboard from Portland, Maine, to St. Mary's, Georgia.[26]

While these steps were being taken to discharge the forces extemporaneously raised, McHenry was trying to evolve means for bettering the army that remained. The constant threat from foreign countries had made the thoughtful realize that we must be able to do something more than crush the Indians and deal effectively with domestic distempers. McHenry appreciated that better facilities must be established to instruct our young officers and help our older ones become acquainted with the progress of military art. In keeping with this idea, he recommended to the President on January 5, 1800 that a

[25] *American State Papers, Military Affairs,* I, pp. 132, 146-151.
[26] *Ibid.,* I, pp. 139-141.

"Military Academy" be established consisting of "The Fundamental School," "The School of Engineers and Artillerists," "The School of the Navy," "The School of Cavalry and Infantry." Instruction at the Fundamental School was to cover two years, usually would be required of all cadets, and must be completed before attending any of the other three. The more specialized courses would be conducted for a similar length of time, except that the advanced course would last only a year for cavalry and infantry. Officers would be eligible for these schools and be placed where their capacity and training warranted. Even sergeants might attend according to McHenry's plan. He wanted enough additional sergeants to fill the requirements of an army of 50,000 men. They were to alternate between school and troop duty. Thus emergencies would be partially cared for. The cost of such thoughtful insurance against the future would be slight. McHenry estimated that buildings for "The Fundamental School" and "The School of Artillerists and Engineers," which were first to be established, would cost a minimum of about $40,000 and a maximum of $80,000. The salaries of professors would amount to $10,489 a year. He hoped to save some $25,000 from current appropriations through reorganization. He might have pointed out that since 1794 Congress had set aside $620,000 for fortifying our ports, a sum so large that only $512,381 of it had been spent by October 1, 1799.[27] The balance remaining would have been more than enough to establish his system of schools—an idea without political appeal that proved entirely too good for adoption. Brick, mortar, and iron were more tangible and had popular support.

Along with such recommendations, McHenry made others of less value. He strongly urged the organization of a regiment of horse-artillery, one of engineers, and one of foot-artillery in place of the two existing regiments of artillerists and engineers. Under this plan the horse-artillery would have no horses except in time of war, the engineers no enlisted personnel except four companies of

[27] *Ibid.*, I, pp. 133-139, 142-144.

artificers and miners, and the foot-artillery would function much like the artillery of the past—as infantry that knew how to keep field pieces in some sort of order and how to fire them when necessary.[28] Members of Congress were not impressed with these suggestions. They paid more attention to his request to make our harbors impregnable. They made money available for this purpose. During April 1800 they gave a slight increase of pay and allowances to the paymaster and assistants of the adjutant general. In the next month they took steps to prevent interruption of work at public arsenals and armories. The employees in both were exempted from military and jury duty. To lure employees away from their job would cost the offender $50 and three months' imprisonment. Sabotage or failure to do assigned work entailed a forfeiture of $20.[29] A larger and more dependable supply of munitions was expected to result.

While such changes were being discussed or put in effect, Wilkinson was on his way back to the capital. He was the only general officer left after the army had been reorganized and the temporary forces discharged. It was well to consult him concerning the administration and disposition of the troops that remained. News from the Southwest would be especially helpful, for in this area the government was still having trouble with Indians and lawless whites. In coming north on the *General Green*, a 32-gun frigate, he stopped over a few days at Havana, where he learned something of the money and perquisites that the officials of Spain were accustomed to enjoy. He also found himself looking upon their women "with strong emotions of admiration and desire." If this information did not help the War Department, he doubtless had other that did.[30]

Wilkinson reached Georgetown early in July 1800. Here he found the War Department under new direction. On May 5, the President had called in McHenry, roundly abused him, and demanded that he resign as secretary. He offered the position to John Marshall, who immediately

---

[28] *Ibid.*, I, pp. 135-139.   [29] J. F. Callan, *op. cit.*, pp. 139-140.
[30] J. R. Jacobs, *Tarnished Warrior*, pp. 192-193.

refused it. Adams was especially angry because he believed that McHenry, under Hamilton's influence, was covertly trying to prevent his reelection. Many of the public wanted a change for more convincing reasons. Wilkinson, as we have seen, regarded McHenry as a "mock minister," knowing little or nothing about the service. Hamilton considered him "wholly insufficient for his place," with the additional misfortune of not having the "least suspicion of the fact." He declared that his incompetence was "so great as to leave no probability that the business of the War Department can make any tolerable progress in his hands"—a condition with which both the President and Congress were acquainted.[31] Washington himself held a similar opinion; according to him, McHenry's "talents were unequal to great exertions or deep resources." Indeed, he confessed that they were not expected to be; his selection as Secretary had been purely a Hobson's choice.[32]

With war in prospect, McHenry was certainly not the type "to ride the tempest or command the storm." Without unusual mental gifts he groped along, frequently losing himself in a mass of details. He reached conclusions slowly —never through the short-cuts of a penetrating mind. When defending any cause, he entirely lacked dynamic qualities. The support that he enjoyed largely resulted from his genial manners and assiduity as a politician, both of which enabled him to acquire friends and recognition from the members of the Federalist party. In spirit and intelligence, he was among the followers, not the leaders, of men. Unfortunately he had climbed to a position of prominence where the smallness of his stature was only too apparent. Few would have known his shortcomings had he been content to hold a lower office.

With McHenry out and John Marshall not interested, Adams needed another secretary of war to serve at least

[31] A. J. Beveridge, *The Life of John Marshall*, II, p. 485; Wilkinson to Pratt, Dec. 27, 1799, *Pratt Papers*, Connecticut State Library; Hamilton to Washington, July 29, 1798, in B. C. Steiner, *op. cit.*, pp. 319-320.

[32] Washington to Hamilton, Aug. 9, 1798, in B. C. Steiner, *op. cit.*, p. 322.

until the next inauguration in 1801. The position was offered to Samuel Dexter, who accepted it the very day that McHenry's resignation became effective, May 13. He did not immediately come to Washington. The climate and accommodations were better elsewhere, Congress was not then in session, and most of the War Department's work during the summer could be done by Wilkinson and other subordinates. General Wilkinson, in fact, continued in or around Georgetown until some time in December. While attending to matters of army routine, he did not fail to strengthen his friendship with the Democratic Republicans who were soon to sweep into office. He especially appealed to the far-traveled and ever-curious Jefferson. Few knew the great Southwest as well as Philip Nolan, whose trips along the Mississippi and into Texas the general had frequently underwritten. Wilkinson and Nolan, being in Washington during the summer of 1800, skillfully kindled the interest of the incoming President in the country across the Mississippi that lay ready for taking. They exhibited articles that disclosed its interesting character—maps of various sorts, Indian weapons and tools, meteorological records, plants of the region, and objects that nature had turned to stone. Nolan told of the innumerable wild horses, some of which he hoped to bring into Louisiana and sell at a profit. Apparently encouraged by Jefferson and Wilkinson, Nolan returned to the Southwest and ventured once more into Texas. There the Spaniards soon killed him as a filibusterer, cutting off his ears to send to their governor as proof that he would disturb them no more.[33]

After seeing his protégé depart on this fatal journey, Wilkinson did administrative chores. According to him, McHenry had left papers in confusion, and these had to be straightened out.[34] The task was probably just what he wanted. He was rather adept at it, and he preferred to stay in Washington until he could call the turn in politics.

Soon Wilkinson's labors were lightened in a rather

[33] J. R. Jacobs, op. cit., p. 194.
[34] Wilkinson to Hamilton, July 28, 1800, in *Hamilton Papers*, LXXVIII, The Library of Congress.

surprising way. On the evening of November 8, 1800, the building partly occupied by the War Department was burned, and practically all of its records were turned into ashes. Some said sparks had come from the chimney of an adjoining room not occupied by government offices; others declared this surmise impossible, for there a corpse was laid out and the fire on the hearth had burned very low. What actually occurred has never been proved. When the Treasury Department suffered a similar disaster in January 1801, tongues wagged more violently than before.[35] By then everyone knew that the Democratic Republicans would soon be in control and would minutely examine all the papers of the out-going Federalists.

Since by December 1800 Wilkinson had done about all that he could and had apparently received some assurance that he would be continued as ranking officer in the army, he left Washington and headed for Pittsburgh, where he remained for several months. At Pittsburgh was Fort Fayette, which had been established shortly after St. Clair's defeat. Its original use for defense against Indians had passed; it now served as a great depot for supplies destined for the Northwest and a stopping point for travelers between the frontier and the cities of the East. At Fort Fayette Wilkinson set his men to repairing, whitewashing, and remodelling the barracks and quarters.[36] He did much to make it a comfortable and attractive post. It delighted him to see buildings and grounds that showed planning and care. Fatigue details, however, did not share in his pleasure. They were happy when he started on his way back to Washington about the first of March. He was eager to be present at the inauguration of Jefferson.

Colonel Hamtramck was left in command. He, too, wanted to know how the army would fare under the incoming administration. Writing to his friend North for an opinion, he was sent a reply that revealed a few pertinent

[35] *American State Papers, Miscellaneous Affairs*, I, pp. 247-252.
[36] *Expenditures in the Naval and Military Establishments*, 1797-1801, *passim*.

suggestions for personal guidance. In part the letter ran: "I think, however, that they (our changed rulers) cannot lessen the little army which now exists. I believe they will not add to it—but let it remain where it is. It is not impossible but Gen. Wilkinson (who it has been said, *entre nous*, was friendly to the politics of the reigning party) may have the fortune to be promoted, if so I think you ought to follow of course. I think, as the new government, or rather the party which have been bellowing and howling against the army, navy and all sorts of expense which the federalists thought necessary for our security, are new in power there will be little hopes of your getting the rank and pay of a Brig.—and as to the rank by brevet it is but a phantom without substance. . . . Gen. W.[ilkinson] is good natured, and I suspect very capable of acting generously by those to whom he is friendly. It is the duty of all to be attentive to those who command them—and it is to their interest to be *well* with the commander-in-chief. His friendship or vanity frequently decides the lot of those who look for promotion. Everything in our political horizon is clouding, or at least changing, whether a clear or a foul day will follow, cannot be seen. Do your duty, and when the time shall offer, if I should [have] a friend of influence in the new Government, I will speak to him of your services and merit which I think of as much as you can wish."[37]

But during the three remaining years that Hamtramck lived, he was not made happy by promotion. When the inauguration occurred, he was presumed, as the senior officer present, to celebrate it in some appropriate fashion. Both he and his wife had come lately from Detroit and had few friends at Pittsburgh. The enmity between political parties and Mrs. Hamtramck's lack of social understanding made matters worse. Finally the colonel decided to have a party for his officers and the leading men of the neighborhood, believing that they, at least, would come. They did, much enjoying a dinner during the afternoon. At the same hour, the very popular Mrs. Wilkinson held a

[37] North to Hamtramck, Feb. 23, 1801, *Hamtramck Papers*, Burton Collection, Detroit Public Library.

reception for the ladies, inviting them to linger afterwards for a fireworks display. They accepted with delight; and the men, now jovial from the numerous toasts at the Hamtramcks, went over to join them. For a time, personal and political differences were forgotten and the Federalists and Democratic-Republicans swore fealty to each other.[38]

38 S. J. Buck and E. Hawthorn, *The Planting of Civilization in Western Pennsylvania*, p. 360.

Like many others in Washington and elsewhere, General Wilkinson was somewhat relieved at the conciliatory tone of the inaugural address, especially upon hearing the President declare, "We are all Republicans, we are all Federalists."[1] And his actions proved equal to his words; no radical steps were taken. Office-holders of the opposite party were not proscribed; the best laws and practices of the preceding administration were retained; those selected for cabinet positions were generally able and of conservative turn.

The new administration soon disclosed its plans for the army. The President favored the maintenance of a force able to defend our people from Indian forays but did not admit the necessity of one competent to meet the initial attacks of foreign troops well trained and skillfully led. Though only a body of regulars adequate in numbers and quality could satisfactorily perform both functions, Jefferson did not accept this point of view. In European armies he had observed many instances of inefficiency and corruption; he was familiar with their use as instruments of tyranny, upholding tottering monarchies and suppressing personal liberty. He was determined that regulars should have no such character or employment in the United States. Therefore, he advocated that they be reduced to the bare minimum required for policing the frontier, guarding arsenals, and performing other federal tasks. He also urged that they be economically administered without any assurance to either officers or men that they would be permanently employed. He wanted none kept in the service any longer than could be avoided. Except for

[1] Jefferson to Congress, Dec. 8, 1801, in J. D. Richardson, *Messages and Papers of the Presidents*, I, pp. 226-232.

artillerists and engineers, he regarded their duties as easily learned; hence, for much of the time, he kept them at work not essentially military, such as road-building, exploring, treaty-making, etc. In keeping with such a hypothesis, he thought that the militia could become very quickly proficient in matters of discipline, tactics, supply, etc. He expected to rely upon them to be the bulwark of our country's defense. To achieve such a purpose, he frequently insisted that Congress pass measures aiding the militia.

During the eight important years of Jefferson's administration Henry Dearborn served as secretary of war. When he took office on March 5, 1801, he was known as a Democratic-Republican of unwavering faith and a veteran soldier with distinguished record in the Revolution. At the outbreak of war he had forsaken his profession as a doctor, raised a company, marched with it to Boston and fought at Bunker Hill. When hardy soldiers were called upon for the invasion of Canada, he had trudged with Arnold through the Maine woods during October and November of 1775. He was taken prisoner at Quebec, where Arnold was wounded and gallant Montgomery was killed in the futile assault on the well-defended ramparts. Misery, discouragement, hunger, cold, small-pox, and defeat were the rewards of this cruel campaign. Exchanged and back in the colonies, Dearborn, with his stalwart and well-led riflemen, the First New Hampshire Regiment, helped to defeat Burgoyne at the bloody battles of Freeman's Farm. Months later he was at Valley Forge, there enduring the hardships of the bitter winter of 1777-1778 with the same fortitude that he had displayed on the heartbreaking march to the St. Lawrence. In the summer of 1779, he served with Sullivan in a merciless campaign that laid waste the fruitful valleys long cultivated by the Indians in New York and Pennsylvania. When the war veered southward he led the van of Washington's army on the road to Yorktown, to fight there and witness the surrender of Cornwallis. Discharged upon the advent of peace he settled in Massachusetts, becoming a major general of its militia and subsequently United States Marshal for the District of Maine.[2]

When he accepted the appointment as secretary of war, Dearborn was fifty years old and one of the few Democratic-Republican politicians from a stronghold of Federalism. He took his religion and politics seriously without being unduly contentious about either. Genial in manner and imposing in appearance, he was about six feet tall, and had gray hair and blue eyes.[3] He was thrifty, practical, and reasonably competent; but his mind had not been enriched by consistent study or extensive travel. Though a familiar and popular figure about Washington and apparently trusted by Jefferson, he never influenced the President so deeply as did the two dominant figures in the cabinet, Madison and Gallatin, who headed the State and Treasury Departments respectively. Like them, Dearborn served Jefferson with unswerving loyalty, consistently putting into practical effect the President's wishes concerning the army, and the work it should do.

The War Department had played an important part in conducting our affairs with the Indians since 1787. In 1801 its attention was called to conditions south of the Ohio, where some of the tribes continued to be sporadically hostile. They were numerous, partially civilized, and occupied highly desirable lands coveted by the whites. The federal government had promised to clear the titles to lands promised to Georgia at its own expense. But first a peaceful and reasonable agreement with the Creeks, Chick-

[2] *Dictionary of American Biography*, V, pp. 174-176. As late as 1944, no real biography of Henry Dearborn had been published. His son, H. A. S. Dearborn, wrote one in seven volumes, but it is still in manuscript at the Maine Historical Society, Portland, Maine. It contains many direct quotations, but has few comments of interpretative value. Most of the official papers of Henry Dearborn as Secretary of War are in The National Archives, Washington, D.C.; some of them may be found, also, in the Public Library of the City of Boston, Chicago Historical Society, The Library of Congress, and The New York Public Library.

[3] Painting in War Department Building, Washington, D.C.; J. W. Hanson, *History of Gardiner, Pittstown, and West Gardiner*, etc., p. 141.

asaws, Choctaws, and Cherokees must be reached.[4] Jefferson hoped to persuade them by liberal gifts of money and annuities, gradually leading them out of their barbarous ways and, incidentally, away from their valuable lands.

In order to help attain these objectives of the President, General Wilkinson left Washington shortly after the inauguration in 1801. He went first to Buffalo to supervise the building of a proposed road between Lakes Erie and Ontario. He left there soon for Tennessee where he expected to make a treaty with the Cherokees. Early in August 1801 he made his way forty miles up the Cumberland. There, at Eddyville in Kentucky, he stopped overnight at the home of his old friend Matthew Lyon, Revolutionary veteran and ex-Congressman from Vermont. This was the same Lyon who had once suffered a sentence of four months imprisonment and a fine of $1,000 for defaming the character of John Adams by charging him with "selfish avarice" and "unbounded thirst for ridiculous pomp and foolish adulation."[5] In a friendly letter to the President, Lyon now told of the general's visit and commended the wisdom of selecting him as a commissioner to the Indians. Thereby, he added, Wilkinson's prestige was enhanced among the savages. His meager pay, too, was considerably augmented by the allowances granted to him and his colleagues—expenses and $8 a day for each of them.[6]

In common with most politicians of the day, Republican and Federalists alike, Lyon overlooked the fact that Wilkinson's primary function as commander-in-chief of the army was the supervision of the army. This was no part-time task, but one that required the strenuous application of all his energy in organizing, training, and supplying widely scattered forces during a highly critical period. When the administration was considering important mili-

[4] A. H. Abel, "The History of the Events Resulting in Indian Consolidation West of the Mississippi," in *American Historical Associations Report*, I (1906), p. 245.

[5] W. M. West, *The American People*, p. 250.

[6] Lyon to Jefferson, Aug. 12, 1801, *Jefferson Papers*, CXV, The Library of Congress.

tary legislation its senior officer and most experienced soldier was banished for two years in the wilderness negotiating with the Indians—work that others could have performed equally well. It is conceivable that neither Jefferson nor Dearborn wanted Wilkinson in Washington, where his advice and influence would not be likely to favor their plans to reduce the military establishment. By a circuitous arrangement to increase his pay, they made his exile more palatable and may have forestalled any protest on his part.

Associated with Wilkinson on this mission were Colonel Benjamin Hawkins, agent for Indian affairs south of the Ohio, "Beloved Man of the Four Nations," and the sixty-two-year-old General Andrew Pickens, "the Red Man's Friend," commonly known as "Skyagunsta," the "Wizard Owl." Early in September, the general joined his two collaborators near Knoxville, Tennessee. With the protection of a few soldiers these three set out for Southwest Point, where they hoped to make settlement easier and to arrange for cutting a road from the highlands to the Tennessee River. Unfortunately, the suspicious Cherokees would have nothing to do with either project, and no meeting with them was held.[7]

After this failure Wilkinson and his party traveled on down the Tennessee, Ohio, and Mississippi in their eight-oared barge, finally reaching the vicinity of Chickasaw Bluffs near the end of October. Here they found that the chiefs of the Chickasaws had arrived and were very peacefully inclined. Made happy with gifts of seven hundred dollars in goods, they willingly granted permission to link the Miró district of Tennessee with the settlements near Natchez by a road running through their territory. Wilkinson made arrangements to build it by successive monthly details of thirty soldiers each. The land was to be cleared for a maximum of sixteen feet, but only for one-half of this distance were the trees to be cut down close to the

7 *American State Papers, Indian Affairs*, I, pp. 648-653, 656-663; and A. Pickens, *Skyagunsta*, pp. 125, 158.

ground and the earth levelled off to make easy traveling.[8]

Successful with the Chickasaws, the commissioners continued on down the Mississippi, arriving in December at Fort Adams, where the Choctaws, a "humble, tranquil, pacific people," had gathered for a conference. They were given conventional annuities and enough rations to feed them on their return journey to their homes. Satisfied with this treatment, they readily consented to the building of a road from Fort Adams to the Yazoo. They accepted the old boundary line and would allow it to be marked once more. By this agreement the overland journey from Natchez to Nashville became both safer and quicker. A few soldiers were sprinkled along the route to give what protection they could to travelers. Mail was rapidly and regularly dispatched by relays of fast post riders, who were expected to cover 120 miles in twenty-four hours. Samuel Mitchell, the agent of the Chickasaws, was provided with medicines for the treatment of those who fell sick along the way.[9]

There remained only the Creeks with whom the commissioners had yet to deal. Negotiations did not commence until May 24, 1802, at Fort Wilkinson, near Milledgeville, Georgia. After the general and his associates had been elaborately received with music and dancing, the conferences began with much eating and drinking and protracted oratory. A treaty was finally signed on June 16 by which the Creeks ceded their lands in Ockmulgee Fork. In return they were given $10,000 in goods and promised generous annuities. The boundaries of the State of Georgia were thus pushed a little farther westward through the peaceful agency of the commissioners sustained by the army.[10]

[8] *American State Papers, Indian Affairs*, I, pp. 651-653; *Public Statutes at Large of the United States of America* (Indian Treaties) VII, pp. 64-65; Secretary of War to Wilkinson, Feb. 18, 1803, in C. E. Carter, *The Territorial Papers of the United States*, V, pp. 186-188.

[9] *American State Papers, Indian Affairs*, I, pp. 648-653; Post Master General to Piatt, Dec. 9, 1805, in C. E. Carter, *Mississippi Territorial Papers*, V, p. 44; Dearborn to Cushing, July 18, 1803, and to Taylor, Oct. 12, 1803, *Military Book, No. 2*, The National Archives.

[10] *American State Papers, Indian Affairs*, I, pp. 668-681; and *Public Statutes*, etc., VII, pp. 68-70.

With the mission to the Chickasaws, Choctaws, and Creeks completed, Pickens returned to his beloved Tamassee and Hawkins to his home among the Indians. Wilkinson set out for Fort Confederation, which the Spaniards had built years before on the Tombigbee. Here he met the Choctaws again, and after presenting them with rifles, ammunition, saddles, bridles, and cloth, he persuaded them to sign another treaty on October 17, 1802. By its terms, they surrendered the lands between the Tombigbee and the Chickasawhay, to the great satisfaction of the neighboring settlers who had long sought to obtain this area. At the same time, the Choctaws permitted the establishment of a trading house among them and a highway that ran through the heart of their country.[11]

From this camp on the Yazoo, Wilkinson supervised the work of establishing boundaries and slashing roads through the forest. W. C. C. Claiborne considered his labors "economical and expeditious." The general himself was not satisfied. Often he was sick with fever and ague, and he was separated from his family and friends. He thought of resigning from the army and becoming governor at Natchez. The position of surveyor general appealed to him also; but Dearborn was distinctly adverse to any such appointment, because Wilkinson, as he said, could then "associate with Spanish Agents without suspicion." Presumably in the army he did so with suspicion.[12]

Our relations with the Spaniards were then on an equivocal footing. With them in control of East and West Florida, supplies for our garrisons in the Southwest either had to pass through Spanish territory or be shipped down the Mississippi and carried a long distance overland by wilderness roads. Merchant vessels whose cargoes passed through Spanish custom houses were charged extortionate duties. On October 18, 1802, Juan Morales, the Spanish

11 *American State Papers, Indian Affairs,* I, pp. 681-683, and *Public Statutes,* etc., VII, pp. 73-74.

12 Dunbar Rowland, *Mississippi Territorial Archives, 1797-1803,* I, pp. 552-555, 581; Smith to Jefferson, Mar. 20, June 21, 1802, *Jefferson Papers,* CIII, CXXIV, The Library of Congress; Wilkinson to Dearborn, May 30, 1802, War Department, The National Archives.

intendant at New Orleans, withdrew the privilege of deposit from American merchants. Secretary of the Treasury Alexander Hamilton proposed that we immediately seize New Orleans and the Floridas. Senator James Ross of Pennsylvania led the Federalists in a series of resolutions introduced on February 16, 1803, asserting the rights of navigation and deposit and authorizing the President to raise 80,000 militia who could take and fortify the mouth of the Mississippi.[18] Wilkinson thought that the Spaniards, aroused by such drastic proposals, might land a thousand men from Cuba in Louisiana. Nevertheless, if reinforcements could be sent to him, he promised to be ready for an offensive whenever the order was given. He wanted Major General John Adair as his principal assistant, but he pointed out that in order to avoid confusion in the matter of command, he would have to be given a brevet of similar grade.[14]

Premonitions of aggression by the Spaniards were entirely without real foundation. Corruption had eaten so deeply into their colonial administrative system that their treasury was without funds and their officials devoid of patriotic purpose. Bribery and intimidation were their chief tools of diplomacy. Wilkinson, likewise skilled in the use of both, was able to obtain dispensations for our vessels when sailing in Spanish waters. Supplies for American garrisons were permitted to pass the King's forts without hindrance.

While Wilkinson was in the Southwest improving our relations with Indians and Spaniards, Jefferson was taking steps to reduce the army. He used for the basis of his decision the report that Dearborn had submitted to the House on December 24, 1801. According to it, the army consisted of ten general staff officers, two companies of dismounted cavalry, two regiments of artillerists and engineers, and four regiments of infantry, aggregating 248 officers, 9 cadets, and 3,794 enlisted men. The tables of

13 A. P. Whitaker, *The Mississippi Question, 1795-1803*, pp. 215-216.
14 Wilkinson to Dearborn, July 24, 1803, *Wilkinson Papers*, The Public Library, Boston, Mass.

organization and previous legislation had called for a total enlisted and commissioned personnel of 5,438; but when vacancies had occurred, no steps had been taken to fill them because of a saving in expense.[15] Presuming that the army merely had to furnish garrisons for the frontier and sea-coast defenses and that both could be accomplished by twenty companies of infantry and an equal number for artillerists and engineers, Jefferson declared that more than these should be dispensed with. Many Congressmen entertained similar notions. No one in high office considered that the army should be of such training and size that in times of emergency it could furnish an adequate nucleus to defend our country against any possible foe.

Out of these conditions came the act of March 16, 1802, in spite of the fact that our relations with France were equivocal and our minister at the Court of St. James was rudely received. By its provisions the army was materially reduced. Cavalry was entirely eliminated. The artillery was organized into one regiment of five battalions. Each of the four companies in a battalion consisted of five officers and seventy-six men. The infantry was also allotted a total of twenty companies; except for one less officer apiece, they were like those in the artillery. They were grouped into two regiments under three field officers each—a colonel, a lieutenant colonel, and a major. The terms colonel and lieutenant colonel were revived for the first time since the days of the Revolution. The engineers were divorced from the artillery and formed into a diminutive corps of seven officers and ten cadets. The staff of this entire force was scaled down to a brigadier general, an adjutant and inspector, a paymaster, three military agents, two surgeons, and twenty-five surgeon's mates.[16]

By June 1, 1802, the army had a total of 172 officers. The authorized enlisted strength was 3,040 men, but fewer than this number were actually present for duty.[17] Ap-

---

[15] *American State Papers, Military Affairs*, I, pp. 154-156.

[16] J. F. Callan, *op. cit.*, pp. 141-149.

[17] T. H. S. Hamersly, *op. cit.*, pp. 49-51; *American State Papers, Military Affairs*, I, p. 156.

proximately seventy-six officers had been discharged since
Dearborn made his report on December 23, 1801. If they
had less than three years' service, they were granted three
months' pay. They received proportionately more if they
had been in the army for a longer time.[18] Louis Tousard,
John Jacob Ulrich Rivardi, and Mahlon Ford found themselves among those discharged. The loss of Tousard was
keenly felt. He was an officer of high attainments and had
been active as colonel of a regiment and inspector of
artillery, having done a great deal to make artillery
matériel better in quality and uniform in kind. Not his
record but his French origin apparently weighed heavily
against him.[19]

Officers generally believed such legislation had treated
them unfairly. They knew that, outside of the army, they
had no profession or trade to which they might turn.
Most of them, entirely too old to start in a new field of
endeavor, viewed their darkening prospects with alarm.
While the law was pending, Montgomery Pike wrote to his
father, expressing an opinion to which many others subscribed.

". . . notwithstanding . . . [you have] grown gray in
service of the country you are to be dismissed with the
noble and adequate provision of three months' pay and
subsistence. . . . Wonderful indeed is the present rage for
economy. . . . Fine encouragement for sons to tread in the
footsteps of their fathers, and unless I can obtain one of
the profitable and honorable staff appointments contemplated in the bill, I have quitting the service strongly in
view; but my plan must be matured and foundation sure."[20]

Luckily for the Pikes, both of them were retained in
the service. Those discharged became constant reminders
to the general public that officers were meagerly paid,
suffered great hardships, and could not depend upon a
reasonable tenure of office. Under the circumstances, the

[18] J. F. Callan, *op. cit.*, pp. 141-149.
[19] W. E. Birkhimer, *Historical Sketch . . . of the Artillery, United
States Army*, p. 32.
[20] Z. M. Pike to Z. Pike, Feb. 28, 1802, in Western Reserve Historical
Society.

ablest young men gravitated into occupations where rewards were greater, the work more attractive, and the
position more secure.

Besides the cheese-paring that had resulted in no
cavalry, no horses for the artillery, and fewer officers and
enlisted men, another venture in economy was tried. It
concerned Wilkinson as commanding general. By the law
of 1802, he received $225 per month, "his full and entire
compensation, without right to demand or receive any
rations, forage, traveling expenses, or other perquisite or
emolument whatsoever, except such stationary as may be
requisite for his department."[21] For the times, such pay,
with allowances, would have been generous; without them,
it was miserly and kept the general from performing one
of his paramount duties—that of inspecting his broadly
scattered troops to improve training or correct abuses.

With such a salary, Wilkinson often teetered on the
verge of bankruptcy. To avoid it, he turned to questionable methods. Apparently by some agreement between
himself and Dearborn, he managed to circumvent the
prohibition concerning rations and travel allowances. He
may have had a few dividends from personal investments.
He also wheedled a considerable sum from the Spaniards
and was occasionally detailed on work where additional
pay and allowances were granted him. When he acted as
commissioner to the Indians he drew $8 a day and liberal
amounts for ration and forage. Tapping all these sources,
his income was still not enough to support his easy spending and open hospitality. In about 1811 William Simmons,
the accountant for the War Department, had Wilkinson
owing the government $7,891.03 for money and supplies
previously advanced.[22]

Although regular troops were fewer, more of them were
required to protect newly established factories and the
roads connecting the frontier garrisons and towns. In case
the United States acquired territory beyond the Mississippi, the army would be faced with an even larger and

[21] J. F. Callan, *op. cit.*, pp. 141-149.
[22] J. Wilkinson, *op. cit.*, II, Appendix, CXXVI.

harder task. In any event, our chain of forts stretching southward from Mackinac to Fort Adams had to be strengthened if honest settlers were to be protected and federal law maintained.

As early as March 9, 1803, Cushing, the inspector general, wrote Hamtramck at Detroit to investigate the possibilities of establishing a post at "Chikago," the Pottawatomie name for skunk. During July troops from Detroit were on their way thither, some traveling overland, others going aboard the schooner *Tracy*, well loaded with supplies. By August 17, they had reached the Chicago river and had ascended from Lake Michigan for about half a mile. Here they began building a fort located on ground lying just south of the river and rising only about eight feet above its sluggish waters. Work proceeded slowly on Fort Dearborn, so named in honor of the new secretary of war. There were not many troops, and some were bilious or weakened with fevers. They also did not have enough horses and oxen to drag the heavy timbers into position to form the palisades and barracks. Fortunately winter was slow in coming and proved to be mild. Next year buildings were completed and members of the garrison were reasonably comfortable. The few French traders living close by were friendly, sometimes harrowing their gardens and doing other favors and chores. Early in 1805 a factory was established there at Fort Dearborn, allowing the purchase of a number of articles at reasonable prices. Butter, raisins, and tobacco sold for fifty cents a pound, tea for five times as much, and whisky for $1.25 per gallon; they were usually beyond the reach of the ordinary laborer who was paid only fifty cents a day or the soldier who had even less. For about nine years, life at Fort Dearborn went on much like that in other frontier posts; then the British captured it, burning the buildings to the ground and massacring most of the garrison.[23]

While the army was being scattered and reduced, Jefferson was unsuccessfully trying to make the state militia the

[23] M. M. Quaife, *Chicago and the Old Northwest, 1673-1835*, pp. 127-144, 287.

bulwark of the nation. Militia members were to be reported to the President annually by the different adjutants general. They were supposed to keep themselves armed and equipped and to assemble on muster or training days when directed. In this way the act of March 2, 1803, was supposed to make a more effective force than the one of 1792. Only for the District of Columbia was a better militia law passed; but it concerned so few that its results for the country at large was negligible. It did, however, give the President a potential force that he might use to quell riot or disorder at the capital. Convinced that men in the militia would neglect to arm themselves properly, Congress set aside $1,500,000 on March 3, 1803, to equip 80,000 militiamen to be ready "to march at a moment's notice." Presumably they would do the correct thing when the marching was over and the fighting began. In addition, on February 24, 1807, the President was authorized to accept 30,000 volunteers. It was understood that they would act as militia. As times became more fearful in 1808, $200,000 were added to the previous $1,500,000 to serve the same purpose.[24]

The militia might be ill-trained and poorly armed when called to active duty, but they were likely to be fairly well fed. For both militia and regulars the chief components of the ration consisted of a pound and a half of meat and eighteen ounces of bread. By the law of March 16, 1802, the amount of whisky was raised from one-half to a full gill, vinegar likewise was doubled, being four quarts to each 100 men. Like that of civilians, the army's food was substantial, but monotonous and poorly balanced. At the same time, double allowances of rations were authorized for the commanding officers of separate posts.[25] They well deserved this addition. In spite of the fact that they had little pay and could ill afford the expense, custom demanded

24 J. F. Callan, *op. cit.*, pp. 150-168, 169, 198-199, 205-206.
25 J. F. Callan, *The Military Laws of the United States*, (revised edition), pp. 141-149. Double rations were authorized for twenty-five posts. Dearborn to Paymaster, June 5, 1802, *Military Book, No. 1*, The National Archives.

that they keep a sort of "open house," especially along the frontier where inns were scarce.

At this time administrative efforts were made to substitute beer and light wines for whisky, rum, or brandy. As early as June 17, 1803, Dearborn directed post commanders, if a majority of their troops consented, to replace spirits with malt liquor from May to October. Such an innovation was expected to be generally beneficial for those serving in a warm climate, but contractors were not pleased because it meant more work and less profit. Each man was to have a good "junk bottle" to keep his daily quart of beer from growing stale.[26] If wine was issued instead, he was to get no less than half a pint.[27] Neither proved popular; and for practical reasons, too, both were definitely abandoned. Most wine came from abroad and could not be readily imported. Men who had enjoyed hard liquor wanted nothing else. Beer had the disadvantage of being very bulky, and, almost of necessity, had to be manufactured locally. Good brew masters were scarce, and the product of amateurs was not always palatable. Frequently it could not be cooled. The troops deserved something better than warm, second-rate beer, especially in a hot climate.

No changes occurred with regard to medicines and general hospital supplies except that they were more systematically and sparingly issued. They were sent all the way from Philadelphia, consigned separately to each company and varied in amount with the section of the country. Dearborn estimated that a southern post of eighty men should have for the year, among other articles, twenty pounds of quinine bark, two of Turkish opium, eight each of mercurial ointment and flowers of sulphur, four quarts of castor oil, twenty gallons of brandy and an equal amount of sherry, sixteen blankets, and half that number of mattresses and sheets. For a northern post of the same size, the supplies mentioned were generally cut fifty

[26] Dearborn to Freeman, et al., June 17, 1803, *Military Book, No. 2,* The National Archives.
[27] Dearborn to Freeman, June 13, 1805, in *ibid.*

per cent, most of the others being issued without reduction.
All medical supplies might be diminished twenty per cent
if a garrison was unusually large. Surgical instruments
were furnished by the government, too, but the post surgeon was responsible for their preservation and care.
Amputating and trepanning sets, weights and measures,
mortars and pestles were expected to last a long time.
Usually there was a shortage of flannel, lint, pins, lancets,
and penis syringes before the year ran its course. In 1802
no new instruments and only half of the usual quantity of
medicines were issued.[28]

When there was an unusual degree of sickness, however,
Dearborn was as liberal as his thrifty nature would allow.
Extra purchases for the sick were sometimes authorized.
Dr. George Dill was even permitted to buy a cow, but he
was distinctly told that only his bonafide patients were
to enjoy the milk.[29] When Samuel Mitchell, federal agent
for the Chickasaws, needed medicines for travelers in his
neighborhood, the army officer nearby was ordered to
supply them.[30] At a time when Colonel Constant Freeman's
troops were nearly all flat on their backs, he was directed
to spare no means to preserve their lives and make them
healthy, although previously he had been begrudged the
purchase of some tea, coffee and raisins for them.[31] A
surgeon at Fort Jay, N.Y., sent in a request for six tin
pans, eight pewter plates, a dozen knives and forks, and a
tea set with cups and saucers. He got what he wanted.[32]
But military patients usually had to use their own mess
equipment, whatever it was. They seldom had beds, customarily sleeping double on straw pallets. Nightshirts

[28] "Regulations for Hospital Supplies" (undated), and Dearborn
to Whelen, Mar. 27, 1803, *Military Book, No. 1*, National Archives.
[29] Dearborn to Dill, Apr. 21, 1803, In *ibid.*, p. 425.
[30] Dearborn to Cushing, July 18, 1803, and to Taylor, Oct. 12, 1803,
Military Book, No. 2, The National Archives.
[31] Dearborn to Freeman, Jan. 21, 1802, *Military Book, No. 1*, and
Dearborn to Freeman, Oct. 9, 1804, *Military Book, No. 2*, The National
Archives.
[32] Dearborn to Beebe, Oct. 13, 1803, *Military Book, No. 2*, The
National Archives.

were not supplied and the sick soldier was lucky if he possessed his own underwear.

The Act of 1802 made no provision for these deficiencies, but it did allow a slight increase in the amount of clothing furnished. The soldier was provided with a pair of half-gaiters and a fatigue suit, in addition to his usual articles. In case he required another hat, coat, shirt, etc., he could draw what he needed, the cost being charged against him on the pay roll at contract price, provided the need had arisen honestly. Otherwise the deduction was twenty-five per cent higher. The paymaster handled all clothing, so the government was seldom a loser. The yearly allowance of a private amounted to $29.66 in the infantry; in the artillery, $31.61. The most expensive item listed was the $6.75 coat of the artilleryman. Shoes for all branches of the service cost $1.10 a pair; overalls and shirts, $1.25; stockings sixty cents and half-gaiters forty-three cents a pair. As a rule neither the coats nor trousers fitted, but they could be altered at twenty-five and eight cents respectively—at the soldier's expense of course. Hats, once made all alike, were ordered fashioned on different blocks, so that a greater number of sizes would be available.[33]

Regulations provided that materials used and methods of fabrication be subject to inspection. Contracts for supplies were let either by the secretary of war or the purveyor of public supplies; the latter was an official of the Treasury Department. When the needlewomen and master tailors completed the clothing, the contractor delivered it to the superintendent of military stores at Philadelphia. From 1802 until 1804 this post was filled by General William Irvine, a veteran of the Revolution with an excellent military record. On February 22, 1802, Dearborn wrote to him asking him to inspect the clothing personally to see that it met specifications. The secretary suggested that he charge a fee of some five or six cents a suit.[34] Irvine ac-

[33] "Regulation for Clothing," Nov. 22, 1802, *Military Book, No. 1*, The National Archives; J. F. Callan, *op. cit.*, pp. 133-139.

[34] Dearborn to Irvine, Feb. 22, 1802, *Military Book, No. 1*, The National Archives.

cepted this task but complaints continued and his relations with Tench Coxe, the industrious and reasonably competent purveyor were not always harmonious. Much of the superintendent's work seems to have been done through slovenly deputies.[35]

Sometimes a soldier might get a little more pay, whisky, and clothing if he worked as an artificer on fortifications or bridges. For every day's actual labor of this kind, he drew fourteen cents and a gill of spirits. He was also furnished a pair of linen overalls and a frock. But none of these additional allowances was granted him unless he worked for sixty days, not including Sundays. Noncommissioned officers and privates who did only ordinary manual labor, not that of artificers, drew similar allowances but were paid only ten cents extra.[36]

Such compensation made soldiers temporarily contented and accelerated the improvement of our national defenses; but it was not as important as retired pay. At first, the regulars enjoyed no pension rights unless they happened to be veterans of the Revolution, no matter how deserving they were. If an officer died from wounds in action, however, his dependents might receive half his pay for five years. Many who served in the campaigns of Harmar, St. Clair, and Wayne against the Indians were prevented by their wounds or other disabilities from continuing in the army or maintaining themselves in civil life. Out of simple justice something had to be done for such individuals. The law of March 3, 1795, gave them the privilege of being placed on the "list of invalids of the United States." Thus an officer might enjoy a maximum pension equal to one half of his pay; in any case it varied with his rank and the degree of his disability. An enlisted man drew five dollars a month for a maximum disability, a smaller amount for one of less degree.[37] During 1806 substantially the same

[35] Coxe to Irvine, Jan. 31, 1804, *Purveyor's Papers*, The National Archives.

[36] "Regulations for Extra Pay and Allowances of Soldiers, etc." June 25, 1801, *Military Book, No. 1*, The National Archives.

[37] Acts of June 7, 1794, and Mar. 3, 1795, in J. F. Callan, *op. cit.*, pp. 105, 111-113.

privileges were extended to Revolutionary veterans. Two years later the federal government took over their payment from the states according to rates of its own. At the same time, similar benefits were confirmed for the regulars and given to the militia and volunteers if disabled while in the service.[38] Until after the war of 1812, no other significant changes occurred in the laws of this type; they were merely applied to any additional troops that happened to be raised.

Since retired pay for officers was small at best and was never granted for years of service but only for physical disability, few could or would take advantage of it, preferring instead to remain on active duty as long as possible. For example, William Whistler, when retired in 1861, had been an officer for sixty years. As a consequence, the army tended to become an almhouse for the decrepit and broken; and some of these, unfortunately, were highest in rank and often most influential in shaping policies. Being decidedly conservative, they saw no virtue in change unless they benefited personally. They lived in a hard narrow world which their opinions reflected. Generally speaking, a court-martial was the only way of getting rid of officers who were physically fit but incompetent. Usually they were clever enough to escape elimination by a nominal performance of their routine duties. Even the ambitious often lost their enthusiasm because of the extreme slowness of promotion, which was strictly in accordance with seniority. Below field grade it was made within the regiment; above, within the "lines of the artillery and infantry."[39] The army stagnated. Officers were averse to new ideas, especially if they encroached on personal liberty or ran counter to long established customs of the service.

On April 30, 1801, officers and men were informed that they must keep their hair short. The purpose was to promote cleanliness and economy and produce a neater ap-

[38] Acts of Apr. 10, 1806, and Apr. 25, 1808, in *ibid.*, pp. 195-197, 206-207.

[39] "Regulations Governing Promotion," May 6, 1801, *Military Book, No. 1*, p. 76, The National Archives.

pearance. Many, however, took pride in their queues and strongly opposed every effort to do away with them. Officers at Fort Mifflin, Pennsylvania, obeyed "the imperious and arbitrary mandate," but with "chagrin and silent indignation."[40] At Wilkinsonville, Georgia, resentment reached a high pitch. There Captain Russell Bissell became deeply embittered at the prospect of losing some of his hair. He wrote out his resignation, but before it could be accepted he had to settle his accounts with the paymaster, about 1,800 miles away. Since he was without funds to make such a journey, he swallowed his pride and appeared as one of the "roundheads" when the commanding general later inspected the post.[41]

Colonel Thomas Butler was much more recalcitrant. For several years he had been stationed in Tennessee, doing almost whatever he pleased. Largely because of his long service, the condition of his health, and his own request, Wilkinson exempted him from the order. Since this dispensation served only to make him more arrogant and neglectful of his duties, it was revoked; and before long he was summoned before a court-martial to explain why he had not cut his hair and reported at Fort Adams in compliance with orders. As a result of the findings, he was sentenced to a reprimand and admonished to be obedient in the future. On being transferred to the Southwest, he became "more contemptuous and disrespectful" than ever before. His conduct could be tolerated no longer. Again he was tried, and this time punishment was heavier: he forfeited all "command, pay and emoluments" for twelve calendar months. On September 7, 1804, thirteen days before the sentence was to become effective, he died of yellow fever. Even in death he remained defiant. It is said that those attending his funeral could see his queue insolently protruding through a hole in the top of his coffin.[42]

40 Wilkinson's order of Apr. 30, 1801, in T. R. Hay, *The Admirable Trumpeter*, pp. 228-229.

41 *Ibid.*, p. 229; and J. R. Jacobs, *op. cit.*, pp. 199-201.

42 T. R. Hay, *op. cit.*, pp. 228-233.

Though not so cantankerous, Colonel Daniel Jackson, at Fort Independence, Boston, was decidedly annoying. During November 1801, Dearborn upbraided him for paying so little attention to frugality and economy. The colonel had altered and repaired barracks without authority. In spite of the fact that long hair was no longer permissible, he continued to issue flour for powdering it. He also ordered an extra half ration of "spirits" for artificers when they happened to be on duty. Hospital stores, too, were mysteriously consumed when troops were undeniably healthy. In defense of his action, Jackson argued that since the regulations did not specifically prohibit his methods they should be approved. To this rather singular brand of reasoning, he added other acts of irritation. He tried various ruses to evade being transferred to some other station, stressing what a hardship it would entail on him and his family. Dearborn proved inflexible. Finally being faced with no other means of winning his point, Jackson sent in his resignation, which was duly accepted on April 30, 1803.[43]

Jackson was more reluctant to give up his friends and interests around Boston than to lose his monthly pay of $75 and the allowances that the army furnished him. The government was not at all generous. Even the commanding general of the army was allowed only four rooms; field officers, two; captains, one; and lieutenants shared rooms in pairs. The general was provided with a kitchen; other officers, if they were above the two lowest grades and were commanding a post, were also provided with kitchens. Captains and lieutenants were entitled to a cord of wood each month between the first of October and the first of April, thereafter one half as much. Every room occupied by eight enlisted men was allotted the same amount. Field officers drew somewhat more. The sick in hospital had what the surgeon recommended. No monetary substitution was allowed in lieu of fuel and quarters. In case barracks or

[43] Dearborn to Jackson, Sept. 4, 1802, Apr. 19, 1803, *Military Book, No. 1*, The National Archives.

quarters needed repairs exceeding fifty dollars, nothing
could be done until Dearborn approved.[44]

The allowances for traveling expenses were even more
parsimonious. Before 1812 army officers often resigned in
preference to changing station. This was especially true
of those who had large families. In 1804 the government
made no provision for the travel or baggage of dependents.
Married or unmarried, all officers of the same grade drew
the same allowances. After paying for their transportation, the government considered $1.00 or $1.25 a day as
adequate reimbursement for additional expenses, depend-
ing upon whether the officer concerned already drew money
for forage.[45] Overland travel was very slow, approximately
twenty miles a day; travel by water was much faster,
except when going upstream. Against the current, sizable
boats seldom made more than fifteen miles in twenty-four
hours. In fact the *President Adams*, a large government
barge, moved even more slowly when en route from Natchez
to the mouth of the Ohio in 1801.[46]

Household effects reached their destination only after
long delay; not infrequently they were badly damaged;
the expense was always very heavy. In 1798 freight from
Philadelphia to Pittsburgh cost about seven cents a pound,
somewhat later a cent or two less.[47] According to Dearborn's regulations of 1802, a colonel was entitled to 750
pounds of baggage, a second lieutenant only one third as
much. Thus if a subaltern wanted to send to Pittsburgh as
much as 750 pounds, he would have to spend much more
than $30, the equivalent of his monthly pay.[48] If he tried
to get it transported free, he would probably find himself
in plenty of trouble. When, in 1811, General Wilkinson

---

[44] "Regulations for Quarters and Fuel," Apr. 28, 1801, *Military
Book, No. 1*, The National Archives.

[45] Dearborn to Bruff, Mar. 31, 1804, *Military Book, No. 2*, The
National Archives; J. F. Callan, *op. cit.*, pp. 141-149.

[46] *Michigan Pioneer and Historical Society Collections*, VIII, pp.
447-449.

[47] *Expenditures in the Naval and Military Establishments by the
Quartermaster General and Navy Agents*, 1787-1801, *passim*.

[48] "Regulations on Travel Allowances," June 28, 1802, *Military
Book, No. 1*, The National Archives.

was court-martialed, among other offenses he was charged with shipping some of his personal property at public expense.[49] Occasionally an officer might take extra things with him on a government barge if there happened to be plenty of room; sometimes the sutler or contractor could be induced to bring a few articles from the Atlantic seaboard at less than the prevailing rate. As a rule, however, officers on the frontier had to be content with bare essentials—food, clothing, equipment, tools, and books. Luxuries were for those whose means were greater and whose places of living were near centers of population.

Like many other officers, Colonel Cushing had to discard many things that he wished to carry with him when he left Washington, D.C., for Natchez, Mississippi, in May, 1805. At the time, he had a family of "four females." This number did not include a slave "wench" who ran away at the prospect of moving. With her gone, his furniture selling at only one third of its value, and the unusual expense incident to the journey, Cushing calculated "on a dead loss of Two Thousand Dollars." Some of his possessions were sent over the Alleghenies by wagon in charge of two privates in Captain John McClellan's company. One of these was the colonel's servant or "striker." He was honest and industrious enough but had "a fine taste for Rye liquor." In spite of this failing, the pair reached Pittsburgh without serious trouble. Here Moses Hooke, the military agent, kept them busy until the Cushings arrived. After arranging for pleasing accommodations for the "females" on one of the government barges, Cushing went aboard and before long was floating down the Ohio, reaching Natchez when peaches were ripening and crepe myrtle and magnolias were in flower.[50]

Even if the government had liberally reimbursed officers for all of their incidental expenses when transferred, some of them would have been unwilling to move, since they did not wish to suffer losses from the sacrifice of local perqui-

[49] J. Wilkinson, *Memoirs of My Own Times*, II, pp. 35-40.
[50] Cushing to Wilkinson, May 4, 1805, Inspector's Office, National Archives.

sites or investments. At Detroit Colonel Hamtramck was financially concerned in the distillery business.[51] Around Loramies, several officers were raising corn and cattle so extensively with soldier labor that they had entirely forgotten their military duties.[52] A few at St. Louis and other points dabbled in real estate and fur-trading ventures. Wherever there were Indians, officers could pick up a few dollars by serving as commissioners or as custodians of annuities. At Michilimackinac, Fort Massac, Fort Adams, and Mobile, an officer could act as "collector of the port." For instance, at Michilimackinac the position yielded from $1,200 to $1,500 a year.[53] Sinecures of this sort were rare, and officers usually had nothing to live on but their inadequate pay. Secretary Dearborn did not bestir himself to have it increased.

Although some posts were popular with officers, there were others that they heartily disliked, especially if they had to help enforce the much hated embargo of December 22, 1807. Along our northern border, they were frequently called on to cooperate with the civil agents of the government in breaking up locally popular and highly remunerative smuggling. In spite of strenuous efforts to the contrary at Niagara, boats loaded with potash passed into Canada. At Oswego two of them sailed without clearance; and, when pursued, they resorted to arms and blatantly defied the authorities. Troops stationed at Sackets Harbor often found their boats cut loose from the moorings, oars stolen, sails destroyed, and timber burned that had been laboriously cut for building barracks. Sentinels were stoned at night and pestered by day. Though constantly harassed and insulted, the lieutenant in command held to his job and his duty, trying to uphold

[51] *Hamtramck Papers*, entries of Aug. 24, 1799, and Jan. 22, 1800, Detroit Public Library.

[52] "General Orders, Loramies," June 12, 1797, in L. Watrous, *A Brief History of the Adjutant General's Department*, p. 5.

[53] Wilkinson himself seems to have been interested in both real estate and fur trade around St. Louis. See J. R. Jacobs, *op. cit.*, p. 219. For Wilkinson as Indian Commissioner, see *ibid.*, pp. 195-198. For port collectors, see Stoddard to Burdick, May 13, 1810, *Letters of Army Officers*, New York City Library.

the law while, without masons or carpenters, he slowly erected temporary shelters to protect his men from an oncoming winter.[54]

One day in September two boats came sailing down Sandy Creek, a few miles from Sackets Harbor, only to be turned quickly about when their masters saw troops on the shore. Next day a detachment found the boats sunk, but the cargoes of potash and a swivel gun had been salvaged and hidden in or around the house of a man named Fairfield who lived close by. The soldiers broke in and carried the contraband away, arousing the anger of Mrs. Fairfield, who was alone in the house at the time. She called on the neighboring magistrate for help. With a warrant and thirty men to sustain him, the constable came and demanded that the troops either fight or surrender. They preferred to fight and soon captured ten of the posse. Later they hunted for the judge who had issued the warrant, but he could not be caught. In retaliation, he induced two citizens to make out charges of felony. This time eighty men came to support the constable. No fight occurred because no armed opposition was offered. The constable was satisfied, but others still burning for revenge, wrathfully demanded that "the felons" be taken who had carried ten "law-abiding citizens" away. At an indignation meeting they drew up a number of caustic resolutions, but did nothing more.[55]

The futility of the embargo soon became apparent. It gained us no better consideration from European countries and it disgusted our citizens at home. Some believed that a larger and more efficient army should be organized. It might help our prestige abroad and would certainly enable us to face England and France with greater assurance. Others, however, were disturbed by the ancient bugbear of militarism. John W. Eppes, son-in-law of Jefferson and a dyed-in-the-wool Democrat, opposed any

[54] *National Intelligencer and Western Advertiser*, Jan. 23. 1809.
[55] J. B. McMaster, *A History of the People of the United States*, III, pp. 304-307.

increase of troops, doing so in the language of political quackery so common in the Congress of that day.

"If we are to have war," he shouted, "this increase of the army will be useless; if peace, I am opposed to it. I am in favor of putting arms in the hands of our citizens and let them defend themselves. . . . If we depend on regular troops alone, the liberty of our country must finally be destroyed by that army which is raised to defend it. . . . I have never yet voted for a regular army or soldier in time of peace. Whenever an opportunity has offered I have voted them down; and so help me God! I will, as long as I live."[56]

Irrespective of any hope of heavenly aid, there were many Democrats in Congress with the same determination. President Jefferson, however, was reluctantly beginning to admit the necessity for a stronger military establishment. On February 25, 1808, a week after Eppes' confession of faith, he sent a request to Congress for an addition of 6,000 men to the regular army. His supporters at the Capitol were thrown into confusion. John Clopton of Virginia approved the proposed increase despite his previous pacifist record. He declared that conditions had changed; little hope for peace remained. George M. Troup of Georgia was of the same mind. He confessed that the militia in his part of the country was "good for nothing." A small standing army was necessary; as Washington had declared, it preserved peace by preparing for war. Nathaniel Macon of North Carolina grudgingly gave his consent only as a war measure.

There were others in the House whose words on the subject almost sizzled with truculence. David R. Williams of South Carolina, who rejoiced in the nickname "Thunder & Lightning," asserted that he had no use for half measures. What we needed, he shouted, was 60,000, not 6,000 additional men. Richard Stanford of North Carolina quoted to his colleagues excerpts from speeches made in 1798 by Eppes, Varnum, Nicholas and Gallatin on re-

[56] H. Adams, *History of the United States during the Administrations of Thomas Jefferson and James Madison*, IV, pp. 211-212.

ducing the army; he accused them of being paragons of inconsistency. John Randolph of Roanoke, a master of sarcasm and ridicule, told the Democrats that they did not know their own minds; they had voted for things impossible to explain. They had built gunboats to protect our shipping and then built forts to protect the gunboats. Their army was a farce and their whole system of defense was diametrically opposed to the embargo. He also declared that "The system of embargo is one system, withdrawing from every contest, quitting the arena, flying the pit. The system of raising troops of whatever sort is another and opposite to that dormant state. They are at war with each other and cannot go on together." Only in one way did he scornfully agree they were mutually helpful—the embargo had resulted in a great surplus of fish. To appropriate federal money to buy the surplus need be considered no longer. Now the 60,000 additional men could eat them, preventing them from rotting on the wharves of Gloucester and Marblehead.[57] In spite of much embarrassment, the Democrats revised their opinions and the bill was finally approved in the House by a vote of 95 to 16. It became a law on April 12, 1808.

The act provided for five regiments of infantry, one regiment of riflemen, one regiment of light artillery, and one regiment of light dragoons, all to be raised for five years only. These were in addition to the existing troops. This increase seemed to require a major general, a rank that Wilkinson ardently coveted. Instead, two brigadiers were appointed and the pay and allowances of their grade were more definitely fixed than by the old law of 1802. Wilkinson, as a brigadier general, had previously received only $225 a month without any other allowances whatsoever. By the new law, he would get only $104 a month as pay, but he was allowed twelve rations a day, or double this number at some posts, and $16 a month for forage when not furnished. A ration was then estimated as worth about twenty cents. Thus he might draw a minimum of

57 For the remarks of Randolph and others in reference to the law of Apr. 12, 1808, see *ibid.*, pp. 212-218.

$192 or a maximum of $264 a month. In addition, he was given quarters, fuel, and reasonable traveling expenses.[58]

The two brigadiers were promptly appointed. Wade Hampton was one of the richest planters in South Carolina. He was proud, irascible and had little capacity as an officer in spite of his Revolutionary experience. Peter Gansevoort of New York had served creditably under Washington and more recently as a military agent. These two appointments as brigadiers, nicely balancing the claims of North and South as to preference, burdened the highest grades in the augmented army with mediocrity. There was no staff to increase the efficiency of administration. If a general desired a staff, officers from the line were detailed for duty. Ordinarily he had no more than a single aide. Besides, none of the new colonels had achieved distinction in the army. Leonard Covington, who was to die gallantly at Chrysler's Field in 1813, gave some promise of efficiency; the others were merely tired old political workhorses. They were appointed from civil life and not promoted from existing regiments. Had they and the field officers been taken from the line of the army, the results might possibly have been better. At least, promotion would have been accelerated and younger men would have found themselves in command of larger units when the war came. The regular officers were naturally not eager to accept commissions in new regiments which might be disbanded at any time, leaving them wholly out of the army. It was this fear, also, that constantly deterred the regulars from being detached from their own regiments to assist in the training of the temporarily raised forces.

Not satisfied with the act of April 12, 1808, the next session of the 10th Congress considered further measures of defense. The session met on November 7 and lasted until March 3, 1809. The day after convening, it received the President's eighth annual message in which he admitted that all of our retaliatory measures against England and France had failed to make either discontinue the violation

58 J. F. Callan, *op. cit.*, pp. 141-149, 200-203; and J. Wilkinson, *op. cit.*, I, p. vii.

of our rights as neutrals. A solution of our troubles must be found.[59] The sole remaining recourse appeared to be war. Congress immediately undertook, as the President suggested, to fix its attention on the country's safety. On December 26, 1808, a committee of the House submitted a resolution "to raise, arm and equip 50,000 volunteers to serve for two years." The cost, which appalled more than a few members, amounted to $2,100,000 for the first year, $800,000 for the second. The bill was hotly debated and bitterly assailed, being passed by the House but defeated in the Senate.[60]

Nor did Congress do anything to make the members of the militia more formidable, although Jefferson urged that they be so well organized and armed that they would furnish "the best security for a people who are free and intend to remain so." Can they, he asked, "repel a powerful enemy at every point of our territory exposed to invasion."[61] Representatives and Senators controlled the means for making this possible. He asked for their action on a matter so important. His request was ignored.

For the regular army no constructive legislation was enacted from April 1808 to March 1809. Instead, self-seeking politicians assailed it in ways that have too often disgraced our democracy. James Wilkinson, the general-in-chief, had laid himself open to criticism, and he got it. Some Congressmen went so far as to declare the enlisted men were too worthless to work and could be tied hand and foot by the inhabitants of any district. Good men would not submit to the whims of tyrannical officers. Why increase the army, anyway? The Democratic-Republicans could never be kicked into war. After all, the army was just a partisan force, an "engine of despotism, made up of underlings of the administration."[62] Half-truths, ignorance, and prejudice prevailed. Nothing was done.

[59] Jefferson to Congress, Nov. 8, 1808, in J. D. Richardson, *A Compilation of the Messages and Papers of the Presidents, 1789-1902*, I, pp. 451-456.

[60] *Annals of Congress*, XIX, p. 910.

[61] Jefferson to Congress, Nov. 8, 1808, in J. D. Richardson, *op. cit.*, I, p. 455.

[62] *Annals of Congress*, XIX, p. 1201.

For the few troops Congress authorized, Dearborn was partly responsible for certain improvements in discipline, training, and equipment. On April 10, 1806, the Articles of War, originally adopted in 1776, were revised in order to conform with the more liberal spirit of the times. In general, they were chiefly concerned with definition of misdemeanors and crimes in the army, how they were to be adjudicated, and what sentences might be imposed. Desertion was to be punished by death or as the court directed. Theft, embezzlement, and insubordination likewise drew heavy penalties. Cashiering or corporal punishment restrained those who would send a challenge or fight a duel. Officers cashiered for cowardice or fraud were to have their names and crimes publicized around the camp and in the state from which they came; thereafter it was scandalous for other officers to associate with them. Anyone in the service accused of a capital offense or any violence against a citizen of the United States was to be surrendered by his commanding officer to the civil authorities for trial. Sutlers, like other camp followers, were subject to the Articles. They were forbidden to keep their shops open after nine o'clock in the evening or to open them before reveille or during divine service on Sundays. A violation usually resulted in the forfeiture of license and exclusion from camp. Any who behaved in unseemly fashion at divine service or swore profanely on any occasion might forfeit a dollar if commissioned, one-sixth as much if enlisted; the funds thus accumulated went to relieve the distress of those in the hospital.[63]

Courts assessing such penalties were of two kinds. The most important was called a general court-martial. It tried the most serious cases and was composed of a maximum of thirteen or a minimum of five officers. A two-thirds vote was necessary for a death sentence, and in times of peace it had to be approved by the President before becoming effective. The dismissal of an officer also had to be referred to the President. The minor court, known as a garrison or regimental court-martial, had a complement

[63] J. H. Callan, *op. cit.*, pp. 170-195.

of only three officers and was allowed to try enlisted men only. Its maximum sentence could not exceed a month's hard labor or forfeiture of pay for a similar period. Neither court could assess more than fifty lashes, and whipping was completely abolished about a month before war was declared in 1812. Courts trying members of the militia were to be composed entirely of their own personnel.[64]

While Dearborn held office, training made little progress except in the branches of engineering and light artillery. For the infantry, the old pattern of Revolutionary instruction continued to be followed; troops were familiar only with von Steuben's "Blue Book." Cavalry and riflemen had no printed manuals. William Duane's *Military Library* was not yet published. If they chose, artillerymen might consult Miller's well known *Treatise*, which had appeared in 1779 and was usually found "in every workship and foundry" where heavy ordnance matériel was manufactured. Its drawings and tables were extensive. One of its plates showed the only style of artillery carriage known. During 1797 Captain William Stevens' *System of Discipline for the Artillery* had become available. It comprised three volumes: the first covered light artillery, the second heavy artillery, and the third the manufacture of ordnance. Though the works of Muller and Stevens were valuable, they were not officially adopted by the War Department.[65] When plans for a larger army were being made in 1798, Alexander Hamilton and C. C. Pinckney drew up training regulations for the artillery. Their manuscript was not published, possibly because the troops for which it was particularly designed were too quickly discharged. It is also possible that it was destroyed in the fire that burned down the War Department building in 1800. During 1808, Wilkinson had a more ambitious program. He compiled a "modern system of movements and maneuvers

64 *Ibid.*, pp. 170-195.
65 W. E. Birkhimer, *Historical Sketch of the Artillery, United States Army*, pp. 224-226; Duane to Eustis, May 1, 1809, in *Senate Document No. 2*, 18th Congress, 1st Session.

for infantry, cavalry and artillery," it was based on translations made from the French.[66] Though Wilkinson billed the War Department for his labors, Dearborn never had the results published, perhaps thinking that other books would serve equally well.

At about this time Kosciusko's *Maneuvers of Horse Artillery* appeared in Paris. Dearborn, who had known the author during the Revolution, saw eye to eye with him on the need of increased mobility for the artillery. The government's acquisition of a number of light pieces from the French at New Orleans may have emphasized this notion. The new pieces were provided with the "most approved Gribeauval carriages, caissons and equipment complete."[67] American field guns usually consisted of 3-pounders and 6-pounders and 5½-inch howitzers mounted on various types of carriages that were moved along by hand traction. All matériel except that requiring a foundry was manufactured by the organization's artificers, who also operated a kind of repair shop for small arms.[68]

The act of April 8, 1808, recognizing the need for an improvement in heavy weapons, authorized the formation of a regiment of light artillery. It did not, however, provide any funds to cover the purchase of horses. Details of equipment were left to the War Department; and Dearborn, always dominated by economy, cautiously began work on this military innovation. No field officers were immediately appointed; in fact, the lieutenant colonel was not commissioned until 1811, the colonel not until the following year. Captain George Peter, an artillery officer, was transferred to the new regiment on May 3, 1808. To him as its senior captain fell the honor of commanding the first properly equipped light artillery company in the United States Army. Three days after he had been designated for this purpose, the secretary of war wrote to him:

"As soon as you can have six-pounders properly mounted, with one ammunition wagon and one light horse

---

[66] W. E. Birkhimer, *op. cit.*, pp. 299-300.

[67] *Ibid.*, pp. 231-232.   [68] *Ibid.*, p. 114.

wagon for conveying four men besides the waggoner, prepared for service, I will order the purchase of a sufficient number of horses for making an experiment with one field piece, with its ammunition wagon containing, say fifty cartridges, ten of which ought to have round shot, and ten of grape or canister. The officers, with one sergeant and three men on horseback, and four men in the light wagon, are to procede at the rate of five or six miles an hour, from Baltimore to this city, and to make some experiments at this place by maneuvering cannon in different directions.... For one six-pounder, one ammunition and one light wagon, and for the officers and others on horseback, it will, I presume, require from thirteen to sixteen horses."[69]

Peter set to work. Ten days later he replied to Dearborn, saying that the horses were in training and the carriages, harness, saddles, bridles, etc., would be ready in a few days. The artificers at Fort McHenry, Maryland, turned out the carriages and limbers following the Gribeauval pattern, assuring a high degree of simplicity and mobility. Twenty-six new uniforms were issued to those who were selected to use this provisional equipment. Soon Peter had his skeleton company rattling over the road to Washington, doing better than six miles an hour. On the fourth of July he led it in a parade along Pennsylvania Avenue; spectators were awed and dazzled as his troops flashed by.[70]

As a result of this initial success, Peter found himself with more men, horses, and guns. By autumn he had a highly efficient and mobile organization. When an army was to be assembled at New Orleans, he was ordered there with his battery. Leaving Baltimore on the day before Christmas, 1808, he set out for Pittsburgh, where he planned to go aboard flatboats and make the rest of his journey by water. Crossing the Alleghenies in mid-winter proved hard but entirely successful. Writing of it to Dearborn, Peter declared, "The performance of the light artillery in the late march has exceeded my most sanguine expectations. The gun carriages, ammunition wagons, fixed ammunition, etc., have arrived without the smallest

[69] *Ibid.*, pp. 34-35.　　　[70] *Ibid.*, p. 35.

injury, and I really believe that the march could have been performed in ten days, could the baggage wagons have kept up with us."[71] Soon after Peter and his men reached New Orleans, Eustis, the new secretary of war, ordered the horses sold, thereby leaving the members of the battery with the hopeless task of dragging their guns by hand through Louisiana mud.[72]

Another of Dearborn's improvements did not end so abruptly. This concerned the artillery guns, especially those designed for use in coast defenses. There 24-pounders and 32-pounders predominated until 1801, when 42-pounders were added. Not until 1811 were there any 50-pounder Columbiads.[73] In 1807 Dearborn reported that there were on hand 927 guns ranging from 18-pounders to 42-pounders, or 235 more than necessary for fourteen different localities requiring defense. Members of Congress seemed to consider his estimates entirely too small, especially after the *Chesapeake* incident; they also knew that some of the guns enumerated were dilapidated relics of the Revolution. In 1808, to allay the fears of some of their constituents along the Atlantic seaboard, they earmarked $1,014,702 for fortifications either to be built or in process of construction. For the same purpose, they appropriated $450,000 on February 10, 1809.[74] If such funds were to be wisely used, more guns had to be furnished. At this time, there was an abundance of the best charcoal and iron ore, but we were entirely dependent on foreign sources for copper and tin. Dearborn, therefore, made a highly desirable and far-reaching change: he discontinued the manufacture of heavy guns from brass and began using iron instead. The iron guns were only a fifth or a sixth as costly, considerably lighter, and no more likely to explode than those of brass.[75]

71 *Ibid.*, pp. 35-36.

72 Eustis to Wilkinson, June 22, 1809, in J. Wilkinson, *op. cit.*, II, pp. 391-392.

73 W. E. Birkhimer, *op. cit.*, p. 277.

74 *American State Papers, Military Affairs*, I, pp. 153-197, 206, 217, 239, 247.

75 W. E. Birkhimer, *op. cit.*, pp. 29-33, 114-115, 266, 271.

To assure a more dependable supply of heavy ordnance, Henry Foxall of the Columbia Foundry was approached by government officials in the hope that he would build a foundry at his own expense on public land near Washington. He demurred, emphasizing the fact that he would probably be unable to convert it to other uses when government business declined because of a change in the times or reasons of political unpopularity. He suggested instead that the government have a foundry of its own, thereby insuring greater uniformity of caliber and design than there had been in the past. He also argued that it would prove very useful in case of emergencies and would furnish valuable data for determining fair prices for work done elsewhere. Failing to reach any agreement with Foxall or others, Dearborn trusted the 500 foundries scattered here and there to meet the demand of war. They could not then, nor did they later, prove equal to it.[76]

The situation with regard to small arms was not more encouraging. The old Charleville pattern of musket prevailed. It was a smooth-bore muzzle-loading flintlock 59½ inches long and weighing nine pounds without a bayonet. Its caliber was .69 inch.[77] At the beginning of 1800, one man working daily could turn out a musket in somewhat less than nine days at either government armory. From 1802 to 1806, 16,234 muskets with bayonets were manufactured at Springfield, Massachusetts, at a cost of $8.945 apiece; at Harpers Ferry, Virginia, only 7,158 were completed and each of them cost $13.435. Even with this difference in expense, Dearborn declared that the former were as highly finished as the latter, and that both of them were equal if not superior to those manufactured elsewhere.[78] Hardly any guns were imported from abroad, even though no duty was levied against them. The same was true of powder. The government, even with the aid of private companies, could not reasonably expect to equip

[76] *American State Papers, Military Affairs*, I, pp. 215-217.

[77] C. A. Miller, "Springfield Arms," in *Army Ordnance*, July-Aug., 1939, opposite p. 14.

[78] *American State Papers, Military Affairs*, I, p. 199.

50,000 militia troops with fundamental arms within two or three years. In fact, not until April 23, 1808, was federal money appropriated to purchase arms for them. It then amounted to only $200,000. A musket cost about $12.00; thus less than 17,000 troops could be equipped if supplies were available. From time to time the states did something to help their militia, but their efforts were consistently casual.

Although Dearborn was a popular and practical soldier of genuine merit, he lacked the varied experience and mental capacity of other great leaders of the early republic. As secretary of war, he remained in office for eight years and two days, a longer continuous period than anyone else in the history of our country. Nevertheless, he did not succeed in making the militia a dependable component of defense or in creating a body of regulars that could furnish a competent framework for a considerable army in case of emergency.

The regulars were definitely not being fitted to meet the requirements of the War of 1812. Few of their officers knew anything about units larger than a company unless they had learned it during the Revolution; and in this case they were so old by Dearborn's time that they could not function efficiently in the field. Battalions had no staff, and not until 1808 were there rudimentary staffs for regiments and brigades. Even for the entire army, laws provided for only an inspector, ten paymasters, a flexible number of assistant military agents, and a lone aide for the general-in-chief; and these were merely a conglomeration of individuals doing routine chores. The difficult problems of supply were in the wrong hands. Three civilians, known as military agents, made purchases for the army but were not subject to its control. They had little interest in strategy or tactics; they worked to show diminished expenditures and a set of nicely balanced books. The necessities of troops were frequently ignored. The contractors, too, were civilians, seldom or never serving the army well if their profits were in danger. Thus while military agents and contractors were demonstrating the evils of the system that engaged them, army officers, to whom these duties rightfully belonged, were not being trained in purchasing and transportation—two matters of supreme importance. In financial matters, the army was only a little better off, being cluttered with regulations for saving pennies. Supervision was so close that a post commander dared not order an expenditure of $50 unless Dearborn first gave approval. In some cases this might require several months because of the distance to Washington. Ruled by such limitations, officers sometimes failed to act in emergencies. As time went on, they became more confirmed in their hesitancy, more hidebound by custom and regulations, almost incapable of making rapid and sound decisions in critical and unusual cases. In fact, the army had cost very little, and its real value was in proportion. Dearborn had clearly shown that he lacked the ability to create an army that would meet the requirements for national defense.

11. *A Military Academy is Founded*

I*n* the Library of the United States Military Academy at West Point hangs a full-length portrait painted by Thomas Sully in 1822. It is of a venerable man slightly stooped, but his head is uplifted and his eyes seem to focus upon faraway things. He may have been recalling the stirring events in which he had stood for those principles that have sustained all peoples since the world began— principles that have not been discarded with fashion like his plum-colored top-coat and the black knee-breeches, which he often wore when riding over his Virginia acres. Neighbors were familiar with his figure and customary dress, but few recognized the outward signs of greatness that the artist has not only perceived but revealed to all who will look and ponder upon the well known features of Thomas Jefferson, the founder of the Academy.

The faculty and cadets of long ago are responsible for this engaging portrait; they themselves contributed the funds that made it possible. They wanted a portrait of Jefferson to remind future officers of the distinguished President who had done so much for their institution. Few donors have had a finer judgment or a better cause.[1]

Although Jefferson established the Academy in 1802, army officers had discussed it for many years. They had often thought of West Point as a desirable location, possibly because it was near the center of population and had long been associated with military engineering. As early as July 1776, Lieutenant Thomas Machim was sent there to lay out fortifications that seem to have been recommended by Colonel Bernard Romans and approved by General Washington.[2] After the surrender of Forts Montgomery

---

[1] T. H. Ormsbee, *The Sully Portraits*, etc., *passim*.
[2] *The Centennial of the United States Military Academy at West Point, 1802-1902*, p. 10; and *MS. Map* 4023.

and Clinton in October 1777, West Point remained the best place along the Hudson to halt hostile movements between New York and Albany. Brigadier General Louis Lebègue Duportail, head of the Corps of Engineers, determined to strengthen its defenses.[3]

One of his very able subordinates was Colonel Thaddeus Kosciusko. After serving Gates with distinction during the autumn of 1777, he was ordered to complete the West Point fortifications that had been haphazardly begun by Putnam and others. He did his work well in spite of difficulties. Before the middle of 1778 the walls of Forts Arnold, Wyllys, Webb, and Putnam were rising against the sky. Emplacements were prepared for a number of guns; in May a few pieces captured from Burgoyne were put in position. After ice had disappeared in the Hudson, a huge iron chain was stretched from West Point to Constitution Island. The links were two feet long, and each of them weighed 140 pounds. Laying such an obstruction in spring and taking it up in autumn required brain and brawn.[4]

Members of the garrison had their full share of toil and hardships. Its first soldier-laborers had little or no shelter, and often the snow was waist high. Using branches from the stunted pines for beds and their own worn blankets for cover, they slept in the open until they had built rude cabins to protect themselves from wind and cold.[5] Small wonder that even after conditions had improved, some stole "rals" to light a warming fire, resulting in an order that anyone "Gilty of such Base Prattis in futur May Depend on Being Severely Punnishitt and the Officer who Kirnife att it will Be called to account."[6] In spite of poor shelter, wretched clothing, and scant rations, fatigue details were large and almost continuous. Usually

[3] T. H. S. Hamersly, *Army Register of the United States*, pp. 272-273.

[4] *The Centennial*, pp. 11-12; W. M. Hornor, Jr., *Obstructions of the Hudson River during the Revolution*, pp. 12-23; Steel Facts, May, 1942, pp. 6-7.

[5] *The Centennial*, pp. 11-12.

[6] *Orderly Book of Benjamin Peabody*, Aug. 31, 1780, p. 35.

they worked from six a.m. to evening gun. For pay, a private drew seven badly depreciated dollars a month. Of this amount sixty-six cents usually went to his washerwoman.[7]

For a while during 1779, when efforts were accelerated to make West Point impregnable, some 2,500 men were employed in laboring there. Once the garrison contained nine regiments exclusive of militia. Duportail believed that 2,880 troops would be needed to man the finished works. Washington considered the place highly important; for a time it was used as his headquarters.[8]

In 1780 Benedict Arnold arrived to assume command. He was then a major general who had already fought brilliantly, lived extravagantly, and carried on a treasonable correspondence with the enemy. At his new post, he completed his program of treachery. In return for his surrender of West Point, the British promised him a commission of brigadier general in their army and a purse amounting to nearly $50,000 in gold. When Major John André, acting as intermediary, was captured near Tarrytown on September 23, Arnold, perceiving that his schemes had failed, immediately fled to the British ship *Vulture* that lay in the Hudson. Though fighting later as a general against the Americans, most of his new allies contemptuously spurned him until the day of his death.[9] After this abortive effort to capture West Point, it attracted little notice for the rest of the Revolution. The War was being waged south of the Potomac. The place became an asylum for those who could no longer withstand the hardships of battle.

A "Corps of Invalids" had been authorized on June 20, 1777. It was to be composed of those who had become casualties. In return for their clothing and keep, they were to serve as immobile garrisons and as a nucleus for training young men who had hopes of being officers in marching regiments. During 1778 some of these invalids began to straggle into West Point. Two years later those from the

[7] *The Centennial*, p. 13.   [8] *Ibid.*, pp. 15-16.
[9] *Dictionary of American Biography*, I, pp. 362-367.

Connecticut and Massachusetts line arrived. Few of them could render any service of value. As a rule, they were pitifully clothed and wretchedly fed. By 1784 most of them had drifted away. Only thirty-eight remained; they were poor and maimed and had no place to go.[10]

Among them was Captain Molly, the only woman in the "regiment" of invalids. Her real name was Margaret Corbin, but she liked her nickname better. It was certainly preferable to "Dirty Kate," which she was sometimes secretly called. Her husband, John C. Corbin, had enlisted as a matross during the Revolution. Accompanying him on campaign, she was accustomed to fill in her time with washing, mending, cooking, and nursing. At the defense of Fort Washington she took her place beside John; while bravely helping to load, fire, and sponge the guns, she was badly wounded with three grapeshot, finally losing the use of an arm. Some time later Pennsylvania gave her a grant of $30. Congress did a little better; it munificently voted her a complete suit of clothes, or its equivalent, and the half pay of a private for the rest of her life. Later the same amount of clothing became annual, but her heartening allowance of liquor was taken away. Bereft of her whisky, disabled, and scantily clad she turned up at West Point, where an order was issued on September 14, 1782, giving her all parts of the ration, half pay for life, and a suit of clothes every year. Since it was retroactive, she now had a due bill for 257 gills of whisky. By such means she was able to acquire a few sundries and make more tumultuous her irascible moods. She could not get about, and for a time was bedridden. Captain Price arranged for her care with boarding-house keepers; one of them was three miles from West Point. Thus he escaped her frequent outbursts of temper, but it did not go so easily for those who had her immediate care. Though deserving much better, she was shabbily kept and sometimes maltreated. The captain supplied her with bed-sacks that others had discarded, and when she needed a shift, he cut up a tent and fashioned it for her. But she seemed to care neither for his material nor

10 *The Centennial*, p. 23.

pattern, so the Captain wrote to the secretary of war, Henry Knox, and asked for three or four shifts. Whether Captain Molly ever received them is not very clear. Upon her death a year or two later, she was drably buried outside the reservation, only to be ceremoniously disinterred in 1926 and placed in final glory beside those who have added heartening pages to the annals of our country.[11]

While West Point was serving as an asylum for the disabled in battle, it was also being used as a depot for storing army equipment not immediately needed. In 1784, 201 cannon were listed on the inventories as fit for service. Five years later 4,146 half, single, and double barrels of powder had been accumulated, according to the records.[12] It was not uniformly good, but it sufficed for issue to Indians or frontier troops. Once in a while a garrison soldier stole a bit for sale to an unwary buyer. Frequently the powder had to be dried out and put in new wooden containers, which civilian coopers were hired to make when artificers were not available. During 1789 the quartermaster had at least one barrel-maker constantly employed, furnishing him a ration and housing in addition to pay of about $7 a month.[13] Other equipment was probably less efficiently cared for. Storehouses were unsuitable. Cleaning and repairing personnel were few and were frequently shifted to other stations. For a time Richard and Joseph Cranch were hired for the purpose. Before 1796 Joseph wanted some twenty-odd cents for cleaning a French, British or Hessian stand of arms; later he asked for double the amount. When repairs or spare parts were required, the price, of course, was increased. Richard charged a dime for glueing a stock or $2.12 for providing a new one of black walnut. He furnished a small screw for seven cents and an English bayonet for $1.32.[14] All parts had to be specially fitted, for exact uniformity had not been achieved.

[11] E. H. Hall, *Margaret Corbin, passim.*
[12] *The Centennial,* p. 23; and *West Point Ordnance Waste Book No. 2.*
[13] *West Point Letter Book No. 2.*
[14] *West Point Ordnance Waste Book No. 4.*

These salvaged muskets, bayonets, belts, cartridge boxes, etc., were often so defective that distant troops were not happy to receive them. It is hoped that the Algerian pirates were even less pleased when they found that their frigate, a singular gift of the United States, was equipped with such questionable ordnance.

If West Point had remained an old soldiers' home and a depot for salvaged supplies, it would never have risen to any marked importance. Fortunately the idea of using it as a training center for the more technical branches of the service had been germinating. On September 23, 1776, Henry Knox wrote to his brother declaring, "We ought to have academies, in which the whole theory of the art of war should be taught, and every encouragement possible be given to draw persons into the army that may give lustre to our arms. As the army now stands, it is merely a receptacle for ragamuffins."[15] Four days later he outlined his ideas more definitely to a Congressional Committee. He proposed that "an Academy be established on a liberal plan...where the whole theory and practice of fortifications and gunnery should be taught, to be nearly on the same plan as Woolwich, making an allowance for the difference of circumstances."[16] About a year afterwards Florberque de la Rocatelle advised Washington to establish a school of military art where a regiment of artillerists, engineers, bombardiers and cannoneers should be stationed.[17] Such a suggestion was timely because of the acute need of artillerists and engineers, but nothing immediately resulted from the efforts of either Knox or Rocatelle. In fact, the army had no training center worthy of note during the Revolution. Sometimes a sort of theoretical instruction was given in the intervals between battles. In 1779, at Pluckemin, New Jersey, Knox induced some of his officers to read lectures on tactics and gunnery. At Pluckemin he

---

[15] H. Knox to W. Knox, Sept. 23, 1776, Noah Brooks, *Henry Knox*, p. 71.

[16] H. Knox to Congressional Committee, Sept. 27, 1776, *The Centennial*, p. 202.

[17] *The Centennial*, p. 208.

also had work huts erected for those who were engaged in making ammunition and other equipment.[18]

When the war ended, Washington thoughtfully considered what should be the size and character of the country's peacetime force and in what way it might best be maintained. During the spring of 1783 a committee of Congress had asked his ideas on this important subject. He in turn sought advice from his colleagues in arms— Steuben, Knox, Huntington, Pickering, Heath, Hand, and Rufus Putnam. Their answers focused on supply, training, and personnel.[19]

Besides other highly important recommendations, Steuben advocated the establishment of an academy and a "manufactory" for military supplies, both of which were to be operated under a director general and a council for the benefit of 120 cadets, who would be required to be over fourteen years of age and would pay the government $300 apiece. High salaried professors would instruct in the subjects of natural philosophy, eloquence, belles lettres, civil and international law, history, geography, mathematics, civil architecture, drawing, French, horsemanship, fencing, dancing, and music. This course was deemed insufficient for those expecting to become artillerists or engineers; they were to be given additional instruction in surveying and gunnery. None would be eligible for a commission in the army except graduates of this academy or former officers of the Revolution.[20]

Steuben was not alone in his desire for an academy. Huntington, Pickering, and others had similar views. Brigadier General Duportail, in reporting on the artillerists and engineers, declared the need for an academy as a "nursery of the corps is too obvious to be insisted on." Under his plan army officers would do the instructing, the course would extend over three years, and some twenty appointed cadets would take it. At about the same time, in 1783, Captain Lewis Garranger urged Congress to

[18] *Philadelphia Packet*, March 6, 1779.
[19] J. M. Palmer, *America in Arms*, pp. 4-9.
[20] *The Centennial*, p. 206.

retain West Point as a place of military education. Philadelphia might be used for the same purpose, as well as
some other place, like Charleston, in the South.[21]

After considering these various ideas, Washington
himself wrote a memorandum to the Committee of Congress.
It was entitled "Sentiments on a Peace Establishment."
It favored a small regular army for protecting the frontier
and magazines, a well organized militia, a series of arsenals
and "manufactories" for military stores, and one or more
academies for instruction in military art.[22] The wisdom of
such a program well deserved approval. But the powers of
Congress were inadequate and the people did not favor laws
of this kind. As for an academy, the Committee declared it
was not worth the expense; the professors attached to the
Corps of Engineers might better give their instruction
wherever they happened to be.[23] The real cause for such
reasoning was that the government was bankrupt, its
credit was gone, and soldiers had already mutinied because
they had not been paid.

From this time until the government under the Constitution was established, the idea of an academy withered
away. West Point had little to distinguish itself from any
other post. Early in 1784 the garrison numbered about
600 men, most of them belonging to the infantry, the rest
to the artillery. General Knox commanded the post for a
while. By May, all of them had been mustered out except
fifty-five, who composed what remained of Alexander
Hamilton's battery, raised in 1776. The number was not
greatly increased for several years. Captain Henry Burbeck's company arrived at West Point during August 1787
and remained there except for a short absence until April
5, 1790. During this period he acted as post commander.
Meanwhile the ground for the reservation had been purchased outright to avoid paying an annual rental of
$437.[24] Thus by the time that Washington was inaugurated

[21] *Ibid.*, pp. 207-208.

[22] Washington, "Sentiments on a Peace Establishment," *Writings
of Washington* (Bi-centennial ed.) vol. 26, pp. 374-398.

[23] *The Centennial,* p. 208.

[24] *Ibid.*, p. 24; and M. Knowlton, *Lands Belonging to the United
States at West Point*, pp. 20-24.

in 1789, West Point had several reasons for being considered as a possible training center. It was centrally located, the land on which it stood was federally owned, and its facilities were particularly adapted for the use of artillerists and engineers.

Knox, as a member of Washington's cabinet and an artillerist of distinction, worked for adequate training. In his recommendations to Congress on January 21, 1790, he urged a "small corps of well disciplined and well informed artillerists and engineers," plus a regular legion and a body of trained militia. Washington, seeing eye to eye with his secretary on the problem of national defense, used him as his mouthpiece. But nothing came from their suggestions except a slight increase in the number of regulars.[25]

When ranking officers complained of the incapacity of their subordinates, Knox saw an ultimate solution in selecting ensigns more carefully, requiring that they be young men of education, character, and spirit. He would have them come from an academy, the foundation for "a respectable army," but he ruefully declared, "the genius of the Republic seems adverse to the permanency of an Army, and every plan which may be proposed to render troops radically good would probably be regarded by many well intentioned citizens as the seeds of a standing army designed to overturn the liberties of the country.

"The army must therefore depend upon itself for its discipline. The officers who possess extensive minds must inculcate the principles of economy, obedience to orders, habitual vigilance, and sobriety and good manners, so essential to perfect discipline and a dignified military reputation subservient to the Laws."[26]

In 1792, several months after Knox had written the above letter to Wilkinson, the question of a military school at West Point was considered by Washington and his cabinet. All favored the idea except Jefferson, who doubted

[25] *American State Papers, Military Affairs*, I, p. 7.

[26] Knox to Wilkinson, July 17, 1792, *Wilkinson Papers*, 1792-1806, Detroit Public Library.

whether such an establishment was in keeping with the Constitution.[27] The decision was left to Congress, which did nothing, largely due to the public apathy and the reasons that Knox had previously given.

But events soon stirred the people from their lethargy and made them appreciate the need for some kind of institution where officers might be trained. With the British impressing our sailors, condemning our ships, and threatening our seacoast towns, those who lived near the Atlantic were strong in their outcry for forts and guns. So few knew anything about either that the government had to employ foreigners to erect our defenses. To prevent the indefinite continuation of such a humiliating condition, a regiment of artillerists and engineers was authorized by the act of May 9, 1794. A school was established at West Point to train the personnel of this new organization. The director was Stephen Rochefontaine, lieutenant colonel commandant and ranking officer of the artillerists and engineers. He had served honorably in the Revolution, winning the brevet of major. His field officers were Louis Tousard, John Jacob Ulrich Rivardi, Henry Burbeck, and Constant Freeman Jr.[28]

Rochefontaine himself arrived at West Point on June 24, 1795.[29] Most of his officers had been commissioned already. As they and the recruits arrived, organization proceeded. At a drawing for colors, the 1st Battalion drew red; the 2nd, green; the 3rd, white; and the 4th, blue.[30] Officers' uniforms were the same as worn by members of the original artillery battalion, then stationed on the frontier. For enlisted personnel, helmets, plumes, and cockades were issued instead of hats. Their coats were blue, faced and lined with scarlet; buttons were yellow and cross belts, white. Pantaloons were to be dark blue in winter and white in summer; half gaiters were black and seven inches high.

[27] *The Centennial,* p. 212.
[28] T. H. S. Hamersly, *Complete Regular Army Register,* p. 275 (2nd part).
[29] *West Point Orderly Book of the Corps of Artillerists and Engineers,* No. 1, p. 30.
[30] *Ibid.,* pp. 32-33.

As late as 1796 only three of the thirty-two cadets authorized seem to have reported to West Point. They were
James Tryplett, Philip Rodrique, and Phillip Landais.[31]
Though doing duty as officers, they drew the uniform,
equipment, and pay of sergeants. Each company went by
its captain's name, which was written on the outside of
the barracks door where it was quartered. On the inside
were listed the corporals in charge of squads. Each man's
name was posted at the head of his bunk.[32]

The regiment enjoyed the distinction of having a band
of twenty pieces. Its members wore black gaiters, helmets
with scarlet plumes, and scarlet coats with dark blue
facings and yellow silk epaulettes. For their instruments
and such gorgeous trappings, the government made no
provision, the cost of both being borne by the officers and
men of the regiment.[33] The musicians, of course, were all
enlisted, most or all of them being drawn from the company
trumpeters. As long as the regiment was concentrated at
one post, the band had a chance of existence.

After these and other details had been arranged, training proceeded. At times Rochefontaine had Tousard and
Rivardi as assistants at West Point. Like him, they were
able but decidedly French in outlook. Instruction went on
with the matériel available. For this purpose, one captain
drew, among other things, a 5-inch howitzer and a half-
dozen brass 6-pounders. Students had to learn the use of
these as well as to know minutely von Steuben's *Regulations*. Beginning on February 10, 1796, officers and cadets
were required to attend "the instruction room" between
eleven and twelve o'clock in the morning, and between four
and five in the afternoon to learn the theory of fortifications. Part of this time was spent in making copies of
typical military works. Paper, pencils, mahogany rulers,
India ink, paint, gamboge, brushes, etc. were supplied.
Orders were issued that none of these articles should be

31 *The Centennial*, pp. 508-509.
32 *West Point Orderly Book of the Corps of Artillerists and Engineers*, No. 2, p. 46.
33 *The Centennial*, pp. 25-26.

accidentally carried away. Senior officers were requested to be present to preserve order and decorum. There were plenty of troublemakers who had no thirst for knowledge and evinced no regard for the Frenchman's technique. After a few months, lectures and lessons ceased for very substantial reasons. During April "the instruction room" caught fire and burned to the ground with all its equipment. Some thought that the theory of fortifications had merely resulted in a practical demonstration of arson. At any rate, no more instruction of this kind was given until 1802, six years later.[34]

The officers of the newly-formed regiment of artillerists and engineers were a difficult lot to control. Most of them were too old for their grade, had little formal education, and were highly critical of Rochefontaine's methods. One April evening in 1796, Lieutenant William Wilson poked his head out of a window and yelled to Rochefontaine that he was a "damned rascal." A duel followed. Three times Wilson fired but without effect; Rochefontaine twice replied with corresponding results. The two then clinched. With no holds barred, the real fight started. The lieutenant lost a good deal of breath swearing at the colonel and yelling that he was going to kill him. In spite of the threat, Rochefontaine escaped with little physical harm; only his feelings and dignity were grossly outraged. In a ferment of mind, he wrote to his friend, Alexander Hamilton, and asked for advice. Apparently the postman, on his four-day round from Peekskill, brought instructions to convene a court of inquiry. Before long the colonel was investigated and restored to his command. At least, this was what Lieutenant N. I. Vischer wrote—the same lovelorn lieutenant to whom the charming Patty Gansevoort had sent twelve dozen kisses engraved on gold leaf. Gossips did not quickly forget Rochefontaine's "recounter," for smiles and chuckles came easily whenever the story of it was told. Another duel at about the same time did not end so for-

34 *Ibid.*, pp. 213-214.

tunately; in it Lieutenant Joseph Elliott was dangerously wounded by Ensign William Scott.[35]

In some respects life in posts along the lower Hudson was less exacting than in those which Indians constantly threatened. In the presence of the enemy, delinquencies had to be treated with more severity. At West Point, a drunkard might incur a bread-and-water diet and confinement in the Black Hole of Fort Putnam for a varying number of hours; perhaps he might also have to suffer twenty-five lashes laid upon his "bare posteriors." While the punishment was being carried out the adjutant, musicians, and a few of the guard were permitted to be present. Sometimes a drunken delinquent was let off by paying a dollar into the company fund.[36] If equipment was lost or destroyed, the cost was charged against the person guilty; he might also suffer a short term of confinement. If a soldier sold government property, his head might be shaved and his outer garments marked with an S. Once in a while a soldier turned up at inspection without a cap because he had left it somewhere as security for a round of drinks. In this case he would have to get it back immediately or suffer a deduction of a dollar and a half for a new one.[37] If not present at tattoo, he might expect some nominal penalty. Once two soldiers who were absent claimed that they had stayed out all night in the company garden to protect it from "cows and other creatures." They were held a day in the guard house for taking such unusual precautions. Corporal Carlton drew even less punishment for more vigorous action. When Eliphalet Worthington's cow innocently grazed on vegetables planted not far from the barracks, the corporal chased her away and "quelled and injured" her. Though Eliphalet was apparently more distraught than she, he obtained no satisfaction except that the corporal had to do duty as a

[35] West Point *MS.*, 418; and C. V. R. Bonney, *A Legacy of Historical Gleanings*, I, pp. 123-124.

[36] West Point *MS.*, 1173, 1216.

[37] *West Point Orderly Book of the Corps of Artillerists and Engineers*, No. 2, p. 69, No. 3, p. 195.

A Cadet before 1812 (from a portrait in the United States Military Academy Library).

private for three days.[38] When a soldier climbed up a tree in a neighboring orchard, and shook down some apples, the owner caught him red handed, gave him a clubbing and called him a rascal. Believing that he had suffered enough for his pilfering, the court did nothing at all.[39] But when Captain Steele with a piece of artillery nearly obliterated the tavern of Esquire North for selling liquor to soldiers, he was assessed damages for his pains.[40] Whether he had to pay them all is unknown. Rochefontaine, after his arrival, was prone to reduce sentences except for the most serious offenses, such as insubordination and desertion.

But even women, in aggravated cases, knew what a whipping meant. When Patty Tooney returned after being drummed out of the garrison three times for disorderly conduct, the court decided to give her the same punishments as before plus twenty lashes upon her naked back. Had she been a mere soldier, she would have bared her buttocks instead. As it was, reasons of "delicacy" prevailed; an officer was even detailed to see that her breasts should suffer no harm.[41] Patty deserved this trifling dispensation and favor. Washing for some fifteen or more men a week brought her only a single ration, a pallet of straw, and a pittance of pay. She might eke out a little more if she were lucky enough to be hired out occasionally by the day. With little before them except a wash-tub horizon, small wonder that Patty and her erring sisters found solace in liquor and frequently bootlegged it to their companions in sin.

The garrison at West Point was larger than at most army posts. During the summer of 1796 at least three battalions took part in parades.[42] After they had been partly organized and trained, they were transferred to

---

[38] West Point *MS.*, 1170.

[39] *West Point Orderly Book of the Corps of Artillerists and Engineers*, No. 1, pp. 157-158.

[40] Harrison Ellery, *The Memoirs of General Joseph Gardner Swift*, p. 30.

[41] *West Point Orderly Book of the Corps of Artillerists and Engineers*, No. 1, pp. 73-74.

[42] *Ibid.*, No. 3, p. 3.

the most important forts that had been built or repaired during the three or four years preceding. By the spring of 1798 only three officers, one cadet, and seventy-three men were present at West Point.[43] The one-armed Tousard, who had won a Congressional brevet of lieutenant colonel and a pension of $30 a month in the Revolution, was sent to supervise the defenses of New York City. Rivardi went to Detroit and later to Niagara; Constant Freeman took station in the South; and Burbeck continued on duty in the northwest. Rochefontaine remained in or about West Point until May 7, 1798, when he was discharged, partly because of the very general antipathy that the army and the public felt against France. In spite of a genuine ignorance of artillery and engineering, Jonathan Dayton made efforts to step into his shoes, but he failed to be appointed. Burbeck was promoted instead. He was a faithful soldier but without the scientific knowledge or interest requisite to head such a corps.[44] Tousard and Rivardi remained in the service until 1802, when the army was reduced and they were discharged.

Although Rochefontaine and his associates had not made an impressive record at West Point, Adams still insisted that facilities must be maintained for the training of officers. On this point he heartily agreed with Washington, who had written Hamilton during the last part of 1799 that "the art of war is at once comprehensive and complicated—it demands much previous study—the possession of it, in its most improved and perfect state, is always of great moment to the security of a nation—for this purpose, an academy where a regular course of instruction is given, is an obvious expedient."[45]

With such thoughts, Hamilton prepared an elaborate plan for training commissioned personnel and sent it to James McHenry, the secretary of war. Concurring in its ideas, the secretary then drew up and forwarded to the

[43] *The Centennial*, p. 6.
[44] W. E. Birkhimer, *Historical Sketch of the Organization, Administration, Material, and Tactics of the Artillery, United States Army*, p. 32.
[45] E. C. Boyton, *History of West Point*, p. 187.

President detailed suggestions on this subject. Bearing the President's recommendation, they were transmitted as a report to Congress on January 14, 1800. By its provisions four schools of fundamental and advanced training for the army and navy were to be established. They were to be located preferably near navigable water and factories for arms.[46] Plenty of equipment was to be provided, a staff of competent instructors was to be engaged, Count Rumford, a great scientist and statesman, was to be offered the position as director of the school. But Congress scrapped the entire plan.[47]

West Point, accordingly, continued much as it had been before—a depot for supplies and a training center of sorts. The garrison usually consisted of only one or more companies with a captain as commanding officer. George Fleming acted as military storekeeper. He drew a salary of $650 a year, lived in a house that General Knox had once used as headquarters, and had charge of all the Revolutionary matériel stored in the long yellow buildings to the northwest near the river. Close by lived Zebina Kingsley, the armorer, and his "exemplary" wife. Mrs. Fleming did not have quite the same reputation. She apparently kept boarders and was inclined to complain. Her husband George may have added to her worries, for he seems to have taken life very much as it came. When she lay sick in her bed, she demanded that the drummers practice where she would not have to hear them. Her neighbor Mrs. Rivardi might have sought a similar favor, not being very well during her pregnancy. When the child arrived she made a somewhat original request of her husband, a rather pliant and henpecked man: to share in her joy she wanted all those in the guard house, except deserters, released from confinement. The post commander acquiesced; thus life and liberty were simultaneously born at West Point on a May day in 1796. Thereafter prisoners naturally yearned for an increase in population and another jail delivery. The large families there gave sub-

[46] American State Papers, Military Affairs, I, pp. 133-139.
[47] The Centennial, p. 215.

stance to hope. Lieutenant and Mrs. Osborn, for example, had a number of children. She was "beautiful," he was studious, and both were popular. They lived in the "White quarters" on the front of the hill overlooking the river.[48]

The Lillies, too, had a large family. There were eight of them, and they were at West Point for most of 1801. The father was a captain, and for a time was post commander. They all had to live very meagerly on the pay that he drew. Often he thought of resigning. He wrote to his friend Samuel Breck in the hope of obtaining civilian employment. When nothing developed from his inquiries, he became greatly discouraged; but he continued to plod along, recalling his remarks of earlier years that "despicable as life is, a man when he has lost it, is not worth half what he was when he had it." His family soon appreciated the full meaning of this bit of philosophy. On September 22, 1801, he was stricken with apoplexy and "died in the arms of his friends." Left without property, Mrs. Lillie decided to move to Milton, Massachusetts, where her poverty might be more easily borne. An officer accompanied the unhappy widow and children to New York City. He would have gone with them farther if she had desired. Master John Lillie remained temporarily at West Point with his friend Lieutenant Harvard, who tried to keep him contented and looked after his schooling. Owing to the influence of friends, John was appointed an army cadet on Christmas eve 1801. He was then only ten years and seven months old. Leaving his home, he returned to West Point where he remained for four years and six months, boarding with some of his friends at the cost of about five dollars a month. He may have stayed with George Fleming, who had written Mrs. Lillie and told her he would be glad to have John. At the same time he disclosed that he had overpaid her $62.42½ when her accounts were settled. Possibly, Samuel Breck, or someone else, paid the debt, or her orphan boy helped to whittle it down with part of the ten dollars that he drew

[48] Ellery, *op. cit.*, pp. 29-30; *West Point Orderly Book of the Corps of Artillerists and Engineers*, No. 2, pp. 95, 115.

each month as a cadet. Whatever occurred, John was not very happy; afterwards he considered this part of his life as spent among the idle, irreligious, dissipated, and uncontrolled. Apparently the hardships of his youth gave bitterness to his observations.[49] He seems never to have been commissioned.

Significant changes were destined to come under Jefferson, but these did not particularly benefit young John Lillie. Soon after becoming President, Jefferson directed his secretary of war, Henry Dearborn, to take the steps necessary to found a military academy. On April 14, 1801, Lieutenant Colonel Tousard, inspector of artillery, was ordered to West Point to help with instruction when his routine duties permitted. At about the same time, George Baron was selected to teach mathematics. Major Jonathan Williams, inspector of fortifications, was chosen to head the "Military School," soon to be established there.[50]

Its purpose was to instruct cadets in preparation for commissions. As early as 1794 cadets had been appointed in the army, occupying a position that was neither commissioned nor enlisted. They helped with drill, paper work, and general police; occasionally they acted as judge advocates in court-martial cases. Their education did not progress far by doing these odd jobs that officers avoided.

When Major Williams reached West Point late in 1801, he had to confer often with George Fleming, the resident storekeeper and acting quartermaster for the garrison. Especially comfortable houses were to be provided for two teachers of mathematics and gunnery and for the two inspectors, one of artillery and the other of fortifications. There was to be a school building measuring twenty by

[49] West Point *MS.*, pp. 272, 275, 277, 280, 295, 402, 471.

[50] Dearborn to Tousard, Apr. 14, 1801; Dearborn to Commanding Officer, West Point, Apr. 15, 1801, *Military Book, No. 1*, pp. 54-57, National Archives.

thirty feet, made of wood and plainly furnished, and consisting of two stories of a single room each.[51]

Cadets began to straggle in about the time of Williams's arrival. The group consisted of promising men in the ranks, sons of army officers, and various civilians. The day before John Adams left office, he parceled out nine appointments.[52] No minimum qualifications were required. Joseph G. Swift, who reported in 1801, has recalled that his classmates ranged in age from twelve to thirty-four years. He might have said that John Lillie was only eleven. Some, he added, were married and had several children, a few were college graduates, one was an ex-British officer, and another had practiced law in the Supreme Court of New York.[53] Though differing so widely in capacity and experience, they seem to have been formed into a single class and followed the same general course of study, usually meeting during the mornings in the small wooden building known as the "Academy." They sat on the long green benches that little John Lillie's father, so recently dead, had arranged to be painted. If John shared in this instruction, it must have been very puzzling to such a young lad. Certainly others did not relish it keenly. During the afternoons, the work was practical and had a wider appeal. Sometimes they practiced surveying, artillery firing, and field exercises. Lectures were given at the "model yard," where Rochefontaine and Rivardi had built a miniature fortress and its auxiliary defenses.

As it was organized, the school certainly could not produce the type of engineer officer that the army acutely needed. The act of March 16, 1802, was designed to improve this condition by creating a Corps of Engineers that was entirely separate from the artillery and consisted of a maximum of twenty officers and cadets. After authorized promotions had been made, this number would be made up

[51] Dearborn to Fleming, May 12, 1801, *Military Book, No. 1*, pp. 70-71.

[52] Sec. of War to Cushing, Mar. 3, 1801, *Military Book, No. 1*, p. 43, National Archives.

[53] H. Ellery, *op. cit.*, pp. 34-35.

of a colonel, a lieutenant colonel, two majors, four captains, four first lieutenants, four second lieutenants, and
four cadets. At first ten engineer cadets were appointed
with an allowance of two rations apiece and the pay of
$16 a month, or $6 more than was granted to those from
any other branch of the service. Promotions in the corps
were to be made on the basis of merit rather than by
seniority, as obtained in the artillery and infantry. Its
personnel were to be stationed at West Point, New York,
for the purpose of forming a "military academy" over
which the principal engineer would preside as superintendent.[54] By this law the United States Military Academy
was founded.

Major Jonathan Williams continued as superintendent.
More than a year passed before all the authorized officers
and cadets of the engineer corps were appointed. Men
fitted for the various grades were hard to find. Though James
Wilson and Alexander Macomb were already first lieutenants they reported to the Academy as students. A
dozen cadets did likewise. Among them were Joseph G.
Swift and Simon Levy, soon to be commissioned. They
were all put to studying Hutton's *Mathematics*, Enfield's
Philosophy, Vauban's *Fortifications*, and Sheet's *Artillery*.[55] Blackboards were used as aids to instruction;
students were stimulated to effort by being warned that
they would be publicly examined at the end of each course.
Necessary books and instruments were acquired from a
variety of sources. Usually they were bought from dealers
at home or abroad or from officers who had some to spare.
Williams and Wilkinson sold a few to the Academy. Swift
did likewise when he needed some money to meet the obligation assumed for a friend who had turned drunkard and
defaulter.[56] When First Lieutenant Robert W. Coburn
was appointed assistant military agent at West Point in
1803, he and George Fleming acted as supply officers; but

[54] J. F. Callan, *op. cit.*, pp. 141-149.
[55] Ellery, *op. cit.*, p. 32.
[56] *Ibid.*, p. 47; and Dearborn to Barron, Oct. 7, 1803, *Military Book,
No. 2*, p. 72, National Archives.

they were so restricted by regulations and the War Department's zeal for economy that they purchased little. To the schoolroom equipment, however, they managed to add a pair of hand irons, a shovel, and a few chairs for officers to sit in.[57] Dearborn was so opposed to spending that he carefully scrutinized all of Williams's requests for books and took him to task for wasting paper and postage by writing a separate letter concerning each subject. Maybe the secretary ruefully recalled that, some three years before, he had approved a bill of $64.00 covering four reams of paper and 500 copies of the *Elements of Fortifications*.[58]

Equipment was hard to obtain, and competent instructors were even more rare. During the spring of 1802, Jared A. Mansfield was appointed a captain of engineers and became a teacher of "natural and experimental philosophy." He enjoyed a high reputation for learning, being a former teacher at Yale, an intimate of Jefferson, and the author of "Motion of Bodies in True Space." Unfortunately he remained at the Academy for only a little more than a year. The stay of Captain William A. Barron was longer. At one time or another he had been a tutor at Harvard and a classmate of John Quincy Adams. With this background, he proved himself an able and engaging teacher of mathematics.[59]

Captain Barron took the place of a civilian instructor named Baron who had been employed in accordance with the act of July 16, 1798. As a former colleague of Charles Hutton of Woolwich, this predecessor of the captain was reputed to be a very able mathematician, but was undoubtedly coarse and impatient. When the youngster Swift declined being a member of his mess in 1801 and joined one operated by the cadets instead, Baron called him a "mutinous young rascal." A fight followed. The Englishman

[57] Dearborn to Fleming, June 13, 1803, *Military Book, No. 3*, p. 455, National Archives.

[58] Dearborn to Williams, June 1, 1805, *Military Book, No. 2*, p. 349, National Archives, and same to same, Jan. 20, 1802, *Military Book, No. 1*, p. 148, National Archives.

[59] Ellery, *op. cit.*, p. 32.

ended his part of it by fleeing to the "Academy" building and bolting the door. Here, from a second story window, he roundly abused Swift in words that were pointedly vulgar. An hour or two afterwards Swift found himself under arrest. Subsequently Dearborn ordered him to apologize, but he refused. Instead, he made counter-charges against Baron, who, in turn, was arrested and his classes suspended. Brought to trial, Baron was found guilty of public and private misconduct. He was dismissed from the service of the United States in February,' 1802. Swift, after being reprimanded for disrespectful words to his superior officer, was restored to duty.[60]

Swift and other cadets seem to have got along better with Francois Desire Masson, the professor of French. Masson was a highly educated emigrant from Santo Domingo. He had been appointed as a teacher during the summer of 1803.[61] He continued until 1810, drawing some forty dollars a month as pay. Since no one had been engaged to give lessons in topographical drawing, he also did this, thereby earning a little more. Under this arrangement, French and drawing classes alternated, being held every afternoon in the week except Saturday and Sunday.[62] In spite of the time spent, results were not satisfactory, probably because no standard of accomplishment was required. Not until somewhat later were cadets able to translate French with accuracy and ease.

They seem to have made much more progress in the theory and practice of surveying, which was obviously essential for engineer officers and certainly of great practical value for any others who might be stationed along the frontier. Under the able guidance of Williams, the country around West Point was mapped and the position and altitude of prominent points determined. Cadets found

---

[60] *Ibid.*, p. 31; and Dearborn to Swift, Oct. 30, 1801, p. 120, Nov. 16, 1801, p. 126, Dec. 5, 1801, pp. 134-135, and Dearborn to Williams, Feb. 11, 1802, p. 150, in *Military Book, No. 1*, National Archives.

[61] Ellery, *op. cit.*, pp. 46-53.

[62] Dearborn to Barron, Dec. 1, 1803; *Military Book, No. 2*, p. 121, National Archives; and Orders of Wadsworth, July 20, 1804, West Point *MS.*, 1071.

"the plain" to be 190 feet higher than the nearby Hudson. Above this level space where the garrison lived, they learned that the Crow's Nest towered some 1,480 feet; Breck Neck, 1,500; Sugar Loaf, 700; and Fort Putnam, 400 feet.[63] Possessed of the elements of surveying, these embryonic officers were at least better off than many of their brothers in arms who were wholly unable to determine the meets and bounds of reservations or the precise location of newly made forts.

Nevertheless, many conditions at West Point were not favorable to learning. During the early 1800's facilities for study were poor and the morale of the cadets was low. For a time they were housed in the "Long Barracks" with the enlisted men of an artillery company. This company was transferred elsewhere in 1803. Little or no money was spent to make quarters attractive and comfortable, especially when there was prospect that the Academy would be moved to some other location. Cadets were without servants until the summer of 1804; then one for every four of them was allowed.[64] Some time still had to elapse before a ration was issued to the women who washed for them all. Perhaps the washerwoman did not relish the government bread and meat anyway. A certain Colonel Colfax was the contractor in 1803, and the provisions were so bad that officers and cadets sent a protesting "memorial" to Dearborn.[65] The government's effort to substitute beer and light wines for whisky was not altogether agreeable. Clothing, too, was a source of complaint. Since engineer cadets drew six dollars more a month than those in the artillery, some argued that they should buy their own uniforms, which would cost from forty to fifty dollars annually if purchased through the Purveyor of Public Supplies. Dearborn held this opinion, declaring that they were very well paid and received their education at government expense. To Williams, the idea

[63] Ellery, *op. cit.*, p. 35.

[64] Orders of Wadsworth, July 20, 1804, West Point *MS.*, 1071.

[65] Dearborn to Barron, May 24, 1803, *Military Book, No. 1*, p. 447, and same to same, July 25, 1803, *Military Book*, No. 2, p. 37.

seemed wrong. He said that as a consequence of this ruling engineer and artillery cadets had different uniforms and wore almost whatever they pleased. He added that all of their ration money and most of their pay was "swallowed up in food," thus leaving them so little for clothing that they went about covered with rags.[66] In spite of several petitions to Congress, Dearborn's opinion prevailed—engineer cadets paid for their own uniforms. Cadets were not busy during the winter. Little or no instruction could be carried on either in or out of doors. For this reason Williams arranged for them to have a vacation from the first of December to the fifteenth of the following March. While away, they were to report their address every month and be ready to return if occasion demanded. For maintenance they drew their usual pay of $16 a month and a small amount of ration money. For their two rations apiece, commutation amounted to about twenty-two cents a day. No allowances were granted for quarters and fuel. When their vacation ended, cadets were enjoined to "punctually return" and resume their "academical pursuits."[67]

While they were on leave, the rest of the garrison did little beside the routine tasks of an ordinary post. In the winter of 1802 only a company of artillery, part of the Corps of Engineers, and a few civilian employees seem to have been present. Williams believed that a few hours of these cold and windswept days might well be devoted to the study and discussion of topics in military science. His idea bore fruit in the founding of the United States Military Philosophical Society on November 12, 1802. Its charter members consisted of the engineer officers then stationed at West Point. None might join unless invited. It was supported by voluntary contributions that ranged from five to twenty-five dollars apiece. Swift, Macomb, Totten, and others were active in its affairs. Thomas Jefferson, John

[66] Dearborn to Williams, Oct. 28, 1805, *Military Book, No. 2*, pp. 392-394, National Archives; and *The Centennial*, p. 509.

[67] Dearborn to Williams, Dec. 3, 1802, p. 330 and same to same, Nov. 6, 1802, p. 310, both in *Military Book, No. 1*, National Archives.

Quincy Adams, W. C. C. Claiborne, Colonel T. H. Cushing and General James Wilkinson were among those in the army and civil life who were carried on its rolls and found interest in its proceedings. At one of the meetings held at West Point during July 1807, Lewis Simond and Count Mimeenitz were present as guests. Biographies of Kosciusko, Pulaski, and DeKalb were discussed. Williams read a paper on field exercises for artillery; and Ferdinand R. Hassler, the new professor of mathematics, offered suggestions on how a map of the United States should be made. The Society flourished for about five years, until the opening of the War of 1812, when its members became widely scattered. The organization withered away; and since its last meeting on November 1813, it has never been revived.[68]

For a time Williams, its moving spirit, was not in the service. He had become irritated at the ruling that prevented him from being post commander even though he was the senior officer present. This meant that a captain or lieutenant of artillery or infantry would perform this duty, even though Williams might be a major or higher. Since the functions of superintendent of the academy and post commander were often interrelated or opposed, friction naturally resulted. Near the end of 1802, Captain George Izard refused to furnish a detachment from his company upon the request of Williams. After Izard and his organization had been ordered to Norfolk, Virginia, to avoid future trouble, only forty-four of the army personnel remained at West Point. There were thirty-two engineers and cadets, a teacher of French, two artillery noncommissioned officers, eight artillery privates, and a surgeon's mate. None seemed to have questioned Williams's authority over a number so pitifully small.[69]

The principle, however, remained at issue. A number of

[68] Ellery, *op. cit.*, p. 71. The records of the Society, consisting of three volumes, were in the New York Historical Society, New York, N.Y., in 1942. Notes from them furnish the basis of this paragraph. I am indebted to Mr. T. R. Hay for this information.

[69] Ellery, *op. cit.*, p. 40; Hamersly, *op. cit.*, p. 279; *American State Papers Military Affairs*, I, p. 175.

those in the engineer corps had been once commissioned in other branches and they resented being deprived of any of their former prerogatives. Even if the corps was small and included only officers and cadets, this should not mean that they were incapable of issuing orders to others. They had been chosen for their mental ability, and their experience was often broader than that of officers in the artillery and infantry. As a rule, their education had been more exacting and their travel more extensive. Frequently they had to work with large groups of men, both enlisted and civilian, in the construction of fortifications along the Atlantic seaboard and elsewhere. Hence Williams contended that when troops of different branches were together the ranking officer present should command them all. This had been the usual practice, and was clearly intended by the 25th and 26th Articles of War.

When the question was referred to Jefferson he upheld the ruling of Dearborn. He declared that engineers should not command troops of a corps other than their own and that they were subject to nobody's order except that of the President, unless he specifically directed the contrary. He argued that engineers were engaged in scientific pursuits and did not have time for routine army duties. He may have understood, but did not add, how resentful others, like Izard, would be in taking any orders from the engineers. As a result, Williams exercised no control except over the Academy personnel, a small fluctuating number of instructors and cadets. The total was slightly increased when a law was enacted in 1803 providing for two teachers of French and drawing, as well as an artificer and eighteen men to do odd jobs around the school. Although Williams had become a lieutenant colonel, he was so disgusted with Jefferson's ruling that he resigned on June 20, 1803.[70]

Major Decius Wadsworth soon afterwards became superintendent at West Point. Siding with Williams, he believed his own future in the army had little to offer. "I find myself," he said, "to be wasting the best of my days

[70] G. W. Cullum, *Biographical Register*, etc., I, p. 27; and T. H. S. Hamersly, *op. cit.*, pp. 278-281.

in the service of my country which professes to make no provision for the gray-headed soldier. I gain nothing but a bare livelihood and I feel willing that some one should take my place."[71] He added that he had not resigned before because he hoped to prosecute his professional studies. Such an opportunity now seemed impossible and the situation was not improving. Thwarted in his ambition and irked by the restrictions on engineers, he joined with four other young officers, Barron, Wilson, Macomb, and Armistead and "memorialized" the President, asking that those in the corps be given the right of command and in turn be subject to the orders of all their seniors.[72] Their efforts proved futile; Jefferson was unwilling to change his orders. On February 10, 1805, Wadsworth resigned.

On April 19, 1805, Williams, upon Jefferson's insistence, was again commissioned, becoming a lieutenant colonel, head of the Corps of Engineers, and superintendent of the Academy for the second time. Since he had general direction of the construction of all the forts along our coast, he was compelled to be frequently absent from West Point on visits of inspection. Therefore, most of the school problems fell on other shoulders. Instruction was of a low order. Teaching personnel was frequently changed. No definite course of study was possible as long as new cadets had to meet only one general qualification, that of being males. Their length of attendance varied greatly, from six months to six years according to their energy, capacity, and previous training. Even after finishing their ill-defined course, they had no positive assurance that they would be commissioned. This was a matter that depended on the judgment of the superintendent and the existence of an unpromised vacancy.[73]

Under the circumstances, cadetships were not so eagerly sought as in subsequent years. A few seem to have been

[71] Wadsworth to Williams, Aug. 12, 1803, West Point *MS.*, 1190.
[72] Wadsworth and others to the President, Dec. 24, 1804, West Point *MS.*, p. 43.
[73] Dearborn to Williams, June 19, 1805, *Military Book, No. 2*, pp. 343-344, National Archives.

like Matthew N. Whyte who was tendered an appointment as artillery cadet in 1804. After he had been directed "to repair" to West Point, Dearborn fervently added that, "This mark of confidence with which the President of the United States has been pleased to honor you, will, I presume, excite in you an emulation to excell in the profession to which you have thus early devoted yourself."[74] Apparently the two were not of the same mind: Whyte did not accept; he did not "repair" to West Point. Others reacted differently. As a gesture of friendship after the purchase of the Louisiana Territory, Jefferson decided to give cadetships to some of the leading families around St. Louis.[75] One Gratiot and two each from the Chouteau and Lorimier families accepted. Dearborn promised that a place would be found for them in the artillery in case they failed to qualify as engineers. For years afterwards, the artillery and infantry had to take the leavings of the engineer corps.

Displeased with the character of instruction and irked with the restrictions imposed upon the Academy, Williams made a number of recommendations to Dearborn on March 14, 1808. One of the most important called for Congress to cease trying to control the academy by legislative acts and leave "the site, the buildings, the number and kind of professors, and all other matters connected with the institution" entirely to the judgment of the President. He and Jefferson apparently agreed that the Academy should be located in Washington, where it would be more directly under government control and would have better opportunity to impress Congress with its value. The instructing personnel, he urged, should be increased and made permanent. Instructors should enjoy definite rank, pay, and allowances; their work should be supplemented by several part time civilian experts. So organized and with the addition of "proper buildings, apparatus, library, etc." he believed that more cadets and minor officers of the navy should be admitted to the academy. Cadets not

---

[74] Dearborn to Whyte, Nov. 8, 1804, *ibid.*, p. 270.
[75] Dearborn to Stoddard, May 16, 1804, *ibid.*, p. 236.

commissioned in the army would become officers in the militia, greatly improving its efficiency.[76]

Although the wisdom of Williams's suggestions was unquestioned, Congress did nothing to put them in effect while Jefferson was President. A deep-rooted prejudice against the academy blinded many to its virtues. Spoil-seeking Democratic-Republicans did not relish the academy because Jonathan Williams was a Federalist. Politicians south of Mason and Dixon's line would do nothing until the academy was moved near their hustings. Some party leaders wanted the distribution of commissions to rest in their hands. With such opinions prevailing, the academy continued to be "a puny, rickety child" without any hope for the immediate future.[77]

[76] Williams to Dearborn, Mar. 14, 1808, in *American State Papers, Military Affairs*, I, pp. 228-230.

[77] Most of the material for this chapter was obtained from the Library of the United States Military Academy at West Point. It not only contains numerous manuscripts of interest and value relating to the Academy but has copies of many others that are scattered throughout the United States. As a guide to research, *The Centennial of the United States Military Academy at West Point, 1802-1902*, and G. W. Cullum, *Biographical Register of the Officers and Graduates, etc.* are invaluable. Also, the W.P.A. of the State of New York has compiled a helpful list of manuscripts at West Point; a copy of it may be found there as well as in the National Archives at Washington, D.C. Unless otherwise indicated, manuscript material used in this chapter is found at the U.S. Military Academy, West Point, New York.

12. *The Army and the Louisiana Purchase*

THE year 1803 witnessed the consummation of the most stupendous transaction in real estate ever recorded on the pages of history. For $15,000,000, President Jefferson, ably abetted by James Monroe and Robert Livingston, purchased for the United States approximately a million square miles, thereby increasing the national domain by about 140 per cent. The cost of this fabulous tract came to about four cents an acre.

The precise boundaries of this immense domain known as the Louisiana Purchase were matters of guesswork to both buyer and seller. The Mississippi River provided an acceptable eastern limit and the Gulf of Mexico defined the southern extent of the regions involved. But on the west there was only a nebulous area that vaguely ended in "the mountains." On the southeast, the line defining the Spanish possessions in Florida was almost equally uncertain. Probably not more than 80,000 inhabitants, exclusive of Indians, were to be found in the two great administrative divisions of Louisiana. Of these, fully one-fourth were resident in or near New Orleans, the sole municipality larger than a frontier village in the entire Purchase.

Concerning their vast acquisition the President and his secretary of state, Mr. Madison, knew very little in detail but much in general. It was certain that the western banks of the Mississippi and the forests and prairies beyond were settled with savages. Many of these were decidedly warlike and dangerously resentful of the white man's intrusion. The civilized inhabitants were mostly French or Spanish Creoles. There was a sprinkling of rough American frontiersmen lured thither by the hope of trade with the Indians or the grant of cheap land under the easy-going Spanish rulers. The immediate task of taking over the Purchase, relieving and replacing the garrisons along the numerous rivers, and asserting the civil authority of the United States, would have to be entrusted largely to the regular army.

The Province of Louisiana was divided into two districts, one administered from New Orleans and the other, the sub-province, from St. Louis. Arrangements were made to have the army, with the American commissioners, move into each of these towns. To take possession at New Orleans, two representatives of the United States government were appointed by President Jefferson. The youthful governor of Mississippi territory, William C. C. Claiborne, and Brigadier General James Wilkinson, general in chief of the army, were the civilian and military legates directed to receive the newly bought empire from Napoleon's commissioner. Governor Claiborne, escorted by mounted militia of the territory, proceeded to meet the general at Fort Adams near Natchez. A large force of volunteers enlisted in Tennessee had made the 400-mile march from Nashville to Natchez in the expectation of possible resistance on the part of the Spaniards in Louisiana. General Wilkinson decided that there would be no need for their services and sent them back home. From the garrison at Fort Adams he detached three companies of regular artillery under Lieutenant Colonel Constant Freeman; and with these and Claiborne's dragoons, he started for New Orleans. The commissioners and the regulars floated down the river in barges, the mounted militia went by road. After a five-day trip the flotilla arrived at a point about two miles north of the city gates, and the troops landed and went into camp. Then ensued a cheerful and ceremonious round of official calls during which arrangements were made for the transfer ceremony on December 20.[1] Three weeks only had elapsed since the French commissioner, M. de Laussuat, had received the province from Spain. He was now, in his turn, to hand it over to the Americans. He prepared to perform this duty with deep reluctance and justifiable misgivings as to Napoleon's business acumen in disposing

[1] J. R. Jacobs, *Tarnished Warrior*, pp. 201-203.

so cavalierly of such a priceless empire. M. de Laussuat had no very exalted opinion of the two representatives of the United States in the transaction. Three months later he was writing to Admiral Decrès that Claiborne had estimable private qualities but little capacity and much awkwardness, defects making him far from equal to his high station. As for the general, the fluent but none too discerning Frenchman spoke of him as, a "flighty rattle-headed fellow, often drunk," not understanding a word of French or Spanish and utterly "without delicacy."[2]

Shortly after noon on the 20th of December, 1803, the cession of the Province of Louisiana to the United States was accomplished. Governor Claiborne and General Wilkinson at the head of their escorting troops rode into the city of New Orleans by the Tchoupitoulas Gate. They were greeted with the thunder of a 24-gun salute. The gunners who manned this ordnance were the not yet repatriated soldiers of His Most Catholic Majesty of Spain. They gave their services in the absence of any of Napoleon's troops. In the council hall of the Cabildo, M. de Laussuat received the American commissioners and shortly thereafter led them to a balcony overlooking the Plaza de Armas. Most of the inhabitants had sadly assembled in the square below to view the ceremony. Speeches were delivered by the chief actors of the drama and as a fitting finale, the great tricolor floating at the flagstaff in the center of the Plaza was hauled down to make way for the Stars and Stripes. For the last time men saw the colors of France wave above the soil that La Salle, Radisson, Marquette and a host of gallant Frenchmen had won for the glory of their empire.[3]

For several months, while Congress wrangled over legislation intended to give territorial status to the purchase, the government in Lower Louisiana and New Orleans consisted, in practice, of the young governor, a judicial body of seven justices appointed by him, and some former

---

[2] Laussuat to Decrès, Apr. 8, 1804, in C. E. A. Gayarre, *History of Louisiana*, III, pp. 10-11.

[3] A. Fortier, *A History of Louisiana*, II, pp. 277-288.

Spanish-French local officials who had consented to continue to function until displaced by American appointees. General Wilkinson remained at Claiborne's elbow and supplied the officers who were delegated to take over the existing military posts. The Spanish garrisons still remained in most of these, their commanding officers usually acting also as intendants and civil commandants of the neighboring districts.

On January 2, 1804, 2nd Lieutenant Henry W. Hopkins, 1st Infantry, was sent with a small detachment of troops to establish American authority in the Atakapas and Opelousas regions. Claiborne appointed him civil commandant there and observed to Secretary Madison that the officer was a young man of prudence, good information, and "possessing some knowledge of the French language." The lieutenant quickly discovered that his new duties involved more than the routine of a frontier garrison. Soon after he arrived in his bailiwick, two of the clergy became involved in a furious controversy over certain jurisdictional claims. The church building itself was threatened with destruction at the hands of opposing factions. Lieutenant Hopkins acted with commendable firmness and decision. He closed the church and forbade those "two servants of the Lord" to exercise their spiritual functions within its doors until they resumed amicable relations—which they presently did.[4]

To take over the military post at Concordia, across the river from Natchez, Wilkinson sent Ferdinand L. Claiborne, the governor's brother and a former army lieutenant. Within the next few months small American detachments relieved other Spanish garrisons scattered along the rivers. As early as December 27, 1803, American troops occupied the brick fort at Placquemines on the Mississippi below New Orleans and the post at the Balize on the Gulf still farther south. To Fort San Esteban de Arkansas, "the Arkansas Post," went 1st Lieutenant

---

[4] Claiborne to Madison, May 29, 1804, in J. A. Robertson, *Louisiana under the Rule of Spain, France, and the United States, 1785-1807*, II, pp. 265-266.

James B. Many of the Regiment of Artillery on March 23. In April, 1st Lieutenant Joseph Bowmar, 2nd Infantry, took possession of Fort Miró on the Washita River. There the ground on which this Spanish work had been built was claimed as private property by the ousted civil commandant. Rather than antagonize the local magnate and his friends by an arbitrary seizure, Bowmar sensibly yielded the point and built himself a log house and a new stockade farther down stream. Within a radius of twenty-eight miles were some 450 settlers who looked to him for protection.[5]

During October, 1804, Fort Miró was visited by William Dunbar, a learned Englishman, whom Daniel Clark described as "the first character in this part of the world" respecting "Science, Probity and general information." He and a certain Dr. George Hunter, accompanied by a sergeant and twelve privates from the New Orleans garrison, composed a party to explore the Washita. While he and the doctor sketched the course of the river, noted the flora and fauna, and accurately mapped important positions, the soldiers, one to an oar, forced their cumbersome barge upstream as far as Hot Springs. Unlike their two leaders, they had little heart for their task and sometimes when the sun rose they lay on their blankets and would not get up until a "good talking to" roused them to action.[6] They were naturally eager to stop at Fort Miró, for this meant a respite from work and the chance of a visit with some of their cronies. First Lieutenant Bowmar was still there as both civil and military commandant. According to Dunbar, he performed this difficult double role to the satisfaction of the army and the neighboring settlers.

Conditions were not equally tranquil at Natchitoches on the Red River. This was the gateway to Texas and the

[5] J. A. Robertson, *Louisiana under the Rule of Spain, France, and the United States, 1785-1807*, II, p. 290.

[6] I. J. Cox, "The Exploration of the Louisiana Frontier, 1803-1806" in *Annual Report, American Historical Association, 1904*, pp. 168-174; "Journal of a Voyage" (by William Dunbar), printed in *Documents Relating to the Purchase and Exploration of Louisiana*, p. 40.

westernmost outpost in Lower Louisiana. After the cession, Wilkinson had promised to occupy it immediately,
but for several months he delayed. While Spanish troops
remained in New Orleans—and many weeks slipped by
before they were finally repatriated—Colonel Freeman
prudently retained the maximum number of troops there.
The Stars and Stripes were not raised at Natchitoches
until April 20, 1804, when Captain Edward Turner, 1st
Infantry, and about 60 soldiers, christened the post Fort
Claiborne. The small Spanish garrison withdrew to Nacogdoches beyond the Sabine River in undisputed Spanish
territory. There a suspicious and alert general of the
Crown had his headquarters. He observed with jealous
and apprehensive eyes the closer approach of the Americans to the undetermined boundary line between Louisiana
and Texas. Fort Claiborne became the most important
of the army's frontier posts; and by the end of 1804, it
had a garrison of 170 regulars in cantonments. Captain
Turner was continually at loggerheads with his Spanish
neighbors. Each commander accused the other of willful
intrusion.[7]

When Turner first arrived at Natchitoches he found
there an American physician, Dr. John Sibley, who was
a Revolutionary veteran, newspaper man, and politician
recently come to Louisiana. He had been sent into the
province in the previous year by President Jefferson,
primarily to gather information about the Indian tribes.
Dr. Sibley was immediately appointed to be a contract
surgeon with the army. He was later an Indian agent and
an influential figure on the border. He evidently took it
upon himself to be a political spy among the troops, for
we find him writing to Claiborne that all the officers of
Captain Turner's command were "non-Jeffersonians," a
not very surprising conclusion when it is remembered that
the President was the leader of the whole movement to
reduce the military establishment to miniature proportions.

Congress provided for the territorial organization and
government of the purchase on March 26, 1804. Under

---

[7] F. X. Martin, *The History of Louisiana*, pp. 330-331.

both French and Spanish rule the Province had been, in effect, administered as two districts, with a governor at St. Louis. Now a clean-cut separation was made and the country lying north of the 33rd parallel was called the District of Louisiana and placed under the territorial government of Indiana. The land south of the same line was organized as the Territory of Orleans. Claiborne was continued as governor there, with command of the militia and the authority to appoint all civil and military officials not designated by the President.

At the time when Laussuat delivered Louisiana to the United States at New Orleans, the sub-province to the north was still under Spanish administration. No formal delivery of the region to the French had been made. Theoretically, Wilkinson and Claiborne had accepted and received the entire province; actually only the Orleans district had shifted allegiance. On January 12, 1804, Laussuat forwarded credentials to an American army officer in the Illinois country. These appointed him Napoleon's agent to receive Upper Louisiana from Spain. The same officer had already been selected by President Jefferson to act as the American commissioner in taking over the country on behalf of the United States.[8] These dual diplomatic duties were entrusted to Captain Amos Stoddard, who was then stationed with his company of artillery at Kaskaskia, on the Mississippi below St. Louis. On February 18, 1804, he obtained a commission from M. de Laussuat appointing him "sole Agent and Commissioner," "to demand and receive" on the part of the French Republic "the quiet and peaceable possession of Upper Louisiana, together with all the military posts at St. Louis and its dependencies."[9] He promptly notified the Spanish lieutenant governor at St. Louis, Colonel don Carlos Dehualt Delassus, that he was sending a detachment of United States troops up the river by boat and would precede them himself by land, in order to make the necessary arrangements for fulfilling his mission. Stoddard did

8 A. Fortier, *op. cit.*, II, pp. 317-318.
9 J. F. Scharf, *History of St. Louis and County*, I, pp. 259ff.

not mention the fact that he had also in pocket a commission from President Jefferson designating him as the American commissioner to accept the transfer from the French commissioner, namely himself.

The choice of Stoddard for this dual role was a peculiarly happy one. The captain was then forty-one years old; he had served three years in the Revolution as an enlisted man in the artillery, and since the peace of 1783 had been a successful lawyer and a member of the Massachusetts legislature. Commissioned in the regular army in 1798, he proved to be an efficient and enterprising officer. He spoke French fluently and was not without some claim to recognition as a writer and orator. Had he, rather than the immature and colorless Claiborne, been selected as governor of the New Orleans territory, probably many of the difficulties in securing the cooperation of the resentful Creoles would have been avoided.

The detachment of the 1st Artillery, sent up the river from Kaskaskia, landed at Cahokia across from St. Louis; and there they camped for several days while Captain Stoddard was conferring with the lieutenant governor. On February 25, 1804, he handed to Colonel Delassus the formal demand for the delivery of Upper Louisiana to France, and on March 9, his left hand, acting for the First Consul, transferred to his American right hand, the same territory. The official ceremony was similar to though less pretentious than the one previously enacted in New Orleans. The American troops, under the immediate command of Lieutenant Stephen Worrell of the Artillery Regiment, were ferried over from Cahokia and marched to the Government House, where Stoddard, with Worrell acting as his adjutant, received the Spanish governor and his retinue. At the American commissioner's side stood a third officer, wearing the uniform of an infantry captain.[10] Tall, soldierly, dignified, with a long, pointed head, thin lips, and a prominent nose, Captain Meriwether Lewis was one whose name was to be linked forever with those

[10] L. Houck, *A History of Missouri*, II, pp. 355-363.

boundless stretches of unknown country about to come into the possession of our Republic.

Stoddard and Delassus exchanged the necessary documents, passed the inevitable compliments and made the equally inevitable speeches. The captain reminded the inhabitants of Upper Louisiana that they were now divested of the character of subjects and clothed with that of citizens, a civic change that to most of them was anything but gratifying. He likewise invited their attention to the significant fact that, "in all free republics . . . permanent armies of any considerable extent were justly deemed hostile to liberty, and therefore the militia is considered the palladium of their safety . . . every soldier is a citizen and every citizen a soldier."[11] It was a fair warning that henceforth their newly-acquired citizenship put them permanently on call for military services previously provided by the King's professional mercenaries.

When the speechmaking was concluded, Worrell marched his blue-clad artillerymen up the hill to the fort where the troops of Spain were drawn up to receive them. The red and yellow standard of Castile was lowered from the staff and the red, white, and blue were flung to the Missouri breeze. The Spaniards moved out of the fort and were quartered in the town until they could travel down the river on their way to Florida. Colonel Delassus seems to have made every possible effort to be helpful. He notified the commanding officers of New Madrid, St. Genevieve, Cape Girardeau, Carondelet and other villages, that they were to surrender their posts when American officers appeared. He also furnished Stoddard with a complete list of all the civil officials in the sub-province, commenting on their administrative abilities as well as their personal habits and character.[12]

Captain Stoddard now assumed the duties of civil and military commandant of Upper Louisiana. His immediate superior was Governor William Henry Harrison of Indiana Territory, whose capital was at Vincennes. The new commandant exercised his gubernatorial functions with sound

[11] L. Houck, *op. cit.*, II, p. 370.   [12] *Ibid.*, II, pp. 362-364.

good sense and conspicuous success. In compliance with his instructions from President Jefferson, he made few changes in the existing methods or personnel of the local government. There were in the district half a dozen influential and comparatively wealthy French families, the Lorimiers, the Chouteaus, the Gratiots, the Valles, and others. Stoddard was clever enough to make friends with them and secure their loyal cooperation in effecting the change from Spanish to American control. Colonel Delassus remained at St. Louis with his troops until October, when he departed for Pensacola, taking with him the Spanish archives and all munitions of war not included in the transfer. Stoddard continued as military commandant until the arrival in July of a senior officer, Major James Bruff, of the artillery, who continued as civil governor until October 1, when he was succeeded by Colonel Samuel Hammond of Virginia.[13]

In New Orleans, Governor Claiborne and General Wilkinson were not as successful as Stoddard. During the first year of American occupation they were immersed in a sea of miscellaneous anxieties and embarrassments. The inhabitants of New Orleans were not entirely happy to become American citizens. Proud and sensitive, the Creoles saw little cause for rejoicing in the sale of their fatherland to a nation identified in their minds with the rude and boisterous frontiersmen who descended the Mississippi in great broadhorns and made nights hideous along the waterfront with their drunken carousing. The soldiers of the American garrison had no trouble in getting along with the peaceable well-behaved Spanish troops who still lingered—some twenty officers and 200 men—but their continued presence was a nuisance and a cause of annoyance and distrust to the inexperienced Claiborne. With the French, both civilians and militia, the story was different. The governor termed them "mischievous, riotous, and disorderly." Military and civil authorities were constantly wrangling over innumerable matters. The mayor of New Orleans quarreled fiercely with Lieutenant Colonel Con-

[13] *Ibid.*, II, pp. 364-381.

stant Freeman of the Artillery Regiment, commandant under General Wilkinson of the American troops in the city. Governor Claiborne finally abandoned all hope of keeping the peace while United States soldiers remained in town and urged the President to remove them: "The troops situated here have," he complained, "conducted themselves as well as an army ever did similarly situated, but it is impossible for any commander to maintain discipline among men posted in a city where the temptations to dissipation are so various, and the means of evading the attention of officers is so easy."[14]

The militia of the new territory, numbering about 10,000, were also another source of anxiety. They were, of course, solidly French. There were at least two companies of "free people of color" whom the governor hesitated to embody in our own militia service.

In Upper Louisiana, where the level-headed Stoddard was at the helm, every practicable effort was being made to win the friendship and loyalty of the most prominent French families. A number of their young men were appointed cadets at the United States Military Academy at West Point. Charles Gratiot and Auguste P. Chouteau, sons of the wealthiest and most influential families between the Missouri and New Madrid, entered the academy between July 1804, and May 1805, and were eventually graduated and commissioned. Pascal Vincent Bouis, appointed in July 1804, was graduated in March 1806; Louis Valle finished in 1808 and declined his commission on graduation. Of these youngsters, Gratiot passed from West Point into the Corps of Engineers and by 1828 was Chief Engineer of the United States and a brigadier general by brevet. Unfortunately he became involved in a military *cause célèbre* concerning an alleged irregularity in the settlement of his account and was dismissed from the service in 1838.[15]

14 *Louisiana Executive Journal*, I, p. 287.

15 For appointments, see F. B. Heitman, *Historical Register and Dictionary of the United States Army*, I, pp. 232, 300, 470, 979.

For the details of the Gratiot case, see *Senate Reports*, 32nd Congress, 1st session, II, p. 357.

Very soon after the purchase and occupation of Upper and Lower Louisiana it became apparent that additional military posts would have to be established if the Indians were to be controlled profitably by their new overlords. The reports submitted to the War Department by the officers who headed the various exploring expeditions that cross-hatched the Trans-Mississippi country invariably recommended sites suitable for the establishment of forts and trading houses, commonly known as factories. From the first, President Jefferson was eager to extend our trade with the Indians and to obtain definite and detailed information about the vast uncharted wilderness west of the settlements along the Mississippi and the Missouri. Even before the news arrived from Monroe that the deal with Napoleon had been closed, Jefferson had made an arrangement to send an exploring party under regular officers into Upper Louisiana to follow the unknown reaches of the Missouri River and push on, if possible, to the Pacific. From Congress he obtained, after urging it in a confidential message, an appropriation of $2,500 for expenses. Jefferson selected his private secretary, Captain Meriwether Lewis, 1st Infantry, to lead the party. Lewis, desiring a military coadjutor, suggested his friend, William Clark, an ex-officer and younger brother of the celebrated George Rogers Clark, to be co-commander. This pair of soldiers was perfectly suited to provide the kind of leadership and management that their mission required.[16]

Their preparations were commenced under War Department orders but remained a military secret until it was definitely known that the Missouri River country was no longer Spanish territory. The President obtained passports for the party from the French and British ministers at Washington, but he met with strong remonstrance from Señor Yrujo who represented the King of Spain at the capital. After arranging a "quiet understanding"

[16] R. G. Thwaites, *Original Journals of the Lewis and Clark Expedition*, I, Introduction, pp. xxiii-xxx.

with Yrujo, Jefferson anticipated no interference on the part of the remaining Spanish garrisons in the West. Late in 1803 a camp was established on the Illinois side of the Mississippi and there the party of Louis and Clark passed the winter in rigorous training for the ordeal ahead. At Louisville, where the two leaders first came together, they selected nine young Kentuckians for the trip; and, by a process of ruthless elimination, fourteen enlisted men from the regular army garrisons at Fort Massac, Kaskaskia, and Southwest Point were accepted from hundreds of eager volunteers. These, with a French interpreter, a hunter, nine voyageurs, and Clark's Negro servant, made up the force that was to "push on to the Pacific." A corporal and six privates of the army were detailed to act as an escort only as far as the Mandan villages.[17]

The thirty-three-year-old Clark was a veteran Indian fighter and woodsman, a first-class military topographer and sketcher. He was enthusiastic about the task assigned him. His formal education, particularly in spelling, was poor; but he knew how to handle soldiers and Indians and was content to leave reports and higher mathematics to Lewis. He had been out of the army since 1796, but Jefferson sent him, for the purposes of the expedition, a new commission as a 2nd lieutenant of artillery. His men steadfastly insisted on calling him "Captain" Clark, and Lewis unfailingly accorded him full recognition as a co-equal commander.

On May 14, 1804, after Captain Lewis had lent his presence to Captain Stoddard's inauguration as civil commandant of Upper Louisiana and signed the transfer documents as principal witness for the United States, his party, packed in clumsy boats, headed up the Missouri current, "under a jentle brease." From the moment that the third and last of the bateaux disappeared around a bend, the explorers were almost as completely separated from civilization as if they had left the earth. Their two years in the wilderness, their perilous adventures, their cruel hardships, and their meticulous fulfillment of their

[17] R. G. Thwaites, *op. cit.*, I, pp. 3-17.

primary mission is a story of compelling interest. Let it suffice here to say that they made their toilsome way up the Missouri to the Mandan villages, the site of Bismarck, North Dakota. There they went into winter quarters, building a little stockade of cottonwood logs that they called Fort Mandan. Here they picked up a friendly Frenchman named Charbonneau and his wife, a Shoshone woman of intelligence. The couple agreed to accompany them on the westward trek and to act as guides and interpreters. For five months Lewis held his men at Fort Mandan while he prepared reports, sent out hunting parties, and collected all available information about the country and the Indians. By April the river was clear of ice and the explorers again started their voyage into the unknown. At the mouth of the Yellowstone more data were gathered and filed in the voluminous notebooks kept by both leaders. By June 25, they had come to the three forks of the Missouri, investigated their sources, and named them in honor of the statesmen who sponsored the expedition, Jefferson, Madison, and Gallatin. On November 7, after months of struggle in the rocky mountain passes and courses of the roaring northwestern streams, they emerged on the shores of the broad Pacific. So carefully had the men been selected, so watchful and prescient were the two commanders, and so firm was the military control imposed and submitted to, that the party had suffered only a single casualty, and he had died from a "Bilious chorlick," possibly appendicitis.[18]

Delinquencies on the part of the men were severely dealt with according to the military code of the time. Since there were only two officers in the party, courts-martial were instituted with sergeants and even privates sitting as members in cases of minor infractions of duty or disregard of regulations. One such court sentenced a soldier to receive fifty lashes on his bare back for a brief absence without leave and some disrespectful language to his superiors on his return. In the cases of capital offenses —and there were a few—the two leaders sat as a court,

[18] R. G. Thwaites, *op. cit., passim.*

one of them doubling in the capacities of member and judge-advocate. A private whom they convicted of sleeping on guard they sentenced to have 100 lashes laid on his back "at four different times in equal proportion." Every evening for four days the unlucky soldier was triced up and given his punishment. Yet such occasional severities in no way lessened the devotion or loyalty of the men. A soldier found guilty of using mutinous expressions was given 75 lashes and discharged as a member of the permanent party. After expressing repentance and begging to be taken back he showed excellent spirit and became very useful. But he was not permitted to go beyond the Mandan town; Lewis enlisted a French voyageur in his place.

The first clearly-marked trail from the Mississippi to the Pacific had now been blazed by the army, and a vast amount of information about the country traversed had been gathered and recorded. While the control of the party by both Clark and Lewis had been tactful and considerate, the essentially military character of the project was never forgotten. They were soldiers of the regular army sent upon a well defined mission, and neither weather nor hardships nor hostile savages nor heartbreaking obstacles prevented them from accomplishing it.

On September 23, 1806, after covering more than six thousand miles and being absent two and a half years, the members of the Lewis and Clark Expedition debarked at St. Louis, where they were enthusiastically welcomed by a delighted public that was eager to know about their travels. To satisfy this curiosity, Clark, the map-maker and artist of the party, prepared for publication the diaries kept by the officers and men, as well as the written and pictorial records. In 1814, after careful revision and editing, these were published.[19] On February 27, 1807, Clark again resigned his regular army commission to accept appointment as brigadier general in the Louisiana

[19] The publication was printed at Philadelphia and entitled *The History of the Expedition under the Command of Captains Lewis and Clark*. During 1904 and 1905 a very fine edition of the journals was published in eight volumes under the direction of R. G. Thwaites.

militia and Superintendent of Indian Affairs at St. Louis. In 1813, he became Governor of Louisiana Territory. Captain Lewis also handed back his army commission after he had reported to the President in Washington. Jefferson immediately made him Governor of Louisiana Territory. He returned to St. Louis, where he proved as competent as a territorial executive as he had been as an explorer and pathfinder. During his brief term he effected many reforms, organized the militia, and set the territorial administration on its feet. Unfortunately his melancholy temperament seems to have affected his mind. While in Tennessee, en route to Washington in 1809, he either committed suicide or was murdered in a wayside cabin where he was staying for the night.[20]

While Lewis and Clark were preparing for their wilderness journey, Brigadier General Wilkinson was planning to visit the national capital where he might tell of his disposition of federal troops and gain information of personal and professional value. Leaving Claiborne to struggle with the knotty problems of government in New Orleans, the general departed by sea on April 25, 1804. During the following summer and autumn he had much to say to the President—and a good deal as well to the Vice-President, the unpredictable Colonel Aaron Burr. His visit proved fruitful early in 1805. He was appointed Governor of Louisiana Territory, now detached from Indiana, at a salary of $2,000 per annum in addition to his army pay. It took him from April 10 until the latter part of June to reach St. Louis. There he was respectfully received by Major Bruff, the military commander, and cordially welcomed at a civic dinner given by the leading citizens of the frontier settlement.[21]

While in Washington, Wilkinson had discussed many times with Jefferson how to obtain additional information about the Louisiana Territory. He had scarcely warmed his official chair at St. Louis before he was organizing and

[20] *Dictionary of American Biography*, IV, pp. 141-144; XI, pp. 219-222.

[21] J. R. Jacobs, *op. cit.*, pp. 215-218.

sending out detachments on widely varying missions. He
had discussed the necessity for reconnaissance of the north
country several times with the President. He was aware
that Jefferson wanted this done by the army.[22] Dearborn
had inquired about the sources of the Mississippi, and
he urged that the Indians in that neighborhood should be
reminded that they were now wards of America rather than
of Spain, France, or England. A profitable trade in furs
was then being carried on in the region which is now Minnesota, Wisconsin, and Iowa. It was monopolized by the
British Northwest Company whose goods and supplies
were flowing in from Canada without American customs
examinations or duty payments. No attempt had been made
by either France or Spain to organize or govern the regions
lying west of the Mississippi and north of the Missouri.
The only flag displayed in those limitless forests and
prairies was the British Union Jack flying from the staffs
of the company factories. Jefferson, Dearborn, Wilkinson,
and certainly Secretary of the Treasury Gallatin, agreed
that the situation required investigation at least.

To ascertain the facts, an excellent officer was chosen—
1st Lieutenant Zebulon Montgomery Pike from the dependable 1st Infantry. He was twenty-six years of age,
"five feet, eight inches tall, eyes blue; light hair; abstemi-
ous, temperate and unremitting in duty." He had entered
the army as a cadet in his father's company about 1794
and had been promoted to ensign and first lieutenant in
1799. His orders from Wilkinson directed him to "proceed
up the Mississippi with all possible diligence." Ten days
after receiving his instructions he was off. He carried
orders to make topographical notes and enter them in a
diary; to record the numbers and locations of the Indians,
sparing no pains to make friends with them; to ascertain
suitable sites for military posts; and to follow the main
branch of the Mississippi to its source. Apparently these
directions originated at Monticello, but General Wilkinson
added a significant postscript of his own: "You will be

[22] Dearborn to Pike, Feb. 24, 1808, in *American State Papers, Miscellaneous Affairs*, I, p. 944.

pleased to obtain permission from the Indians who claim the ground, for the erection of military posts and trading houses at the mouth of the River St. Pierre, [St. Peter, or Minnesota River], the Falls of St. Anthony [Minneapolis], and every other critical point which may fall under your observation."[23] Such a comprehensive exploratory program was to be in addition to Pike's "other duties," as his instructions ran. The general confidently expected him to be back at St. Louis before the Mississippi froze in late autumn.

Lieutenant Pike started from his camp near the city at 4:00 p.m. on Friday, August 9, 1805, in a keel boat seventy feet long, provisioned for four months and manned by a sergeant, two corporals, and seventeen privates. On September 4 he arrived at Prairie du Chien on the Wisconsin side and there exchanged his keel boat for two bateaux. Seventeen days later he reached the mouth of the Minnesota River, pitched camp, and began diplomatic negotiations with a war party of 150 Sioux who happened to be in the neighborhood. After considerable discussion and the friendly stimulation of the chiefs by discreet distribution of certain "fees," he obtained their signatures to a legally phrased but wholly illegal conveyance. Under its terms the government acquired some 100,000 acres of valuable land, one tract at the mouth of the St. Croix River, the other from the confluence of the Minnesota and the Mississippi to as far north as the Falls of St. Anthony. How much money might be received by the Sioux Nation was left blank in the treaty. However, besides this unspecified sum there were more tangible and immediate gifts of tobacco and liquor. The United States Senate subsequently filled in the blank with the words "two thousand dollars."[24]

After making this highly satisfactory deal, Pike carefully informed the Sioux that their Great White Father now resided in Washington instead of across the Great Salt Water as formerly; that the sale of rum or whisky to

---

[23] Wilkinson to Pike, July 30, 1805, in *American State Papers, Miscellaneous Affairs*, I, p. 942.

[24] W. W. Folwell, *History of Minnesota*, I, pp. 91-94.

them by the white man of whatever nation was strictly prohibited; and that the Sioux and the Chippeway peoples,
long mortal enemies, must live in peace and amity henceforth. Resuming his way northward, he came to the Falls
of St. Anthony where a century later a great city of half
a million people was to straddle the river.

Navigation became very difficult because of shoal water
and rapids; the soldiers therefore earned their pay many
times over. Several fell sick and Pike ordered these to
march along the banks. On the 16th of October, 1805, he
reached the site of the later town of Little Falls. Here, at
the mouth of the Swan River, the lieutenant decided to
establish winter quarters. His men began to build a log
house, forty feet square and enclosed with strong pickets,
ending up with a fort so solid and strong that he said he
"would have laughed at the attack of 800 or 1000 savages."
With a safe base established he prepared at once to penetrate farther into the forests in search of the source of
the great river. Selecting only Corporal Bradford and a
small detail, he left behind his sergeant, one Henry Kennerman, in command of the fort, ordering him to conserve the
stores of food and drink and remain on friendly terms with
the Indians. Using wooden sleds, Pike, Bradford, and their
men struggled northward in blinding snowstorms and with
temperatures ranging near zero. Every night before he
slept, the conscientious lieutenant entered on the pages of
his journal the day's occurrences; sometimes "the cold
was so severe as to freeze the ink" in his pen.[25]

On the 8th of January, 1806, Pike and Corporal Bradford, ahead of the rest, came late at night to the gates of
the Northwest Company's stockade trading post at Sandy
Lake. There they remained twelve days, hospitably entertained by the company's agent. The laggards of the detachment came up after five days, and Pike put them to
work constructing *traineaux de glace*, or toboggans, for
use during the remainder of the trip. On February 1, with
a single enlisted companion, the lieutenant came to the

25 *Ibid.*, pp. 94-97.

Northwest Company's important post at Leech Lake,
erroneously supposing that he had now reached the source
of the Mississippi. Believing this part of his mission fulfilled, he began informing the British traders as to their
rights, responsibilities, and derelictions. To Hugh Mc-
Gillis, the director of the Fond du Lac Department of the
Company's northwestern empire, who was then at Leech
Lake, Pike wrote and personally delivered a courteous but
unmistakably authoritative letter. The factor was made to
understand that his business was being carried on in United
States territory. No more British goods should be introduced from Canada without the payment of customs
duties at Mackinac. The trading posts of the company
must cease to fly the British flag and their agents must
refrain from any political dealing with the Indians. The
company's actions must conform with American commercial law.

McGillis, after giving the communication a week of
prudent Scotch consideration, replied by a letter couched
in equally formal terms. He cheerfully conceded every
point as justly made and promised that, so far as he could
manage, the company would conform. Soon the British
colors came down from the post flagstaff—Pike had his
riflemen shoot away the iron pin to which they were
fastened. Then this assiduous United States marshal assembled the neighboring Indians and laid down the law to
them in unequivocal fashion.[26]

On February 18 the doughty lieutenant began his long
journey back. When he reached the fort near Little Falls
he was infuriated to find that his carefully hoarded supplies
had been squandered by the faithless Sergeant Kennerman
in an orgy of riotous living and entertainment of both
soldiers and Indians. Most of the provisions had been
eaten; even the keg of superior whisky reserved for the
personal use of the commanding officer had been traded
to the savages. The sergeant was promptly shifted to the
guardhouse and two days later tried and stripped of his

[26] *Ibid.*, pp. 97-98.

chevrons, Corporal Bradford being given them instead. A month later, on April 7, 1806, the entire party left for St. Louis. There Pike made the final entry in his journal.

> "April 30—Arrived about 12 oclock at the town (St. Louis) after an absence of eight months and 22 days."[27]

In October 1805, or about two months after Pike had left to find the source of the Mississippi, General Wilkinson sent his son, 1st Lieutenant James Wilkinson, and forty men up to the Missouri River with the ostensible object of establishing a fort at the mouth of the Platte. They carried along $2,000 worth of traders' goods in which the general himself, Mrs. Wilkinson's brother-in-law (the factor at Bellefontaine) or one of the Chouteaus had some important personal interest. After the members of the expedition had covered about 300 miles in the wilderness, they fell in with hostile Indians and suffered a casualty. This was enough to deter them from all ideas of building a fort or exchanging the rest of their goods at a profit. By the latter part of December they were all back in St. Louis.[28]

In the following year another better organized party set out for the upper reaches of the Red River. William Dunbar, who had helped explore the Washita in 1804, helped in preparation, but he did not accompany the expedition. It was led by Thomas Freeman, a civilian engineer and surveyor who had charted the boundary line between the United States and the Spanish possessions to the west. Accompanying him was a naturalist named Peter Custis. The military escort included Captain Richard Sparks, 2nd Infantry, Lieutenant Enoch Humphreys of the Artillery, a "young officer of considerable talent," two non-commissioned officers, seventeen privates, and a Negro servant. In April 1806, they set out from Fort Adams, reach-

[27] *Ibid.*, p. 99.
[28] I. J. Cox, "Opening the Santa Fe Trail," in *Missouri Historical Review*, XXV, p. 41; and Kate L. Gregg, "Building of First American Fort West of the Mississippi" in *ibid.*, XXX, pp. 361-362.

ing Red River on May 3. By the 19th they had arrived at
Natchitoches, where they conferred with Dr. John Sibley,
the Indian Agent, and Captain Turner, the commanding
officer of the recently occupied fort. Sibley had been up the
Red River in 1803 as far as the site of the later city of
Shreveport. He declared that the Spaniards in Texas had
learned of Sparks's expedition and had sent out a force
to intercept and drive it back. The captain then asked
Turner for reinforcements. Twenty soldiers under Ensign
John J. Duforest, 2nd Infantry, were furnished him. With
provisions for nine months in their flatboats, they left
Natchitoches on June 2. Five days later they were over-
taken by an Indian courier dispatched by Sibley with
information that a strong body of Spanish troops had
left Nacogdoches and would endeavor to cut them off at
the Caddo Villages. Sibley himself arrived soon after his
messenger, and then the whole situation was canvassed.
Freeman, although he had strict orders from President
Jefferson to avoid hostilities if possible, agreed with
Sparks that they should push on. They soon learned that
about 300 Spanish dragoons had reached the Caddo Villages and were awaiting them there. A friendly Caddo
chief came down to meet them and complain of the mis-
treatment suffered by his people at the hands of the arrogant Spaniards. He said that he had informed the Spanish
commander that he wished to live in peace with both white
peoples and that if they intended to do any fighting they
must go elsewhere for battle. Someone else brought word
that the Spanish now numbered more than a thousand and
had hauled down the American flag at the Villages, sub-
stituting the red and yellow standard of Spain. Although
apparently headed for trouble, Sparks was not yet ready
to return. After caching his papers and extra provisions,
he cautiously continued his march. On June 29, 1806, his
advance guard flushed the Spanish outposts at a point
635 miles above the mouth of the Red River. The pickets
fled immediately, but within a short time dragoons came
galloping forward. Sparks, Humphreys, and Duforest
made dispositions to take them in flank or rear in case

the camp was charged. At this juncture Don Francisco Viana, commander of the Spanish troops and the garrison at Nacogdoches, appeared with a flag of truce. Then followed a lengthy interview with Freeman and the American officers. He informed them that his force was ten times greater than theirs and that he had received positive orders from Governor Cordero of Texas to prevent the Americans from advancing any further up the Red River. He insisted that they must fall back. Sparks and his men decided, in the light of their instructions and the small size of their force, that they had better comply with this ultimatum at least temporarily. They thought it best to return to Natchitoches and perhaps later continue their investigations upstream with a more formidable escort. The Spaniards were obviously disturbed by the repeated American endeavors to penetrate what they regarded as Spanish territory west of the Sabine.[29]

Soon they were to have even greater anxiety. Very shortly after Pike had returned from the upper Mississippi, Wilkinson decided to send him on another expedition into the Southwest. He had on his hands a number of Osage Indians who had been recently ransomed from the Potawatomie, and were to be restored to their kinsmen in western Missouri. There was also a group of Osage and Pawnee chiefs whom Captain Peter had visited in 1805. He had persuaded them to accompany him on a visit to Washington. They had now returned to St. Louis and wanted to go home. The duty of escorting these Indians to their country was properly one for the army. The general welcomed it as an opportunity to carry out several different missions on a single expedition across the plains. Diplomatic conferences with some of the warring prairie tribes might serve to bring about peace between them. A show of flag and uniform, combined with gifts of gaudy but inexpensive baubles, might impress the Indians with the fact that the Great White Father was their ruler.

[29] R. G. Thwaites, *Early Western Travel*, XVII, pp. 66-76; I. J. Cox, "The Exploration of the Louisiana Frontier, 1803-1806" in *Ann. Rept. Amer. Hist. Assn., 1904*, pp. 168-174.

Incidentally, the route southwestward to New Spain might be investigated, and perhaps the elusive sources of the Red and Arkansas Rivers—so much an object of President Jefferson's interest—might be discovered and mapped.[30]

Wilkinson asked Pike, recently back from the North, to take command of the escorting troops and carry out the secondary objects of the expedition. After some hesitation at the prospect of again leaving his family for a long while, the energetic and ambitious lieutenant consented to go. He cherished the hope that he might eventually be selected to head a commission to survey and establish the western boundary of the Louisiana Purchase. He therefore welcomed this chance to familiarize himself with this unknown part of the Spanish frontier. He began his preparations immediately; and by the middle of June he was ready to leave, delayed only because some of the ransomed Osages had fallen sick.[31]

It is possible that General Wilkinson expected to derive from Pike's information something that would help to promote certain obscure and possibly sinister designs of his own. This has been a subject of much speculation by historians. The official instructions given to Pike were contained in two letters, both of entirely innocent content. But Pike and the general had numerous confidential conversations and discussions before they parted. Almost every project sponsored by Wilkinson inevitably comes under the suspicious scrutiny of those interested in his clouded career.

In addition to returning the Indians to their homelands, Pike received written instructions:

a. To effect a permanent peace between the warring Osage and Kansas tribes.

b. To seek out the Comanches and visit the towns of the so-called Pawnee Republic and bring about peace and amity between them.

[30] Jefferson in 1818 stated that he had nothing to do with Pike's expedition to the Southwest. See Jefferson to Wilkinson, June 25, 1818, in Jefferson, *Works* (Ford edition), XII, pp. 98-99.

[31] Pike to Wilkinson, Apr. 20, 1807, in *Zebulon Pike's Arkansas Journal*, edited by S. H. Hart and A. B. Hulbert, pp. 183-185.

c. To avoid giving offense to the Spaniards along their frontier.

d. To note "the geographical structure, natural history, and population" of the country through which he passed, preserving interesting specimens of minerals and plants.

e. To keep notebooks, make astronomical observations, and collect data to satisfy the deep interest of the President in the direction, extent, and navigation of the Red and Arkansas Rivers.

He was given, for expenses, the sum of $600 in trade goods to be used in Indian commerce.[32]

Early in July 1806, the Osage prisoners and chiefs were ready to leave for their homes. Pike had selected his soldiers; seventeen of them had been his companions on the trip up the Mississippi. He even took along Henry Kennerman, the faithless sergeant formerly reduced to the ranks for squandering supplies at Swan River. As the sole commissioned officer to accompany Pike, the general selected his own son, 2nd Lieutenant James Biddle Wilkinson, 2nd Infantry, instructing him to leave the main body when it reached the Arkansas River. He was to descend it to Natchez, investigating and reporting on the country through which the Arkansas flowed. With naïve paternal anxiety, the governor warned the hardy and indefatigable Pike not to overwork the boy. He wrote: "My son has the foundation of a good Constitution, but it must be tempered by degrees—do not push Him beyond his capacity in hardships too suddenly. He will, I hope, attempt anything, but let the stuff be hardened by degrees."[33]

A certain Dr. John H. Robinson, a civilian physician, was added to the party as a volunteer surgeon. He also had the task of collecting a debt owed a St. Louis merchant by an absconding trader if and when they found themselves in the neighborhood of Santa Fé, New Mexico. The

[32] Wilkinson to Pike, June 24, 1806, in *American State Papers, Miscellaneous Affairs*, I, p. 943.

[33] Wilkinson to Pike, July 18, 1806, in *American Historical Review*, XIII (1907-1908), p. 815.

complete personnel of the expedition, when it left Bellefontaine Landing, fourteen miles north of St. Louis, on
July 15, 1806, was as follows:

> 1st Lieut. Zebulon M. Pike, 1st Infantry,
> 2nd Lieut. James B. Wilkinson, 2nd Infantry,
> Dr. John Hamilton Robinson, volunteer surgeon,
> Sergeant Joseph Ballenger,
> Sergeant William Meek,
> Corporal Jeremiah Jackson,
> Sixteen privates,
> Baroney Vasquez, French and Spanish interpreter,
> 51 Osages and Pawnees.[34]

Pike and his troops ascended the Missouri in two boats
while the Indians marched along the banks guarded by a
detail of soldiers. At the mouth of the Osage River, the
party left the Missouri and proceeded up the Osage to
the Grand Osage Village in what was later known as
Vernon County, Missouri. The Indians were reunited with
their relatives and friends; and Pike, who had found them a
nuisance on the tedious trip, was glad to be rid of them
and go on to more important work. Only one of the soldiers
had fallen by the wayside; the worthless Kennerman
deserted almost at the start and never was heard from
again.[35]

Pike's next stop was the principal village of the Pawnee
Nation on the Kansas-Nebraska border and the Republican
River. There he marched with his men, accompanied by a
large delegation of Osage warriors. Pike thought them thieving and quarrelsome, a "faithless set of poltroons, incapable of a great and generous action." At the Pawnee capital
in northern Kansas extended conferences were held with
the chiefs, from whom Pike was surprised and disturbed
to learn that very recently a strong Spanish force had
visited the vicinity, evidently in search of him. In fact,
Don Nemecio Salcedo, captain general of the Internal
Provinces of New Spain, whose headquarters were at

---

[34] *American State Papers, Miscellaneous Affairs*, I, p. 943.
[35] *Op. cit.*, pp. 19, 20, 39, 50.

Chihuahua, had received ample warning of both Pike's and
Freeman's incursions into what he regarded as the King's
dominion.[36] As a consequence, he had sent out, under a
Spanish lieutenant, Don Fecundo Malgares, a reconnoitering party of 360 regular dragoons and New Mexico militia with orders to strengthen the allegiance of the northern
Indians to Spain. He was either to intimidate the American
explorers or drive them back. As we have seen, Governor
Cordero of Texas had succeeded in intercepting Freeman
and Sparks on the Red River. Malgares went far into
American territory searching for Pike, missing him only
by a few weeks. Afterwards he had returned to Santa Fé,
leaving on the grassy prairies a broad and unmistakable
trail which Pike easily followed, knowing that it would
lead him by the best route to the Spanish frontier.

The protracted pow-pow with the Pawnees was over by
the end of the first week in October, and Pike headed south
through Kansas to the Great Bend of the Arkansas. There
Lieutenant Wilkinson, with Sergeant Ballenger and four
privates, began their descent of the river while Pike turned
westward. Before they parted, young Wilkinson expressed
misgivings about ever getting home again, giving to Pike
a letter full of petulant complaints at the meagerness of
his equipment. The doughty explorer was glad to lose sight
of Wilkinson, who did not have the qualities required of a
successful pioneer. He had already delayed the progress
of the party on several occasions when he suffered from
headaches and fever.[37]

Still searching for the headwaters of the Red River,
Pike made his adventurous way into Colorado by easy
stages. During the winter of 1806, he and his men, badly
equipped for the severe weather, suffered extraordinary

[36] Wilkinson in his "Reflections" of April, 1804, may have given the
Spaniards warning of such incursions. However, Pike states that in-
formation of his expedition to the Southwest came to Chihuahua from
"Spanish emissaries" in St. Louis. See I. J. Cox, "The Louisiana-
Texas Frontier," in *Southwestern Historical Quarterly*, XVII, p. 31;
and A. B. Hulbert, *Zebulon Pike's Arkansas Journal*, pp. 78-79.

[37] E. Coues, *The Expeditions of Zebulon Montgomery Pike*, II,
passim.

hardships until they finally came to the San Luis Valley and built a rude fort on the Conejos River. He had completely failed to find the Comanches. Although indisputably in Spanish territory, he claimed that he was unaware of the fact. Before long the authorities in New Mexico learned of his presence and sent out troops to arrest him. After his capture, they took him to Santa Fé and later to Chihuahua, treating his party with much kindness but confiscating most of his notes and papers. After a sojourn of many weeks in Mexico, during which the observant lieutenant learned much about the country and its people, he was sent home by way of Texas, arriving safely at Natchitoches on July 1, 1807. In 1810, against the advice of Wilkinson, he published an account of his journey, establishing his fame as an able soldier and daring explorer.[38]

While daring explorers were stripping the West of its secrets and others were preparing to establish trading houses among the Indians, Wilkinson was spending most of the time in St. Louis, frequently discharging his duties as Governor of Upper Louisiana with more vigor than discretion. Numerous local civilians and army officers turned against him. Without their cooperation he could not expect to be of much future use there. Accordingly on May 16, 1806, he was ordered to leave for New Orleans "with as little delay as possible." The Spaniards were proving obstreperous along the southwestern boundary, and measures had to be taken to make them behave.

In spite of the need for haste, Wilkinson procrastinated, not reaching Natchez until September 7, 1806. Meanwhile a few Spanish soldiers had advanced east of the Sabine River, claiming the land that they had occupied for His Most Catholic Majesty. Their bravado continued until Wilkinson went out to meet them with a small force of his own. Then they sluggishly withdrew to their former position west of the river. Their leader, Simon de Herrera, was shrewd enough not to call on any of his poorly paid, ill-fed, undependable soldiers to do any real fighting over a

[38] *Ibid., passim.*

questionable cause. Wilkinson likewise wanted peace. At Natchitoches a face-saving agreement was effected. By its terms the Americans would not advance beyond the Arroyo Hondo; the Spaniards would not cross the Sabine. The intervening territory, which neither would enter, was declared to be neutral.

Before reaching this singular compromise, Wilkinson received a letter from Aaron Burr that fired his mind with a fantastic scheme of his own. The letter was dated July 29, 1806, and delivered to Wilkinson sometime during the early days of October. It told of a nebulous plan of buc-caneering adventure in which he, Burr, and a "host of choice spirits" might share. By the middle of November from 500 to 1,000 men, "the best blood" of the country, would be on the way from the Falls of the Ohio to the Southwest. Early in December they expected to reach Natchez, where they could then determine whether to seize Baton Rouge or pass it by. When they reached New Orleans, they could decide on the next step to be taken. In any event, part of the British and United States navies would be "in at the Mississippi" ready to help. At their ultimate destination, the "choice spirits" would be wel-comed, provided the inhabitants were allowed freedom of religion and no longer made subjects of a foreign power. This "glory and fortune" could be achieved in three short weeks were they worthy of it. With his "life and honor," Burr guaranteed success.

But Wilkinson did not relish the idea of being guilty of treason in the hope of being a secondary figure in a new state of illegitimate birth. He preferred to make solid capital and substantial reputation out of the schemes of the ex-Vice-President and his band of deluded followers. He would magnify the danger to his countrymen until they were stricken with terror, then he would step forth as their deliverer, ruthlessly crushing the freebooters who were coming down the river to loot New Orleans and establish an empire on the ruin of a conquered Mexico and a dismembered Union.

On October 20 and 21 Wilkinson wrote to Jefferson

telling him what horrors were in the offing. From 8,000 to 10,000 men were to rendezvous at New Orleans, where with the aid of a fleet they would form an expedition to seize Vera Cruz. Just what would happen to the territory of Orleans he could not say. He declared "the magnitude of the enterprise, the desperation of the plan, and the stupendous consequences with which it seems pregnant, stagger my belief . . . for this reason I shall forbear to commit names, because it is my desire to avert a great public calamity, and not to mar a salutary design or to injure any one undesignedly." He said that he did not know the prime mover or what the ultimate objective could be. He had been told, however, that the President connived at the plan and that the country would approve. His own orders did not permit him to do so. He would thwart the descent of such bandits by moving neighboring troops to a point along the Mississippi about fifteen miles below the mouth of the Ohio. In addition warships should be stationed where the Mississippi flows into the Gulf of Mexico in order to prevent the coming and going of unauthorized vessels. And on land a force of regulars should be organized to hunt down the freebooters and make them surrender.

Jefferson was not terrified, but he was impressed when these astounding letters reached him from his commanding general. The President and his Cabinet determined to prevent all armed bodies from traveling down the Mississippi; to warn all army posts to be on their guard; to call out militia if needed; to seize any boats suspected of being built for Burr; and to grant Wilkinson extraordinary powers to deal with the fearful situation.

If Jefferson responded in a way that Wilkinson hoped, others did not. To the Viceroy of Mexico, Iturrigaray, Walter Burling carried a letter telling how the general had succeeded "at the risk of his life, fame, and fortune" in preventing Burr and his followers from conquering the land of the Montezumas. For such an estimable service the bill was $110,000. The viceroy was not deceived by this ruse. Burling soon started home empty-handed; he carried no more than a message of thanks and good wishes to

Wilkinson in return for his efforts and "righteous intentions." For backing this singular errand, the general was out of pocket some $1,500; he subsequently charged this sum to the government and received reimbursement.

Similar letters were addressed to Governor Vincente Folch at Mobile and Pensacola—a previous source of financial gain. They told how Wilkinson had protected the Spanish possessions from lawless United States citizens who were immediately threatening Baton Rouge and ultimately the Mexican provinces. Wilkinson claimed that by employing all available means he had averted a catastrophe and prevented this foul blot upon the good American name. In spite of such mendacious fluency, no Spanish dollars were sent in return.

Meanwhile Wilkinson had reached New Orleans, arriving there November 25, 1806. He wanted the inhabitants to think that the upriver bandits would soon be at their gates to overturn the government and ransack the city. In flamboyant words he warned the populace, and with ruthless zeal he rid the place of Burr's associates. Erich Bollman was thrown in jail, and soon sent north consigned to the President. Samuel Swartwout and Peter Ogden suffered a similar fate. General John Adair was dragged from his dinner, suffered confinement, and shipped away for federal investigation. As Jefferson later conceded, Wilkinson trod the law in the dust, flaunted the judges, and "swaddled" Governor Claiborne "in his sack and laid him to bed like a great baby." Others declared his acts were "too notorious to be denied, too illegal to be justified, too wanton to be excused."

Certainly the actual events did not warrant such high-handed measures. Starting for the West sometime in August 1806, Burr had journeyed down the Ohio, visiting Wheeling, Cincinnati, and a few other places, always beguiling his group of would-be-settlers of the Bastrop grant with alluring plans of greater adventure. They might have a king and a court in Mexico; they might build an empire from United States territory and adjacent provinces of Spain. But recruits and money came slowly, especially after Jefferson's November proclamation warning all to refrain from joining any enterprise hostile to Spain. Burr himself fell under suspicion; he was investigated in Kentucky but no indictment was made. Finally he and sixty men went aboard nine boats and started down the Ohio from a point not far from the mouth of the Cumberland. They had little beside farming tools and supplies. Upon reaching the neighborhood of Natchez, Burr again was brought before a grand jury and again escaped charges. He knew, however, that if Wilkinson ever caught him a court-martial would follow, and the results might not be so easy. Burr, therefore, abandoned his deluded followers and fled, only to be apprehended near Fort Stoddert, Alabama, on February 19, 1807. His followers, stranded, hopeless, and bitter, settled where they could and started life anew.

During the next month, Burr was taken as a prisoner to Richmond, Virginia, where he was examined by John Marshall, Chief Justice of the Supreme Court. In June a grand jury began investigating. Twice in the previous eight months Burr had faced a similar tribunal. On the 13th, Wilkinson arrived from New Orleans to offer incriminating testimony. He was corpulent, redfaced, a little wheezy, and gorgeously arrayed in the colorful uniform of the general in chief of the army. No one was more fully determined to convict Burr, that "damned and pickled villain." Soon the "little arch traitor" was indicted for treason and misdemeanor. After considering the evidence given by a few genuinely honest witnesses and a number of "chore boys," self-seekers, and shameless hypocrites, the trial jury failed to convict Burr of treason. He never was brought into court on the lesser charge.

Burr's reputation, however, was ruined; never again would the public trust him. Wilkinson, the general in chief of the army, had also lost prestige, not because he had failed to bring a talented rascal to book, but because of his unsavory connection with the Spaniards and his more recent acts of highhanded folly. Opposition to him was growing. Until the last days of January 1809, he remained in or around Washington, believing that there he could best defend himself from the incessant attacks of his rancorous enemies.[39]

Meanwhile the army, now familiar with the general features of the territory of the Louisiana Purchase, continued to establish garrisons at strategic points, following the pattern established between 1803 and 1805 at Chicago, Bellefontaine, Arkansas Post, and Natchitoches. In 1808 troops started building Forts Madison and Osage. At all of these places factories were erected where Indians might obtain blankets, guns, traps, etc. in exchange for their tallow, beeswax, and skins of deer, beaver, otter, muskrat, raccoon, and bear. Jefferson strongly believed that such agencies would help toward permanent peace; he also wanted the best trading posts located west of the Mississippi River so that the tribes east of it would migrate thither, leaving their coveted lands to the whites. By these factories the President also hoped to drive out competing British traders, who were often familiar with the language of the savages, sometimes married squaws, and usually had goods superior to ours. The plan did not prove entirely successful. Some of the traders were incompetent; regulations forbade the sale of whisky and the extension of credit; and fixed store-houses were not as accessible as wandering peddlers.[40] Many years would elapse before the tribes of the mountain and plain would become relatively tranquil and consider the President as their "Great White Father in Washington."

[39] See J. R. Jacobs, *Tarnished Warrior*, pp. 209-240, for the relations of Burr and Wilkinson during this period.

[40] R. L. Fisher, "The Western Prologue to the War of 1812," in *Missouri Historical Review*, Apr. 1936, pp. 267-281.

Dᴜʀɪɴɢ the last part of 1808 and the opening months of 1809, officers and men of the army were scattered in posts along the Atlantic seaboard, the Mississippi Valley, and the Canadian border. Their distribution had little to do with the preparation for a war that threatened with England. Only around principal harbors had defenses been strengthened with a few guns and small garrisons. Between the Gulf of Mexico and the Great Lakes, American troops, except for the concentration at New Orleans, were mostly engaged in pushing the Indians westward, trying to stifle objections with traders' goods and government annuities. Along the Great Lakes and the St. Lawrence, they functioned more as policemen for the enforcement of the embargo than as soldiers standing ready to halt a hostile irruption from Canada.

Such was the disposition of troops when Madison became President. He, like Thomas Jefferson, was a man of peace. Both the country and the party were divided. This was a serious situation when war seemed close and our means for waging it were contemptible. The times required strong leadership which Madison could not provide. The changes that he made in the cabinet merely added to its weakness. Robert Smith was given the portfolio of the State Department; Paul Hamilton became secretary of the navy; Albert Gallatin continued with the treasury, William Eustis took over the direction of the War Department. Excepting Gallatin, not a cabinet member was a man of distinguished ability.

Eustis had rendered loyal and indefatigable service as a doctor during the Revolution. When it was over, he returned to Boston, where he practiced his profession with reasonable success. From time to time he took a turn at local and national politics, serving as a representative from Massachusetts in Congress from 1800 to 1805. There he supported the policies of the Democratic-Republicans, placing himself in a strategic position for their subsequent favors. When Madison distributed offices in accordance with the sectional demands of his party, Eustis was chosen as a beneficiary from New England. On March 9, 1809, he became secretary of war.[1]

On May 22, 1809, the Eleventh Congress assembled. Madison, wishfully thinking that our relations with England and France were improved, had ordered most of our gunboats tied up and the militia freed from readiness for immediate service. At the same time he wondered whether or not the army and navy should be reduced.[2] Madison was essentially a kindly man, fumblingly trying to maintain peace by blowing on a paper trumpet and brandishing a wooden sword. He wanted to effect a major operation by an "unremitting application of poultices and frequent doses of chicken broth." His character did not suit him to lead his people with a warrior's unfaltering resolution.

The President's uncertainty was John Randolph's opportunity. On May 24 he vehemently demanded that the House discharge the organizations temporarily raised by the act of April 12, 1808, and use the funds thus saved to arm the militia. The proposal was voted down by northern members who were unwilling to allow the majority of the money to be spent in the South, where it was more obviously needed.[3] Thus Eustis, the secretary of war, was left with eight new and two old regiments. He did not know their numerical strength and was only slightly familiar with their relative efficiency. He was not even sure of the location of the different companies, scattered as they were between Mackinac, Portland, and New Orleans.

At this time New Orleans had the largest number of

---

[1] *Dictionary of American Biography*, XII, pp. 190-191; and *Journal of the Executive Proceedings of the Senate*, etc., II, p. 120.

[2] Madison to Congress, May 25, 1809, in J. D. Richardson, *Messages and Papers of the Presidents, 1789-1802*, I, pp. 468-471.

[3] *Annals of Congress, 11th Congress, 1st and 2nd Session, 1809-1810*, pp. 60-73.

troops at any one place. Into this "burying ground of the Old South" Dearborn had ordered the 3rd, 5th, and 7th Infantries, a battalion of the 6th, and all of the Riflemen, Light Dragoons, and Light Artillery recruited south of New Jersey, so that they could frustrate any hostile movements that the British might make against "New Orleans and its dependencies."[4] The officers of these organizations had been commissioned directly from civil life, and except for a few in the grades of field rank, they had no military knowledge or experience. After recruiting their companies in the East, they usually started for New Orleans with their men, traveling via the Ohio and the Mississippi or the Atlantic. On March 26, 1809, Colonel Alexander Parker of the 5th Infantry arrived at New Orleans with 300 men and assumed command.[5]

Meanwhile General Wilkinson had been ordered to New Orleans on December 2, 1808. He did not leave the East until the last days of January because he was busy with personal affairs and with learning what official errands Jefferson would have him perform. He lingered en route for a few days at Baltimore and Charleston, enjoying the hospitality of the people and vigorously airing his political opinions. He was always a politician first and a general afterwards. When his ship, the *Hornet*, touched Havana, he assured the Spaniards that they need not fear the concentration of troops at New Orleans unless they permitted the use of West Florida for our injury; he also expressed the President's hopes that none of Spain's possessions should fall into the hands of either England or France. After delivering this message of good will and disposing of some apples and flour that he had brought with him in spite of the embargo, he left for Pensacola, where he hoped to see Governor Folch of Florida. This hope was never realized.[6]

On April 19 he reached New Orleans. Some hailed his

[4] Dearborn to Wilkinson, Dec. 2, 1808, in *American State Papers, Military Affairs*, I, p. 272.

[5] Deposition of Alexander Parker, in *American State Papers, Military Affairs*, I, pp. 284-285.

[6] J. R. Jacobs, *Tarnished Warrior*, pp. 248-250.

arrival with derision, describing him as "His Serene Highness," the "Grand Pensioner de Goday," the friend of "Field Marshall Possum" (Colonel Parker) and "King Solomon" (Governor Claiborne). They said the bells even rang: "The Pensioner is come, um, um, um." They were not sure of his future plans, but they knew that there would be a prodigious banquet where His Serene Highness would cut plenty of capers.[7]

Wilkinson had made many bitter enemies at New Orleans during the Burr conspiracy. They constantly ridiculed him, overlooking no opportunity to thwart his purposes or damn his reputation. At a time when civilian cooperation with the army was essential, Wilkinson had little of it.

On April 16 the enlisted force consisted of 1,733 sick and demoralized men. In a city where prostitutes and raw liquor were cheap, troops showed little restraint in their frequent hours of idleness. The officers were too ignorant and inexperienced to exercise sane control and to direct their energies into healthful channels. Of the noncommissioned officers and privates, 553 were unable to do any duty because of chills, fevers, dysentery, diarrhea, and other diseases. Since the 10th, the sick had increased 25 percent, not counting about 200 officers, many of whom were ill. Only three doctors were well enough to give them medical attention. The hospitals, though filled with the bedridden, had few stock remedies to hasten recovery.[8] During May the heat and the rains, heavy and "almost incessant," made the climate almost unbearable.

Wilkinson saw clearly that he must find a better location for his troops. Dearborn had given him full authority on December 2, 1808, to move them elsewhere. On April 30, 1809, Eustis advanced the same idea, declaring that the health of the troops came first and strongly recommending that they be removed to the vicinity of Fort Adams and Natchez.[9] Wilkinson procrastinated, meanwhile the sick

[7] *Federal Republican and Commercial Gazette* (Baltimore), May 30, 1809.

[8] J. Wilkinson, *Memoirs*, II, appendix CIII.

[9] Dearborn to Wilkinson, Dec. 2, 1808 in *ibid.*, pp. 242-243 and Eustis to Wilkinson, Apr. 30, 1808, in *American State Papers, Military Affairs*, I, p. 273.

increased. Finally, on May 29, he announced that his command would be transferred to Terre aux Boeufs, situated twelve miles below New Orleans on the left bank of the Mississippi. He said that the land was dry there, although actually it was three feet below the surface of the river. The site, he added, was healthy, furnished "the best water of the country," was near the market, and had strategic advantages for the protection of the city.[10] Certainly the first statement was untrue, and the others were at least open to question. Much labor would be required to redeem Terre aux Boeufs from jungle and make it fit for a camp. In fact, Major Pike kept details of several hundred men busy for a week clearing the land and digging ditches for drainage. For the use of about thirty acres, as well as for pasturage and timber close by, Jean Delassize received $640.34 for the three months that troops were there.[11] The rent was unquestionably high.

Why Wilkinson selected Terre aux Boeufs is not clear. Suggestions from others usually irked him, especially from Eustis for whom he had little respect. Although Fort Adams and Natchez were places acceptable from the standpoints of health and strategy, Wilkinson seemed not to focus his mind on these most important considerations. Apparently personal reasons intruded. By remaining in or near New Orleans, he could counteract the schemes of his enemies while enjoying the conviviality of old friends. His dwindling finances could be more easily recouped here than elsewhere. Here he could also profitably dispose of the eleven horses sent him from Kentucky and the merchandise that he had brought with him from the East. The place was also convenient for meeting the Spanish Governor of the Floridas, Vicente Folch, who might be tricked into paying highly for fictitious services. And, of course, purchases for the army were being constantly made. In the city, he would be in the best position to take a personal interest in them if his scruples permitted.

10 Wilkinson to Eustis, May 29, 1809, in J. Wilkinson, *op. cit.*, II, pp. 358-361.
11 *American State Papers, Military Affairs*, I, pp. 280, 294, 295.

On June 9, 1809, the first contingents reached Terre
aux Boeufs. Retaining embankments kept the Mississippi
from flooding the area. Encircled by river and swamp,
troops pitched some 400 to 500 tents, flooring them with
the boards composing the chalons that had brought them
down from New Orleans. In these shelters they arranged
their equipment, made their pallets of straw, and disposed
their few personal belongings. The rains came, the river
rose, the tents leaked, and the sinks overflowed. The ground
was deep in mud and littered with filth. Flies were everywhere, and toward evening mosquitoes were even more
numerous. The heat was intense. There were only a few
shade trees. An arbor was erected where men might loiter
and eat their food, but it gave no comfort to those who
were too weak to leave their stifling tents. Those who died
were buried nearby in graves so shallow that a nauseating
odor sometimes pervaded the camp.[12]

For a place and climate of this kind, the men needed a
few things that are now regarded as essential for health
and comfort. Pantaloons and shoes were soon worn out
and replacements were very hard to obtain. Men went
about in rags, and Wilkinson confessed that their appearance was disturbing when they paraded on July 4. Usually
clothing was shipped in casks from Philadelphia directly
to company commanders, who were held strictly account-
able for its issue. As a rule, posts kept no large supply on
hand from which emergency issues might be made. Only
very limited supplies were available at Terre aux Boeufs;
these came from companies that were much under authorized strength. From this or another source, some of the men
obtained a few articles after their inexperienced officers
had complied with bookkeepers' regulations. Underclothes,
of course, were not issued. Other articles were like those
worn at posts in Maine or Michigan, for no matter if the
climate was hot or cold, the regulation clothing was the
same. With such a shortage, clothing was not only threadbare but dirty. Men had no money to pay others to do their
laundry, and they were often too sick to do it themselves.[13]

[12] *Ibid.*, I, pp. 280-289.   [13] *Ibid.*, I, pp. 278-289.

Four pounds of soap were issued with every 100 rations. It is significant that James Morrison, the contractor, was paid for 28,436 extra rations of whisky but only two additional pounds of soap.[14] Some of the whisky seems to have been exchanged for vegetables to supplement the bread and pork diet of hospital patients.

Many of the sick stayed in their tents unattended except for the awkward efforts of their well-meaning companions. They lived wretchedly, and many of them died. By day they had no relief from heat and flies. The tents had no screening of any kind. When mosquitoes swarmed at night, the entrance was covered with an improvised curtain; but it proved of little use, for men were constantly going and coming on account of dysentery and diarrhea. Mosquito nets would have helped greatly, but they cost $2.50 apiece, half a month's pay for a private soldier; and although Wilkinson asked for approval to purchase them, Eustis never granted the needed authority.[15] Years later, in the same locality, the settlers screened their barns to make life bearable for their horses and mules.

If shelter was poor, the food was no better. In that climate flour quickly became moldy and full of lumps. It was old, colored like brimstone, and often alive with worms and bugs. Not infrequently the pork was rusty and the beef was not fit to be eaten. Whisky was about as good as usually issued. Except for the sick, men did their own cooking, generally in small groups of a half-dozen or more. Facilities at Terre aux Boeufs were crude, and few knew how to make the best use of them. No vegetables were issued except to those in the hospital; of course, they could be bought, but few had any money at all, for pay had been long in arrears. From such a monotonous diet, men sought release with whatever they could get. Once some convalescents gorged themselves with catfish and cucumbers; they died very soon.[16]

[14] Ration voucher in J. Wilkinson, *op. cit.*, II, p. 510.

[15] Wilkinson to Eustis, May 12, 1809, in J. Wilkinson, *op. cit.*, II, pp. 351-356; and *American State Papers, Military Affairs*, I, pp. 286.

[16] *American State Papers, Military Affairs*, I, pp. 278-290; and J. Wilkinson, *op. cit.*, appendix, CVII.

When Eustis learned that rations were below standard, he ordered Wilkinson to investigate and inform him so that, if need be, deductions could be made from the contractor's account.[17] He dreaded the report that he would have to make Congress on army expenditures; he knew only too well that they would come under the microscopic scrutiny of highly critical Federalists. The Federalists, not the imminence of war, seemed to disturb him.

Wilkinson was reluctant to take decisive measures because of his business connection with James Morrison, the contractor, who had sent him eleven horses from Kentucky. He had sold them at good prices in New Orleans. Alarmed at complaints, Morrison wrote confessing that any profits in his contract depended upon Wilkinson; he also declared that, when it was completed, arrangements would be made "satisfactory" to the general. Meanwhile, he asked that no examination of the flour be made except "in the last resort," for he had directed his agents to purchase sweet flour and mix with the rest so that all of it would be palatable. No drastic measures were taken. When Morrison failed to supply any flour at all for two or three days, Wilkinson did arrange for the purchase of 100 barrels at New Orleans. The general declared that this flour was not any better than what had been issued before. When fresh beef was similarly obtained, a part of it was so bad that it had to be condemned. The local prices were extremely high. Of course, the bill would be charged against the account of Morrison who was paid only sixteen cents for a single ration with all its components. Knowing that rations were bad, Eustis vigorously complained to the contractor but did nothing more.[18]

With such a system, troops could never expect to be well fed. A contract was awarded to the person who agreed to supply rations for a particular area at the lowest price. Sometimes a congressman might help a friend to obtain

[17] Eustis to Wilkinson, Aug. 12, 1809, in *Military Book, No. 4*, National Archives.

[18] Morrison to Wilkinson, July 28, 1809, *Wilkinson Papers*, III, Chicago Historical Society; Eustis to Morrison, Jan. 1810, *Military Book, No. 4*, National Archives.

a contract. For the entire army there might be several contracts, each involving perhaps $100,000 or more. The cost of the ration varied. In 1809 it was fifteen cents in Maryland and a cent higher around New Orleans.[19] By the act of January 11, 1812, it was commuted at twenty cents. If the contract was faithfully observed, the profits were small and might result in losses, especially when provisions had been carelessly packed or transportation costs proved greater than anticipated; on the other hand, they might be considerable if the contractor was able to have sub-standard meat and bread accepted and could evade furnishing some of the vinegar, soap, candles, or whisky. Too often the soldier suffered, the contractor profited, and the commanding officer could do nothing about it.

Obviously those who were sick needed better food than Morrison's wretched ration allowed. Besides medicines, instruments, and bedding, hospitals usually had certain amounts of sugar, rice, chocolate, tapioca, wines, brandy, etc., but the hospital at New Orleans was very scantily supplied. When the supply on hand was exhausted, Wilkinson authorized the military agent, Andrew McCulloch, to purchase replacements as well as some chickens at sixty cents apiece and eggs around thirty-five cents a dozen. These, with port and madeira wine at from $4 to $5 a gallon, Eustis declared to be "inadmissable charges" against the War Department, so informing both the military agent and the hospital surgeon on August 10, 1809.[20] Thereafter none were bought. Patients subsisted, for the most part, on the regular ration and what vegetables could be obtained in exchange for the whisky component.

Eustis was not ignorant of the conditions at Terre aux Boeufs. The monthly reports were revealing and officers on leave filled his ears with what was happening there. On June 22, 1809, he took action: he peremptorily ordered Wilkinson "immediately to embark" his men for "the high

[19] Inspector's Office to Johnson, Sept. 28, 1809, War Department Letters, National Archives; and J. Wilkinson, *op. cit.*, II, p. 510.

[20] Eustis to McCulloch and Spencer, Aug. 10, 1809 in J. Wilkinson, *op. cit.*, II, pp. 451-452.

ground in the rear of Fort Adams and Natchez."[21] Though compliance could not be escaped, Wilkinson procrastinated, giving plausible reasons for delay. Not until September 10 did the army start moving up the Mississippi.

Again bungling prevailed. Wilkinson was sick and did not accompany the troops on their long hard, 300-mile journey on the river. Many important details were neglected or ignored. Only a few drew part of their arrears of pay and had a little money to spend on the way. The paymaster was hidebound with regulations and Wilkinson feared that if the soldiers had any money they would desert. The military agent had no funds for contingent expenses, not even for the sick. The brigade quartermaster, 2nd Lieutenant Thomas H. Jesup, had a few dollars left over from the sale of the artillery horses, but he fell ill and remained in New Orleans.[22] No new clothing was issued; it was thought better to wait until troops arrived at Natchez. Only those who were very ill were left behind in the hospital; the hardiest were set to marching overland, often through swamp and jungle; the rest were crowded on a few boats, which had no facilities for bed-ridden passengers.[23] They might have fared much better traveling in small groups over a period of time instead of in a simultaneous movement of approximately 1,500 men.

Many of the sick never reached Natchez. They were placed on the decks exposed to rain and sun, except for a little protection furnished by improvised awnings. No straw was issued; it cost $60 a ton at New Orleans. They lay on thin, worn blankets, which they also used for cover at night. Their usual diet was the same as before—bread, meat, and whisky. When a hundred pitifully weak soldiers, mostly boyish recruits and broken veterans, were put off at Point Coupée, officers raised $100 for them. But it did little good, for many of them soon died. When the boats pulled into the shore, tied up for the night, and prepared the only hot meal of the day, the burial squads made their

[21] Eustis to Wilkinson, June 22, 1809, in *American State Papers, Military Affairs*, I, p. 274.

[22] J. Wilkinson, *op. cit.*, II, p. 473.

[23] *American State Papers, Military Affairs*, I, pp. 280-290.

rounds and gathered up those who had died since morning, wrapping them in blankets and placing them in shallow graves beside the river. When the sun rose, the same service was again performed.[24]

Finally, in the last days of October, the remnants of what once had been an army reached Fort Washington. Here Colonel Thomas H. Cushing, 2nd Infantry, had done little to prepare accommodations for them. In spite of new clothing, receipt of pay, and much better climate, many failed to recover from the sickness afflicting them. Casualties were almost as numerous as during the rout of St. Clair. Of some 2,036 noncommissioned officers and privates, losses had aggregated over a 1,000 between February 1809 and January 1810. One hundred sixty-six deserted; the rest died. To these must be added approximately forty officers who resigned or died.[25]

Most of the responsibility for such a ghastly condition must fall upon the shoulders of the two ex-doctors, Eustis and Wilkinson. Wilkinson was never entirely governed by his mission, that of keeping his men competent and properly disposed to defend New Orleans. Other factors often influenced his decision. He complained that he was frequently thwarted by the restrictions which Eustis imposed. The secretary of war had no trust in the general; and, although Eustis was far away and burdened with the preparation for war, he constantly interfered in matters of detail. He was so disturbed by expenditures at New Orleans that he lost all sense of army requirements and functions. When hay was high, he ordered the artillery horses sold. Soon there were none for the guns or for doing any hauling about the camp. When he saw the bills for renting buildings in New Orleans, he directed Wilkinson to "put an end to it." When the hospital surgeon bought

---

[24] *Ibid.*, pp. 280-290.

[25] Total deaths and desertions are given as 930 in J. Wilkinson, *op. cit.*, II, p. 372; but this number does not include deaths at Fort Adams (*American State Papers, Military Affairs*, I, p. 283), losses at Point Coupée (*ibid.*, p. 283), and resignations and deaths of commissioned officers (T. H. S. Hamersly, *Complete Regular Army Register of the United States*, pp. 61-62).

his patients chickens and wine he declared these delicacies to be "inadmissable charges" against the War Department and said that their purchase must cease. The military agent was expected to obtain the approval of the secretary before he made any expenditure amounting to as much as $50 except in case of emergency; in any event payment could be made only for things actually delivered or services received.[26] Under the circumstances, it is not surprising that the military agent would not furnish Wilkinson with $500 for contingent expenses when troops started for Natchez. Notwithstanding Eustis's repeated directions for retrenchment to Wilkinson, the military agent, and the surgeon, he declared to the House on April 10, 1810, that it was inexplicable to him why all articles necessary for the health and accommodation of troops had not been purchased, particularly when the military agent was expected to get whatever the general requested.[27] The whole truth would have proved embarrassing to Eustis; and so he had lied —a piece of mendacity inspired by the meanest motives.

In November 1809, Wilkinson left New Orleans to rejoin his shattered command at Natchez. There he remained until sometime in February, mostly engaged in obtaining evidence to clear himself in an investigation pending in the House of Representatives. At the same time he was trying to bring Captain Winfield Scott to book because Scott had publicly proclaimed him a traitor, liar, and scoundrel. Soon Scott was brought before a court-martial for speaking in this fashion of his commanding general and for withholding pay from some of his men for over a year. He was found guilty of both charges and was sentenced to the loss of all rank, pay, and emoluments for a year. Although the charges had arisen apparently from personal animosity, they did disclose that Scott could not hold his tongue in a tavern and that he had failed to give his own

[26] Eustis to Wilkinson, June 22, 1809, in J. Wilkinson, *op. cit.*, II, pp. 391-392; Eustis to McCulloch and Spencer, Aug. 10, 1809, in *ibid.*, pp. 451-452; Dearborn to Abrahams, Apr. 26, 1808, in *ibid.*, pp. 433-434.

[27] Eustis to Newton, Apr. 4, 1810, in *American State Papers, Military Affairs*, I, p. 275.

men the money that rightfully belonged to them.[28] Neither can be condoned simply because Scott was youthful and indiscreet.

After a year's enforced absence from the army, Scott returned to the Southwest, becoming a staff officer of Brigadier General Wade Hampton, who had assumed command of the troops in that area after Wilkinson's departure. One of Scott's duties was that of judge advocate. In the course of time, he was directing the prosecution of Colonel Thomas H. Cushing, whom Hampton had arraigned on charges of opening his letters, disobedience of orders, and various other delinquencies. In spite of the fact that Wilkinson had tried to ingratiate himself, Hampton thoroughly disliked Wilkinson and his partisans. Cushing, who was one of these, was held in arrest so long that Eustis wrote to Hampton directing him to settle the issue. On March 20, 1812, the trial began. Cushing was found guilty and ordered to be censured.[29] Apparently his reputation did not suffer. Much to the disgust of Hampton, Cushing was later made adjutant general of the army, a position from which he could readily pay off a few old grudges. It is significant that Hampton subsequently challenged Eustis to a duel and that the friendship between Cushing and Wilkinson continued unbroken.[30]

While Wilkinson was traveling to the East in 1810, two committees in the House of Representatives were busily investigating his conduct with regard to Burr, the Spaniards, and the great mortality of troops at New Orleans. Both collected a mass of data, but no punitive measures against Wilkinson were taken. Nevertheless, he wanted to put an end to such investigations—so disturbing to his reputation and finances. Eustis, too, was eager to have them settled; Wilkinson was a constant embarrassment to an already harassed administration. On June 1, 1811, Wilkinson was ordered to appear before a court-martial

28 C. W. Elliott, *Winfield Scott*, pp. 31-34; and J. R. Jacobs, *Tarnished Warrior*, pp. 160-161.

29 *The Trial of Thomas Cushing, passim*, in United States Military Academy Library.

30 M. J. Wright, *General Scott*, pp. 12-13.

and defend himself against eight charges and twenty-five specifications. The Spaniards had evidence that would incriminate him, but of course they did not testify. Since Burr had been acquitted four years before, no great punishment could be expected to fall on Wilkinson even if he were proved to be an accomplice. The other charges concerning disobedience, negligence, etc. were so tied up with ambiguous orders and regulations that nothing could be proved. On February 14, 1812, Wilkinson was found not guilty on all counts. The President reluctantly approved the verdict.[31] Eustis now had to find a place for his senior brigadier general, the third ranking officer in the army, one in whom no one had much confidence. Finally Wilkinson was ordered back to New Orleans. He did not arrive there until three weeks after war had been declared.

Courts-martial and courts of inquiry were matters of common occurrence. Commissioned officers usually appeared before one or the other if they continued in the service for many years. Charges might be grave or frivolous. Major James Bruff showed his contempt for General Wilkinson, and that was enough to cause his suspension from the army for a year without any pay. After Jefferson became President, Captain Nathaniel Leonard damned him in the presence of troops; charges followed, partly for this reason. Major William MacRea got into trouble because he required a soldier who was on duty as orderly and wearing sidearms to act as his personal porter and his daughter's footman on the streets of New Orleans. Colonel Henry Gaither was forced into retirement because he put an infant on the payrolls and drew rations accordingly. Captain James S. McKelvay found it hard to explain why he took a government boat and ran it aground, especially when on the same evening he and a few of his cronies had been on a "frolic" with some of the "sporting women" of Charleston. Even after the declaration of war, 1st Lieutenant William Depoistu had to face a judge advocate who wanted to know why he had declared that the Baltimore volunteers were nothing but a lot of tailors and shoe-

31 J. R. Jacobs, *Tarnished Warrior*, pp. 266-275.

makers, noted for horsestealing and not worth a damn.[32]

The frequency of army courts-martial for officers may be ascribed partly to the fact that they not only tried essentially military cases but also frequently took cognizance of those that were of a civil nature. In addition, all posts were small, and officers often became irritated at each other. Personal dislikes grew into morbid hatreds, frequently resulting in court-martial charges or duels. Isolated and inured to hardship, commanding officers usually had narrow views. They seemed to prefer meticulous compliance with the letter of orders and regulations rather than a reasonable observance of the spirit.

The petulant use of courts injured the service. Besides keeping a number of officers very busy on a duty that often produced only bitterness, it sometimes wrecked the teamwork of large commands, especially when high-ranking officers with large personal followings were its victims. The army had not yet learned that efficiency and high morale thrive best on a minimum of punishments, impartially applied.

While wrangling and incompetence were thwarting our plans for the defense of the Southwest, settlers in the Northwest were becoming more fearful that the Indians would take to the war path. The Shawnee chief, Tecumseh, and his one-eyed brother, The Prophet, had determined to stop further immigration along the Ohio and the upper Mississippi. In 1805 Tecumseh began urging all tribes to unite and agree to dispose of no land unless all of the others acquiesced. Chiefs who independently bartered their heritage away were to be deposed and punished. The land, he declared, had come to them from heaven, and theirs it was going to remain forever. They must shun civilized ways and live simply as they had done in the past. The Prophet added that he often held council with the Great Spirit, who had told him that all the whites in

[32] For Bruff, see *American State Papers, Miscellaneous Affairs*, I, p. 576; for Leonard, *Old Records, Adjutant General's Office*, National Archives; for MacRea, *ibid.*, for McKelvay, *ibid.*; for Depoistu, *ibid.*; for Gaither, *American State Papers, Miscellaneous Affairs*, I, p. 604.

America would be destroyed within a few years. When his miraculous powers were questioned, he declared that he would blot out the sun. He had learned that an eclipse was due on June 16, 1806. When it occurred, the savages' faith in him was unbounded. In all their plans Tecumseh and The Prophet seemed to have the blessing of the British as well. At Fort Amherstburg chiefs enjoyed royal entertainment and munificent gifts; but at Vincennes they fared poorly and the American annuities were shoddy and cheap.[33]

In the spring of 1808 Tecumseh and his followers established the village of Prophetstown, located at the juncture of the Wabash and the Tippecanoe rivers about 200 miles north of Vincennes by the water route. Shortly after the treaty of Fort Wayne in 1809, Tecumseh declared that he would not permit the survey of the land which had been recently ceded. Dark rumors also circulated that the Indians were planning to take nearby forts and towns and massacre the inhabitants. In the hope of peace, William Henry Harrison, Governor of Indiana Territory, asked Tecumseh to come and talk with him at Vincennes. Tecumseh came with some 400 warriors and immediately declared that the Indians had been wrongfully deprived of their lands and that he was going to punish the chiefs who had signed the treaty of Fort Wayne. Harrison repudiated any act of injustice, only to be called a liar by Tecumseh, who later apologized. Yielding nothing, Harrison agreed only to refer the whole matter to the President. Thus the conference ended. Another followed in July 1811; Tecumseh complained as before. Harrison immediately wanted to know why there had been murders and raids in Illinois, and finally he asked if the whites would be prevented from settling in the country ceded by the Weas. After receiving only evasive replies, Harrison asserted that the moon might sooner fall out of the sky than the President would permit his people to be murdered with impunity. He would also prefer to dress his warriors in petticoats rather than yield any land that had been justly acquired. Tecumseh

[33] F. Cleves, *Old Tippecanoe*, pp. 53-58.

left and journeyed south, where he endeavored to secure the Creeks and Cherokees as allies. War seemed close at hand.[34]

While discussions were going on at Vincennes, Eustis had ordered the 4th Infantry, about 600 strong, to descend the Ohio from Pittsburgh and report to Harrison for duty. But while the troops were en route, Eustis directed the regiment to halt near Cincinnati, except for one company which should continue on to Vincennes. Harrison could not reconcile this change with the previous instructions that he should attack if hostilities threatened, and do so with a force sufficient to insure success. He therefore sent word for the entire regiment to assemble at Vincennes. At about the same time he ordered all the Indiana militia mobilized, instead of only four companies as Eustis had directed. The secretary acquiesced after he had learned of the real conditions through Judge Benjamin Parke and Chancellor Waller Taylor.[35]

On September 19 the 4th Infantry arrived under the command of Colonel John P. Boyd, a native of Massachusetts who had been commissioned in 1808 and had previously served the Moguls of India for a dozen or more years as a soldier of fortune. His regulars caught the eye with their brass buttons, skin-tight pantaloons, long tail coats, stovepipe hats, chin straps, and red, white, and blue cockades. In spite of the fact that their uniforms were better for the stage than the wilderness, they acquitted themselves well. The militia and volunteers wore clothing more suitable—rough caps, hunting shirts, and breeches. Harrison was dressed similarly except that his beaver hat was decorated with an ostrich plume.[36]

With the Indians continuing to murder and steal, Harrison started his 1,000 troops northward from Vincennes

[34] L. Esarey, *Messages and Letters of William Henry Harrison*, I, pp. 535-546.

[35] For orders of Eustis, see Eustis to Boyd, July 17, 22, and Aug. 21, 1811, in *Military Book, No. 5*, in National Archives; and Eustis to Harrison, July 17, 20, 1811, in L. Esarey, *op. cit.*, I, pp. 535-537. For Harrison's action, see F. Cleves, *op. cit.*, pp. 88-90.

[36] F. Cleves, *op. cit.*, pp. 88-89.

on September 19, just as he had threatened to do. By the first of October they had reached Terre Haute. Three miles north of this spot they began building a fort. The work with shovel and ax was hard and monotonous, and those who were lazy complained loudly. With an inclination toward flogging for petty offenses, Colonel Boyd made matters worse. Harrison, better understanding his militia, volunteers, and regulars, assembled and told them kindly but firmly of the hardships that they must mutually share. Those who would escape suffering had better go home and claim from their sweethearts and friends the rewards of a deserter. They shouted that they were with him, and went back to their work with more zeal than before. That night they were issued an extra ration of whisky, and before the blazing camp fires they wrestled and chortled and swore. By the 27th a rude block house had been finished with barracks, bastions, and pickets. A bottle of bourbon was broken over the main gate, and Fort Harrison became a frontier post.[37]

Leaving the sick and a few able-bodied men at the new fort, Harrison crossed the Wabash and moved north along its western bank. His troops were in good spirits. Seventy-six mounted riflemen had just joined the regiment, and more volunteers from Kentucky were marching to reinforce him. Since the Indians continued to murder and steal, Harrison ordered his troops to shoot any of them on sight. On November 2, they reached the mouth of the Vermillion, remaining there long enough to throw up breastworks and transfer supplies from boats to wagons. On the 6th they pitched camp on a ten-acre piece of ground, three-quarters of a mile from Prophetstown. That evening it was turning cold, and chill autumn rain began to fall. They were 950 strong including 300 regulars. They lay on their arms, bayonets fixed, and cartridge boxes ready. In case of attack, they were ordered to hold their position until they were relieved. Harrison was not going to be surprised; he did not trust The Prophet's promise of peace and a conference on the following day.[38]

[37] *Ibid.*, pp. 91-93.   [38] *Ibid.*, pp. 95-97.

While Harrison's men were keeping alert, The Prophet, taking advantage of the absence of Tecumseh, was haranguing his warriors. He declared that he had made them invulnerable; he swore that Harrison's men were half dead, their powder harmless, and their bullets soft like rain. All this he had done through a magic potion he had brewed and an enchantment he had perfected.[39] Believing his words, the Indians moved forward to attack Harrison's camp, which was shaped like a flatiron with the end cut away. The blunted end and base represented the right and left flanks respectively. In the rear lay Burnet's creek and in every other direction were scattered thickets and marshy prairie. Wagons, horses and supplies had been placed in the center of the camp. Regulars and militia were sandwiched in the front and rear lines; the flanks were protected by mounted riflemen.

At about 4:00 on the morning of the 7th, rustling in the willows near the left rear of the camp disclosed the fact that Indians were there. The Battle of Tippecanoe was on. The savages began yelling and rushing the lines. Several of the bravest managed to gain the center of the camp and took a few scalps. One hundred warriors had been detailed to kill the white chief who rode a gray horse; fortunately Harrison happened to be mounted on a black one instead. He escaped unscathed, though constantly moving about giving orders as calmly as at drill or parade. Colonel Abraham Owen on a "remarkably white horse," Major Joseph Hamilton Daviess in a white surtout, and several other officers equally conspicuous were soon killed. The Indians, their black paint making them difficult to see in the half-light, pushed the attack with vigor. Three times they charged, and three times they were driven back. When day broke they hesitated to make another trial of strength against such bravery and skill. Then Harrison had his opportunity; he ordered a counter-attack from both flanks. The Indians fled. Those whom the infantry could not overtake, the dragoons tried to ride down before they found refuge in the swamps.[40]

39 *Ibid.*, pp. 98-99.   40 *Ibid.*, pp. 99-103.

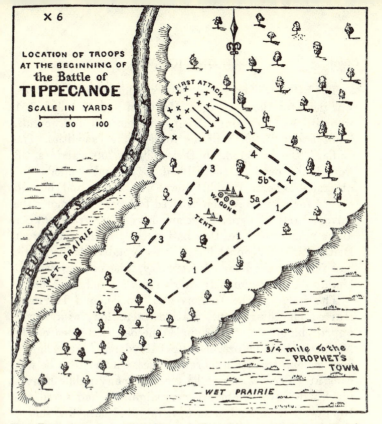

THE BATTLEFIELD OF TIPPECANOE (based on contemporary data).

1. Front line. The troops faced toward The Prophet's town and were composed of one battalion, 4th Infantry, Major G. R. C. Floyd commanding, and three companies of Indiana militia, one on the left, two on the right of Floyd's battalion, Colonel J. Bartholomew commanding.

2. Right flank troops were composed of mounted riflemen, Captain Spier Spencer commanding.

3. Rear line troops were composed of one battalion, 4th Infantry, Captain W. C. Baen commanding, and four companies of Indiana militia on the right of Baen's battalion, Lieutenant Colonel L. Decker commanding.

4. Left flank troops were composed of mounted riflemen, Major Samuel Wells commanding.

5a and 5b. Support and reserve. Two troops of dragoons were on the left rear of the front line, Major J. H. Daviess commanding. A troop of cavalry was near Daviess, facing the left flank, Captain B. Parks commanding.

6. Prophet's Rock, from which The Prophet exhorted his warriors.

The battle was over and victory achieved, but the price was dear for those engaged. Harrison had 37 killed, 151 wounded, and 2 missing. Twenty-nine more died of wounds. Thus about one-fifth of his forces were casualties. The Indians, too, suffered. Of their 560 to 700 warriors, 36 were found dead on the field of battle and a number of others elsewhere. Prophetstown was taken and burned except for what Harrison ordered to be saved. Among the salvaged articles were a large amount of high-grade powder and a number of rifles that had recently come from Great Britain.[41] The Prophet himself was repudiated; his magic had failed in the hour of extremity. The savages trussed him up and ignominiously carried him around like a baby.

The spirit of the Indians was broken, and Harrison started marching home. Rations were low, winter was approaching, and the wounded needed better care. By November 12 he had reached Fort Boyd, and here he halted long enough to obtain more supplies. On the 18th he was back at Vincennes, where he received many public honors for his decisive two-month campaign. He had saved the Northwest from an Indian uprising, and he well deserved the praise that was given him. Congress believed in his ability and before long would make him a general. Those who had become casualties at Tippecanoe were granted pensions. Enough rangers were to be raised so that the frontier would be adequately protected in the future.

Tippecanoe helped arouse the people to the needs of defense. For over two years they had been indifferent. From Madison's inauguration on March 4, 1809, until December 24, 1811, only one federal law had been passed affecting our military establishment, and it provided that recruiting should cease for the eight additional regiments authorized in 1808. Although our relations with England, France, and Spain were in a critical condition, the 11th Congress smugly neglected to prepare for war. In three sessions aggregating 285 days, it ignored the requests of

---

[41] The official account of the battle of Tippecanoe is given in Harrison to Eustis, Nov. 8, 18, 1811, in L. Esarey, *op. cit.*, I, pp. 614-631. For British powder and rifles, see *Western Sun* (Vincennes), June 25, 1812.

the President, who wanted the militia made adequate for
emergencies, a volunteer force of 20,000 men prepared for
"actual service," and an additional military academy
established at the capital or elsewhere.[42] Instead, members
of Congress wasted time in acrimonious debate, discussing
Non-Intercourse, the navy, the Indians, the British prime
ministers, the Bank of the United States, etc. They failed
to recharter the Bank, thereby making the financing of
war appreciably harder. One committee investigated Wilkinson at great length; another endeavored to ascertain
why so many soldiers had died at New Orleans. Nothing
really constructive resulted. Without leaders of strength
and vision, both the House and the Senate floundered about
like rudderless ships in heavy seas.

The secretary of war, William Eustis, did not help by
vigorous espousal of definite plans. He was essentially a
military tinker. What changes he effected in the army were
generally small and of a routine nature. He concerned
himself with details so much that he lost track of missions
and principles. Such infirmity of purpose had been disclosed very clearly when he dealt with troops at New
Orleans and in the Northwest.

Nevertheless Eustis must be credited with several
desirable changes at the Military Academy, even if he
later reduced it to no more than a name. Apparently acting
on Williams's advice, he fixed entrance requirements and
the general nature of the curriculum. No cadets were to be
admitted under fifteen or over twenty years old. They had
to be of good health and character and to be well versed
in writing, arithmetic, and the English language. The
length of the course was established at four years. At the
end of this time cadets had presumably learned the elements of algebra, geometry, trigonometry, surveying, and
conic sections; they could speak French "tolerably" and
translate it accurately; and they knew thoroughly the
current manuals on artillery and infantry. If they demonstrated competence in these subjects, they were to be

---

[42] Madison to Congress, Jan. 3, Dec. 5, 1810, in J. D. Richardson,
op. cit., pp. 478-479, 482-487.

given certificates that would put them in line for a commission. Study and instruction extended from eight o'clock in the morning until four in the afternoon with an hour's interval for the noon-day meal. Afterwards drill and practical exercises continued until sunset. From sunset to taps was set aside for additional study. Each year a vacation from December 15 to March 15 was allowed.[43]

After these constructive measures had been effected, Eustis began to ignore Williams and the best interests of the Academy. Civilian instructors were shabbily treated, three of them being ordered to live on the salary of two. They resigned when able to obtain positions elsewhere. Cadets were treated with similar parsimony and sometimes put on the same basis as those in the ranks. When ordered to go and see fortifications under construction at New York, cadets had to bear all the expenses of "their transportation, quarters, or any other items." Eustis directed Williams to "learn" them "to subsist on small means"; he wanted them to understand that they were "to labor or at least to be near to laborers so as to be able to work if it should be necessary." Upon finishing their training, cadets were ordered to join companies where they would do duty as soldiers and demonstrate their fitness to become officers. Some were even sent away earlier for this purpose. None could feel sure that he would ever be commissioned.[44] Not until April 29, 1812, was legal provision made for cadets to be carried as supernumerary officers.

Under these circumstances the Academy could scarcely be popular or efficient. When it opened on April 1809, forty-two cadets were on its muster rolls, but only thirty seem to have been present.[45] Some of them attempted to set the barracks on fire, and three were expelled as a result

[43] Regulations for the U.S. Military Academy issued by Eustis, Apr. 30, 1810, in Copied War Department Letters at U.S. Military Academy Library; G. W. Cullum, *Biographical Register of the Officers and Graduates of the U.S. Military Academy,* etc., III, pp. 535-538, 585.

[44] Eustis to Williams, date lacking, quoted in G. W. Cullum, *op. cit.,* III, p. 524; and Eustis to Williams, May 18, 1810, in Copied War Department Letters at U.S. Military Academy Library.

[45] G. W. Cullum, *op. cit.,* III, p. 524.

of the ensuing investigation. Those who remained were often absent from classes in mathematics, French, and fortifications. Sometimes there was no one present at all in drawing.[46] Standards sunk lower and lower. At one time in 1810, the corps had dwindled to fifteen cadets and two instructors—one in French and one in mathematics. Of the 206 cadets authorized between January 18, 1810, and April 29, 1812, only two were appointed; neither seems to have attended the Academy.[47] On March 1, 1811, eighteen cadets were commissioned without any examination. Some were even less deserving. After Williams had expelled Cadet Burchard for assault and battery and opposing an officer, Eustis kept him in the service and commissioned him in 1811. In the same year regular academic instruction ceased, teachers and cadets being equal in number and totaling four. By March 1812 only one of the former remained, 1st Lieutenant Alden Partridge.[48] On July 31, 1812, Williams resigned for the second and last time, not so much because of conditions at the Academy, but because he was not allowed to take command of the principal forts defending New York City. By then the Academy had passed through its darkest days; its prospects had already begun to brighten. Williams's most important recommendations were realized by the law of April 29, 1812. Authority was granted for an increase of three professors, six engineer officers, and the creation of a company of "bomadiers, sappers and miners." Cadets were not to exceed 250, and they were to be commissioned as supernumeraries if no vacancies existed when they were graduated. Money was provided for the establishment of a library and the purchase of other equipment, and hereafter the President might choose whomever he wished to head the Academy.[49]

[46] Eustis to Williams, June 18, 1809, in Copied War Department Letters in the U.S. Military Academy Library.

[47] Eustis to Simonds, May 23, 1809, in Copied War Department Letters in U.S. Military Academy Library; G. W. Cullum, *op. cit.*, III, pp. 527, 533, 547.

[48] G. W. Cullum, *op. cit.*, III, pp. 544, 558, 560.

[49] J. F. Callan, *The Military Laws of the United States* (revised edition).

This piece of legislation was the work of the 12th Congress that met for the first time on November 4, 1811. The new legislators were entirely different from their predecessors. The apathy that people felt toward Great Britain had passed. Vigorous young men from the West and South had joined the House of Representatives and they demanded that our potential forces be prepared to defend our rights on land and sea. The querulous old men who had previously led their colleagues into timidity and vacillation were relegated to quiet corners, and their places were taken by Clay, Calhoun, Grundy, and others who, aggressive and dynamic, preferred war to a continuance of supine submission to Great Britain. They vehemently urged that the resources of the nation be consecrated to the means of defense. Their efforts helped, but they came too late to be of maximum benefit.

During the remaining six months before war began on June 18, 1812, fifteen laws were enacted to strengthen the fighting forces. Nothing was done for the militia. The President, however, was authorized to accept and organize 30,000 volunteers. Since few volunteered, the time of enlistment was reduced to eighteen months for one-half of them.[50] The results proved no better. The state governors were then called on to supply the deficiency. Some acted indifferently; others did nothing at all.

Steps were taken to increase the number of regulars greatly, to make the service more attractive, and to create a better system of supply. All existing organizations were to be brought up to maximum strength. Ten new regiments were to be raised and a corps of artificers recruited. Recruits were encouraged to enlist by the offer of a $16 bounty. Those who served faithfully until discharged were promised a bonus of three months' pay and 160 acres of land.[51] If disabled in line of duty, privates and noncommissioned officers might draw a maximum pension of $5 a month; a pension for officers might amount to the equivalent of half pay. Dependents of anyone dying from wounds in service

[50] W. A. Ganoe, *The History of the United States Army*, p. 118.
[51] Act of Jan. 11, 1812, in J. F. Callan, *op. cit.*, pp. 212-215.

were entitled to half his pay for five years. Pay for
enlisted men was never to be in arrears more than two
months; travel allowances were liberalized; the ration
when not received was commuted at twenty cents; flogging
was abolished; and clothing when needed could be obtained
more easily than before.[52] With these improvements it
was hoped that the ranks would be quickly filled in old and
new organizations. Unfortunately there were very few
competent instructors for recruits. Officers were commissioned from civil life and knew almost nothing of their
duties.

For this army of 1812, the rudiments of a staff were
created. The two major generals were each allowed two
aides; other general officers were allowed one only. Military
agents and the Purveyor of Public Supplies were discarded. A Commissary General of Purchases, with his
deputies, took their places, buying whatever the army was
allowed. They were civilians under the immediate direction
of the secretary of war; only "in cases of necessity" were
the deputies permitted to make purchases for the commanding general, the quartermaster general, or his assistants. The quartermaster general himself was given the
rank, pay, and emoluments of a brigadier general. His
assistants might be taken from the line of the army and
given additional pay. His primary function was to house
and transport supplies; he could buy them only when
authorized by the secretary of war.[53] The new system had
the same defects as the old one—purchase and distribution
were placed in different departments. Not until both were
put under a single military head would troops in field and
garrison be competently supplied.

For "the better regulation of the ordnance," a Commissary of Ordnance was to be appointed with the rank, pay,
and emoluments of a colonel of infantry. He was to execute
all orders of the secretary of war and, in times of hostilities,
those of any general officer in respect to providing troops

[52] Acts of Jan. 11, 1812, Apr. 1812, and May 16, 1812, in J. F.
Callan, *op. cit.* (revised edition), pp. 212-228.

[53] Act of Mar. 28, 1812, in J. F. Callan, *op. cit.*, pp. 217-220.

with munitions. He was also to inspect ordnance, ammunition, gun carriages, etc. to see that they were uniformly and properly made.[54] Through him and his assistants, the War Department could always tell what weapons and related equipment were on hand. Since the discharge of Tousard in 1802, no one had had responsibility for the work of the Commissary of Ordnance. When the army was increased, the need for such an officer became imperative.

No thoughtful person regretted laws designed for the improvement and enlargement of our national defense, but he might well lament that they had not been enacted before. There was not sufficient time to carry out the plans of Congress, and we lacked men of outstanding military experience and capacity. Those on whom the responsibility fell soon found themselves hampered by the bickering of the states and the interference of politicians. Even after the army had been organized, its disposition could not always be governed by principles of strategy. Too often sectional interest had to be satisfied. Our desire for victory was great, but our reluctance to pay the price was greater.

[54] Act of May 14, 1812, in *ibid.*, pp. 226-227.

14. *A Country Unready for War*

On June 18, 1812, our twenty-nine years of peace with Great Britain ended. War was upon us. For our part, it had resulted from sectional passion and party interest, not from solid, well-calculated foreign policy that could expect unanimous support because of deep and widespread resentment. Although the British had spurned our ambassadors, blockaded our harbors, confiscated our ships, impressed our sailors, and incited the Indians to attack our settlements in the Northwest, we were not whole-heartedly united in a firm resolution to fight for the rights that we believed to be ours on land and sea. When the declaration of war reached New England, meetings of indignation were held, bells were tolled, and flags were flown at half-staff. In spite of the fact that this section owned one-half the specie of the country, it was to do little in the floating of war loans, subscribing to only three of the forty-one millions of dollars needed by the Treasury. Massachusetts, Rhode Island, and Connecticut soon restricted the use of militia troops to their states. Some localities even continued to send flour and beef to British garrisons along the St. Lawrence. Thus, of the 7,239,881 inhabitants of the United States, many gave no more support to the war than they had given to previous laws relating to non-intercourse and the embargo.[1]

The country invited attack. It was extensive, highly desirable, and not well defended. In the West Indies were strong, hostile bases, admirably suited for the concentration of men and ships. A large armed force might be based

[1] J. T. Adams, *The March of Democracy*, pp. 246-247; E. Channing, *A History of the United States*, IV, p. 457; J. B. McMaster, *A History of the United States, from the Revolution to the Civil War*, III, pp. 549-555. *Sixteenth Census of the United States: 1940*, p. 15.

there; the greatest navy in the world stood ready to furnish its escort. When cities along the eastern coast were captured, raiding parties could easily harry the adjacent country for a radius of fifty miles or more. None could foretell where such a blow might fall. Many places offered prospects of hostile success. The border of our domain, either jutting out into the Atlantic or lying next to Spanish Florida, measured approximately 2,805 miles from Passamaquoddy Bay to the mouth of the Mississippi.[2] Somewhere between these two points the British might strike, probably in the more thickly settled sections where booty and loot were greater. In 1810 the center of population was forty miles northwest of Washington, D.C.[3] Philadelphia had the largest number of inhabitants of any city. New York, Boston, Norfolk, Charleston, Savannah, and New Orleans were also important. They were all situated on the Atlantic or connecting bodies of water. The last four cities did not have wealth or industry comparable to the others, but they exercised great influence in the slaveholding areas south of the Potomac. New Orleans, since its acquisition in 1803, had shown symptoms of turbulence; Great Britain might attack there in the hope of winning new lands and subjects for the Crown.

The possibility of an attack along the shoreline of the Atlantic or the Gulf had long disturbed us. Ever since the Revolution we had envisaged such a contingency. From thirty to forty of the most important harbors had been allotted federal funds to improve their defenses. Between 1794 and 1805, $1,166,429.60 had been used for this purpose. For 1808 alone, $1,014,702 was spent, the size of the disbursement being mainly due to indignation over the Chesapeake affair; it was the maximum for any one year prior to the war of 1812. After 1808 appropriations dwindled. In 1811, $160,303.86 was believed enough to make the harbors safe.[4]

In the allotment of funds, political rather than military

2 *American State Papers, Military Affairs*, I, p. 791.
3 *Sixteenth Census of the United States: 1940*, p. 9.
4 *American State Papers, Military Affairs*, I, pp. 206, 239, 296.

considerations too often governed. The leaders of the administration and the aggressive champions of defense usually came from the South. They were insistent that their section should not suffer. No general strategic plan governed the selection of the areas to be fortified. Often they were poorly built on ill-selected sites. There were entirely too few competent engineers to supervise construction. Laborers, too, were ignorant and varied in industry as their patriotic fervor ebbed and flowed. Although the resulting works seemed to satisfy the local inhabitants, they were scarcely adequate against determined attacks. Heavy guns were often antiquated, improperly placed, and insufficiently manned. No dependable infantry stood by to operate with the artillerists. The militia were supposed to help, but they had little or no training and were chronically unreliable.

Since our harbors were poorly defended, we could not use them to best advantage as bases for privateers harrying British merchantmen upon the open sea. In 1810 we had plenty of sailors and about 1,000,000 tons of shipping. This was in spite of the embargo, Berlin and Milan decrees, Orders in Council, and the stern application of the Rule of War of 1756.[5] With such men and equipment it was possible to make British trade hazardous in parts of the Atlantic.

The Navy Department had been organized only since 1798, and by 1812 the navy had no more than seven frigates and nine smaller ships. When Jefferson became President he induced Congress to provide for 278 auxiliary gunboats; they were to be hauled upon the beach during days of peace and to be run in the water and extemporaneously manned in time of war. A tornado washed one of these singular ships into a Georgia cornfield; another went down en route to the Barbary Coast; all of them were nearly as futile as their opponents had prophesied.[6] With such a small navy, we could not send an

[5] E. Channing, *op. cit.*, IV, p. 350.
[6] *The Encyclopedia Americana*, vol. 27, pp. 372-373; J. B. Mc-Master, *op. cit.*, III, pp. 195-200. *Dictionary of American History*, II, 429.

expeditionary force to seize any point in the British West Indies or along the coast of Canada.

Our western frontier was less susceptible to attack except along its northern or southern edges, near New Orleans or the Great Lakes. The sparsely settled intervening territory was traversed by the great waterway of the Mississippi and protected by forts at St. Louis, Massac, Chickasaw Bluffs, Natchez, and Loftus Heights. Any invading force coming from the south would be lucky if it ever reached Natchez. Some 80,000 persons lived in the Louisiana Purchase and many of them would rally to prevent hostile forces from advancing farther inland. Progress would be exceedingly slow at best because only flat-boats and keel-boats were available for transportation. These could make only a few miles a day against the current. A descent from Canada on New Orleans would have been less practicable. For this purpose hostile supplies would have to be accumulated on the Great Lakes, carried overland to the Mississippi, and then down its waters. Such a scheme presumed British control of the Lakes, which furnished the only feasible line of communications to the far away bases of Quebec and Montreal, from which no roads continued westward into the wilderness. In spite of these difficulties, the Spaniards had feared in 1797 that the British and Americans would unite and sweep southward through the Mississippi Valley and take New Orleans.[7] Together they might have done so. But in 1812, the Americans were against the British, not with them. The only aid that the British might obtain would have to come from the Indians, who could conduct sporadic raids upon the western settlements. This, though hard to bear, would have no real effect upon the war.

The decisive fighting must come elsewhere. There were indications that it would occur in the vicinity of the Great Lakes and the St. Lawrence River. Canada was the only British possession that could be reached overland; all others lay across seas that hostile ships completely ruled.

[7] For the fears of the Spaniards in 1797, see J. R. Jacobs, *Tarnished Warrior*, pp. 163-166.

Ever since war had been imminent, "On to Canada" had been a popular slogan among the younger and more aggressive politicians in the South and West. Perhaps our failure to win it as the "Fourteenth Colony" had made us more determined than ever. Certainly its land and people were much like our own, and we confidently believed we could readily organize a greater republic reaching to the North Pole. If this were accomplished, we could monopolize the fur trade and eliminate Indian raids in the Northwest. It was also apparent that Great Britain, shorn of this dominion, would not be in such a strategic position to thwart any American policies inimical to her interests. Canada appeared to be a highly desirable fruit, temptingly close, and ready for picking.

In 1812, Canada was divided into Upper Canada and Lower Canada. Of the two sections, the former was more thinly populated and almost devoid of roads. It lay west and south of the Ottawa River. Practically all its settlers lived on the shores of Lakes Ontario, Erie, and Huron, near the narrow waters that connected them, and along the banks of the St. Lawrence. This chain of waterways furnished the only practicable means by which they could take their products eastward to Montreal and Quebec, where they exchanged them for the necessities of their western homes. If we captured Montreal and Quebec or controlled this line of communications, the rest of Canada could be taken easily.

Several factors had to be considered before attempting such an operation. A majority of the 4,500 British troops were stationed in Lower Canada, the region north and east of the Ottawa River. Most of the 500,000 Canadians lived here and furnished the great bulk of the militia who were of about the same dubious quality as our own.[8] As long as the British held the St. Lawrence, men and supplies could be transported from England to Montreal and Quebec more easily than we could forward them to Sackets Harbor, Oswego, or some other advance base. Of course, England

8 W. Wood, *Select British Documents of the Canadian War of 1812,* I, pp. 11-12.

could afford to furnish little help while she was desperately trying to save herself from the armies of Napoleon. But once this danger had passed, large reinforcements might be expected. Hence the quicker an invasion of Canada began, the better were American chances of victory. Perhaps those of French origin living in the valley of the St. Lawrence might not strongly oppose us, for they deeply disliked British rule and religion. These and other Canadians near the border were often friendly with settlers in our north country. They were bound to each other by strong commercial ties. For years they had exchanged wheat, beef, potash, furs, and manufactured goods. The Great Lakes and St. Lawrence furnished an easier route to good markets than the one, largely by land, that led to Boston, New York, Philadelphia, or other eastern cities.[9] Probably there would be many both in Canada and the United States who would be very reluctant to do any hard fighting. The United States had to reckon with the fact that in the section that would have to furnish most of its troops and supplies great numbers of citizens were in this frame of mind.

In marching against Montreal, we could go via the Hudson, Champlain Valley, and the Richelieu. Although the most direct route, it had been used with only questionable success during the Revolution. A difficult portage intervened between Albany and Lake George. The rest of the way to Plattsburg, the most advanced base, offered less trouble. The adjacent country, however, was thinly populated and barren of supplies. From Plattsburg to Montreal there were sixty-odd miles more through rugged hostile wilderness or an even greater distance following the Richelieu and the St. Lawrence.

The obstacles to such an advance from Albany were so formidable that few advocated it, least of all the inhabitants of the West. They were bitterly opposed to the withdrawal of any troops in the areas south of the Great Lakes in order to augment the number available for an

---

[9] For this trade between Canada and the United States, see J. B. McMaster, *op. cit.*, II, pp. 464–465.

offensive movement in the East. They were fearful that their frontier towns would be raided by British and Indians.

In order to keep our northern soil free of invaders, it would be necessary to control, at least, Lakes Erie and Ontario, the isthmus between, and the upper reaches of the St. Lawrence. In such a strategic plan, Presque Isle, Buffalo, Niagara, Oswego, and Sackets Harbor had vital importance. A small army and fleet vigorously led and properly disposed might hold them all. There was an abundance of raw materials for the army and navy. The militia would be effective if properly trained and adequately supplied. Sailors and shipbuilders were plentiful along the Atlantic coast and were eager to be employed. If brought to Presque Isle, Oswego, and Sackets Harbor, they could be set to building and manning ships fashioned from timber cut from the neighboring forests. Therefore we were mainly concerned with assembling enough men of the proper type in these critical areas and providing them with the rations and equipment that they would need in order to work or fight.

It would be necessary to depend on two well-known supply routes. One ran from Philadelphia to Pittsburgh; another from New York to Albany, Utica, Sackets Harbor, Oswego, and Buffalo. By the first of these, the distance to the nearest point on the Lakes was longer, more difficult to travel, and ended too far from the most important centers of British resistance, Montreal and Quebec.

Pittsburgh, however, would prove to be an important depot for the whole Northwest, just as it had been during the campaigns of Harmar, St. Clair, and Wayne. It was also the point of departure for supplies going down the Ohio and Mississippi to New Orleans and less distant points. From Philadelphia to Pittsburgh was about 310 miles, requiring a long, hard journey, especially over steep hills which might be covered with snow and ice. In the winter, pack-horses were about the only practical means of transportation; during the rest of the year wheeled vehicles frequently appeared along the way. As a rule,

neither traveled as rapidly as the regular stage that came
from Philadelphia twice each week in about six days.
Passengers paid $20 for fare and were allowed twenty
pounds of baggage.[10] Express riders generally made the
trip in a little more than half this time.[11] Small bodies of
troops, such as a company or battalion, usually marched
about twelve miles a day; thus they might be expected to
reach Pittsburgh in about four weeks. As in all overland
traveling, freight rates were high, varying from $100 a
ton, or five cents a pound, to twice that much or more.[12]
Erie, the site of Fort Presque Isle, was the town on the
Great Lakes nearest to Pittsburgh. If goods were destined
for this more remote area, they would have to be transported 160 miles more. The route followed the course of
the Allegheny River to French Creek, then along it to
Le Boeuf, or Waterford, Pennsylvania, then across country for about fifteen miles over a fairly good road that had
been improved by a turnpike company and the unwilling
efforts of the local drunkards. Erie itself was a shabby
little town of about 400 people living around a small fort
protecting an excellent harbor in which ships trafficking
between Detroit and Buffalo found good protection from
high winds and thick ice.[13] Incoming vessels brought salt,
furs, and other articles that were destined for places in
the interior of Pennsylvania and New York; departing
vessels bore cargoes of manufactured goods that had been
freighted from Pittsburgh at a cost of several cents a
pound.[14]

Besides this route, another, even greater, began at
Pittsburgh. From there flat-boats costing around $50
apiece were continually descending the Ohio when the
waters were high and the season favorable. In this way
passengers might travel to New Orleans for a fare of $60,

[10] Buck, A. J. and E. H., *The Planting of Civilization in Western
Pennsylvania*, p. 241.

[11] E. Wilson, *Standard History of Pittsburgh*, p. 81.

[12] B. H. Meyer, *History of Transportation in the United States
before 1860*, p. 78; J. B. McMaster, *op. cit.*, III, p. 463.

[13] L. J. Sanford, *The History of Erie County, Pennsylvania*, pp.
108-109.

[14] *Ibid., passim.*

carrying freight along with them at an additional cost of $6.75 per 100 pounds.[15] The trip consumed about thirty days. Returning by the same route was about three times as long and much more expensive. In 1812 most of the powder, shot, and other supplies required by the settlers in the valleys of the Ohio and the Mississippi would have to come from Pittsburgh rather than from New Orleans, where sea-borne commerce with the eastern cities had greatly diminished on account of British naval supremacy.

The same eastern cities also furnished munitions to the Lake Ontario region, which was constantly threatened with attack. Supplies could be most easily forwarded over the route that began at New York, passed through Albany, and terminated at Oswego or Sackets Harbor. Lately it had become more important because steamboats had appeared on the waters of the Hudson, thereby greatly shortening the time required to cover the 165 miles from New York to Albany. Some 232 miles still remained between Albany and Oswego. This part of the trip was also by water except for portages between Albany and Schenectady, around the falls of the Mohawk, and between the Mohawk and Wood Creek. From Three Rivers to Oswego was a discouraging stretch of twenty-four miles. Here navigation was "extremely dangerous and tedious" on account of the shoals, rapids, and falls; boats took three days, required a crew of four men, and could carry no more than thirty barrels of produce at a time.[16] Owing to these and other hazards, wagon transportation to and from points west of Albany was sometimes preferred, even though the cost was greater in money and time. Generally the minimum rate from New York to Oswego ranged from $2.25 to $2.50 for each 100 pounds. From New York to Buffalo, a distance of about 500 miles by land and water, it approximated $100 a ton or 5 cents per pound—an amount three times more than the usual market value of wheat, six times that of corn, and twelve times that of oats. Flour, bringing an even higher price, could not stand the cost of wagoning

15 B. H. Meyer, *op. cit.*, p. 103.
16 *American State Papers, Miscellaneous Affairs*, I, pp. 836, 877.

for 150 miles.[17] Since a great deal of wheat was raised in the area just south of Lake Ontario, bread enough for a small army could be purchased locally. This was a considerable factor in determining where we would concentrate our forces.

Obviously if the army operated anywhere on the northern frontier, transportation would be difficult and exceedingly expensive.

Nor was this all. Even at established bases, enough essential supplies would be hard to accumulate. Adequate stores of food would doubtless be easiest, because the nation was largely agricultural. The ration was simple, consisting mainly of bread, meat, and whisky. Of these components, good meat would be difficult to purchase and keep in quantity. This was due more to the fact that it was often poorly cured and packed rather than to any real scarcity in the country. Hogs and cattle were plentiful in Kentucky, Ohio, Pennsylvania, and New York; often droves of them cluttered the roads that led to the eastern cities. A great deal of wheat was also grown along the frontier, where it was generally milled and sold. The resulting flour, however, would deteriorate rapidly unless kept in watertight containers. Whisky was issued only in very small quantities; and even if a shortage prevailed, the army would suffer little in consequence. Hence, the troops had prospects of being reasonably well fed if the contractors would keep their agreements. In the past they had often escaped responsibility and tried to swell their profits at the expense of the soldiers.

Getting enough cloth for uniforms was much more of a problem. Our manufacturers of textiles could not meet our peacetime needs. Many wondered where we would get the shirts, pants, coats, and tents for the troops. They would require more than the usual number of these articles if they were to wage war in the north country. Good blankets, also, were scarce. Better and cheaper ones came from abroad. We did not produce the right wool to make the best kind.[18]

[17] B. H. Meyer, *op. cit.*, p. 103.
[18] Irvine to Calhoun, *American State Papers, Military Affairs*, II, pp. 42-43.

The embargo of 1807 had made us appreciate our deficiency in domestic manufactures. Numerous societies were founded to help overcome this lack. Members of many organizations promised to wear clothing only of domestic weave. In some states companies organized to turn out cotton and woolen goods were granted a long exemption from taxes. With this encouragement, progress followed, only to diminish when the embargo ceased and cheaper British imports managed to reach the markets in spite of obstructing laws. Different sections demanded protective tariffs, but they were not always granted. In 1812 the best thread, blankets, and uniform cloth continued to be imported, even after we knew that our ships would soon be swept from the seas. No surplus was laid by to meet the unusual demands of war. The master tailors and their assistants lacked the materials, which, under the best circumstances, could not be turned into uniforms and issued to troops within less than several months.

Prospects for small arms and associated equipment were better. If properly encouraged, our steel and iron industry might produce quantities of rifles, muskets, and bayonets. In addition there were many on hand, but not all were in serviceable condition. Springfield Arsenal would be able to make and repair about 18,000 muskets a year.[19] Factories at Harpers Ferry and other places should be able to turn out many more. The constant demands for powder, especially from the frontier, had resulted in almost enough mills to meet wartime needs. Leather was available for making plenty of belts and cartridge boxes. Enough shoes would be harder to supply.

We had a reasonable number of heavier guns. They were composed of mortars, howitzers, and 24, 32, and 50-pounders, and were situated in forts along the Atlantic and the Gulf of Mexico. We could scarcely expect to increase the number of these pieces in the area south of the Potomac because of transportation difficulties, but the defenses of our coastal cities in the East might, at least, be strengthened. Such a task should prove easier than

19 *American State Papers, Military Affairs,* II, p. 478.

before because we had lately begun to manufacture heavy ordnance of iron; also a little progress in standardizing calibers had been made. Ammunition, although not always the best, was good and serviceable and could be provided in reasonable quantities.

Many lighter guns, such as small howitzers and 4-pounders and 6-pounders, would be needed for the field artillery. These, too, were being made of iron, and could probably be supplied. But they had to be mobile to function properly, and this was possible only to a very limited degree. Carriages varied with the maker, and there was little or no idea of interchangeable parts. The horses of the only light artillery regiment were sold in 1809 because of their expensive upkeep. No provision was made to provide more until February 24, 1812.[20] Men pulled the guns along with drag ropes. It would be a wonder if they reached the right place at the right time. Certainly if the field artillery was to function properly, we would require more guns, an adequate number of horses, and an increased personnel that was thoroughly trained and dependable.

No branch of the service had such personnel available when war was declared. The regulars numbered only 6,744, although 35,000 had been authorized six months before.[21] With few exceptions, the newly appointed officers were grossly ignorant. They stumbled along with their subordinates, simultaneously learning and teaching as best they knew. No camps or schools existed to instruct them in the fundamentals of their profession. The Military Academy might have been used for this purpose, but Eustis had almost destroyed it. By June 18, 1812, only eighty-nine cadets had ever finished its course; and of these only sixty-five were serving with the army when hostilities began.[22] Being few in numbers and low in rank, they could exert no decisive influence. The law of April 29, 1812, enlarg-

[20] Eustis to Wilkinson, June 22, 1809, in J. Wilkinson, *Memoirs*, etc., II, pp. 391-392; J. F. Callan, *Military Laws of the United States* (rev. ed.), p. 216.

[21] *American State Papers, Military Affairs*, II, p. 46.

[22] G. W. Cullum, *Biographical Register of the Officers and Graduates*, etc., III, p. 588.

ing the Academy was passed too late to improve the situation.

The militia, our sole remaining military asset, was much less competent. In 1795, the President had been specifically authorized to employ them to suppress insurrection or repel invasion. While in the service they were to be paid, organized, and controlled much like the regulars. If they did not comply with the President's orders, they might be fined a year's pay.[23] Nevertheless, some politicians questioned the legality of sending militia beyond the borders of their respective states; more contended that they should not be ordered outside of the country, for example, into Canada. Unless these two ideas were entirely eradicated, they could not be used for offensive operations; and the time, money, and equipment expended on them might better be spent on the regulars.

In addition, the militia were of little value in war because of certain long-established practices. They had no real training or discipline. The few days annually set aside for the purpose were a farce; they were used instead for convivial reunion. Usually the officers were abysmally ignorant of tactics, seldom developing their organizations into efficient military units but frequently using them as active political machines.

With a few changes of detail, the militia were often like those whom C. H. Smith of Georgia described many years later:

"We used to have general musters all over the State twice a year. The militia was ordered out to be reviewed by the commander-in-chief, who was the governor. The constitution required him to review 'em, and as he couldn't travel all around in person, he had to do it by proxy, and so he had his proxy in every county, and he was called the governor's aide-de-camp with the rank of colonel. This gave the governor over a hundred aides-de-camp, and they all took it as a compliment and wore cocked hats with red plumes, and epaulets, and long brass swords, and big brass spurs, and pistols in their holsters, and rode up and

23 J. F. Callan, *op. cit.*, pp. 108-110.

down the lines at a gallop, reviewing the militia. The militia were in a double crooked straight line in a great big field and were armed with shot guns, and rifles, and muskets, and sticks, and cornstalks, and thrashpoles, and umbrellas, and they were standing up and setting down, or on the squat, or playing mumble-peg, and they hollered for water half the time, and whisky the other; and when the colonel and his personal staff got through reviewing he halted about the middle of the line and said, 'Shoulder arms —right face—march,' and the drums rattled, and the fifes squeaked, and several guns went off. These colonels held rank and title while the governor held office, and they were expected to holler hurrah for the governor on all popular occasions, and they did. The next governor appointed a new set until the state was chock full of them."[24]

With these conditions too often prevailing, only the regulars had a knowledge of war. A vast gulf lay between the regulars and the militia, and Congress made no real effort to bridge it through appropriate legislation. When emergencies brought them together, they spent altogether too much time in mutual recrimination and wrangles over precedence. When they separated, they were convinced more than ever that neither had real reason for existence. The militia did not realize that the regulars were the only real source of the information that they must have if they were to prove able in battle; the regulars did not appreciate that in war they alone were too few for victory, and if they ever were to attain it the militia and volunteers must furnish the bulk of the fighting forces. In order to succeed, the military leaders had to break down this animosity between the regulars and temporary troops and obtain legal authority to use both groups in the most profitable way as long as an emergency existed.

We could scarcely expect as much from the men in high office at the time of the outbreak of hostilities. In the hierarchy of command, President Madison stood first. At heart he was a pacifist whom politicians had bulldozed into war. He did not possess dynamic, aggressive characteris-

24 C. H. Smith, *Bill Arp's Scrap Book*, p. 236.

tics and was entirely unfitted for the role that was expected of him. His principal subordinates could not supply Madison's deficiencies.

The secretary of war, William Eustis, had only a second-rate mind that dwelt on petty things; most of the time he thought in terms of schemes rather than principles. He had a kind of smartness, but no real ability. He could not discard local or sectional thinking in favor of national interest. Constantly remembering who had given him office, he always consulted the oracles of his party before making any military decision. In taking the auspices, he habitually interpreted them for the benefit of the Democratic-Republicans. As a political haruspex he was admirable; as secretary of war, he was a piddling incompetent. Few, however, could have made the War Department function efficiently as it was then organized. It was cluttered with responsibilities that other departments did not care to have. Indian affairs, government lands, and invalid pensions all came under its direction. Ten or twelve subordinates did all of this work and at the same time tried to prepare the country for war. The previous administration had complained that War Department personnel were entirely too few, but Congress had provided no more. No one in the War Department could supply the military knowledge that Eustis obviously lacked.

Just below Eustis stood Henry Dearborn. After eight years in Jefferson's cabinet and three as the Collector of the Port of Boston, he had become senior officer in the army on January 27, 1812, with the rank of major general. He was then sixty-one years old and without the qualities required for a general in chief. Some thirty years had elapsed since he had seen active service in the Revolution. Although his bodily vigor had passed and his mind had grown rusty in office routine, he was still worthy of being consulted in matters of practical detail and general administration. But he had lingered too long over politics and the flesh-pots of easy living to meet the Spartan hardships and provide the rugged leadership essential for success in a field command.

Even less could be expected of Thomas Pinckney, the other major general. He had been reasonably effective as a diplomat and member of Congress, but had never really distinguished himself as a soldier. In 1812 he was sixty-three years old and had not been associated with the army since the Revolution. His record there was neither extensive nor brilliant.

Of the nine brigadier generals, James Wilkinson was senior and had enjoyed the longest period of service. With the exception of Alexander Smyth, he was probably the most voluble and egotistical high ranking officer. Few trusted him; many hated him; more doubted his honesty and military ability. He was essentially a political opportunist with a military sheen. Wade Hampton had been in the army since 1809. He was wealthy and had a strong political following, but the little that he knew about his profession was nullified by his contentious and vindictive spirit. John P. Boyd was younger than either of these two, being only forty-eight. He was a blustering soldier of fortune who had served for twenty years under potentates of India. Joseph Bloomfield, James Winchester, William Hull, Thomas Flournoy, and John Chandler were without greatness. They were either to bring disgrace to the army or fade away into innocuous obscurity. The thirty-nine-year-old William Henry Harrison was far more promising. He had served efficiently as a lieutenant in the army from 1791 to 1797, had enhanced his reputation as Governor of Indiana Territory, and in 1811 had badly defeated the Indians at Tippecanoe. More of his kind were badly needed.

The so-called "General Staff" was no better than the field command, probably knowing even less of its characteristic duties. Thomas H. Cushing, the adjutant general, was in such poor health that he could scarcely get about. The inspector general, Alexander Smyth, was just a commonplace braggart without redeeming qualities. Morgan Lewis was quartermaster. Although he was a person of character, he had only a microscopic conception of the wide range and extreme difficulties of his task. The adjutant and inspector, A. Y. Nicoll, had the rank only of a major and his contribution to the service was in proportion. Robert Brent, the paymaster, possessed a knowledge of peacetime routine, but that was about all. As a rule, the "General Staff" functioned as individuals, not as a team.

Why were such men selected as leaders? The answer is simple; there were few or none better. The chief source of supply was the regular army, which for years had been exceedingly small. In 1802 there were only thirteen field officers for combat units; within seven years only nine of these remained. Jefferson believed that the army had little need of those beyond the grade of captain. In 1809 the army reached its maximum strength before 1812, having thirty-six field officers, exclusive of engineers, who were not permitted to command troops except by specific orders of the President. When war was declared only twenty-nine field officers were still in the service.[25] At the very best they had been afforded only three opportunities to see as many as 1,000 men under arms since 1783; this occurred during the campaigns of St. Clair and Wayne and at the concentration at New Orleans in 1809. In the last case, more than half of the troops were bedridden, and the energy of all was employed in the care of the sick. Consequently, field officers were not familiar with their function. Many of them were also too old for vigorous work on campaign and too deeply sunk in the ruts of peace routine to meet the constantly changing situations of war.

Nor were field officers available elsewhere. We had been so busily engaged in conquering a wilderness and building a republic that we had paid no attention to the effective preparation of the new militia for a war that was imminent. Neither the public nor Congress insisted on improvement. In mere numbers they seemed to be formidable enough. Since they were potentially capable, we failed to see that they were entirely worthless for immediate fighting. We would not acknowledge that they needed training, involving only a little expense, inconvenience, and time. We com-

[25] For figures on field officers, T. H. S. Hamersly, *Army Register of the United States*, pp. 55-80.

placently allowed them to continue as untrained as ever. We were soon to suffer for pursuing such an unreasoning course; for in time of war, ignorance of strategy and tactics demands a fearful cost in the lives of men. Unfortunately we do not seem to learn from history, for this was neither the first nor the last time that we drifted into war unprepared.

BIBLIOGRAPHY

I. PRIMARY SOURCE MATERIAL

A. UNPUBLISHED

Army Officers, Letters. New York City Library.

Autograph Letters. The Pennsylvania Historical Society (Philadelphia).

H. C. Castellano Scrap Book. The Library of the Cabildo (New Orleans).

William C. C. Claiborne Papers. Mississippi Department of Archives & History (Jackson).

Adjutant John Crawford, Orderly Book. Detroit Public Library.

Darlington Collection. University of Pittsburgh.

Henry Dearborn Papers. Boston Public Library.

Henry Dearborn Papers. The Maine Historical Society (Portland).

Durrett Manuscripts. University of Wisconsin (Madison).

Andrew Ellicott Papers. The Library of Congress.

1st U. S. Infantry Order Book. Detroit Public Library.

Peter Gansevoort, Jr., Papers. The New York City Library.

Gratz Collection. The Pennsylvania Historical Society (Philadelphia).

J. F. Hamtramck Papers. Detroit Public Library.

Josiah Harmar Papers. William L. Clements Library (Ann Arbor, Michigan).

Josiah Harmar Papers. The Historical Society of Wisconsin (Madison).

Jonathan Heart Orderly Book of Sept. 7, 1785 to May 2, 1788. National Archives.

Samuel Henley Papers. Detroit Public Library.

Harry Innes Papers. The Library of Congress.

David Jones Papers. Detroit Public Library.

Jacob Kingsbury Papers. The Library of Congress.

Henry Knox Papers. The Massachusetts Historical Society (Boston).

Military Book, No. 1, No. 2, No. 3, No. 4, No. 5. National Archives.

Military Book, No. 154. The National Archives.

Northwest Territory Papers. The Library of Congress.

Old Records, Adjutant General's Office. National Archives.

Old Records, Inspector's Office. National Archives.

Papeles Procedentes de Cuba. The Library of Congress. These papers concern James Wilkinson's relations with the Spaniards.

Benjamin Peabody, Orderly Book of. U. S. M. A. Library.

Timothy Pickering Papers. Massachusetts Historical Society (Boston).

David Porter Papers. Library of Congress.

John Pratt Papers. The Connecticut State Library (Hartford).

Purveyor's Papers. National Archives.

Quarter Master General Ledger A, July 1796-November 1797. Library of Congress.

Regular Army in *Miscellaneous Papers.* Library of Congress.

Arthur St. Clair Papers. Detroit Public Library.

Arthur St. Clair Papers. National Archives.

Winthrop Sargent Papers. The Massachusetts Historical Society (Boston).

Winthrop Sargent Papers. Mississippi Department of Archives & History (Jackson).

War Department Letters (copied). U. S. M. A. Library.

Anthony Wayne Papers. The Historical Society of Pennsylvania (Philadelphia).

West Point Letter Book, No. 2. U. S. M. A. Library.

West Point Orderly Book of Artillerists and Engineers, No. 1, No. 2, No. 3. U. S. M. A. Library.

West Point Ordnance Waste Book, No. 2, No. 4. U. S. M. A. Library.

John Wilkins Papers. Detroit Public Library.

James Wilkinson, Order Book, 1797-1807. National Archives.

James Wilkinson Papers. Boston Public Library.

James Wilkinson Papers. Chicago Historical Society.

James Wilkinson Papers. The Library of Congress.

James Wilkinson Papers. Detroit Public Library.

James Wilkinson Papers. The Historical and Philosophical Society of Ohio (Cincinnati).

James Wilkinson Papers. The Massachusetts Historical Society (Boston).

James Wilkinson Papers. The Missouri Historical Society (St. Louis).

James Wilkinson Papers. The Newberry Library (Chicago).

William Woodbridge Papers. Detroit Public Library.

B. Published

1. BOOKS, PAMPHLETS, ARTICLES

John Adams' Works. Edited by C. F. Adams. 10 vols. Boston: 1850-1856.

American State Papers. Foreign Relations, vol. I. *Indian Affairs,* vol. I. *Miscellaneous,* vol. I. Washington, 1832-1861.

Erkuries Beatty Diary in *Magazine of American History,* vol. I.

Lieutenant Henry Boyer, "A Journal of Wayne's Campaign" in J. J. Jacob, *Life of Michael Cresap,* etc. Cincinnati, 1866.

Captain Daniel Bradley, Journal of. Edited by Frazer E. Wilson, Jobes & Son, Greenville, Ohio, 1935.

William Clark, "Journal of General Wayne's Campaign" in *Mississippi Valley Historical Review,* vol. I.

Congress, Annals of. Washington, D.C. 1834-1856.

Continental Congress, 1774-1789, Journals of. Edited by Library of Congress, Washington, D.C., 1934.

Continental Congress, Letters of Members of the. Edited by E. C. Burnett, Carnegie Institution of Washington, Washington, D.C., 1921-1936.

"Zachariah Cox, Documents Relating to." Edited by I. J. Cox and in *Quarterly Publications of Historical and Philosophical Society of Ohio,* vol. VIII.

"Major Ebenezer Denny, Military Journal of" in W. H. Smith, *St. Clair Papers,* vol. II.

Expenditures in the Naval and Military Establishments by the Quarter Master General and Navy Agents. Neither publisher nor date of publication given. A copy is in the War College Library, Washington, D.C.

"Captain Isaac Guion, 1797-1799, Military Journal of" in *Fifth Annual Report . . . of Archives . . . Mississippi.*

Alexander Hamilton, Works of, 12 vols. Edited by Henry Cabot Lodge, G. P. Putnam's Sons, New York, 1885-1886.

Captain Jonathan Heart, Journal of. Edited by Consul Willshire Butterfield, Joel Munsell's Sons, Albany, 1885.

John Heckewelder, "Narrative of His Journey to the Wabash in 1792" in *Pennsylvania Magazine of History and Biography,* vol. XII.

Thomas Jefferson, Writings of, 10 vols. Edited by Paul Leicester Ford, G. P. Putnam's Sons, New York, 1905.

Legislative History of the General Staff of the United States. Edited by R. P. Thian, Government Printing Office, Washington, D.C., 1901. Composed entirely of extracts from laws governing the General Staff.

William Maclay, Journal of. Edited by C. A. Beard, Albert & Charles Boni, New York, 1927.

James Madison. *Writings Comprising His Public Papers and Private Correspondence.* 9 vols. Edited by Gaillard Hunt, G. P. Putnam's Sons, New York, 1900-1912.

"McDowell's Story" in H. Howe, *Historical Collections of Ohio,* vol. II.

The Military Laws of the United States, Revised Edition. Edited by J. F. Callan, Philadelphia, 1863.

"Captain Samuel Newman, The Journal of" in *Wisconsin Magazine of History,* vol. II.

Messages and Papers of the Presidents, 1789-1902. Edited by J. Richardson, Bureau of National Literature and Art, 1904.

Winthrop Sargent, "Diary" in *Ohio Archaeological and Historical Society Publications,* vol. XXXIII.

Lieut. Governor John Graves Simcoe, The Correspondence of, etc. Edited by E. A. Cruikshank, Ontario Historical Society, Toronto, 1925.

Von Steuben, *Regulations for the Order and Discipline of the Troops of the United States.* Philadelphia, 1779.

Arthur St. Clair, *Narrative,* etc. Philadelphia, 1812.

Thomas Irwin, "St. Clair's Defeat" in *Ohio Archaeological and Historical Society Publications,* vol. X.

Arthur St. Clair Papers. Edited by William H. Smith. 2 vols. Robert Clark Company, Cincinnati, 1882.

General Joseph Gardner Swift, Memoirs of. Edited by H. Ellery. Privately printed, 1890.

John Cleves Symmes, Correspondence of. Edited by B. W. Bond. The Macmillan Company, New York, 1926.

Thomas Taylor Underwood, Journal of. Edited by the Society of Colonial Wars in the State of Ohio. Cincinnati, 1945.

The Territorial Papers of the United States. Edited by C. E. Carter, Washington, D.C., United States Printing Office, 1936.

Benjamin Van Cleve, "Memoirs, etc." in *American Pioneer,* vol. II.

George Washington, Writings of, 14 vols. Edited by W. C. Ford, G. P. Putnam's Sons, New York, 1889-1892.

Anthony Wayne, "Order Book" in *Michigan Historical Collections*, vol. 34.
James Wilkinson, *Memoirs of My Own Times*, 3 vols. and an atlas. Philadelphia, 1816.

2. NEWSPAPERS AND MAGAZINES

Albany Register (Albany).
American Museum (Philadelphia).
The American Pioneer (Cincinnati).
Augusta Chronicle and Gazette of the State (Augusta).
Aurora (Philadelphia).
The Centinel of the Northwest Territory (Cincinnati).
The Cincinnati Miscellany (Cincinnati).
Columbian Centinel (Boston).
Federal Republican and Commercial Gazette (Baltimore).
Gazette of the United States (Philadelphia).
Kentucky Gazette (Lexington).
Maryland Gazette (Annapolis).
Maryland Gazette (Baltimore).
National Intelligence (Washington, D.C.).
New York Journal and Patriotic Register (New York).
Niles Register (Philadelphia).
The Palladium (Frankfort, Ky.).
Philadelphia Packet (Philadelphia).
Western Sun (Vincennes, Ind.).
Western World (Cincinnati).

II. SECONDARY SOURCE MATERIAL

Adams, Henry. *History of the United States.* 9 vols. Scribner's, New York, 1921.
Adams, J. T. *The March of Democracy.* Scribner's, New York, 1932.
Adams, Randolph G., and Peckham, Howard H. *Lexington to Fallen Timbers, 1775-1794.* University of Michigan Press, Ann Arbor, 1942.
Albion, Robert Greenhalgh, and Pope, Jennie Barnes. *Sea Lanes in Wartime.* W. W. Norton and Co., Inc., New York, 1942.
Babcock, K. C. *The Rise of American Nationality.* In the American Nation Series. Harpers, New York, 1906.
Balch, Thomas. *The French in America during the War of Independence of the United States, 1777-1783.* 2 vols. Porter and Coates, Philadelphia, 1891.

Baldwin, Leland D. *Pittsburgh, the Story of a City*. University of Pittsburgh Press, 1937.

Belcher, Henry. *The First American Civil War*. 2 vols. Macmillan, London, 1911.

Bemis, S. F. *Pinckney's Treaty*. The Johns Hopkins Press, Baltimore, 1926.

Beveridge, Albert J. *The Life of John Marshall*. 4 vols. Houghton Mifflin, New York, 1916.

Birkhimer, William E. *Historical Sketch of the Organization, Administration, Matériel and Tactics of the Artillery, United States Army*. James J. Chapman, Agent, Washington, D.C., 1884.

Blakeslee, F. F. *Uniforms of the World*. E. P. Dutton & Co., New York, 1929.

Bolton, C. K. *The Private Soldier Under Washington*. Scribner's, New York, 1902.

Bond, B. W. *The Civilization of the Old Northwest*. Macmillan, New York, 1934.

Bonney, Catharina V. R. *A Legacy of Historical Gleanings*. 2 vols. J. Munsell, Albany, 1875.

Bowers, Claude F. *Jefferson in Power*. Houghton Mifflin, Boston, 1936.

Boyd, Thomas A. *Mad Anthony Wayne*. Scribner's, New York, 1929.

Boyton, E. C. *History of West Point*. 1863.

Brice, W. A. *A History of Fort Wayne from the Earliest Known Accounts of this Point to the Present Period*. 1868.

Bruce, W. C. *John Randolph of Roanoke*. 2 vols. Putnam's, New York, 1922.

Buck, S. J. and E. H. *The Planting of Civilization in Western Pennsylvania*. University of Pittsburgh Press, 1939.

Burt, A. L. *The United States, Great Britain, and British North America*. Yale University Press, New Haven, 1940.

The Centennial of the U. S. Military Academy, 1802-1902. 2 vols. Government Printing Office, Washington, D.C., 1904.

Channing, E. A. *A History of the United States and its People*. 7 vols. Macmillan, New York, 1921-1932.

Christian, P. W. *General Wilkinson and Kentucky Separatism, 1784-1798*. A Northwestern University Ph.D. thesis, 1935.

Cleaves, Freeman. *Old Tippecanoe*. Scribner's, New York, 1939.

Coues, Elliot. *The Expedition of Zebulon Montgomery Pike.* 3 vols. Francis P. Harper, New York, 1895.

Cox, I. J. "Opening the Santa Fe Trail" in *Mo. Hist. Review,* XXV.

"The New Invasion of the Goths and Vandals" in *Miss. Hist. Assn. Proceedings,* VIII.

"The Pan-American Policy of Jefferson and Wilkinson" in *Miss. Valley Hist. Rev.,* I.

The West Florida Controversy, 1798-1813. Johns Hopkins Press, Baltimore, 1918.

"Wilkinson's First Break with the Spaniards" in *Biennial Report, Dept. of Archives and History of the State of West Virginia, 1911-1912, 1913-1914.*

"General Wilkinson and his Latin Intrigues with the Spaniards" in *Amer. Hist. Rev.,* XIX.

"The Exploration of the Louisiana Frontier, 1803-1806" in *Annual Report of the American Historical Association for 1904.*

Craig, O. J. "Ouiatanon" in *Indiana Historical Society Publications,* vol. II, No. 8.

Cronan, Rudolph. *The Army of the American Revolution and its Organizer.* Pub. by Rudolph Cronan, 340 E. 198 St., New York, 1923.

Cullum, G. W. *Biographical Register of the Officers and Graduates of the U. S. Military Academy.* 2 vols. D. Van Nostrand, New York, 1868-1879.

Dawson, H. B. *Battles of the United States by Sea and Land.* 2 vols. New York, 1858.

Dictionary of American Biography. Edited by Allen Johnson and Dumas Malone. 20 vols. Scribner's, New York, 1928-1937.

Dillon, John B. *A History of Indiana from its Earliest Exploration by Europeans to the Close of the Territorial Government in 1816,* etc. Indianapolis, 1859.

Downes, Randolph Chandler. *Frontier Ohio, 1788-1803.* The Ohio State Archaeological and Historical Society, Columbus, 1935.

Drake, Benjamin. *Life of Tecumseh, and His Brother the Prophet, etc.* Cincinnati, 1856.

Drake, Francis S. *Life and Correspondence of Major-General Henry Knox.*

Drewry, E. B. *Episodes in Western Expansion as Reported in the Writings of James Wilkinson.* Cornell University Ph.D. Thesis, 1935.

Dupuy, R. E. *Where They Have Trod.* Frederick A. Stokes Co., 1940.

Elliot, Charles Winslow. *Winfield Scott, the Soldier and the Man.* Macmillan, New York, 1937.

Fisher, Robert L. "The Western Prologue to the War of 1812" in *Mo. Hist. Rev.,* April, 1936.

Fiske, John. *The Critical Period of American History, 1783-1789.* Houghton Mifflin, Boston, 1897.

Fortescue, J. W. *A History of the British Army.* 10 vols. Macmillan, London, 1899-1920.
The British Army, 1783-1802. Macmillan, London, 1905.

Fortier, Alcée. *A History of Louisiana.* 4 vols. Goupol and Co., Paris, 1904.

Ganoe, W. A. *The History of the United States Army.* Appleton, New York, 1932.

Gardiner, A. B. "The Uniforms of the American Army" in *Magazine of American History,* August, 1877.

Godfrey, Carlos Emmor. "Organization of the Provisional Army of the United States in the Anticipated War with France, 1789-1800" reprinted in *Pa. Mag. of Hist. and Biog.,* vol. 38, April 1914.

Gregg, Kate L. "Building of the First American Fort West of the Mississippi" in *The Missouri Historical Review,* vol. XXX, July 1936.

Hall, E. H. *Margaret Corbin.* The American Scenic and Historic Preservation Society, New York, 1932.

Hamersly, T. H. S. *Complete Regular Army Register of the United States.* Wm. K. Boyle, Printer, Baltimore, 1880.

Hamilton, P. J. "Early Roads of Alabama" in *Transactions of the Alabama Historical Society,* 1897-1898, II.

Hansen, M. L. *The Atlantic Migration, 1607-1860.* Harvard University Press, Cambridge, 1940.

Harlow, R. V. *The History of Legislative Methods in the Period before 1825.* Yale University Press, New Haven, 1917.

Harpster, J. W. *Penn Pictures of Early Western Pennsylvania.* University of Pittsburgh Press, 1938.

Hatch, L. C. *The Administration of the American Revolutionary Army.* Longmans, Green and Co., New York.

Hay, Thomas Robson, and Werner, M. R. *The Admirable*

Trumpeter. Doubleday, Doran, and Co., Inc., Garden City, 1941.

"General Wilkinson—the Last Phase" in *La. Hist. Quarterly,* XIX.

"Some Reflections of the Career of General James Wilkinson" in *Miss. Valley Hist. Rev.,* XXI.

Hazard, Samuel. *United States Commercial and Statistical Register.* vol. 1, July 1839 to Jan. 1840. Philadelphia, 1840.

Heitman, F. B. *Historical Register and Dictionary of the United States Army.* Government Printing Office, Washington, D.C., 1903.

Hicks, James E. *Notes on United States Ordnance.* 2 vols. Pub. by James E. Hicks, Mount Vernon, N.Y., 1940.

Houck, Louis. *A History of Missouri.* 3 vols. R. R. Donnelley and Sons Co., Chicago, 1908.

Hulbert, A. B. *Historic Highways of America.* The A. H. Clark Co., Cleveland, 1905.

The Paths of Inland Commerce. vol. 21 of *The Chronicles of America,* Yale University Press, New Haven, 1921.

Hutcheson, Harold. *Tench Coxe.* The Johns Hopkins Press, 1938.

Jacobs, J. R. *Tarnished Warrior.* Macmillan, New York, 1938.

Kapp, Friedrich. *The Life of Fredrick William von Steuben.* Mason Bros., New York, 1859.

Kite, Elizabeth S. *Brigadier-General Louis Lebègue Duportail.* Institut François de Washington. The Johns Hopkins Press, Baltimore; The Dolphin Press, Philadelphia; 1933.

Knowlton, Miner. *Lands Belonging to the United States at West Point.* Washington, D. C., 1839.

Landham, Charles. *Dictionary of the United States Congress and General Government.* Hartford, 1865.

McAfee, R. B. *History of the Late War in the Western Country.* Lexington, 1816.

McClaeb, W. F. *The Aaron Burr Conspiracy.* Dodd Mead, New York, 1903.

McLaughlin, A. C. "The Western Posts and the British Debts" in *Am. Hist. Assn. Annual Reports for 1894.* Washington, 1905.

McMaster, J. B. *A History of the People of the United States, from the Revolution to the Civil War.* 8 vols. Appleton, New York, 1913.

The Maumee Valley through Fifty Years, 1763-1813.

Bulletin No. XXXIII of the William L. Clements Library, Ann Arbor, 1940.

Meyer, B. H. *History of Transportation in the United States before 1860*. Carnegie Institution of Washington, Washington, D.C., 1917.

Palmer, J. M. "General Marshall Wants a Citizen Army" in *The Saturday Evening Post*, December 23, 1944.

Pickett, Albert James. *History of Alabama*. 2 vols. Charleston, 1851.

Prentiss, Charles. *The Life of the Late Gen. William Eaton*. Brookfield, 1813.

Prentiss, H. P. "Timothy Pickering as the Leader of New England Federalism, 1800-1815" in *Essex Institute Historical Collections*, January and April, 1933, and April 1934.

Quaife, M. M. *Chicago and the Old Northwest, 1673-1835*. University of Chicago Press, 1913.

Raff, George W. *A Manual of Pensions, Bounty, and Pay*. Cincinnati, 1862.

Robertson, J. A. *Louisiana under the Rule of Spain, France, and the United States, 1785-1807*. 2 vols. The A. H. Clark Co., Cleveland, 1911.

Sandford, L. G. *The History of Erie County, Pennsylvania*. Pub. by the author, 1894.

Scharf, J. T. *History of St. Louis City and Country*. 2 vols. L. H. Everts and Co., Philadelphia, 1883.

Schreve, R. O. *The Finished Scoundrel: General James Wilkinson*. Bobbs Merrill, Indianapolis, 1933.

Scott, M. T. "Old Fort Massac" in *Transactions of Illinois State Historical Society*, 1903.

Sipe, C. H. *Fort Ligonier and its Times*. Telegraph Press, Harrisburg, 1932.

Smith, Charles H. (Bill Arp). *Bill Arp's Scrap Book*. James P. Harrison and Co., Atlanta, 1884.

Sparks, Jared. *The Library of American Biography*. vol. XV (Biography of Z. M. Pike), Boston, 1845.

Spaulding, Oliver S. *The United States Army in War and Peace*. Putnam, New York, 1937.

Steiner, B. C. *The Life and Correspondence of James McHenry*. The Burrows Bros. Co., Cleveland, 1907.

Stoddard, Major A. *Sketches, Historical and Descriptive of Louisiana*. Philadelphia, 1812.

Turner, T. J. *The Frontier in American History*. Holt, New York, 1921.

Verhoeff, Mary. *The Kentucky Mountains: Transportation and Commerce, 1750-1911*. Filson Club Publications, No. 26, Louisville.

Volstorff, V. V. *William Charles Cole Claiborne, A Study in Frontier Administration*. Northwestern University Ph.D. Thesis, 1933.

Wandell, S. H., and Minnigerode, M. *Aaron Burr*. 2 vols. Putnam's, New York, 1927.

Waugh, E. D. J. *West Point*. Macmillan, New York, 1944.

Wegand, Maxime. *Histoire de L'Armée Française*. Ernest Flammarion, Paris, 1938.

Whitaker, A. P. *The Mississippi Question, 1795-1803*. Appleton-Century Co., New York, 1934.

Wildes, Harry Emerson. *Anthony Wayne*. Harcourt Brace, New York, 1941.

Wilkinson, James. "General James Wilkinson" in *La. Hist. Quarterly*, vol. I, No. 2.

Wilson, Erasmus. *Standard History of Pittsburgh, Pennsylvania*. H. R. Cornell and Co., Chicago, 1898.

Wilson, F. E. *The Peace of Mad Anthony*. Charles R. Kimble, Greenville, 1909.

Wilson, J. G. "Sketch of the Life of Lieutenant James Strode Swearingen, etc." in *New York Herald*, October 4, 1903.

Wilstack, Paul. *Jefferson and Monticello*. Doubleday Doran and Co., New York, 1940.

Wissler, Clark. *Indians of the United States*. Doubleday Doran and Co., New York, 1940.

Wood, Edwin O. *Historic Mackinac*. 2 vols. Macmillan, New York, 1918.

Wright, L. B., and Macleod, J. A. *The First Americans in North Africa*. Princeton University Press, 1945.

INDEX

Adair, J., pursues Indians, 160; proposed Wilkinson assistant, 251; at New Orleans, 339

Adams, George, and Slough, 103

Adams, John, inaugurated, 193-194; and France, 206; and Wilkinson's schemes, 217-218; meets cabinet, 222; appoints Washington, 223; and generals, 224; halts preparedness, 236; and Matthew Lyon, 247; West Point for training, 294; appointments to West Point, 298

Adams, John Quincy, member Philosophical Society, 304

Adventure, Wayne travels in, 185

Alexandria, Va., defense of, 166

Algerian pirates, captures by, 166; U.S. frigate, 285

Allegheny County, in Pa., 67

America, or Americans, Boscawan to, 70; as engineers, 166; northward sweep of, 175; occupy Ft. Mackinac, 185; and Carondelet scheme, 203

Amherst, Jeffrey, St. Clair with, 70

Ancient and Honorable Artillery Company, 6

André, John, capture of, 282

Anglo-Saxons, in America, 3

Antigua, vessels seized, 165

Armistead, Walker K., and President, 306

Armstrong, John, and squatters, 22; escape of, 58; at Fort Hamilton, 147-148

Arnold, Benedict, at West Point, 127; Dearborn with, 245; treachery of, 282

Articles of War, first, 6; revision of under Dearborn, 272-273

Auglaize River, army reaches, 171

Augustin, Matias, and taffia, 216-217

Austin, Wm., and Little Turtle, 210

Bachus, James, tells of Hartshorn, 57

Balize, La., American troops at, 312

Ballenger, Joseph, of exploring party, 334-335

Baltimore, Md., defense of, 166-167; troops around, 231-232

Barbee, Joshua, at Fallen Timbers, 173

Barlow, Joel, Scioto Company, 28

Baron, George, as mathematics teacher, 297

Barron, Wm. A., teacher at Academy, 300; and President, 306

Bayou Tara, Wilkinsons and, 219

Beatty, Erkuries, payment of troops, 37; "Military Chest" of, 77

Bedford, Pa., militia behavior at, 19

Bedinger, Michael, "little queen" Polly, 140

Bellefontaine, Mo., garrison at, 341

Bellerophontia, camp near Licking mouth, 155

Bermuda, vessels seized at, 165

Big Bottom, Wyandots and Chippewas attack, 67

Big Tree, at Legionville, 150

Billy, and St. Clair, 89

Bissell, Daniel, at Presque Isle, 188

Bissell, Russell, hair cutting order, 262

Blazing Star, at Bedford, Pa., 19

Blinn, principles of, 155

Bloomfield, Joseph, estimate of, 384

Blount, Wm., and Cherokees, 66; plot of, 194

"Blue Book," and Eaton, 135

Blue Jacket, attacks Fort Recovery, 168, 170; to Greenville, 180; at Detroit, 185

Board of Treasury, on pay and clothing, 37-38

Bockongelas, to Greenville, 180

Boscawan, Edward, St. Clair with, 70

Boston, Mass., troops in, 6; "Bunch of Grapes Tavern," 28; ships from, 165; defense of, 166; troops around, 231-232

Bowdoin, James, Mrs. St. Clair, half sister of, 70

Bowles, Wm. Augustus, and Creeks, 235

Bowmar, J., and Fort Miró, 313

Boyd, Ensign, attack on, 160

Boyd, John P., and 4th Inf., 358; estimate of, 384

Bradford, Corporal, with Z. M. Pike, 328

Brandywine, Pa., St. Clair at, 70

Brant, Joseph, to Philadelphia, 151

Breck Neck, N.Y., height of, 302

Breck, Samuel, and the Lillies, 296

Brent, Robert, of "General Staff," 385

British, attitude of, 149; encourage Indians, 164; anger against, 165; warships of, 166; at Fort Miami, 177; evacuate Fort Mackinac, 187; relations with, 195; Wilkinson and, 204

British N. W. Co., monopoly by, 325; investigation of, 325

"Brown Bess," Americans and, 7

Brown, J., Spanish pensioneer, 217

Brown, Montgomery, store of, 186

Bruff, J., Wilkinson to, 198; of Upper Louisiana, 318; and Wilkinson, 324, 355

Buffalo Creek, Procter reaches, 73

Bunker Hill, Mass., Dearborn at, 245

Burbeck, H., at Mackinac, 187; at West Point, 287, 289; in the northwest, 294

Burling, Walter, carries letter to Iturrigaray, 338

Burr, Aaron, and Wilkinson, 324; letters to Wilkinson, 337; expedition of, 339-340; indicted, 340

Butler, Edward, and camp site, 99; and Slough, 102; arrogance of, 156

Butler, Pierce, protection for Georgia, 45

Butler, Richard, Indian commissioner at Ft. McIntosh, 22; down the Ohio, 24; corn to Indians, 33; president of board of inquiry, 63; dislike of Sargent, 80; Knox instructions, 83; reaches Northwest, 86-87; differences with St. Clair, 91-92; and Slough, 102-104; Indians attack, 106; death of, 108; Wayne's regard for, 156

Butler, Thomas, to Tennessee, 195, 215; hair cutting order, 262

Caddo Villages, Spaniards at, 330

Cahokia, Ill., 1st Artillery at, 316

Calhoun, John C., in 12th Congress, 365; action against Gr. Britain, 366

Campbell, Joseph, at Fort Adams, Tenn., 196

Campbell, R. M., and recruits, 135; at Fallen Timbers, 173-175

Campbell, Wm., at Fort Miami, 175-177

Canada, Wayne in, 127; irruption from, 228; smuggling, 266; importance of, 372, 373; divisions of, 373; invasion of, 374-375

Caribbean, privateers in, 165

Carlisle, Pa., detachment from, 138

Carlton, Corporal, punishment of, 292-293

Carmichael, J. F., at Legionville, 133-134, 136

Carondelet, Baron de, and Wilkinson, 186; Wilkinson bribes from, 189; and Power, 203-204; succeeded by Gayoso, 216; Kentucky and Tennessee, 217

Carpenters' Hall, sick militia in, 19

Carrington, E., for Sec. of War, 191

Casa Calvo, Marquis de, and Wilkinson, 235

Chandler, John, estimate of, 384

Charleston, S.C., ships from, 165;

defense of, 166-167; place for military education, 287

Charleville musket, Americans prefer, 8; character of, 277

Cherokees, and Blount, 66; Wm. Moultrie, 126; land reserved to, 195; and Guion, 196; in Tennessee, 221, 247, 248

Chesapeake, incident of, 276, 370

Chickasaw Bluffs, Spaniards warned, 185; Spanish plans and, 196; and War Department, 246-247; Wilkinson and Indians at, 248-249

Chickasawhay River, lands near ceded, 250

Chickasaws, trade with, 47; Robertson and, 66; twenty join army, 98; and Guion, 196; treaty with Wilkinson, 248-249; Mitchell and, 258

Chippewas, and St. Clair, 47; attack Big Bottom, 67; to Greenville, 179, 180

Choctaws, S. C. Yazoo Company and trade with, 45-46; towns of, 216; and War Department, 246-247; treaty with, 249

Chouteau family, cadet appointments from, 307

Cincinnati, Ohio, founding of, 31; Fort Washington at, 75; ration price at, 85; as a rendezvous, 144; soldiers at, 145-146; forts north of, 149; Wayne's army reaches, 153-154; dissipation at, 156; Wilkinson family at, 210

Cincinnati, Society of, Washington and Knox members, 42

"City Tavern," Wayne at, 183

City Troop, 6

Claiborne, F. L., to Concordia, 312

Claiborne, W. C. C., opinion of Wilkinson's work, 250; member of Philosophical Society, 304; governor in Louisiana, 310, 312, 315-316, 319

Clark, George Rogers, Indian commissioner, 24; expedition against Indians, 25; grant to, 181; and Power, 204

Clark, Wm., brother of Geo.

Rogers Clark, 320; co-commander with Lewis, 320-321; map-maker, 322; as brigadier-general Louisiana Militia, 323; Supt. of Indian affairs, 324

Clay, Henry, in 12th Congress, 365; opposition to Great Britain, 366

Clopton, John, increase of troops, 268

Coburn, Robert W., assistant military agent, 299

Colfax, Colonel, as contractor, 302

Collins, Joseph, messenger of Wilkinson, 219

Columbia College, students from, 167

Columbiads, first of, 276

Commissary of Ordnance, appointed, 367

Commissary General of Purchases, takes place of Purveyor of Public Supplies, 367

Concordia, La., and Wilkinson, 219; F. L. Claiborne to, 312

Congress of the Articles of Confederation, apathy of, 13; army legislation, 34-35; on army pay, 37-38; decline of, 40; St. Clair president of, 70; on an army, 287

Congress of the Constitution, or Congressmen, grant to Frenchmen, 28; 1st Congress and army, 43-44; law of April 30, 1790, 50; Senecas, 67; 1st Congress and defense, 68-69; and St. Clair's defeat, 118-119, 124; and law of March 5, 1792, 125; foreign relations, 182-183; 4th Congress, 189-193; French relations, 206; war preparations, 207-208, 222; laws of 1798 and 1799, 224-227; and fortifications, 237-238; act of March 16, 1802, 252-253; 10th and defense, 270-271; and Captain Molly, 283; Knox's recommendations to, 288; McHenry's plan, 294; 11th Congress, 362; 12th Congress, 365-367

Connecticut, militia from, 16;

character of militia of, 45; prisoners of, 137

Conner, Lydia, punishment of, 201

Constitution, made and adopted, 41; on trial, 149

Constitution Island, chain to, 281

Continental Army, Sargent in, 70

Continental Congress, Second, Articles of War, 6

Corbin, John C., husband of Captain Molly, 283

Cordero, Governor, and American explorers, 335

Cornplanter, at Fort Harmar, 48; to Philadelphia, 67; at Legionville, 150

Corps of Engineers, Congress of Articles on, 287; creation of, 298-299; Williams recommissioned in, 306

Corps of Invalids, at West Point, 282-284

Coudray, Tronson du, role in Revolution, 11

Covington, Leonard, efficiency of, 270

Cox, Tench, and clothing, 260

Cox, Zachariah, and Tenn. Land Co., 194-195; and Wilkinson, 215-216

Cranch, Joseph and Richard, repairing equipment, 284-285

Crawford, John, Sargent on, 114

Creeks, trade and treaty with, 46-47; visit Robertson, 66; and Spain, 221; and Bowles, 235; and War Department, 246; treaty with, 249

Creoles, in Louisiana, 309, 316

Crow's Nest, N.Y., height of, 302

Cuba, troops from, 251

Cumberland river, troops up, 195; Indian raids along, 211

Cushing, F. H., character, 143; problems of, 234; founding of Ft. Dearborn, 255; family movement of, 265; member Philosophical Society, 304; at Ft. Washington, 352; prosecution of, 354; adjutant general, 384

Custis, Peter, on expedition of 1806, 329

Cutler, Manasseh, Ohio Company and Scioto Company, 28

Dalrymple, principles of, 165

Darke, William, Harmar's board of inquiry, 63; character of, 92; at St. Clair's defeat, 107, 109

Daviess, J. H., killed at Tippecanoe, 360

Dayton, Jonathan, Symmes writes to, 32; Pickering prefers, 224

Dearborn, Henry, army health, 232-233; early career and appointment as Sec. of War, 245-246; and Wilkinson, 248; disapproves appointment of Wilkinson, 250; report of December 1801, 251-252; and decrease of army, 252-254; rations, supplies, and pay, 256-261; hair cutting order, 261-262; army allowances, 263-265; revises Articles of War, 272-273; light artillery company, 274-275; coast artillery, 276-277; directed to found an academy, 297; on spending, 300; orders to Swift, 301; cadet rations and clothing, 302-303; engineers and command, 305; and cadet appointments, 307; New Orleans troops, 344-345; character of, 383

DeButts, as aide, 173

Decrès, Admiral, and de Laussuat, 311

DeKalb, Johann, Baron, biography of, 304

Delassize, Jean, land rental, 346

Delassus, Colonel don C. D., and Louisiana Purchase, 315, 317, 318

Delaware, recruits from, 71

Delawares, to Fort Harmar, 48; and women, 90; at St. Clair's defeat, 107; fears of, 138; for war, 158; attack Fort Recovery, 168; to Greenville, 179, 180

Democratic Republicans, Wilkinson and, 240; prospects of control, 241; and Federalists, 243;

Dearborn as, 245; and war, 271; and Academy, 308

Democratic Society, of New York City, 166

Democrats, Jeffersonian, 184; and preparedness, 269

Denny, Ebenezer, aide of St. Clair, 102; messenger of St. Clair, 116-117

Depoistu, Wm., Baltimore, volunteers, 355

Detroit, Mich., Dick family to, 67-68; commissioners to, 158; troops from to Chicago, 255; Hamtramck at, 266; Rivardi to, 294

Dexter, Samuel, appointed Sec. of War, 240

Dick, Thomas, family captured, 67

Dickinson, John, Harmar's letter to, 23-24; constitutional convention, 40

Dill, George, 258

Diven, Wm., attempt to kill, 139; and courts, 154

Dominica, vessels seized at, 165

Dorchester, Lord, Seven Nations, 164

Doughty, John, at West Point, 15; "Doughty peach," 27

Doyle, F., founding Fort Massac, 211

Duane, Wm., Military Library, 273

Duer, Wm., as contractor, 80, 83, 119-120

Duforest, John J., and expedition of 1806, 330

Dunbar, W., and Fort Miró, 313; description of, 313, and Dr. Hunter, 313; and Red River expedition, 329

Duportail, Louis Lebègue, in Revolution, 11-12; fortifications at West Point, 281; garrison at West Point, 282; on an academy, 286

Duquesne, Pa., 5

Eaton, Wm., and "Blue Book," 135

Edinburgh, Scotland, St. Clair in, 70

Eel River, Miamis on, 74; tribes of, 151

Elements of Fortifications, copies of, 300

Elizabethtown, Pa., on suggestions for army, 172

Ellicott, A., and Gayoso, 213-214; medicine of, 215; to Pickering, 217; and Wilkinson, 218-219

Elliott, Joseph, and Wm. Scott, 292

Elliott, Matthew, shelters commissioners, 158

Elliott & Williams, ration contractors, 36; 161, 162

Enfield, Philosophy of, 299

England, contraband, 165; John Adams, 194

Eppes, John W., and troops, 267-268

Eustis, Wm., army health, 232-233; Peter's battery, 276; appointed Sec. of War, 342-343; recommends removal of troops, 345; orders investigation Terre aux Boeufs, 347; orders troops to Fort Adams and Natchez, 350-351; responsibility for Terre aux Boeufs, 352-353; orders 4th Inf. to W. H. Harrison, 358; a military tinker, 363; changes at Academy, 363; and Cadet Burchard, 364; and Military Academy, 380; character of, 383

Exchange, tallow and chandlers from, 166-167

Fairfield, Mrs., and contraband, 267

Fallen Timbers, battle of, 173-176; fruit of Wayne, 178; peace offers before, 180; Wayne revisits, 184; Newman, 190-191; horses of, 195

Falls of the Ohio, immigrants to, 31; Clark grant, 181

Farmer's Brother, of Senecas, 151

Faulkner, Wm., and "Whisky Boys," 130

Federal, Wayne and Wilkinson, 184

Federalists, and Wayne, 184; Mc-Henry, 191; and Democratic Republicans, 243; Jefferson and, 244; J. Ross leads, 251; Williams and, 308

Ferguson, William, repairs for Harmar's men, 53; work at Fort Washington, 81; character of, 92; at Fort Jefferson, 93; death of, 108

Fifth Regiment, troops for, 236

Filson, John, Losantiville, 30

Findlay, Potawatomie Camp, 180

Finney, Walter, travels down Ohio, 24

First American Regiment, character of, 39

First City Troop, and Wayne, 184

First New Hampshire Regiment, at Freeman's Farm, 245

First Regiment, Major Wyllys and, 58; recruits for, 71; strength, 76, 427; clothing of, 78; haversacks of, 81; morale of, 95; pursues mutineers, 98; and pack train, 112; discipline of, 116; officers of, 142; men of, 145-146; returns from, 228

Fitzsimmons, Thomas, and St. Clair committee, 118

Fleming, George, storekeeper at West Point, 295; and the Lillies, 296; as quartermaster, 297-298, 299-300

Flournoy, Thomas, estimate of, 384

Folch, Vicente, and Wilkinson, 346

Ford, M., and Hodgdon, 142-143; artillery of, 195; discharge of, 253

Fort Adams, Miss., established, 213; treaty at, 249; collector of the port at, 266; Claiborne at, 310; 1806 expedition, 329

Fort Adams, Tenn., christened, 196

Fort Arnold, at West Point, 281

Fort Boyd, Harrison at, 362

Fort Claiborne, establishment of, 314

Fort Clinton, surrender of, 280-281

Fort Confederation, Ala., treaty with Choctaws, 250

Fort Dearborn, founding of, 256

Fort Defiance, Wayne builds, 172; Wayne strengthens, 177; Wayne revisits, 184

Fort Detroit or Detroit, Wayne reaches, 185; sloop, 187-188; Wilkinson at, 198-199; Hamtramck and Abbott at, 231; winter transportation to, 232

Fort Fayette, headquarters of Wayne, 128; Wilkinson at, 208; proposed abandonment, 228

Fort Finney, establishment of first and second, 24-25; Kersey to second Fort Finney, 31

Fort Franklin, founding of, 32-33

Fort Greenville, established and life at, 159-163; Wayne at, 162; Wayne leaves, 171; Wayne returns, 178

Fort Hamilton, army builds, 87-88; and Fort Jefferson, 93; fugitives reach, 114; communications with, 141; and St. Clair, 145; supplies at, 146-147; pay of men at, 156; Wayne speech near, 162

Fort Harmar, established, 26-27; traffic by, 29; Marietta settlers, 30; ration price at, 36; 1789 Indian conference at, 48; treaty of, 48-49, 71, 180; troops from, 76

Fort Harrison, established, 359

Fort Independence, Mass., and D. Jackson, 263

Fort Jay, N.Y., sick at, 258

Fort Jefferson, Ohio, building of, 93-94; life at, 94-96; flight to, 110-112; communications with, 141; Wilkinson's men at, 144; and Fort St. Clair, 145; supplies at, 148; Wilkinson at, 163

Fort Knox, established at Vincennes, Ind., 26; ration price at, 36; Indian depredations near, 47; expedition from, 51-52; troops from, 76; supplies, 148, 149; proposed abandonment, 228

Fort Mackinac, Americans occupy, 185; Wayne visits, 186; winter transportation to, 232

Fort Madison, established, 341

Fort Massac, life at, 186-187; Guion reaches, 196; Wilkinson at, 211; medicines at, 229; collector of the port at, 266

Fort McIntosh, Federal commissioners and treaty of, 22; ration price at, 36; treaty of, 48

Fort Miami, army approaches and passes, 172-175; Wayne at, 184

Fort Mifflin, Pa., hair cutting order, 262

Fort Miró, and Wm. Dunbar, 313

Fort Montgomery, surrender of, 280-281

Fort Niagara, necessities at, 231

Fort Osage, established, 341

Fort Oswego, proposed abandonment, 228

Fort Panmure, Miss., Cox confined in, 215

Fort Pickering, at Chickasaw Bluffs, 229

Fort Pitt, garrison in 1783, 14; in 1783 and travel between Forts Pitt and McIntosh, 20-21; discharges at, 23; ration price at, 35; troop assembly at, 71

Fort Presque Isle, proposed abandonment, 228; necessities at, 231; winter transportation to, 232

Fort Putnam, at West Point, 281; Black Hole of, 292; height of, 302

Fort Recovery, founded, 163-164; attack on, 168-171

Fort St. Clair, building of, 145, 149

Fort Stanwix, treaty of, 48, 67

Fort Steuben, established near Wheeling, Va., 26; Indian dep-

redations near, 47-48; troops from, 76

Fort Washington, Ohio, St. Clair arrives, 50; Harmar's expedition from, 51, 53-54; board of inquiry at, 63; troops to, 71; Indian squaws at, 74; settlers around, 75; troops assemble at, 76-77; Hodgdon arrives, 80; workshop at, 81; horses at, 82; distance from St. Clair battlefield, 99; fugitives to, 114; no pay at, 116; posts north of, 141; entertainment at, 143-144; Wilkinson's men return to, 144; pay of men at, 156; Wayne reaches, 184; horses at, 195; Guion leaves, 196, reformation of, 197; Little Turtle at, 210; ten boats to Ft. Massac, 211; proposed abandonment, 228; supplies at, 231

Fort Washington, Miss., troops reach, 352

Fort Wayne, near St. Clair defeat, 99; established, 177-178; Indians to, 179; Wilkinson at, 198; proposed abandonment, 228

Fort Webb, at West Point, 281

Fort Wilkinsonville, Ga., Creek treaty at, 249; hair cutting order, 262

Fort Wyllys, at West Point, 281

Fourth Regiment, to Tennessee, 195

Foxall, Henry, and foundry project, 277

France, alliance with, 10; and John Adams, 206; equivocal relations with, 252

Francis, Tench, as purveyor, 234

Frankfort, Ky., Wilkinson at, 186

Franklin, Benjamin, at Constitutional Convention, 40

Freeman, C., and sick, 258; at West Point, 289; to the south, 294; Louisiana Territory, 310; Fort Claiborne, 314; at New Orleans, 318

Freeman, F., and Ellicott, 218; Red River expedition, 329

Freeman's Farm, Dearborn at, 245

French, privateers, 165; traders, 175; cessions to the, 180; artillery from the, 274

French Broad river, and Cherokees, 66

French Directory, apology and bribes, 221; overthrown, 236

French Store, Harmar reaches, 56

Gaither, Henry, retirement of, 355

Gallatin, Albert, Jefferson and, 246; on reducing army, 268-269; Sec. of Treasury, 342

Gamelin, Pierre, envoy to Indians, 50

Gano, J. S., Fort St. Clair, 145

Gansevoort, Peter, appointed brigadier general, 270

Garranger, Lewis, on military education, 286-287

Garrison Way, in Pittsburgh, 129

Gates, Horatio, ex British Officer, 6

Gayoso de Lemos, Wilkinson to, 209; Ellicott and, 213-214; Cox and, 216; character of, 116; Wilkinson cultivates, 217-219; cooperation of, 235

Gazaway, Ensign, clothing of, 132

Gazette of the United States, on Army, 45

General Green, Wilkinson abroad, 238

Genet, Edmund Charles, and Fort Massac, 211

Georgetown, Md., Wilkinson at, 240

Georgia, Indian raids, 67; Indians restless, 185; crooked legislature of, 194-195; new troops in, 236; boundaries extended, 249

Germans, Romans and, 159

Gerry, E., and France, 206

Gibson, Alexander, defends Fort Recovery, 169

Gibson, George, Harmar's board

of inquiry, 63; character of, 92; and slough, 102-104

Girty, Simon, attacks St. Clair, 106; Fort Recovery, 168

Goforth, Wm., arrest of Harrison, 146

Gordon, A., refuses Procter's request, 73

Governor's Island, defense of, 166

Grand Banks, 165

Grand Glaize, tribes at, 151

Grasson, Victor, death of, 108

Gratiot Family, cadet appointments from, 307

Great Britain, and northwest forts, 16; Indian alliance, 158; surrender of posts, 182-183; end of our peace with, 369

Great Lakes, shipping on, 232

Great Miami, squatters on, 22; troops arrive at mouth of, 24; Symmes grant, 30; army reaches, 87; Fort Hamilton on, 146

Greene, Nathanael, and du Coudray, 11; and Wayne, 127; Fort Greenville, 160

Greenville, Ohio, St. Clair reaches, 97; convoy to, 169; peace treaty at, 180-181; Wayne reaches, 184; treaty of and frontier, 194

Gribeauval, equipment, 274

Grundy, Felix, in 12th Congress, 365-366

Guasutha, at Legionville, 150

Guion, Isaac, to cover Mississippi, 196; at Natchez, 214; arrests Cox, 215; and Ellicott, 218

Gunn, James, on Georgia and Indians, 46

Hall, Horatio, operation with Wyllys, 58

Hamilton, Alexander, New Orleans and Floridas, 251; training regulations, 273; battery of, 287; Rochefontaine to, 291; Washington to, 294

Hamilton, H., meeting, 139

Hamilton, Paul, Sec. of Navy, 342

Hammond, S., Governor of Upper Louisiana, 318

Hampton, Wade, appointed brigadier general, 270; Wilkinson and Eustis, 354; estimate of, 384

Hamtramck, John, Fort Steuben- and Fort Knox, 26; Patrick Brown and, 48; failure of his expedition, 52; character of, 92; and pack train, 112; Wea and Eel River tribes, 151; at Fallen Timbers, 173; at Fort Wayne, 178; at Detroit, 199; at Fort Fayette, 241-243; founding Fort Dearborn, 255; at Detroit, 266

Hamtramck, Mrs. John, at Fort Fayette, 242-243

Hand, E., for general, 126; Washington asks advice of, 286

Hardin, John, on reconnaissance, 56; on raid, 57-58; death of, 151

Harmar, Josiah, early career, 18; opinion of Ft. McIntosh, 20; and Pennsylvania squatters, 22; Pennsylvania quota, 23; ordered down Ohio, 24; federal surveyors, 26; at Ohio Co. dinner, 30; orders to Kersey, 32; supplies for, 36; Knox advises, 52; his expedition en route, 53-55; sends out Hardin and Trotter, 56-57; retreat of, 59; results of his campaign, 60; disgusted, 62; board of inquiry, 63-64; defeat of, 68; opinion of St. Clair, 70; St. Clair helps, 71; and St. Clair's campaign, 96; and supplies, 119; lessons from, 121; veterans under, 260

Harpers Ferry, Va., armory at, 277; supplies from, 279

Harrison, Wm. H., character of, 143; and artificers, 146; as governor, 317; instructions from Jefferson, 318; and Tecumseh, 357; moves against Indians, 359; Battle of Tippecanoe, 360-362; estimate of, 384

Hartshorn, A., escape, 57-58; death, 170-171

Harvard University, W. A. Barron, tutor at, 300

Harvard, Lt., and John Lillie, Jr., 296

Hassler, Ferdinand R., at Academy, 304

Hawkins, Benjamin, associate of Wilkinson, 248; back to Indians, 250

Heart, Jonathan, at Fort Franklin, 32-33; and son, 89

Heath, Wm., Washington asks advice of, 286

Hedrick, Captain, for peace, 151

Henrico County militia, 6

Herrera, Simon de, and Wilkinson, 336

Hibernia, sons of, 136

Hobson's Choice, Wayne names, 154; departure from, 158

Hodgdon, Samuel, as quartermaster, 80-82, 86-119; revisionary report, 121; Wilkinson's opinion of, 142; succeeded by O'Hara, 192

Holston River, and Cherokees, 66

Hooke, Moses, military agent, 265

Hopkins, H. W., and Louisiana Territory, 312

Hopkins, Sgt., 136

Hornet, carries Wilkinson, 344

Houdin, M. G., failure of mission, 73

House of Representatives, thanks Wayne, 178; Dearborn's report to, 251; act of April 12, 1808, 269; and Burr, 354; 12th Congress, 365

Howard, J. E., for Sec. of War, 191

Howe, William, fears Valley Forge fortifications, 11

Howell, Joseph, Jr., as paymaster, 116; succeeded by C. Swan, 193

Huger, Isaac, S. C. Yazoo Co., 46

Hull, Wm., estimate of, 384

Humphreys, Enoch, 1806 expedition, 329

Hunter, G., and Fort Miró, 313

Huntington, J., for general, 126; Washington asks advice of, 286

Hurons, at Detroit, 185

Hutton, Charles, *Mathematics* of, 299; and W. A. Barron, 300

Illinois, Indians of, 101, 151, 179

Indiana, Dist. of Louisiana under, 315

Indians, tactics of, 4; and treaty of 1783, 16; depredations near Forts Knox and Steuben, 47-48; result of Harmar's Campaign on, 62; James Robertson, 66; Rufus Putnam, 67; offensive against, 68; after Fort Harmar Treaty, 71; plans concerning, 71-72; emissaries to, 73; recruits fear of, 77; troops clothing to Indians, 78; and 50 militia, 97; attack St. Clair, 105-110; attack Kentuckians, 124-125; for fighting against, 137; Knox's assurance to, 141; at Fort St. Clair, 145; lands north of Ohio, 149; peace efforts with, 151-152; cavalry training against, 154-155; commissioners to, 157; precautions against, 159; convoy, 160; visit Greenville, 164; attack Ft. Recovery, 168-171; Fort Defiance and May, 172; at Fallen Timbers, 173-176; to Greenville, 179; in Southwest, 185-186; and land grabbers, 195; and War Department, 210; at Natchez, 214; Wilkinson tells of, 227; Americans and Spaniards, 235; in Pennsylvania and New York, 245; and Wilkinson, 247-250; pay of commissioners to, 254; veterans against, 260

Innes, Harry, on Indian depredations, 48; Wilkinson to, 145, 190

Irvine, Wm., and army clothing, 259-260

Iturrigaray, Viceroy, and Burling, 338

Izard, George, and Williams, 304-305

Izard, Ralph, protection for Georgia, 45

Jackson, Daniel, and Dearborn, 263

Jackson, Jeremiah, on expedition, 334

Jamaica, vessels seized, 165; attack from, 235

Jay, John, treaty of, 180, 184, 185; treaty of and frontier, 194

Jefferson, Thomas, and standing army, 12; Wm. Blount, 194; and Nolan, 240; inauguration and army plans, 244-245; and Dearborn, 246; and Wilkinson, 248; army reduction, 254; increase of troops, 268; strengthening of militia, 271; founder of U.S. Military Academy, 280; opposition to Academy, 288-289; founds the Academy, 297; and Mansfield, 300; member Philosophical Society, 303-304; engineers and command, 305; cadet appointments, 307; Williams recommendations to, 307-308; and Louisiana Purchase, 309; representations of, 310; and Sibley, 314; and Stoddard, 315; and Harrison, 318; exploring parties, 320, 325; route to new Spain, 332; Burr's scheme, 337-338; and ships, 371; and army, 385

Jesup, T. H., brigade quartermaster, 351

Kaskaskia, Ill., 316

Kayashuto, Jonathan Heart, 33

Ke-Kiong-gay, Wayne reaches, 177

Kennedy, Charles, punishment of, 201

Kennerman, Henry, at Little Falls, 327; disobeys orders, 328; and Pike, 333-334

Kentucky and Kentuckians, as prisoners, 179; Carondelet, 203-217; Lyon in, 247

Kentucky Gazette, and deserters, 85

Kentucky River, Scott's troops assembled at, 73

Kersey, Wm., at North Bend, 31; at Ft. Adams, Tenn., 196

Kickapoos, disregard treaties, 47; Scott to harry, 73; Chickasaws hate, 98

Kingsbury, Jacob, at Fallen Timbers, 173

Kingsley, Zebina, exemplary wife of, 295

Knox, Henry, bookstore at Boston, 5; training, 6; and du Coudray, 11; discharging from army, 14; organizing of militia, 16; and Symmes, 32; as Secretary at War, 38-39; sketch of, 42; his suggestions for a peacetime army, 44; Knox advises Harmar, 52; dissatisfied with Harmar, 62; peace, 66; treaty of Fort Stanwix, 67; on defense, 68; and St. Clair, 70; plans July offensive, 71; thanks Wilkinson, 74; on pay, 77; on troop clothing, 78, 94; on supply, 80, 83, 86; and ration certificates, 94; news of St. Clair's defeat, 117; and Hodgdon, 119; and Duer, 120; revisionary report, 121; and Wayne, 127-128; Legion of the United States, 131; clothing supply, 132; instructions to Wilkinson, 141-142; Wilkinson's correspondence, 142; Six Nations, 151; orders to Legion, 152; son of R. Butler, 156; orders to Wayne, 158; engages engineers, 166; Wayne as successor, 182; Wayne to, 190; Major General, 224; on a military academy, 285; at West Point, 287; on military training, 288

Knoxville, Ky., troops near, 195; Indian commissioners meet near, 248

Kosciusko, Thaddeus, *Maneuvers of Horse Artillery*, 274; West Point fortifications, 281; biography of, 304

Lachrymae Christi, and Wilkinson, 163

Lafayette, contribution of, 10-11

Lake Erie, Fort Miami near, 172; Wayne on, 185, 188; road between and Ontario, 247

Lake Huron, and Ft. Mackinac, 187; Swan visits, 202-203

Lake Michigan, and Fort Mackinac, 187; Swan visits, 203

Landais, Phillip, cadet at Academy, 290

L'Anguille, attack on, 51; burned, 74

LaSalle, and Louisiana Territory, 311

Lee, Arthur, at Fort McIntosh, 22

Lee, Charles, ex-British officer, 6

Lee, H., for general, 126; wants Sec. of War, 191; and Adams, 224

Lee, Richard Henry, on regulars, 46

Legion of the United States, origin of, 126, 131; abolished, 192

Legionville, Pa., founding of, 130-131; policing of, 132; deserters from, 138-139; chiefs at, 150

Leonard, Nathaniel, and Jefferson, 355

levies, character of, 93; contention of, 95

Levy, Simon, at Academy, 299

Lewis and Clark Expedition, arranged for, 320; Senior Yrujo and, 320, 321; start of, 321; extent of, 322-324

Lewis, Meriwether, and delivery of Upper Louisiana, 316-317; exploring party, 320

Lewis, Morgan, as quartermaster, 384

Lewis, Thomas, at Fallen Timbers, 173

Liberty Avenue, in Pittsburgh, 129

light house, of Philadelphia, 183

Lillie, John, and family, 296-297

Lillie, John, Jr., as cadet, 296-298

Lincoln, Benjamin, on Washington's plans for an army, 44-45; for general, 126; commissioner to Indians, 157

Little Turtle, and L'Anguille, 74; attacks St. Clair, 106; attacks Fort Recovery, 168; program of, 175; to Greenville, 180; at Detroit, 185; to Pittsburgh, 205; and Wilkinson, 210

Livingston, Robert, and Louisiana Purchase, 309

Loan Office of Pennsylvania, army pay, 38

Loftus Heights, Miss., site of Fort Adams, 313; Freeman at, 218

London, England, St. Clair in, 70

long barracks, cadets in, 302

Lorimier Family, cadet appointments from, 307

Louisburg, 5; Amherst at, 70

Louisiana, and Carondelet, 186; Power on way to, 205; and Nolan, 240; invasion of, 251; boundaries and population of, 309; divisions of, 310; cession and government of, 311, 314; and Stoddard, 317; post needed in, 320

Louisville, Ky., John Hardin expedition from, 49

Lowry, John, attack on, 159

Luce, Francis, detachment of, at North Bend, 32

Ludlow, Israel, agent of Duer, 83; St. Clair and, 90-91

Ludlow's Station, army and, 84-86

Lyon, Matthew, 247

Maclay, Wm., on regulars and Knox, 46

Machim, Thomas, fortifications at West Point, 280

MacMahon, Wm., Indians attack, 169-170

Macomb, Alexander, at Academy, 299; member Philosophical Society, 303; and President, 306

Macon, Nathaniel, on troops, 268

MacRea, Wm., troubles of, 355

Madison, James, Constitutional Convention, 40; and Wayne, 128; and Jefferson, 246; and the Louisiana Purchase, 309, 312; as President, 342; a pacifist, 342, 382

Maine, District of, and Dearborn, 245, 246

Malgares, Fecundo, and American expedition, 335

Mansfield, Jared A., teacher at Academy, 300

Manual of 1764, 6

Many, J. B., to Arkansas Post, 312-313

Marietta, Ohio, founding of, 29; St. Clair reaches, 70; and army of Wayne, 153

Market Street, and Wayne, 183

Marquette, and Louisiana Territory, 311

Marshall, J., and France, 206; refuses to be Sec. of War, 238-239

Maryland, recruits from, 71, 77

Massachusetts, fugitives from, 14; militia quota of, 18; character of militia, 45; recruits from, 77; highway robbery, 137; new troops in, 236

Masson, Francois Desire, at Academy, 301

Maumee River, Indian villages of, 49, 52, 58; Fort Greenville on, 159; British fort on, 164; army reaches, 171; tribes on, 177; Wayne down, 184

May, Wm., capture by Indians, 172

Mayflower, arrival at Marietta, 29

McClary, J., and Ellicott, 218

McClellan, John, privates of company of, 265

McCulloch, Andrew, military agent, 350

McDowell, Margaret, to Wayne, 157

McGillis, H., and Pike, 328

McGillvray, Alexander, makes treaty for Creeks, 47-48

McHenry, J., appointed Sec. of War, 191; Wilkinson's opinion of, 205; in cabinet, 222; opinion of Wilkinson, 227; army health, 232-233; on supplies, 234; recommends Military Academy, 236-238; resigns, 238-239; Hamilton to, 294-295

McHenry's Tavern, Harrison at, 146

McIntosh, L., for general, 126

McKee, Alexander, on Maumee, 164; store, 173; his and Indian losses, 175; house at Detroit, 185

McKelvay, James S., scandal, 355

Meek, Wm., of Osage Indian Party, 334

Mercer County, Ohio, site of St. Clair camp, 99

Mercer, John, Company of, 32

Mexico, 217

Miamis, disregard treaties, 47; and Harmar, 60; post in villages of, 72; on Eel River, 74; and women, 90; fears of, 138; and Fort Knox, 149; for war, 158; attack Fort Recovery, 168; capital of, 177; to Greenville, 179, 180; Little Turtle Chief of, 205

Michilimackinac, 202; collector of the port at, 266

Middle States, attitude toward army, 34

Mifflin, Thomas, Governor of Pennsylvania, 168

Militia, inheritance from Indians, 4; quotas from Connecticut, New York, New Jersey, Pennsylvania, 16; defects of, 64, 92; desertion of, 95; mutinous, 98; from Kentucky, 211; arms and accoutrements, 223; Jefferson favors, 245, 256, 271

Mimeenitz, Count, Philosophical Society, 304

Mississippi River, money via, 189; forts on lower, 196; Carondelet scheme, 203; navigation and deposit, 250, 251; protection of, 372

Mississippi Territory, W. Sargent, governor of, 213; medicines for, 229

Mitchell, S. M., son of, 205

Mitchell, Samuel, and Cox, 216; medicines for, 249, 258

Mitchell, William, punishment of, 201

Mobile, Ala., commissary at, 230; collector of the port at, 266

Mohawks, Brant of, 151

Molly, Captain, at West Point, 283-284

Monroe, James, Indian Commissioner, 24; and Louisiana Purchase, 309

Montgomery, Richard, Dearborn with, 245

Montreal, Canada, importance of, 373, 374; center of resistance, 375

Montserrat, vessels seized at, 165

Morales, Juan, intendant at New Orleans, 250-251

Morrison, James, as contractor, 347; and McCulloch, 350

Moses, to Greenville, 180

Mott, Corporal, at St. Clair's defeat, 111

Moravian Town, squatters, 23

Moultrie, Alexander, S. C. Yazoo Company, 46

Moultrie, Wm., for general, 126

Mount Vernon, meeting at, 40; Washington at, 223

Muller, treatise of, 273

Murray's Wharf, Creeks arrive at, 47

Muskingum River, squatters on, 23; Fort Harmar on, 26; Big Bottom on, 67

Nacogdoches, Tex., Spanish troops leave, 330

Nance, "Red-headed," at St. Clair's defeat, 111

Napoleon, U.S. friendship, 236; and Louisiana, 310

Nashville, Tenn., road to, 249

Nassau, vessels seized at, 165

Natchez, Miss., Guion reaches, 196; character of, 214-215; and Cushing, 234; road from to Tennessee, 248, 249; Cushing reaches, 265

Natchitoches (on Red River), gateway to Texas, 313-314; expedition at, 330

Navy Department, ships of, 371

Nawiatchtenos, death at Fort Washington, 150

New Arrow, at Legionville, 150

Newburgh, address at, 14

New England, attitude toward army, 34; recruits from, 71; Sargent of, 76; War of 1812, 369

New Jersey, militia from, 18; new troops in, 236

New Lights, around Fort Washington, 75

New London, Conn., defense of, 166

New Madrid, Mo., fears for, 221

Newman, R., and Wilkinson, 190-191

New Orleans, La., Wilkinson and Spaniards, 141; traffic with, 186; right of deposit, 208; Wilkinson in, 220; fears for, 221; supplies through, 235; French artillery at, 274; Peter's battery to, 275; and transfer to U.S., 309-316; troops at, 345-346

New York City, Redcoats in, 6; St. Clair visits, 53; ships from, 165; defense of, 166-167; troops around, 231-232

New York State, and Vermont, 13-14; militia from, 16; recruits from, 71; Indians in, 245

Niagara, Gordon at, 73; commissioners reach, 157; smuggling at, 266

Nicholas, Wilson C., on preparedness, 268-269

Nicoll, A. Y., and the general staff, 385

Ninth Street, in Pittsburgh, 129

Nolan, Philip, and Jefferson, 240

Norfolk Militia Discipline, mentioned, 5-6

North Bend, Symmes founds, 31

North Carolina, cession of lands, 66; Indian raids, 67

North, Esquire, and Captain Steele, 293

Northern Liberties, 18th Irish Infantry in, 6

Northwest Ordnance, genesis of, 25; passage of, 29

Northwest Territory, St. Clair, governor of, 70, 180; women of, 90

Ockmulgee Fork, lands in ceded, 249

Ogden, Peter, and Wilkinson, 339

O'Hara, James, ration contractor, 36, 197; quartermaster, 161; successor of Hodgdon, 192

Ohio Company, founding of, 28; Sargent, secretary of, 70

Ohio River, immigration along, 27-28; Shawnee treaty, 28-29; "Territory South of," 66; chieftains north of, 67; garrisons along, 71; settlers north of, 76; ducking in, 132; supplies by, 149; as boundary, 158; Fort Massac on, 186; Butler down, 196; and Carondelet scheme, 203; Fort Massac on, 211

Ohio State, treaty of Greenville, 181

Old Coffee House, grocers from, 167

Oldham, Wm., joins with recruits, 89; character of, 92; and Slough, 102-103; death of, 108

Olle, funeral of, 150

Omeetown, burning of, 56

Osborn, Samuel, at West Point, 296

Oswego, N.Y., smuggling at, 266

Ottawas, at Fallen Timbers, 175; to Greenville, 180

Owen, Abraham, killed at Tippecanoe, 360

Pacific Ocean, Clark reaches, 322

Painted Pole, of Shawnees, 151

Parker, Alexander, at New Orleans, 344

Parsons, G. H., judge of Northwest Territory, 70-71

Partridge, Alden, at Academy, 365

Peas upon a Trencher, at Detroit, 199

Peat, John, and children, 75-76

Pensacola, Fla., British threaten, 235

Pennsylvania, Indian raids and militia from, 16-19; Allegheny, 67; St. Clair settles in, 70; recruits from, 77; rebellion in, 149, 168; Indians in, 245

Peter, George, light artillery, 274-276; and Indians, 331

Philadelphia, Pa., 18th Irish Infantry in, 6; Cornplanter to, 67; St. Clair leaves, 70; Procter returns to, 73; Congress at, 118-119, 124; Mrs. Wilkinson to, 146; chiefs to, 151; ships from, 165; defense of, 166; Wayne in, 183-184; physicians of, 187; 4th Congress at, 189; Wilkinson in, 190; troops around, 231-232; supplies from, 234; freight from, to Pittsburgh, 264; military education at, 287

Piankashaws, attack on, 48; to Greenville, 180

Pickens, Andrew (Skyagunsta), associate of Wilkinson, 248; to Tamassee, 250

Pickering, Timothy, commissioner to Indians, 157; in War and State Depts., 191; Ellicott to, 217; and W. S. Smith, 224; Washington asks advice of, 286

Pike, Z., at Ft. Massac, 186; receives Guion, 196; at Fort Pickering, 229

Pike, Z. M., at Massac, 187; to his father, 253; Mississippi expedition, 325-329; expedition to Southwest, 331-336; at Terre aux Boeufs, 346

Pinckney, C. C., for general, 126; for Sec. of War, 191; expelled from France, 206; major general, 224; training regulations, 273

Pinckney, F., treaty of, 183, 185; treaty of and frontier, 194; treaty of, 196, 208-209, 211, 217; described, 384

Pittsburgh, militia to, 19; garrison at, 20; Indian atrocities near, 68; troops held at, 77, 86; "Whisky Boys," 128; detachment to, 138; deserters, 139; Mrs. Wilkinson to, 146; Whisky Rebellion near, 168; *Federal* at, 184; Wilkinson at, 189; goods at, 231; Fort Fayette at, 241; Peter's battery to, 275; depot, 375

Placquemines, La., fort at, 312

Pluckemin, N.J., training at, 285-286

Portland, Me., defense of, 166, 236

Portsmouth, N.H., defense of, 166

Posey, Gen., thanks to, 162

Potawatomies, to Greenville, 179-180

Power, Thomas, and Wilkinson, 203-205, 219

President Adams, government barge, 264

Presque Isle, Wayne dies at, 188

Price, Captain, death of, 108

Price, Wm., at Fallen Timbers, 173; and Captain Molly, 283-284

Princeton, N.J., St. Clair at, 70

Procter, Thomas, failure of mission, 73

Prophet, and Indians, 356-357, 360

Prophetstown, established, 357; burned, 361

Protestants, around Fort Washington, 75

Pulaski, Count Casimir, biography of, 304

Putnam, Israel, fortifications at West Point, 281

Putnam, Rufus, Ohio Company, 27-28; arrival at Marietta, 29; Indian chieftains tell, 67; to Indians, 151; Washington asks advice of, 286

Quebec, Canada, Wolfe at, 70; Dearborn at, 245; importance of, 373, 375

Radisson, Pierre, and Louisiana Territory, 311

Randolph, Beverly, commissioner to Indians, 157

Randolph, John, on preparedness, 269, 343

Rapids, of Maumee, 184

Ray, James, aid to fugitives, 59

Red Feather, to Greenville, 180

Regulars, character of, 92-93; at Fort Recovery, 168-169; and Jefferson, 244; Dearborn and training of, 278; benefits for, 366-367

Republican or Republicans, bakers, 167

Revolution, troops before, 6; uniform, infantry, and heavy weapons in, 7-8; Wayne in, 127; Dearborn in, 245; veterans and pensions, 260

Rhine, Germans on, 159

Rhode Island, fugitives to, 14

Richardet's Tavern, and Wayne, 184

Rivardi, J. J. U., discharge of, 253; at West Point, 289, 294-295; model yard of, 298

Robertson, James, of Tennessee, 66

Robinson, John H., on Osage expedition, 333-334

Rocatelle, Florberque de la, school of military art, 285

Rochefontaine, Stephen, at West Point, 289-294; model yard of, 298

Rodrique, Philip, cadet at Academy, 290

Romans, Bernard, fortifications at West Point, 280

Romans, principles of, 159

Ross, James, leader of Federalists, 251

Rumford, Count, and an academy, 295

Russ, Abraham, family killed, 68

Sackets Harbor, N.Y., smuggling, 266-267

St. Clair, Arthur, training, 5; family of, 29-30; and Chippewas, 48; invitation to Indians, 48; Pierre Gamelin, and Indians' reply, 50; helps Harmar, 52-53; Harmar's court findings to, 63; report on Harmar, 68; governor and major general, 69; experience, 70; Indians and troops, 70-71; instructions to, 71-72; sickness of, 72; and Wilkinson, Procter and Scott, 72-73; thanks Wilkinson, 74; sickness of, 74-75; collects troops, 76-77; pay and clothing of troops, 77-78; recruits of, 79; subordinates of, 79-80; builds Fort Hamilton, 87-88; Billy, 89; Ludlow, 91; unfitness for campaign, 96, 97; troubles of, 98; camp of, 99-101; action of Butler, Gibson, Oldham, 103-104; Indians attack, 105-110; retreats to Ft. Jefferson, 112-113; to Fort Washington, 113-114; losses of army of, 115-116; reaches Philadelphia, 117; estimate of, 121-122; escorts for, 143; misfiring of men of, 155; formations of, 158; cannon of, 169; Findlay, 180; veterans under, 260; horses of, 195

St. Josephs River, valley of, 177

St. Kitts, vessels seized at, 165

St. Louis, Mo., fears for, 221; business ventures at, 266; cadet appointments around, 307

St. Mary's, Ga., defense of, 236

St. Marys River, valley of, 177

St. Patrick, holiday, 136

Salcedo, Nemecio, and Pike, 334-335

Sandusky, no vessel to, 73

Santo Domingo, F. D. Masson from, 301

Sargent, Winthrop, Secretary of Northwest Territory, 70; unpopularity of, 76, 91; Oldham's recruits, 89; inspects militia, 104-105; escorts for, 143; with Wilkinson expedition, 144; governor of Mississippi Territory, 197; at Natchez, 214-215

Savannah, Ga., defense of, 166

Scioto Company, founding of, 28

Scioto River, squatters on, 23; Potawatomie camp on, 180

Scotch-Irish, around Fort Washington, 75

Scott, Charles, expedition of authorized, 72; results of expedition, 73; popularity of, 76; St. Clair campaign, 96; lessons from, 121; for general, 126; reaches Greenville, 171; at Fallen Timbers, 174

Scott, Wm., and J. Elliott, 292

Scott, W. S., and Wilkinson, 353; and Cushing, 354

Seavey, Henry, punishment of, 201

Sebastian, B., Spanish pensioneer, 217

Second Infantry, at Pittsburgh, 128-129

Second Regiment, recruits for, 71; clothing of, 78; casualties at St. Clair's defeat, 107; discipline of, 116; returns from, 228

Secretary at War, work in Revolution, 7

Senate, Harmar's defeat, 68; W. Blount, 194

Senecas, to Fort Harmar, 48; Cornplanter, 67; no vessel for, 73; chiefs of, 151

Seven Nations, Lord Dorchester, 164

Sevier, J., Pickering prefers, 224

Shaumburgh, B., at St. Clair's defeat, 111; and Power, 205; at Ft. Stoddert, 229-231

Shaw, John Robert, travel on the Ohio, 21-22

Shawnees, treaty of 1786, 28-29; disregard treaties, 47-48; report from, 56; and Harmar, 60; and women, 90; at St. Clair's defeat, 107; fears of, 138; against peace, 151-152; for war, 158; attack Fort Recovery, 168; at Fallen Timbers, 175; to Greenville, 179, 180

Shaylor, Joseph, at Fort Jefferson, 93-94

Shay's Rebellion, and Constitution, 41

Sheet, *Artillery* of, 299

Sibley, John, at Natchitoches, 314; and 1806 expedition, 330

"Sign of the Plow and Oxen," tavern of, 74

Simcoe, J. G., hospitality of, 157

Simmons, Wm., Wilkinson pays, 254

Simond, Lewis, Philosophical Society, 304

Sixtieth Foot, St. Clair in, 70

Slough, Jacob, patrol of, 102-103

Smith, Ballard, 140

Smith, C., first judge advocate, 192

Smith, Captain, at St. Clair defeat, 108

Smith, C. H., describes militia, 381

Smith, Robert, Secretary of State, 342

Smith, W., adjutant general, 224

Smyth, Alexander, and Wilkinson, 384

Snipes, William Clay, S. C. Yazoo Co., 46

South Carolina, recruits from, 71

South Carolina Yazoo Company, 45; slave killing, 137

Southern States, attitude toward army, 34-35

Southwest Point, Tenn., proposed meeting at, 248

Spain, friendliness for, 217; anxious, 221

Spaniards, at New Orleans, 141; in the Southwest, 149, 183, 185;

and W. Blount, 194; Cox, 195; fort evacuation, 195; plans of, 196; and Carondelet scheme, 203; Wilkinson's advice to, 204-205; posts and boundaries, 208-209; Wilkinson's citizenship, 209; hope of pay from, 217; Wilkinson tells of, 227; "imbecility" of, 228; and army supplies, 235; kill Nolan, 240; and U.S. shipping, 251; in Louisiana, 310; withdrawal of, 314

Sparks, Richard, on 1806 expedition, 329-330

Springfield, Mass., garrison at, 34; armory at, 277, 379

Stanford, Richard, on increase of troops, 268-269

Steele, Captain, and Esquire North, 293

Steuben, Baron von, training by, 8-9; for general, 126; Legion of the United States, 131; *Regulations*, 134, 199; on an academy, 286; learning of *Regulations*, 290

Stevens, as assistant to Purveyor, 234

Stevens, Wm., *System of Discipline for the Artillery*, 273

Stillwater, Ohio, flight to, 111

Stoddard, A., role in Louisiana territory, 315-318, 321

Stony Point, N.Y., Wayne at, 127

Sugar Loaf, N.Y., height of, 302

Sullivan, John, and du Coudray, 11; Dearborn with, 245

Swan, Caleb, paymaster, 193; to Michilimackinac, 202-203

Swartwout, Samuel, and Wilkinson, 339

Swift, Joseph G., at the academy, 298-299; and Baron, 300-301; member Philosophical Society, 303

Symmes, John Cleves, his opinion of Vincennes inhabitants, 112; grant of, 30-31; judge of N.W. Territory, 71

Talleyrand, and envoys, 221

Tchoupitoulas Gate, at New Orleans, 311

Tecumseh, and Indians, 356-357; absence of, 360

Tennessee, Indian raids into, 16; and James Robertson, 66; cavalry for, 185; plotting in, 194-195; troops to, 195-196; and Carondelet, 203, 217; Cox to, 216

Tennessee Land Co., Cox and Georgia, 194-195

Tennessee River, Indian raids along, 211; road to, 248

Terre aux Boeufs, troops at, 346-348

Texas, Nolan killed in, 240

Third Regiment, Z. M. Pike cadet of, 187; troops for lower Mississippi, 196; Kersey of, 196; returns from, 228-229

Thorpe, John, superintendent of artificers, 54

Ticonderoga, 5; St. Clair at, 70; Knox at, 86; Wayne at, 127

Tippecanoe, battle of, 360-362

Todd, Robert, at Fallen Timbers, 173

Tooney, Patty, at West Point, 293

Tories, colors of, 7

Totten, Joseph G., member Philosophical Society, 303

Tousard, Louis, discharge of, 253; at West Point, 289-290; to New York City, 294; ordered to West Point, 297; work of, 367

Tracy, from Detroit to Chicago, 255

Train, The, 6

Treasury Department, contracts, 162; building burned, 241; army clothing, 259

Treaty of Fort Stanwix, and Senecas, 67

Trenton, N.J., St. Clair at, 70; Knox at, 86

Trotter, James, on reconnaissance, 57

Troup, George M., increase of troops, 368

Trueman, A., death of, 151

Tryplett, J., cadet at Academy, 290

Turkey Creek, Harmar reaches, 53

Turnbull, Marmie, & Co., contract of 1786, 35-36
Turner, Edward, as an officer, 314; at Natchitoches, 330

United States, southwest tribes and Carolina cession, 66; and Chickasaws, 98; tradition of army of, 107; Six Nations, 158; defense of, 166; army of, 176; Jay and Greenville treaties, 180-181; flag at Ft. Miami, 184; Spanish evacuate area of, 216; Spaniards and aims of, 235; strength of regulars, 236; and regulars, 244; first light artillery company, 274
United States Military Academy, and McHenry, 236-237; founder of, 280; Knox on an academy, 285; Act of March 16, 1802, 298-299; instruction at, 306; and Washington, 307; appointment of cadets, 319; changes by Eustis, 363-364; increase of, 365; results of Eustis' work, 380
United States Military Philosophical Society, founded, 303-304
Upper Canada, Simcoe governor of, 157

Valley Forge, von Steuben at, 8-9; fortifications at, 11; huts at, 130; Steuben at, 199; Dearborn at, 245
Van Cleve, at St. Clair's defeat, 111
Van Rensselaer, Solomon, dragoons of, 195
Varnum, Joseph B., on preparedness, 268-269
Varnum, J. M., judge of Northwest Territory, 70-71
Vasquez, Baroney, with Pike, 334
Vauban, *Fortifications* of, 299
Venango, Pa., Fort Franklin at, 32
Vermillion, proposed attack on, 51; Hamtramck reaches, 52
Vermont, and New York, 13-14
Viana, Francisco, at Nacogdoches, 331

Vincennes, Ind., Fort Knox at, 148; conference at, 357
Virginia, drafts from, 77; and H. Lee, 126
Vischer, W. I., and Patty Gansevoort, 291
Volunteer Greens, and Wayne, 184
Vulture, Arnold flees to, 282

Wabash Indians, Pierre Gamelin to, 50; and Putnam, 151
Wabash River, St. Clair's camp on, 99; supplies by, 149
Wadsworth, Decius, superintendent of Academy, 305-306
Walnut Hills (Vicksburg), Spaniards' plans, 196
War Department, hold troops at Pittsburgh, 86; ration certificates, 94; St. Clair writes to, 99; contracts, 162; Swan, clerk in, 193; friendship for Indians, 210; and Wilkinson, 216, 238; building burned, 241; and Indians in Georgia, 246-247; and Simmons, 254; Hamilton's regulations, 273; light artillery, 274; commissary of ordnance, 367
Washington, D.C., character of, 240; and Jefferson, 244; Cushing leaves, 265; first light artillery in, 274; and Academy, 307; center of population, 370
Washington, George, training and books, 5; Valley Forge fortifications, 11; resigns command, 13; at Constitutional Convention, 40; inaugurated, 41; his 1786 suggestions for an army, 44; treaty of Fort Stanwix, 67; opinion of St. Clair, 70; urges haste, 86; news of St. Clair defeat, 117; on selection for general, 126; desire for peace, 149-150; "Emortal," 158; Whisky Rebellion, 168; thanks Wayne, 178; support of Wayne, 181; selecting Sec. of War, 191; at Valley Forge, 199; birthday of, 200; and Wilkinson, 220; as

lieutenant general, 223; on standing army, 268; West Point fortifications, 280; importance of West Point, 282; "Sentiments on a Peace Establishment," 287; on a military academy, 288, 294

Washite River, exploration of, 313

Wayne, Anthony, for general, 126-127; appointment of, 128; at Pittsburgh, 129-130; to Legionville, 130; training at Legionville, 131-140; and Indian chiefs, 150; army of to Cincinnati and training there, 153-157; orders to advance, 158; precautions of, 159; founds Fort Greenville, 160; and contractors, 161-162; invitation to, 163; founds Fort Recovery, 163-164; Fort Recovery attacked, 168-171; leaves Greenville, 171; builds Fort Defiance and "Citadel," 172; Fallen Timbers, 173-175; and W. Campbell, 176-177; and peace treaty, 180-181; departure of, 181-182; returns to Northwest, 185-187; death of, 188; Wilkinson's opinion of, 190; desires Sec. of War, 191; and horse purchases, 195; veterans under, 260

Wea or Weas, attack on, 51; tribes, 151; attack Fort Recovery, 168; to Greenville, 180

Weedon, G., for general, 176

Weed's Tavern, and Wayne, 184

West Indies, privateers in, 206

Wheeling, Va., squatters, 23; Fort Steuben, 26; army of Wayne, 153

West Point, N.Y., and Duportail, 11; garrison at, 15, 34; Wayne at, 127; as early post, 280-298; mapping of, 301-302

Whigs, colors of, 7

"Whisky Boys," near Pittsburgh, 128; Wm. Faulkner, 130

Whisky Rebellion, near Pittsburgh, 168

Whistler, Wm., sixty years an officer, 261

Whitehall dock, coopers from, 167

White Pigeon, to Greenville, 180

Whyte, Matthew N., appointment as cadet, 307

Wilkins, John, Jr., quartermaster, 192; at Detroit, 199

Wilkinson, James, advice to Harmar, 62-63; consults with St. Clair, 72; L'Anguille expedition, 74; popularity of, 76; St. Clair campaign, 96; lessons from, 121; in the Revolution, 141; in the Northwest, 141-147; disregard for Wayne, 154; James Morrison, 162; invitation to Wayne, 163; at Fallen Timbers, 173; assumes command, 182; confers with Wayne, 184; money from Carondelet, 186; stories about, 186-187; visit to Philadelphia, 190-194; Tennessee troops, 195; inspects and reforms, 197-203; and Power, 203-205; at Pittsburgh, 208; to Sargent and Gayoso, 209; and Little Turtle, 210; down the Mississippi, 211-212; establishes Ft. Adams, 213; and Z. Cox, 215; and Ellicott, 218-219; and Gayoso, 219-220; confers with Hamilton, 227-229; returns to Southwest, 234-235; at Havana, 238; in Washington, 240-241; at Fort Fayette, 241; and Indian treaties, 247-250; pay of, 254, 267-270; criticism of, 271; training regulations, 273-274; Knox to, 288; sale of books, 299; member Philosophical Society, 304; and Claiborne, 310, 312, 315, 318; in St. Louis, 324-325, 329, 331-333, 336; and Burr, 337-341; in New Orleans, 344-345; at Terre aux Boeufs, 346; court martial of, 354-355; Congress investigates, 362; estimate of, 384

Wilkinson, Mrs. J. B., frontier hospitality, 143-144; to Philadelphia, 146; and Wayne, 163; at Cincinnati, 210; and Sargent, 215; and Gayoso, 219; at Concordia, 220; at Fort Fayette, 242-243

Wilkinson, James B., up the Missouri, 329; and Pike, 333-335

Williams, David R., on increase of troops, 268-269

Williams, Jonathan, as head of Academy, 297-305; recommissioned, 306; recommendations to Jefferson, 307-308; and Eustis, 363-365

Wilson, James, at Academy, 299; and President, 306

Wilson, Wm., and Rochefontaine, 291

Winchester, James, estimate of, 384

Wolfe, James, at Quebec, 70

Woolwich, England, Charles Hutton of, 300

Worrell, Stephen, and Upper Louisiana, 316-317

Worthington, Eliphalet, 292-293

Wyandots, to Fort Harmar, 48; attack Big Bottom, 67; fears of, 138; for war, 158; attack Fort Recovery, 168; at Fallen Timbers, 175; to Greenville, 180

Wyllys, John P., accompanies Hardin, 58-59

Wyoming Valley, devastation of, 13

Yale, Mansfield as teacher at, 300

Yazoo, and Carondelet scheme, 203

Yrujo, Senor, 320, 321; Lewis and Clark expedition, 320-321

Yorktown, and Duportail, 11; St. Clair at, 70; Dearborn at, 245

Zeigler, David, accompanies Hardin, 56; Wilkinson's opinion of, 142

81
83
85
88